Markus Bestehorn

Evaluation of Spatio-Temporal Queries in Sensor Networks

Markus Bestehorn

Evaluation of Spatio-Temporal Queries in Sensor Networks

Processing Spatio-Temporal Queries Based on Object Detections by Sensor Nodes

Südwestdeutscher Verlag für Hochschulschriften

Imprint
Any brand names and product names mentioned in this book are subject to trademark, brand or patent protection and are trademarks or registered trademarks of their respective holders. The use of brand names, product names, common names, trade names, product descriptions etc. even without a particular marking in this work is in no way to be construed to mean that such names may be regarded as unrestricted in respect of trademark and brand protection legislation and could thus be used by anyone.

Publisher:
Südwestdeutscher Verlag für Hochschulschriften
is a trademark of
Dodo Books Indian Ocean Ltd., member of the OmniScriptum S.R.L Publishing group
str. A.Russo 15, of. 61, Chisinau-2068, Republic of Moldova Europe
Printed at: see last page
ISBN: 978-3-8381-2514-5

Zugl. / Approved by: Karlsruhe, Karlsruhe Insttitute of Technology, Dissertation, 2011

Copyright © Markus Bestehorn
Copyright © 2011 Dodo Books Indian Ocean Ltd., member of the OmniScriptum S.R.L Publishing group

Acknowledgements

Several people contributed significantly to this dissertation. With this section, I would like to express my deep gratitude towards these people and acknowledge their respective contributions.

Klemens Böhm is the person behind the research and the quality of this dissertation. He was the person that taught me research from the beginning to the end and how to publish results. Furthermore, I am grateful for his tireless editorial effort that improved the quality of my papers and thus this dissertation: Whenever there was a graph with a font that is too big or to small, a sentence too long or a verb that could be active instead of passive, Klemens was there to edit it. In this context "whenever" is meant literally: Looking through my inbox, I found mails with editorial comments on papers ranging from 7 am to 12 pm, from Mondays to Sundays. Needless to say, we never got a paper back from reviewers where the quality of presentation was not mentioned in a positive way. This dissertation would have been a shadow of itself without his help.

The KIT database group, especially *Erik Buchmann*, *Thorben Burghardt* and *Mirco Stern*, has been a constant source of inspiration, expertise and amusement. Most members of the database group had to take time out of their schedules to read one of my papers at one point or another. Erik always had valuable ideas for research and Mirco was a valuable sparring partner regarding papers or opinions on different topics related to sensor networks. Thorben, in addition to being a great colleague, co-designed a practical course with me which was valuable, because it made recruiting students and getting them interested in sensor networks much easier.

The members of the ZeuS project, funded by the Landesstiftung Baden-Würtemberg, also influenced this dissertation. Both papers on query dissemination are joint work with *Zinaida Benenson* and *Felix Freiling* from the University of Mannheim. ZeuS helped to establish this connection and was the initial basis for my interest in query dissemination. Furthermore, our energy measurements to verify our results would not exist without the help of the Institute of Telematics, in particular *Mario Pink* and *Anton Hergenröder*.

I also have to thank all my students who did a lot of coding, had to endure me as a supervisor and conducted hundreds of experiments: The diploma thesis of *Marek Jawurek* is the foundation for our papers on query dissemination. *Matthias Klein* implemented a mechanism that allows us to collect evaluation statistics of arbitrary granularity from Sun SPOT sensor nodes over the air. *Olga Ulmer* worked on the evaluation of spatio-temporal predicates with a relational database system which is the baseline for all evaluations regarding spatio-temporal queries in sensor networks. *Thomas*

Thieringer implemented and evaluated our approach for in-network processing of spatio-temporal predicates and developments. *Tobias Schneider* evaluated the spatio-temporal query processor on Sun SPOT sensor networks and had to endure a lot of frustration while debugging software in large sensor networks. Furthermore, I would like to thank my student assistants that helped me to implement various pieces of software on Sun SPOT sensor nodes and publish a lot of software: *Sven Meisinger, Johannes Röder, Jürgen Czerny.*

There are two exceptional students that are missing in the paragraph above. This is because their work goes so far beyond anything one could expect from a student or a co-worker that it deserves a separate paragraph: *Stephan Kessler* and *Andreas Leppert.* Andreas implemented and evaluated a lot of existing query dissemination mechanisms which is frustrating because most of them only work on paper. Stephan greatly influenced my work on spatio-temporal queries and designed and implemented detection neighbor approximation mechanisms. In the early days, when Sun SPOTs were not even available in Europe and most of the software was "beta" at best, they helped me to get a start on programming these little sensor nodes. Stephan and Andreas co-designed and implemented a large portion of the KSN software which is currently used by Sun SPOT users in more than 40 countries all over the world.

I would also like to thank the people from Sun Microsystems and Syntropy, in particular *John Daniels, Roger Meike, Dave Cleal, David G. Simmons* and the other staff members of the Sun SPOT project at the Sun Labs. Their responses to hundreds of questions by my students and me on the developer mailing list as well as on forums have been a great help. In addition I would like to thank *Frank Schlichting* who magically delivered Sun SPOTs directly into my office at a time when buying them was not possible.

As with any success in life, one's family and friends are those that make the success possible. In particular, I would like to thank my parents, *Maike* and *Kurt*, for pushing me to stay at the university and complete a doctoral degree. Furthermore, in cooperation with my sister *Tina* and my brother *Max*, they always helped me to get my head up again when work frustrated me. My family helped me to see the positive aspects whenever something negative happened. And finally I would like to thank that unknown person that invented golf: In combination with my family and friends, this game helped me through the worst setbacks during my doctoral work, because the hole world collapses into a sphere of 42.67 millimeters and all computer science is left outside.

Contents

1 Introduction   **11**
1.1 Application Examples 12
    1.1.1 Application Example 1: Surveillance 13
    1.1.2 Application Example 2: Animal Tracking 14
    1.1.3 Scope and Assumptions 15
1.2 Contributions and Outline of this Dissertation 16

2 Technical Background   **19**
2.1 Sensor Network Platforms and Architecture 19
    2.1.1 State-of-the-Art on Sensor Nodes 19
    2.1.2 Communication in Sensor Networks 24
    2.1.3 Energy Supply and Consumption 26
    2.1.4 Impact of Future Developments 28
    2.1.5 Summary 29
2.2 Fundamentals of Moving Object Databases 30
    2.2.1 Point-Set Topology 30
    2.2.2 Spatial and Spatio-Temporal Predicates 32
    2.2.3 Spatio-Temporal Developments 34
    2.2.4 Moving Object Databases vs. Sensor Networks 36
2.3 Processing Relational Queries in Sensor Networks 37
2.4 Summary 38

3 Semantics of Spatio-Temporal Queries   **41**
3.1 Node and Detection Model 42
3.2 Point-Set Topology for Sensor Networks 45
3.3 Deriving Predicate Results from Object Detections 48
    3.3.1 Predicate Results for Regions 51
    3.3.2 Predicate Results for Zones 55
    3.3.3 Static and Dynamic Zones 58

		3.3.4	Summary	59
	3.4	\multicolumn{2}{l}{Spatio-Temporal Developments}	60
		3.4.1	Irregularity of Zones and Concatenation	60
		3.4.2	A Canonical Collection of Spatio-Temporal Developments	62
		3.4.3	Formal Description of Object Detection Sequences	71
		3.4.4	Detection Terms	73
	3.5	\multicolumn{2}{l}{Summary}	80

4 Query Dissemination in Sensor Networks — 81

    4.1 Problem Statement 81
    4.2 Dissemination of Spatio-Temporal Queries 83
    4.3 Performance Study on Existing Dissemination Approaches 84
        4.3.1 Existing Dissemination Approaches 85
        4.3.2 Experimental Setup 90
        4.3.3 Results and Analysis 92
        4.3.4 Discussion 99
    4.4 Optimizing Probabilistic Query Dissemination 99
        4.4.1 Topology Information 100
        4.4.2 Reachability Prediction 104
        4.4.3 Estimating Energy Consumption 106
    4.5 Evaluation 107
        4.5.1 Simulation 108
        4.5.2 Break-Even Analysis 113
        4.5.3 Sun SPOT Case Study 114
    4.6 Summary 116

5 Energy-Efficient Processing of Spatio-Temporal Queries — 117

    5.1 Preface 117
    5.2 Data Structures and Algorithms 118
        5.2.1 Detection Scenario Computation 120
        5.2.2 Memory Requirements and Management 121
    5.3 Centralized Strategy 122
    5.4 Distributed Object-Information Collection 123
        5.4.1 Reactive Strategy 127
        5.4.2 Proactive Strategy 129
        5.4.3 ZIP – Zone Information Protocol 131
        5.4.4 Detection Neighbor Approximation 134
        5.4.5 Failure Handling 135
        5.4.6 Distributed Notification Filtering 136
    5.5 Evaluation 141

		5.5.1	Static Zones – Evaluation	141
		5.5.2	Dynamic Zones – Evaluation	147
	5.6	Summary		148

6 Conclusion and Future Work   149
- 6.1 Summary . . . 149
- 6.2 Future Work . . . 151
  - 6.2.1 Queries with non-identifiable Objects . . . 151
  - 6.2.2 Detection Cost Optimization . . . 152
  - 6.2.3 Object-Object, Region-Region and Region-Zone Predicates . . . 152
  - 6.2.4 Approximation of Detection Neighbors . . . 153
  - 6.2.5 Advanced Concatenations and Predicates . . . 155
  - 6.2.6 Querying the Movement of Humans with Privacy-Related Position Obfuscation 155

List of appendices

A Energy Consumption Profile of Sensor Nodes   157
- A.1 Experimental Setup . . . 157
- A.2 Results and Analysis . . . 158
  - A.2.1 Impact of Communication on node lifetime . . . 158
  - A.2.2 Energy consumption of sending and receiving . . . 159
  - A.2.3 Impact of energy-aware MAC protocols . . . 161
- A.3 Lessons Learned . . . 163

B Spatio-temporal queries with relational operators   165
- B.1 Relational Schema . . . 166
- B.2 Expressing a Spatio-Temporal Query using SQL . . . 166
  - B.2.1 **Step 1** – Computing `OutsideDetected`^{v} . . . 167
  - B.2.2 **Step 2** – Computing `InsideDetected`^{v} . . . 169
  - B.2.3 **Step 3** – Computing `DisjointView`^{v} . . . 171
  - B.2.4 **Step 4** – Computing `InsideView`^{v} . . . 175
  - B.2.5 **Step 5** – Assembling the subqueries . . . 177
- B.3 Relational Schemas and Regions . . . 177
- B.4 Lessons Learned . . . 178

C The Karlsruhe Sensor Networking Project   179
- C.1 KSN Testbed . . . 179
- C.2 KSN Serialization and Collections . . . 180
  - C.2.1 The KSN Serialization Process . . . 182
  - C.2.2 Study of Serialization Overhead . . . 188

C.3	KSN Radio Stack	191
	C.3.1 Design Targets and Overview	193
	C.3.2 Layers of the KSN Radio Stack	194
	C.3.3 Evaluation and Summary	203
C.4	KSN Simulator	204
	C.4.1 Components of the Simulator	204
	C.4.2 Squawk Adaptation Layer	205
C.5	KSN Management Application	208
	C.5.1 Main Concepts	208
	C.5.2 Evaluation	210

D A Topology Discovery Protocol — **215**
D.1 Overview – Echo-based Topology-Discovery 215
D.2 Expansion wave 216
D.3 Contraction wave 219

List of Figures — **221**

References — **224**

Index — **235**

Chapter 1

Introduction

A *sensor network* consists of many sensor nodes deployed over an area to acquire data through sensing. Typically, *sensor nodes* are battery-powered, miniature computers equipped with application-specific sensing hardware and a wireless communication interface. These devices have several advantages over traditional *passive sensors* which modulate a voltage based on some environmental parameter, e.g., temperature: Sensor nodes do not require any infrastructure such as wiring to forward measured values or a permanent power supply. This reduces deployment costs by up to 90% [127]. Furthermore, they can be applied to scenarios where data must be acquired from remote areas where such infrastructure is unfeasible, e.g., Antarctica [32] or on glaciers [59, 87]. Additionally, the computational capabilities and wireless communication allow sensor nodes to filter, combine and preprocess data acquired by sensing.

These advantages led to numerous deployments of sensor networks for scientific [19, 22, 32, 59, 63, 69, 70, 85, 123], industrial [43, 56, 76, 88] or surveillance [6, 52, 57, 58, 77, 138] purposes. Each of these applications has different requirements, e.g., regarding sensing hardware or the capabilities of the nodes. These different requirements resulted in the development of a large number of different sensor nodes [2, 34, 40, 97, 120, 131] programmed in various languages [49, 100, 111] using different types of sensing hardware [3, 18, 80, 114, 119] and software platforms [33, 61, 116, 121]. Thus, the notion of a sensor network is by no means well-defined and reusing software developed for one application is difficult unless the exact same nodes with the same sensors are used. Hence, for most applications software and sometimes even hardware had to be developed from scratch. This, in combination with the complexity of programming applications for such distributed systems using unreliable, wireless communication is in the way of easy deployment and usability of sensor networks.

Research on sensor networks has demonstrated that accessing sensor networks using *declarative queries* similar to database systems is a promising approach to solve these problems [16, 17, 50, 133]: Users view the sensor network as a *relational database* and describe the data they are interested in using a query language, e.g., SQL. A query processor installed on each node takes care of sensing, collecting, aggregating and routing the requested information. This declarative approach provides a uniform way to access the data acquired through sensor networks, can be reused in different applications and frees the user from details on node platforms, communication protocols or sensing hardware.

So far, the focus of research on declarative query processing in sensor networks has been relational queries [1, 27, 30, 65, 66, 81, 82, 84]. This is problematic for a significant portion of sensor networks, namely those deployed to track moving objects, e.g., animals [22, 69, 85] or vehicles [6, 58, 138]. Users of these sensor networks are interested in the movement of objects, i.e., their queries have a *spatio-temporal semantic*. However, expressing spatio-temporal semantics using relational operators results in very complex queries [130] that are "hopelessly inefficient to process" [53]. This is because modeling movement over time requires special data types and operators not offered by relational databases and the existing query processors for sensor networks as well. This dissertation is the first that addresses the semantics and processing of spatio-temporal queries in sensor networks.

For traditional database systems, researchers have proposed *Moving Object Databases* which support spatio-temporal queries [21, 39, 54, 125]. As this dissertation shows, a straightforward application of these research results is not possible due to well-known limitations of sensor networks: for example, moving objects databases model objects as a single point and regions as point sets. This implies that information on moving objects and regions is complete and accurate. We investigate the relevant properties of sensor networks and show that only a fraction of sensor networks can acquire information of such quality. This dissertation provides semantics for spatio-temporal queries applicable to all types of sensor networks. This is challenging, because these semantics must cope with the intricacies of sensor networks, e.g., node failures, incomplete object trajectories and different precisions of sensing hardware. Furthermore, we address the energy-efficient dissemination and processing of spatio-temporal queries.

The remainder of this chapter is organized as follows: Section 1.1 reviews existing deployments and introduces two application examples for object tracking sensor networks which serve as an example throughout this dissertation. In Section 1.2 we point out the contributions of this dissertation and outline its content.

1.1 Application Examples

Generally, sensor network applications can be classified as either *monitoring* or *tracking* applications [83]. Monitoring applications use sensor nodes to observe phenomena and report data on these phenomena to the user, i.e., users are interested in a set of sensor readings. One example for a monitoring application is [87]: For this deployment, sensor nodes were deployed on top, inside and below a glacier to monitor pressure, temperature and tilt. A user of this system could be interested in the temperatures measured inside the glacier. Viewing such a sensor network as a table/relation is simple and the aforementioned research has shown that accessing the information obtained using relational queries is promising.

In a sensor network deployed for tracking, users are interested in the movement of objects. We describe two applications of object-tracking sensor networks in detail and provide examples for spatio-temporal queries in sensor networks in the following. Additionally, we use these scenarios to limit the scope of this dissertation and introduce a set of assumptions. Furthermore, the examples allow us to introduce the four general types of spatio-temporal queries in sensor networks. This dissertation shows that each type has different requirements regarding the capabilities of the sensor network.

1.1.1 Application Example 1: Surveillance

Figure 1.1 illustrates an application from vehicle-target detection and classification called "A line in the Sand" [6]. In this application, sensor nodes are deployed to track vehicles moving in an area. An example for a spatio-temporal query in this application is "Which vehicles $\mathbf{V}_i$ have entered the restricted access region $\mathbf{R}$?".

Each node is equipped with sensing hardware to detect and classify moving objects, i.e., a node can determine if an object is a pedestrian or a vehicle. [6] discusses several approaches for detection of vehicles and humans: Sophisticated hardware like radar or laser scanners allows precise localization of objects. Ultrasonic range finders determine the distance of objects to the detecting node, but not their exact position. Contrary to this, acoustic or thermal sensing hardware only allows nodes to determine if an object is in the vicinity of the node. Hence, while there exist detection mechanisms that determine if a detected object is inside the region, on the border or outside, this is not true for a large portion of detection mechanisms used in sensor networks. The semantics for spatio-temporal queries must be defined in a such way that they take into account different precisions of detection mechanisms.

Another issue discussed in [6] is the possibly *uncontrolled deployment* of sensor nodes for surveillance applications: Particularly for military applications it is often unfeasible to deploy nodes manually, e.g., because the observed area is controlled by enemy forces. Hence, sensor nodes may be dropped out of an airplane which might result in unobserved areas and other anomalies [5]. These areas must be taken into consideration when processing spatio-temporal queries in sensor networks.

For the query above, the region $\mathbf{R}$ is a set of points specified by a polygon. Since the polygon implicitly enumerates all points inside the region and does not change over time, we refer to this type of region as *static region*. Another possible way to define a region is the specification of constraints for measurable values, i.e., the set of points inside the region changes over time. For example a set of constraints could identify underwater oil-spills and define the region based on this constraint. In this case, the user is interested in the movement of objects, e.g., boats or animals, in relation to the oil-spill. We refer to this type of region as *dynamic region*.

We show that sensor networks must meet relatively strict requirements to provide accurate results for spatio-temporal queries related to regions. Particularly dynamic regions are problematic and we show that sensor networks typically cannot make a statement regarding the topological relation of a

1.1. APPLICATION EXAMPLES

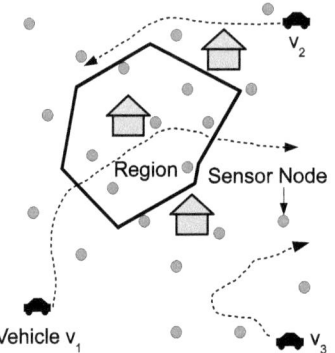
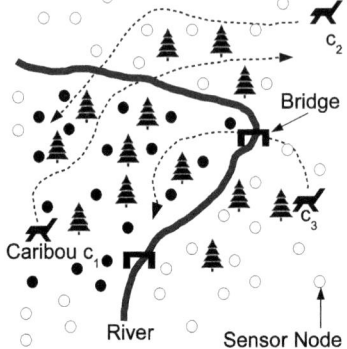

Figure 1.1: Illustration of a surveillance application

Figure 1.2: Illustration of an animal-tracking application

moving object and a dynamic region. Users of sensor networks address this issue by observing object movement in relation to a set of nodes as the second application example shows. For static regions, we provide an approximation approach that is applicable to any kind of detection mechanism and prove that this approximation is optimal regarding result quality.

1.1.2 Application Example 2: Animal Tracking

Tracking animals at large temporal and spatial scales is important for understanding their behaviour and the influence of external factors on their habitat [22, 74]. Sensor Networks are well suited to allow this, because they can be deployed over large areas and allow observation of vertebrates such as caribous [91, 110] without intrusion. The following query is an example for a spatio-temporal query scientists studying caribous using a sensor network as illustrated in Figure 1.2 could issue: "Which caribous C_i have moved into the tree-covered swamp area on the south-western side of the river?"

The swamp area that is covered by trees on the south-western side of the river can be modeled as set of points. Thus, processing the spatio-temporal query would require exact recording on the location of trees, the swamp and the river. For most sensor network deployments this is impractical. Instead, the majority of these scientific applications use a *controlled deployment*, i.e., deployments are typically carefully planned to observe an area of interest [47]. The controlled deployment allows recording properties of the surroundings for each node during deployment, i.e., before the nodes start sensing. Examples for such properties are, if a node is deployed inside the forest or in a treeless area, close to food resources, in the swamp or in a calving area. This information allows users to derive a set of nodes that are inside the area of interest: for example, all nodes in the tree-covered swamp area on the south-western side of the river (black colored circles in Figure 1.2). It is sufficiently accurate for the purpose of such an installation if the sensor network observes caribou movement in relation to this set of nodes. We refer to such a set of nodes as *zone* to distinguish it from the term "region" which describes a point set. In Figure 1.2, the zone is represented by all black-colored circles and users of these sensor networks typically express their interest as follows: "Which caribous C_i have entered the zone $\mathcal{Z}$?" This dissertation is the first to address spatio-temporal queries regarding zones and we define the semantics for these queries in Chapter 3.

If the zone is determined based on deployment data, the zone does not change over time, i.e., it is a *static zone*. Users can also define a zone based on constraints on measurable phenomena. An example of such a zone is the set of nodes that currently measure temperatures below $0°C$. Similar to the spatial extend of a dynamic region, the nodes in this zone can obviously change over time and thus we refer to this type of zone as *dynamic zone*.

1.1.3 Scope and Assumptions

The applications above limit the scope of this dissertation. We are interested in a declarative interface for sensor networks that observe moving objects. Thus, we limit our discussion to queries regarding the spatio-temporal relationship between a moving object and the following four types of regions/zones:

Static region: A set of points that is constant over time.
Dynamic region: A set of points whose shape and size changes over time.
Static zone: A set of nodes that is constant over time.
Dynamic zone: A set of nodes where nodes are added/removed over time.

We leave aside queries aimed at the topological relationship of two regions, lines and regions, lines and lines etc.

Additionally, the applications also include implicit assumptions: We assume that nodes are stationary, i.e., they do not move after the deployment is finished and the nodes start sensing. Once sensing has started, nodes are able to distinguish between query-relevant objects and irrelevant ones. This means that if the query is interested in vehicles, the detection mechanism allows each node to distinguish vehicles from any other kind of moving object, e.g., pedestrians or animals. This assumption is feasible, because detection mechanisms are typically designed for a specific type of object. For example, mechanisms for the detection of animals, e.g., acoustic animal recognition [80], already filter irrelevant events. Other detection mechanisms for animals rely on collars [69, 91] attached to individuals of the observed species, i.e., animals without a collar remain undetected.

The detection technologies mentioned above typically allow the identification of these individuals as well which is important for complex spatio-temporal queries. For instance, if node S_i detects a certain object and another node S_j detects the same object later on, the sensor network can derive that the same object was detected twice. Such an identification is typically available, e.g., through identification numbers on the collars, characteristical noise patters or ferro-magnetical signatures (cf. [6] for several examples).

1.2 Contributions and Outline of this Dissertation

This dissertation is the first that addresses spatio-temporal queries in sensor networks and its major contributions are as follows:

C.1 Spatio-Temporal Semantics: We define the semantics of spatio-temporal queries in sensor networks based on object detections by sensor nodes. First, we develop a formal model that provides a layer of abstraction for the information acquired through object detection mechanisms of arbitrary precision. Based on this abstraction we define the semantics of spatio-temporal queries involving regions as well as zones. We integrate these semantics into the foundations of moving object databases which is challenging because the semantics also have to take into account the properties of sensor networks, e.g., unobserved areas, node failures or inaccurate object detection. The integration is important, because it allows the application of existing results for Moving Object Databases to sensor networks, e.g., spatio-temporal query languages like [38].

As we show, particularly regions are problematic in combination with inaccurate detection mechanisms and unobserved areas. To solve this problem, we propose an approximation approach that partitions objects detected into three subsets: Objects that definitely conform to a spatio-temporal query, objects that might conform and objects that definitely do not conform. We formally prove for this approximation approach that it is optimal, i.e., that a sensor network cannot provide a better result under non-restrictive assumptions.

In addition, we investigate the semantical depth of our approach in the context of regions as well as zones and compare it to moving object databases.

C.2 Query Dissemination: There has been a plethora of research aimed at efficient broadcasting techniques and query dissemination. In many cases, the existing mechanisms have been solely evaluated using simulations. We conduct a performance study of a representative subset of the existing mechanisms using a Sun SPOT deployment to disseminate spatio-temporal queries. The most important result of this study is that particularly highly sophisticated mechanisms often cannot cope with the nature of sensor networks.

Based on the results of the performance study, we derive that probabilistic broadcasting is a promising approach. With this approach, upon receiving a query, every node has a probability P to forward the query. Finding a minimal value for P where all nodes receive the query is an optimization problem. We develop an optimizer for probabilistic query dissemination and demonstrate its efficiency using simulations as well as a Sun SPOT deployment.

C.3 Efficient Processing: Based on the semantics (**C.1**), we develop a spatio-temporal query processor for sensor networks that derives results for spatio-temporal queries efficiently. To derive results, sensor nodes must collect information on objects and their movement. A naive approach to do so is sending all information about detected objects to the base station. But we show that this is prohibitive regarding energy consumption. Thus, we propose two strategies which allow in-network computation of results. These strategies differ in the way they collect from nodes close to each other. By combining the spatial correlation of object detection and the semantics of spatio-temporal queries, both strategies reduce the number of messages significantly. Our evaluation based on simulations as well as several Sun SPOT deployments shows that in-network strategies reduce communication by 45% to 89%, compared to collecting all information at the base station.

The remainder of this dissertation is organized as follows: Chapter 2 explains the basic concepts of Moving Object Databases and investigates the challenges of processing spatio-temporal queries in sensor networks. Additionally, Chapter 2 reviews related work and discusses the impact of future developments regarding the hardware used in sensor networks. Chapter 3 defines the semantical foundations of spatio-temporal queries in sensor networks (**C.1**). The details of our work on query dissemination (**C.2**) are presented in Chapter 4. This includes a performance study of a representative subset of existing approaches for query dissemination in a real sensor network. After the queries has been disseminated to sensor nodes, spatio-temporal queries must be processed with as little energy consumption as possible. Chapter 5 provides in-network processing strategies for spatio-temporal queries (**C.3**). We conclude in Chapter 6 and sketch directions for future research on spatio-temporal query processing in sensor networks.

Parts of this dissertation were originally published in shortened form in [12] (Semantics), [7, 11] (Query dissemination) and [13, 14] (Energy-efficient processing).

1.2. CONTRIBUTIONS AND OUTLINE OF THIS DISSERTATION

Chapter 2
Technical Background

In this chapter, we provide further information on moving object databases, relational query processing in sensor networks and sensor node hardware in general. Most importantly, we review related work and show that neither existing query processors for sensor networks nor moving object databases are feasible alternatives for accessing object tracking sensor networks declaratively. Additionally, we show that the challenges addressed in this dissertation will persist even if future developments on node hardware, communication protocols etc. are taken into account.

2.1 Sensor Network Platforms and Architecture

The term "sensor network" is by no means well-defined, because the applications they are used for have a big impact on the actual hardware and architecture used. For our purpose, a sensor network is a collection of hundreds or thousands of stationary sensor nodes and at least one base station. The base station serves as a central point of access from which query results must be sent to the user. Each node is equipped with sensors, memory, a processor, wireless radio and a battery. This section investigates the major challenges of sensor network deployments at present and how these challenges will evolve with future developments in hardware or architecture.

2.1.1 State-of-the-Art on Sensor Nodes

For our deployments and experiments, we used Sun SPOT sensor nodes [120] and Mica motes [131]. We describe both platforms in detail and provide an overview of other, currently available sensor nodes. Based on this overview, we derive a set of constraints that affect query processing in sensor networks in general and abstract from concrete platforms. Our mechanisms address these constraints instead of being tailored towards a specific hardware platform which ensures that they are applicable to any object tracking sensor network.

2.1. SENSOR NETWORK PLATFORMS AND ARCHITECTURE

Example Platform: Sun SPOTs

Sun SPOTs are a development platform published by Sun Research. Each node measures about 70×41×23 millimeters and consists of three components as shown in Figure 2.1 (from top to bottom): the *sensor board*, a *main board* and a rechargeable 3.7V lithium-ion battery with a capacity of 750 mAh.

Figure 2.1: A Sun SPOT sensor node and its components

The default sensor board is equipped with sensors for light, temperature and acceleration. In addition, the default sensor board has eight programmable LEDs for debugging as well as two buttons to trigger events on the sensor node. To allow easy extension, pins to attach additional hardware to the sensor board, e.g., additional sensors for humidity, RFID readers or GPS receivers, are available as well. Even though a real deployment would tailor the sensors installed to the needs of the application, the default board is useful during the development process of an application. Furthermore, the modular architecture of the SPOTs allows the replacement of the default sensor board with other extension boards or custom sensors ranging from sound, barometric pressure or magnetic fields to cameras and laser scanners.

The main board contains a 32-bit ARM920T processor which executes at 180MHz max. clock speed. Furthermore, 512KB RAM and 4MB flash memory are used to store data. Even though access to flash memory consumes non-negligible amounts of energy, we disregard this, since all our mechanisms run exclusively on RAM. SPOTs are IEEE 802.15.4 [64] compatible and use a CC2420 radio chip for communication. To reduce energy consumption, different components of the hardware can be switched off and several *sleep states* of the whole node are supported. This allows a full-charged Sun SPOT to operate up to 900 days, but naive usage of CPU, LEDs and radio can reduce this to a few hours (cf. Appendix A).

The main board also contains two AT91 timer/counter units operating at different frequencies. These allow scheduling of operations with high temporal precision and serve as a clock to determine the current date and time. There are several ways to synchronize the clock: Whenever software is installed on a SPOT, the clock is synchronized with the clock of the computer from which the software is installed. For most deployments, this synchronization is sufficient, since the deviation of the clock is so small that the batteries are depleted before the deviation becomes significant. Furthermore, there exists protocols which allow fine-grained synchronization of sensor node clocks [37]. Time synchronization is important for our purpose, because it allows two sensor nodes to determine if they detected an object at the same time. Furthermore, existing protocols to conserve energy by switching off radio and other devices require clocks to coordinate waking and sleeping.

Software for SPOTs is written in Java (CLDC 1.1 compatible) and executed using a Squawk virtual machine which is specifically designed for platforms such as sensor nodes. The Squawk VM is Java ME compatible and thus, code developed for this dissertation could be easily used on other Java platforms.

Example Platform: Mica Motes

One of the first sensor nodes that were commercially available were *Mica motes*. Mica motes have a 4MHz, 8bit ATMEL ATmega128L processor and 4KB of RAM. Additionally, 512 KB of non-volatile flash memory is installed on Mica motes.

By default, Mica motes do not have any sensing hardware installed, but there are several sensor boards available. Mica Motes have a 51-pin connector which allows the attachment of these boards to the nodes. Sensor boards contain different sensors of varying complexity for different physical phenomena.

The most important difference between motes are the batteries and their impact on the form of the mote as illustrated by Figure 2.2: Mica2 motes are powered by two standard AA batteries. With a size $58 \times 32 \times 7$ millimeters (excluding batteries), their form precisely matches the form of the two AA batteries. Contrary to this, Mica2DOT nodes use 3V coin cells to power the same hardware. This results in a coin-shaped form and reduces the size of the mote to 25×6 millimeters (exclusive batteries). Sleep states and shutdown of different components of the hardware is supported as well and allows motes to run for up to a year.

Another difference between different versions of Mica motes is their radio chip: Similar to Sun SPOTs, the MicaZ motes [131] use a use the CC2420 chip, while Mica2 and Mica2Dot motes use CC1000 chips.

The operating system used for Mica motes is TinyOS [61]. TinyOS is an open-source operating

2.1. SENSOR NETWORK PLATFORMS AND ARCHITECTURE

Figure 2.2: Mica motes: Mica2 (left) and Mica2Dot (right)

system specifically designed for sensor nodes with energy and memory constraints as they appear on Mica motes and other platforms. Programs for TinyOS are written in a C-like programming language called *nesC* [49]. In this context, the term "operating system" is different from its typical meaning for computers since TinyOS lacks many features that typically define an operating system: Features like process isolation, scheduling, memory management or multi-threading are not included in TinyOS and its main feature is a set of library interfaces that provide convenient software abstraction to access hardware. These and many other features known from traditional operating systems have been removed to reduce the memory footprint of TinyOS to the absolute minimum.

Other Sensor Node Types

There are multiple platforms for sensor networks that have been designed for different applications. We discuss them here briefly to provide a broader perspective on sensor nodes and their evolution over time.

Intel™ Motes [97] have been developed with the aim of providing higher bandwidth, more computational capabilities, smaller size and longer periods of operation for industrial or military applications. The circuit board of an Intel mote has a size of 30 × 30 millimeters which integrates all components of the mote: A 12 MHz CPU, 64KB RAM, a radio with a range of approximately 30 meters and several connectors to allow the attachment of sensors and other hardware, e.g., LEDs. The latest generation of Intel motes [2], has significantly higher computational capabilities than its predecessor at almost the same size (48 × 36 millimeters): 32MB RAM and 32MB flash memory allow single nodes to store significant amounts of data. The 32-bit Intel PXA270 XScale CPU allows processing of such data, even if they are streamed at high temporal resolution. To keep power consumption low, this CPU supports frequency scaling in the range of 13–416 MHz. Similar to SPOTs and Mica motes, Intel motes use the CC2420 radio chip, and in addition Intel motes support Bluetooth [115].

The ETH Zürich has developed its own sensor node platform called BTnode [40]. There have been several revisions of the hardware which generally increased memory capacity or communication capabilities. The current revision 3 uses an ATmega128L micro-controller running at 8 MHz with 244KB RAM and additionally 128KB flash memory. In addition to the CC1000 low-power radio chip, BTnodes support Bluetooth for communication. Similar to Mica2 motes, BTmotes are powered by two AA batteries and thus their size of 58.15 × 33 is also similar.

For further information on different node platforms see [78].

Sensing Hardware and Detection Mechanisms

A large number of different sensors have been reported to work in sensor networks; from simple passive devices whose resistance varies with environmental conditions such as temperature, humidity or light, to more complex sensors like magnetometers and even radar. Since this dissertation focuses on object tracking sensor networks, we limit our review to sensing hardware that has been used for detection of moving objects. This allows the identification of important properties of these detection mechanisms that must be taken into account when processing spatio-temporal queries in sensor networks.

Target and object detection has received a lot attention from research [6, 18, 35, 57, 58, 80, 114, 119, 138]. For example, [58] uses magnetometers to detect the magnetic field generated by moving vehicles. According to their results from an outdoor deployment of 70 nodes, the magnetometers are able to reliably detect a vehicle at a distance of 8-10 feet. So far, the existing approaches on object detection are aimed at increasing the accuracy of detection or the efficiency, particularly if readings from several nodes must be combined to detect an object. The spatio-temporal query processor proposed in this dissertation builds on top of these approaches: The existing detection mechanisms try to detect objects and our approach provides users with a declarative way to access this information on moving objects. In the following, we discuss important lessons learned from the aforementioned object detection approaches which we must take into account for our approach.

In [80], microphones have been installed on sensor nodes to detect, classify and identify animals, in this case frogs. Acoustic approaches have been applied to vehicles as well [18, 119], where the noise of engines or propulsion gear has been used to detect vehicles. Similarly, [91] tracks caribous using radio-collars. All of these mechanisms share that they cannot determine the exact position of an object detected. This is different with other detection mechanisms that allow distance estimation like Laser Scanners or even provide precise locations for detected objects like radar [35].

Several limitations regarding detection of vehicles and humans using magnetometers and micropower-impulse (MI) radar (TWR-ISM-002-I) have been reported by [6]: Their magnetometers became desensitized over time and this process was accelerated if the sensor node was exposed to heat for longer periods of time. While this could be fixed by circuitry that re-calibrated the magnetometers at certain intervals, the area observed by a sensor node was significantly reduced temporarily. Furthermore, the MI-radar and the magnetometer influenced each other when differ-

2.1. SENSOR NETWORK PLATFORMS AND ARCHITECTURE

ent nodes where deployed close to each other. While the documentation [3] of the TWR-ISM-002-I mentions a maximum range of 60 feet, the actual range of the radar was usually significantly less and external influences, e.g., rain, reduced the range even more. Hence, one has to take into account that detection ranges change over time resulting in areas that temporarily or permanently unobserved. These and other intricacies of object detection must be taken into account when processing spatio-temporal queries in sensor networks.

2.1.2 Communication in Sensor Networks

Wireless communication is one of the key features of sensor nodes because it allows data transport without wiring. This section reviews the hardware and the energy consumption characteristics as well as mechanisms that allow multi-hop communication.

Radio Hardware

As apparent from the review above, the CC2420 [26] and CC1000 [25] radio chips are commonly used for sensor nodes. While the CC2420 operates at 2.4 GHz, the CC1000 operates at frequencies below 1 GHz. The radio chips are half-duplex which means that the radio-chip can only either listen to the wireless medium or send a message, i.e., a node can never listen to its own message. This is important because nodes sending messages cannot determine if a collision occurred by themselves. Therefore, sensor networks require measures to avoid collisions as described below.

According to the data sheets of both radio chips, the typical communication distances range from a few meters to 50 meters. External influences have a significant impact on the actual communication range: For example, the communication ranges of the Sun SPOTs deployed in the KSN Testbed described in Appendix C.1 were significantly influenced by metal fire doors (cf. Figure C.1). If the fire doors were opened, there were nodes that could communicate directly with each other, while communication between these nodes required relaying of messages by intermediate nodes if the doors were closed. Generally, we were never able to observe communication ranges of more than 20 meters indoors and 35 meters outdoors.

Changes in communication ranges and temporarily unavailable nodes must be taken into account by the design of any mechanism for sensor networks. Typically, this issue is resolved by routing protocols which will be discussed next, but in some cases errors must be handled at application level.

Communication Standards and Protocols

Most communication protocols developed for sensor networks are based on the IEEE 802.15.4 [64] standard. 802.15.4 specifies the two lowest layers of the OSI-model for low-rate wireless personal area networks (WPAN): the physical layer (PHY) and the medium access control (MAC) layer. There exist several different protocols based on 802.15.4 that provide high-level protocols, e.g., for routing or compression. We discuss different 802.15.4-compliant implementations of these two layers first and then describe high-level protocols.

Physical and Medium Access Layer The physical layer (PHY) ultimately provides the transmission service and access to communication hardware. Among other tasks, the main task of PHY is encoding the digital information into an analogue signal for sending and decoding incoming analogue signals into digital information while receiving. There are several different encoding schemes and 802.15.4 uses direct-sequence spread spectrum (DSSS). Generally, the aim of these schemes is to protect the analogue signal from corruption or noise. For all of these schemes this protection comes at the cost of bandwidth, i.e., the encoded signal takes up more bandwidth than the digital information that is encoded. This is one of the reasons for the difference between the bandwidth of the radio chip and the actual bandwidth of a sensor node. For example, the CC2420 radio chip has a maximum bandwidth of 250 kbps, but one can observe 40 kbps at most in reality.

The MAC layer handles all access to the physical radio channel and device. One of the important tasks of this layer is contention control: When more than one node attempts to send a message at the same time, a collision occurs, i.e., receivers of the message cannot decode the message correctly and therefore discard it. To avoid unnecessary retries and the resulting energy consumption, 802.15.4 specifies a *carrier sense multi access with collision avoidance protocol (CSMA/CA)*. Before sending a message, a node waits a random time and listens to the wireless medium. If the medium is busy, i.e., at least one other node is already sending, the message is delayed for a random time. When the node determines that the medium is clear, it tries to send the message. Waiting or delaying messages obviously further reduces the radio bandwidth and thus, the MAC layer also contributes to the reduced bandwidth observed in reality. CSMA/CA reduces the chance of collisions, but does not prevent or detect them, e.g., because of the hidden terminal problem [45, 109].

The wireless medium is a broadcast medium, i.e., when a message is sent, all nodes in range of the sender can receive the message. The MAC layer also allows unicast communication by attaching the unique identifier of the node to a every message. Nodes decode this identifier and discard the message if it does not match their own identifier. Contrary to broadcast communication, the unicast communication supports link-level acknowledgements, i.e., the sender can determine if the message was received by the intended neighbor node.

802.15.4 based High-Level Protocols Due to the ad-hoc nature of sensor networks and the limited range of radio communication, it must be taken into account that certain nodes cannot communicate with each other directly. This is the motivation for several high-level protocols [95, 118, 140] that build upon the 802.15.4 specification and provide multi-hop communication, i.e., messages are forwarded by multiple nodes if the sender and receiver cannot communicate directly. The general approach of these protocols is as follows: Each node stores a short list of neighbors, i.e., nodes it can communicate directly with, and some routing information about the connectivity of each neighbor to the rest of the network. This information is then used to make intelligent

2.1. SENSOR NETWORK PLATFORMS AND ARCHITECTURE

routing decision, i.e., forward the message towards the intended receiver efficiently. The main task of such a protocol is therefore to acquire and maintain this information on neighbors and their connectivity. Another feature of these protocols are end-to-end acknowledgements which allow the sender to determine that a multi-hop transmission of a message was successful.

Routing protocols that allow finding and maintaining routes in sensor networks can be classified into *proactive* and *reactive* protocols (cf. [89] for an overview). In this context, reactive means that routes between a sender and a receiver are established only on demand whereas proactive protocols acquire and maintain routes independently of their usage. We briefly describe *ad-hoc on-demand distance vector routing (AODV)* [103, 104] because it was used for our evaluation but other routing protocols could be used as well. Appendix C.3 describes the AODV implementation we used in detail. In AODV, the network is silent until a node wants to send a message, i.e., it is a reactive protocol. At this point, the sender node broadcasts a request for a route. Upon receiving a request, the node stores the identifier of the node it received the request from, checks if there exists an entry for destination of the request and re-broadcasts the request if no such entry exists. If such an entry exists, this is reported back to the original sender of the request which in turn can start sending the message. The KSN Radio Stack described in Appendix C.3 is also based on the AODV protocol and was used for the majority of the evaluations using Sun SPOTs.

2.1.3 Energy Supply and Consumption

Sensor nodes typically are either battery powered or equipped with a solar panel. In the latter case, the solar panel is used to recharge batteries which serve as a power supply during times where no sun light is available [32, 63], e.g., at night or during bad weather. Careless use of the energy resources can exhaust batteries within hours as shown by Appendix A and reported by [27, 83]. Thus, even if solar panels are used, mechanisms must be designed in a way that energy consumption is minimized to increase the lifetime of a sensor network.

Typically, sensing and communication dominate the power consumption by orders of magnitude compared to computation or RAM access [50, 82]. For example, [83] reports that $\approx 94\%$ of the energy consumption for a simple application collecting sensor readings from Mica motes must be attributed to communication. Our measurements in Appendix A confirm this even for the significantly more powerful CPU used in Sun SPOT sensor nodes. Therefore, the key objective regarding energy efficiency is reducing the energy consumed by the communication devices to a minimum.

The general problem with reducing energy consumption of communication devices is that the energy consumed while receiving or sending is almost as high as if there is no communication at all unless the device is completely switched off. For example, [27] reports that several nodes kept their radio switched on at all times due to a software bug. The affected nodes depleted their batteries in a short time while other nodes without the bug of the same deployment ran for weeks. Thus, keeping the radio switched on at all times is not a viable option, but if the radio is switched off, the node cannot communicate at all.

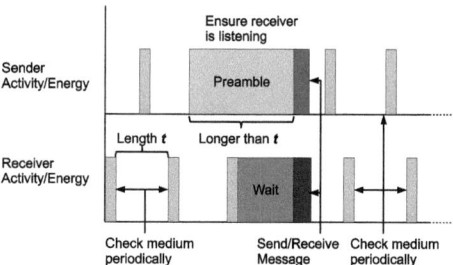

Figure 2.3: Illustration of B-MAC [105]

To address this so called *idle listening*, the networking community has proposed several energy-aware, 802.15.4-compliant MAC implementations [20, 105, 126, 134]. These MAC protocols reduce energy consumption by shutting down the radio whenever it is not needed and defining mechanisms to wake up the radio when it is needed to ensure that communication still works. An example of a state-of-the-art, energy-aware MAC protocol is B-MAC [105]. The core mechanism of the protocol and its impact on energy consumption is illustrated in Figure 2.3: Nodes check periodically if there exists an another neighboring node that would like to send a message and shut down the radio if no such node exists. If a node has to send a message, the node will notify all surrounding nodes of this by occupying the medium and sending a *preamble*. This preamble indicates which node is the intended recipient of the message and the length of this preamble is at least as long as the period that nodes shut down the radio. This ensures that the recipient of the message wakes up its radio at least once during this period and keeps it on until the message is transmitted. The length of the *sleep period* is typically in the order of seconds while the time spent sending the actual message typically takes a few milliseconds. Thus, the energy consumption for the preamble at the sender and waiting for the message at the receiver is orders of magnitudes larger than sending the message. This pays off because sensor nodes are typically idle for more than 90% of the time, i.e., neither sending nor receiving.

The schema illustrated above applies to all energy-aware MAC protocols [55]: They exploit the ratio between idle time and active time of sensor nodes to switch the radio off, but induce an overhead that is large compared to sending the actual message. From a query processing perspective, the number of times such a MAC layer is forced to wake up the radio is the only influence query processing has on energy consumption, i.e., the number of times messages are sent or received. The actual amount of energy consumed for sending/receiving a message depends on several factors that are outside of the control of the query processor, e.g., actual MAC implementation or occurrence of collisions. Therefore, we use the number of messages sent and received as a proxy to evaluate the energy efficiency of our measures. In particular, we do not count the number of

2.1. SENSOR NETWORK PLATFORMS AND ARCHITECTURE

bytes sent or received. This is because the time the radio is switched on and thereby the amount of energy consumed for sending a message is only marginally affected by the size of the message but mainly depends on the MAC protocol as shown above. Appendix A provides an evaluation that investigates the energy consumption in relation to message size.

2.1.4 Impact of Future Developments

So far, we studied the properties sensor networks as they are in use today. This section examines technology trends that will shape research on sensor networks in the future. Predicting these trends is important, because it allows researchers to distinguish problems that will continue to be important in the future from problems that become obsolete with further advances in hardware and software.

Wireless Communication

The most important point regarding the development of radio hardware is that multi-hop communication will be required even with future developments taken into account. Assuming hardware with infinite range, the energy required for sending a signal over a distance d is d^k where k is the *path-loss exponent*. The actual value of k depends on several factors, e.g., the length of the antenna or if there are obstacles between the sender and the receiver. Realistic values for k are between 2 and 4 with sensor networks usually tending to 4, particularly for indoor deployments [108]. Thus, multi-hop communication and the energy-efficient routing protocols will remain important in sensor networks.

Even though low-power radio development could reduce power consumption of radios by one order of magnitude [108], energy consumption related to communication will still dominate the overall energy consumption. In particular the predicted energy savings possible in other areas, e.g., CPU or memory [24, 41, 62, 86], exceed those possible for communication devices. Therefore, even with technological advances regarding the energy consumption of different hardware components taken into account, reducing communication will remain an important design target for query processing in sensor networks.

Computational Capabilities

The *International Technology Roadmap for Semiconductors (ITRS) [68]* is an annual prediction of the technology trends in semiconductor technology for the following 15 years. For the time between 1999 and 2014, the ITRS report has predicted an increase of transistor density by a factor of 30. This prediction has been accurate so far and the most recent report of 2009 predicts a continuation of this trend. Thus, it can be expected that the computational capabilities of sensor nodes will also increase. This is already apparent with the development history of the Intel motes [2, 97] described above.

Another prediction for 1999–2014 of the ITRS is that while transistor density increases by a factor of 30, the energy consumption of these chips will only double. This means that increasing the computational power by a factor of 15 in sensor nodes does not increase power consumption compared to the chips in sensor nodes today. With the introduction of power saving features into CPUs used in sensor nodes [2, 86], e.g., frequency scaling, the actual energy costs for computation has outperformed this prediction of the ITRS.

In addition to the increased computational power of sensor nodes, it is expected that memory capacity will increase by a factor of 1000 between 1999 and 2014. This trend has matched the actual performance of semiconductors and the ITRS report of 2009 confirms this trend for the future. Comparing the 4 kilobytes in Mica motes with 512 kilobytes of Sun SPOTs substantiates this trend. For sensor nodes, this means that the memory constraints will be a matter of the past in the near future with flash memory in the order of gigabytes and several megabytes of RAM.

Even though having large quantities of RAM on sensor nodes will increase their energy consumption [1], one can expect that memory will not be an important constraint in the future. In particular, there have been several proposals for reducing energy consumption of memory chips [24, 41, 62]. Summing up, while the current development of software for sensor nodes has to cope with severe limitations regarding energy consumption and computational power, these problems will cease to exist in the future.

Energy Consumption and Storage

The advances of battery technology are closely tied to the requirements of their electronic applications. However, the time scale for battery improvements is very long compared to electronics. According to [106], battery capacity only doubles in 35 years while the number of transistors doubles every 12–24 months according to Moore's Law [96]. Furthermore, the energy density of batteries as well as their capacity are bounded by chemical and physical limits.

Thus, while the computational capacity of sensor nodes will increase in the near future, the energy constraints will remain a key design target for applications in sensor networks. This also applies to solar powered sensor nodes, since they require batteries to survive time spans without sun light as mentioned above. In such a solar powered system, the limited capacity combined with the energy consumption of radio communication will still deplete batteries within days without sophisticated measures to reduce energy consumption.

2.1.5 Summary

This section has reviewed sensor network technology and the challenges associated with sensor networks in general, but also with object-tracking sensor networks in particular. We have shown that energy efficiency is the most important optimization goal in sensor networks, even with future technological developments taken into account. The largest contributor to energy consumption is communication and the networking community has made major efforts regarding the reduction of energy consumption for communication. These state-of-the-art protocols control and minimize the activity time of the radio chip at hardware level, i.e., they minimize the energy consumption if communication between nodes is required by the application. Our mechanisms built on top of these protocols and minimize the number of messages required by the application, in our case the query processor.

Another challenge of sensor networks that has been addressed by the networking community is reliable multi-hop communication in the context of changing connectivities, node failures and other intricacies. We use these results for query processing and cleanly separate between the routing layer and the query processing layer, i.e., we do not change the routes provided by the networking layer. This allows the application of our measures to different routing mechanisms. Furthermore, most of the errors related to communication are handled by the routing layer. Whenever the error handling of the routing layer is insufficient to obtain correct query results, we show how to detect and handle the error.

Target or object tracking has received a lot of attention in different contexts resulting in different approaches for all kinds of objects. A challenge that has to be solved at the query processing layer is the varying accuracy of detection hardware and the mechanisms that use this hardware to determine if an object has been detected or not. We address this by defining spatio-temporal semantics that cope with this varying accuracy and provide feedback about the accuracy of the query result to the user.

2.2 Fundamentals of Moving Object Databases

Research on moving object databases has shown that relational database systems are insufficient for efficient storage of spatio-temporal data and processing spatio-temporal queries. To address this issue, spatio-temporal data types and operators have been introduced. This section reviews the basic concepts of moving object databases as far as they are relevant for this dissertation. For further information see [39, 53, 54]. Afterwards, we show that the characteristics of sensor networks are in the way of applying these research results in a straightforward way to sensor networks.

2.2.1 Point-Set Topology

The fundamental concepts of moving object databases are based on *point-set topology* [46]. According to point-set topology, a space is composed of infinitely many points, e.g., the d-dimensional Euclidean space $\mathbb{E}^d$. We will use the 2-dimensional space for illustrations but all concepts, those of moving object databases as well as our own, can be extended to three or more dimensions and other spaces.

Point-set topology distinguishes subsets of space, i.e., finite sets of points, which are called entities. For any entity $\mathbf{e}$, there exists a complement $\overline{\mathbf{e}}$, i.e., a set of all points not contained in $\mathbf{e}$. Every entity $\mathbf{e}$ partitions the space into three pair-wise disjoint subsets: the *interior* $\mathbf{e}^I$, the *border* $\mathbf{e}^B$ and the *exterior* $\mathbf{e}^E$. We provide the formal definitions of these concepts for Euclidean spaces in the following (see [36, 46] for more universal definitions). Let $\mathbf{b}(\mathsf{c},\epsilon)$ be an ϵ-ball i.e., a set of points whose distance from the center c in the metric d is less than $\epsilon > 0$:

$$\mathbf{b}(\mathsf{c},\epsilon) = \left\{ \mathsf{p} \in \mathbb{E}^d \mid d(\mathsf{p},\mathsf{c}) < \epsilon \right\} \tag{2.1}$$

Using the concept of a ϵ-ball, the partitions interior and border are defined as follows:

Definition 1 (Interior): The *interior* of an entity $\mathbf{e}$, denoted $\mathbf{e}^I$, is a point set that contains a point $\mathsf{c} \in \mathbb{E}^d$ if there exists an ϵ-ball around c that only contains points in $\mathbf{e}$. □

Definition 2 (Border): The *border* of an entity $\mathbf{e}$, denoted $\mathbf{e}^B$, is a point set that contains a point $\mathsf{c} \in \mathbb{E}^d$ if every ϵ-ball around c intersects with $\mathbf{e}$ and its complement $\overline{\mathbf{e}}$. □

Based on this, the exterior $\mathbf{e}^E$ contains all points that are neither part of the border nor the interior, i.e. in the interior of $\overline{\mathbf{e}}$:

Definition 3 (Exterior): The *exterior* of an entity $\mathbf{e}$, denoted by $\mathbf{e}^B$, is a point set that contains a point $\mathsf{c} \in \mathbb{E}^d$ if there exists an ϵ-ball around c that only contains points in $\overline{\mathbf{e}}$. □

There are three different types of entities: *objects*[1], *lines* and *regions*. We leave aside lines in the following, since they are irrelevant in our context.

Definition 4 (Object): An *object* $\mathbf{o}$ is an entity that is represented by its position $\mathsf{p} \in \mathbb{E}^d$. □

An object partitions the space as follows: The interior $\mathbf{o}^I$ contains only p, the border $\mathbf{o}^B$ is empty, and all points except p are the exterior $\mathbf{o}^E$.

A region is a point set where every point p satisfies a set of conditions that describe an entity covering more than one point of space, e.g., a security area or storm. We denote the set of conditions that define a region $\mathbf{r}$ as $\mathsf{C}_\mathbf{r}$ and the function that checks for a point p if it fulfills $\mathsf{C}_\mathbf{r}$ as $\mathsf{C}_\mathbf{r}(\mathsf{p})$:

$$\mathsf{C}_\mathbf{r}(\mathsf{p}) = \begin{cases} \mathcal{T} & \text{iff } \mathsf{p} \text{ fulfills } \mathsf{C}_\mathbf{r} \\ \mathcal{F} & \text{Otherwise} \end{cases} \tag{2.2}$$

Defining regions as arbitrary point sets is problematic, because such point sets could contain anomalies like dangling lines, cuts and punctures. To avoid this, [122] introduce regularization which adds or removes points from regions until the aforementioned anomalies are corrected. To ease our presentation, we assume that one condition in $\mathsf{C}_\mathbf{r}$ corrects these anomalies, i.e., all regions are assumed to be regular in the following.

Definition 5 (Region): A *region* $\mathbf{r}$ is a set of points which satisfy a set of conditions $\mathsf{C}_\mathbf{r}$:

$$\mathbf{r} = \left\{ \mathsf{p} \in \mathbb{E}^d \mid \mathsf{C}_\mathbf{r}(\mathsf{p}) = \mathcal{T} \right\} \tag{2.3}$$

For a region $\mathbf{r}$, the partitions defined above are illustrated as follows: The border $\mathbf{r}^B$ contains all points of the line encompassing the interior $\mathbf{r}^I$. All points that are neither in $\mathbf{r}^B$ nor in $\mathbf{r}^I$ are part of the exterior $\mathbf{r}^E$.

---
[1] Entities represented by a single point in space are typically called *point* by publications on this subject. We refer to such an entity as *object* to clearly distinguish it from a point which is an element of space.

2.2. FUNDAMENTALS OF MOVING OBJECT DATABASES

$$\begin{pmatrix} a^B \cap b^B & \neq \emptyset & a^B \cap b^I & \neq \emptyset & a^B \cap b^E & \neq \emptyset \\ a^I \cap b^B & \neq \emptyset & a^I \cap b^I & \neq \emptyset & a^I \cap b^E & \neq \emptyset \\ a^E \cap b^B & \neq \emptyset & a^E \cap b^I & \neq \emptyset & a^E \cap b^E & \neq \emptyset \end{pmatrix}$$

Figure 2.4: 9-Intersection Model for two spatial entities **a** and **b**

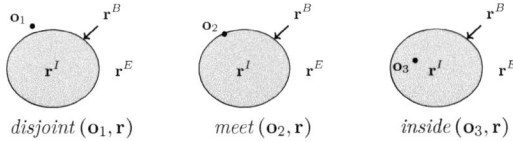

$disjoint(\mathbf{o}_1, \mathbf{r})$ $meet(\mathbf{o}_2, \mathbf{r})$ $inside(\mathbf{o}_3, \mathbf{r})$

Figure 2.5: Spatial Predicates for object/region relations

$$\begin{pmatrix} \mathcal{F} & \mathcal{F} & \mathcal{F} \\ \mathcal{F} & \mathcal{F} & \mathcal{T} \\ \mathcal{T} & \mathcal{T} & \mathcal{T} \end{pmatrix} \quad \begin{pmatrix} \mathcal{F} & \mathcal{F} & \mathcal{F} \\ \mathcal{T} & \mathcal{F} & \mathcal{F} \\ \mathcal{T} & \mathcal{T} & \mathcal{T} \end{pmatrix} \quad \begin{pmatrix} \mathcal{F} & \mathcal{F} & \mathcal{F} \\ \mathcal{F} & \mathcal{T} & \mathcal{F} \\ \mathcal{T} & \mathcal{T} & \mathcal{T} \end{pmatrix}$$

$disjoint(\mathbf{o}_1, \mathbf{r})$ $meet(\mathbf{o}_2, \mathbf{r})$ $inside(\mathbf{o}_3, \mathbf{r})$

Figure 2.6: 9-Intersection representation of spatial predicates (**a** = $\mathbf{o}_i$ and **b** = **r**)

2.2.2 Spatial and Spatio-Temporal Predicates

The 9-intersection model [36] describes the topological relationship of two entities **a** and **b**: As illustrated in Figure 2.4, there are nine possible intersections of the exterior, the border and the interior of **a** with the exterior, the border and the interior of **b**, respectively. Each of these intersections is either empty or not. Hence, a matrix of nine boolean values identifies the relationship of **a** and **b**. The topological relationship of **a** and **b** *matches* a given intersection matrix I, if the partitions of **a** and **b** intersect as described in I.

There exist $2^9 = 512$ unique intersection matrices, but only a few of them make sense. For example, if the interior and exterior of two entities intersect, their borders intersect as well. Each intersection matrix that describes a possible topological relation is associated with a *spatial predicate*.

Definition 6 (Spatial Predicate): A *spatial predicate* $p(\mathbf{a}, \mathbf{b})$ is a function associated with a unique intersection matrix I that returns $\mathcal{T}$, if the topological relation of **a** and **b** matches I:

$$p(\mathbf{a}, \mathbf{b}) = \begin{cases} \mathcal{T} & \text{iff } I \text{ matches topological relation of } \mathbf{a} \text{ and } \mathbf{b} \\ \mathcal{F} & \text{Otherwise} \end{cases} \quad (2.4)$$

For an object **o** and a region **r**, only three intersection matrices make sense which are associated with the following predicates: $inside(\mathbf{o}, \mathbf{r})$, $meet(\mathbf{o}, \mathbf{r})$ and $disjoint(\mathbf{o}, \mathbf{r})$. The intersection matrices associated with each of these predicates are shown in Figure 2.6. Figure 2.5 illustrates each predicate and Example 1 explains the intersection matrices matching the topological relationship shown in each case.

Example 1: The left-most matrix in Figure 2.6 describes $disjoint\,(\mathbf{o}_1, \mathbf{r})$. As mentioned before, the border of an object is empty, i.e., the $\mathbf{o}_1^B$ of $\mathbf{o}_1$ does not intersect with any partition of $\mathbf{r}$. This is reflected by the first row of the 9-intersection matrix for $disjoint\,(\mathbf{o}_1, \mathbf{r})$. The second row implies that $\mathbf{o}_1^I \cap \mathbf{r}^E \neq \emptyset$, i.e., $\mathbf{o}_1$ is outside of $\mathbf{r}$. The last row of the 9-intersection matrix describing $disjoint\,(\mathbf{o}_1, \mathbf{r})$ shows that $\mathbf{o}_1^E$ intersects with all partitions of $\mathbf{r}$.

The matrices for $meet\,(\mathbf{o}_2, \mathbf{r})$ and $inside\,(\mathbf{o}_3, \mathbf{r})$ only differ from the matrix for $disjoint\,(\mathbf{o}_1, \mathbf{r})$ in the second row: The topological relation of $\mathbf{o}_2$ and $\mathbf{r}$ conforms to $meet\,(\mathbf{o}_2, \mathbf{r})$ if $\mathbf{o}_2^I \cap \mathbf{r}^B \neq \emptyset$, i.e., the object $\mathbf{o}_2$ is on the border of $\mathbf{r}$. Similarly, $\mathbf{o}_3^I \cap \mathbf{r}^I \neq \emptyset$ implies that $\mathbf{o}_3$ is inside of $\mathbf{r}$, i.e., $inside\,(\mathbf{o}_3, \mathbf{r})$. ♦

So far, all concepts are purely spatial. To include temporal aspects into a model, one needs a model of time first. We refer to the domain of time as $\mathbb{T}$. *Temporal lifting* [39, 53] models time as a sequence of instants $t \in \mathbb{T}$ where each instant is represented by a real number, i.e., $\mathbb{T} \subset \mathbb{R}$. Lifting models a spatial value α that changes over time as a *temporal function* $\theta\,(\alpha) : \mathbb{T} \to \alpha$.

When entities such as objects or regions move, this is modeled by adding or removing points from their interior, border and exterior. Based on lifting, one can model a *moving object* or a *moving region* as a point set that changes over time, i.e., an entity $\mathbf{e}$ that moves is modeled as a temporal function $\theta\,(\mathbf{e})$.

Definition 7 (Moving Object): A *moving object* $\mathbf{O}$ is a lifted spatial object $\mathbf{o}$, i.e., a function $\theta\left(\mathbb{E}^d\right) : \mathbb{T} \to \mathbb{E}^d \cup \{\emptyset\}$ that models the position of an object over time. If $\mathbf{o} = \emptyset$, i.e., the object does not exist, at some point in time $t \in \mathbb{T}$, the function returns $\emptyset$ for this instant of time. □

The set $\mathbb{P}$ contains all possible point sets and every region $\mathbf{r}$ is an element of $\mathbb{P}$.

Definition 8 (Moving Region): A *moving region* $\mathbf{R}$ is lifted spatial region $\mathbf{r}$, i.e., a function $\theta\,(\mathbf{r}) : \mathbb{T} \to \mathbb{P} \cup \{\emptyset\}$. If $\mathbf{r} = \emptyset$ at some instant $t \in \mathbb{T}$, the region does not exist at this time and thus the temporal function returns $\emptyset$. □

Lifting is applicable to predicates as well: A spatial predicate $p\,(\mathbf{o}, \mathbf{r})$ is a function that returns either $\mathcal{T}$ or $\mathcal{F}$. In the context of $p\,(\mathbf{o}, \mathbf{r})$, the topological relationship of $\mathbf{o}$ and $\mathbf{r}$ is modeled by the boolean return value of $p\,(\mathbf{o}, \mathbf{r})$. Hence, a *spatio-temporal predicate* is a lifted spatial predicate:

Definition 9 (Spatio-Temporal Predicate): A *spatio-temporal predicate* $P\,(\mathbf{O}, \mathbf{R})$ is a lifted version of spatial predicate $p\,(\mathbf{o}, \mathbf{r})$, i.e., $P\,(\mathbf{O}, \mathbf{R}) = \mathcal{T}$ for every instant $t \in \mathbb{T}$ where $p\,(\mathbf{o}, \mathbf{r}) = \mathcal{T}$ and $P\,(\mathbf{O}, \mathbf{R}) = \mathcal{F}$ otherwise. □

To avoid confusion and make notations discernible, we adopt the following convention widely used by the moving object database community for the remainder of this dissertation: We denote purely spatial entities and predicates by lower case letters and start spatio-temporal entities and objects with capital letters. For example, $\mathbf{o}$ is a purely spatial object while $\mathbf{O}$ is a moving object, i.e., a spatio-temporal entity. This applies to predicates as well: $Inside\,(\mathbf{O}, \mathbf{R})$ refers to the lifted

2.2. FUNDAMENTALS OF MOVING OBJECT DATABASES

version of the spatial predicate *inside* (o, r).

2.2.3 Spatio-Temporal Developments

In moving object databases, users formulate a query by describing the movement they are interested in. To express arbitrarily complex changes of relationships between spatio-temporal entities, [39] defines the concatenation operator as follows:

Definition 10 (Concatenation): The *concatenation* of two predicates, $P \triangleright Q$, is true if P is true for some time interval $[t_0; t_1[$, and Q is true at t_1. □

Using this concatenation operator, one can construct *sequences* of spatio-temporal predicates $P_1 \triangleright P_2 \triangleright \ldots \triangleright P_q$. We refer to such a sequence of spatio-temporal predicates as *spatio-temporal development*.

Example 2: In one of the examples in Section 1.1, the user wants to know which vehicles $\mathbf{V}_i$ have moved into region $\mathbf{R}$. To fulfill the query, a vehicle $\mathbf{V}_i$ must be outside of $\mathbf{R}$, then move over the border $\mathbf{R}^B$ into the interior $\mathbf{R}^I$. This query is expressed as follows:

$$\textit{Disjoint}\,(\mathbf{V}_i, \mathbf{R}) \triangleright \textit{Meet}\,(\mathbf{V}_i, \mathbf{R}) \triangleright \textit{Inside}\,(\mathbf{V}_i, \mathbf{R}) \quad (2.5)$$

This spatio-temporal development usually is referred to as Enter $(\mathbf{V}_i, \mathbf{R})$.

$$\textit{Disjoint}\,(\mathbf{V}_i, \mathbf{R}) \triangleright \textit{Meet}\,(\mathbf{V}_i, \mathbf{R}) \triangleright \textit{Disjoint}\,(\mathbf{V}_i, \mathbf{R}) \quad (2.6)$$

$$\textit{Inside}\,(\mathbf{V}_i, \mathbf{R}) \triangleright \textit{Meet}\,(\mathbf{V}_i, \mathbf{R}) \triangleright \textit{Disjoint}\,(\mathbf{V}_i, \mathbf{R}) \quad (2.7)$$

Other sequences are constructed similarly: The spatio-temporal development in (2.6) is typically paraphrased as Touch $(\mathbf{V}_i, \mathbf{R})$ and (2.7) shows a development called Leave $(\mathbf{V}_i, \mathbf{R})$. ♦

Semantical Depth [39] has studied the semantical depth of moving object databases by proposing a canonical collection of spatio-temporal developments. While infinite sequences of spatio-temporal predicates are possible, this study shows that it is sufficient to explicitly consider a canonical collection of 28 developments for moving object databases. These 28 unique spatio-temporal developments form a basic set from which more complex developments can be constructed through concatenation as illustrated by Example 3.

Example 3: Assuming a user is interested in objects $\mathbf{O}$ that enter a region $\mathbf{R}$, move around inside the region and then leave the region. To express this using the aforementioned developments, the user concatenates Enter $(\mathbf{O}, \mathbf{R})$ and Leave $(\mathbf{O}, \mathbf{R})$, i.e., Enter $(\mathbf{O}, \mathbf{R}) \triangleright$ Leave $(\mathbf{O}, \mathbf{R})$. Even though $\triangleright$ is only defined as a concatenation operator for predicates, this is still correct since spatio-temporal developments only paraphrase sequences of spatio-temporal predicates. Hence,

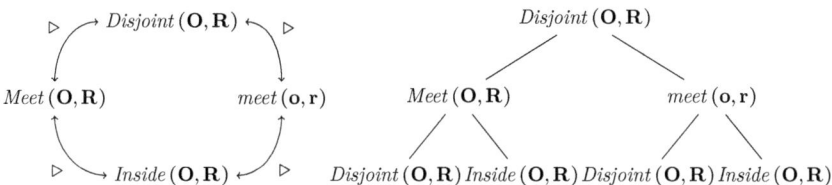

Figure 2.7: Development graph for object-region predicates

Figure 2.8: Development tree for developments starting with $Disjoint(\mathbf{O},\mathbf{R})$

the expression $Enter(\mathbf{O},\mathbf{R}) \triangleright Leave(\mathbf{O},\mathbf{R})$ translates to the sequence in (2.8).

$$\underbrace{Disjoint(\mathbf{O},\mathbf{R}) \triangleright Meet(\mathbf{O},\mathbf{R}) \triangleright Inside(\mathbf{O},\mathbf{R})}_{Enter(\mathbf{O},\mathbf{R})} \overbrace{\triangleright Meet(\mathbf{O},\mathbf{R}) \triangleright Disjoint(\mathbf{O},\mathbf{R})}^{Leave(\mathbf{O},\mathbf{R})} \qquad (2.8)$$

Note that the $Inside(\mathbf{O},\mathbf{R}) \triangleright Inside(\mathbf{O},\mathbf{R})$ occurring at the junction between $Enter(\mathbf{O},\mathbf{R})$ and $Leave(\mathbf{O},\mathbf{R})$ has been summarized to a single $Inside(\mathbf{O},\mathbf{R})$ since $P = P \triangleright P$ [39]. The concatenation $Enter(\mathbf{O},\mathbf{R}) \triangleright Leave(\mathbf{O},\mathbf{R})$ is typically denoted as $Cross(\mathbf{O},\mathbf{R})$. ♦

In the following, we briefly outline how this canonical collection of 28 spatio-temporal developments has been obtained. This is important, because we use a similar approach to measure the semantical depth of our approach and compare it to the semantical depth of moving object databases.

Figure 2.7 shows the so-called *development graph* which expresses the possible topological changes of objects and regions over time. Each vertex is associated with a predicate and an edge corresponds to the concatenation of the predicates connected by the edge, i.e., an edge (P,Q) equals $P \triangleright Q$. There are several important facts in this graph:

1. There are two vertexes associated to the "meet" predicate. In this context, the $meet(\mathbf{o},\mathbf{r})$ means that $\mathbf{o}$ is on the border of $\mathbf{r}$ at exactly one instant of time. Contrary to this, $Meet(\mathbf{O},\mathbf{R})$ is true if $\mathbf{O}$ is on the border for one or more instants of time.
2. There is no edge between $Meet(\mathbf{O},\mathbf{R})$ and $meet(\mathbf{o},\mathbf{r})$. This is because $Meet(\mathbf{O},\mathbf{R}) = meet(\mathbf{o},\mathbf{r}) \triangleright Meet(\mathbf{O},\mathbf{R})$.
3. There is no edge between $Inside(\mathbf{O},\mathbf{R})$ and $Disjoint(\mathbf{O},\mathbf{R})$ and vice versa. The reason for this is that an object has to move over the border at some point of time between $Inside(\mathbf{O},\mathbf{R})$ and $Disjoint(\mathbf{O},\mathbf{R})$.

2.2. FUNDAMENTALS OF MOVING OBJECT DATABASES

Every possible path $(P_1, P_2, \ldots, P_q)$ in the development graph describes a possible spatio-temporal development $P_1 \triangleright P_2 \triangleright \ldots \triangleright P_q$. There exists infinitely many paths through the graph due to cycles. To avoid these cycles and obtain a canonical collection of spatio-temporal developments, [39] construct *development trees* from the development graph. Each development tree corresponds to a predicate P and this predicate is the root the tree. The child-nodes of each node are all predicates reachable from P according to the development graph. To bound the depth of the tree, child-nodes are leaf-nodes in the tree if (1) all possible predicates are already on the path back to the root node or (2) the path to the root node contains a cycle. Figure 2.8 shows the development tree representing all unique developments starting with $Disjoint(\mathbf{O},\mathbf{R})$. This tree contains seven possible paths/developments. The trees where the other three predicates are root nodes are symmetrical to this tree, i.e., there are $4 \cdot 7 = 28$ developments.

2.2.4 Moving Object Databases vs. Sensor Networks

The previous section has reviewed the fundamentals of spatio-temporal query processing for traditional database systems. This section shows that some of the properties of these fundamentals are in the way of applying them to sensor networks in a straight-forward manner. Furthermore, it reviews existing work on spatio-temporal query processing in the context of sensor networks.

Moving object databases model objects as a single point in space. This implicitly means that the exact location of an object is known and for moving objects this implies that the position is known at any point in time. As shown in Section 2.1.1, most of the detection mechanisms used in sensor networks cannot provide this accuracy. There has been some work related to uncertainty regarding the position of objects: For example, [21, 31, 124, 125] have shown how to process spatio-temporal queries if the position of an object is only known an some instants of time, i.e., object positions are sampled over time. First, these methods still require precise object positions from time to time. Second, some are based on relatively strict assumptions, e.g., [125] assume that an object whose position is p_1 at t_1 and p_2 at t_2 moves on a straight line between p_1 and p_2 "at a constant speed".

Modelling regions as well-defined point sets is problematic as well: The border of a region is defined in such a way that it resembles a line that encompasses the region completely. While users of object-tracking sensor networks may define a region similarly, this definition does not take into account that the border of a region may be unobserved. For example, a user may query $Enter(\mathbf{O},\mathbf{R})$. Lets assume that $\mathbf{O}$ moves from the outside of $\mathbf{R}$ into the region, but it is never observed on the border, e.g., because a node that was deployed to observe the border has failed. From a semantical point of view, the object has entered $\mathbf{R}$, but the predicate $Meet(\mathbf{O},\mathbf{R})$ has never been true. Another problem with the border is that the time it takes an object to move over a line is infinitely short, because lines are not "thick". Hence, capturing the moment where the object is on the border would require an infinitely high temporal resolution of the detection hardware.

Capturing the spatial extend of regions is problematic as well in some applications. As motivated by the application examples in Section 1.1, in these cases users formulate queries regarding the object movement in the context of a set of nodes. These types of queries are unique to sensor networks and thus, there exists no previous work on them. Summing up, while concepts like predicates, 9-intersection model and predicate concatenation provide a foundation, a substantial amount of work is required to apply them to sensor networks.

2.3 Processing Relational Queries in Sensor Networks

So far, relational queries have been the focus of research on query processing in sensor networks [16, 17, 30, 50, 66, 81, 82, 84, 133]. Relational approaches are sufficient for queries interested in sets of measured values or aggregates over such values. An example of such a query is "What is the average temperature measured by all nodes?". It has been shown for traditional database systems that expressing spatio-temporal queries using relational systems results in complex [130] queries that are inefficient to process [53]. Appendix B illustrates this for a simple development. This section investigates the reasons for this and shows that they also apply to sensor networks. Most importantly we show that using existing relational query processors for sensor networks like TinyDB [84] or Cougar [133] would result in collecting all data on object detections at the base station. Our evaluation shows that this is inefficient compared to the in-network processing we propose.

One of the main reasons for the aforementioned inefficiency is the lack of continuous or time-aware data types: A value stored in a table is assumed to be constant unless it is updated explicitly. While this is appropriate for storing results, e.g., of temperature measurements taken at distinct instants of time, it is problematic if values change continuously. To cope with these continuous changes, the respective table or attribute value either requires frequent updates or queries are processed based on outdated data. Another problem is the lack of support for point sets: Since relational systems only allow the simple data types like integer, float or string for attributes, point sets are decomposed into separate values stored in many tuples. Processing spatio-temporal queries requires reconstructing these point sets prior to processing the actual query. Appendix B provides a SQL statement for a simple spatio-temporal query in a sensor network and illustrates these problems. The resulting SQL statement contains several subqueries and each of these subqueries contains joins.

Processing joins in sensor networks is a challenging problem which has received a lot of attention from the database community [1, 15, 28, 29, 132, 136, 139]. Join operators are important, because they allow combining a measured value of one node with the measured values of other nodes. This applies to spatio-temporal queries as well, because object detections of different nodes must be joined, e.g., in case of Enter$(\mathbf{O}, \mathbf{R})$ to determine if $\mathbf{O}$ was detected outside of $\mathbf{R}$ before it was detected inside of $\mathbf{R}$. The general problem with join operators in sensor networks is that a single node typically cannot decide if there exist tuples from other nodes that join with those stored locally. Finding out if such tuples exist is communication intensive because these tuples may be arbitrarily distributed over the network.

Most of the aforementioned proposals regarding join processing avoid the problem of arbitrary distributed join tuples by imposing restrictions and focusing on special types of join queries. [1] support the join operator for a relation of sensed data with a pre-defined, static external relation. Thus, the approach is inapplicable to spatio-temporal queries since these require joins of relations that frequently change over time as shown above. Others [15, 29, 135, 136] use distance constraints to ensure that the tuples to be joined are in a small area stored on nodes close to each other. For example [135] consider joins where the join condition uses a constraint like $distance\,(\mathcal{S}_A, \mathcal{S}_B) \leq d$ where d is the distance from node $\mathcal{S}_A$ to node $\mathcal{S}_B$. Their evaluation shows that unless d is smaller than the communication range of the nodes, the join should be processed at the base station. Since the distance between nodes detecting the same object may be arbitrarily large, these approaches would compute the result of a join for a spatio-temporal query at the base station. The analysis in [15] shows that general join operators require collecting all data at a central location. Unless the data is distributed in a certain way, this central location is the base station.

Some approaches use a central location such as the base station for partial computation of the join. An example for such an approach is [132], where the join is computed in two phases: First, the nodes send compressed representatives of their locally stored tuples to a central location. The tuples that fulfill the join condition are identified based on the representatives and the central location sends notifications to the nodes that store these tuples. When a node receives such a notification, only the tuples that are stored locally and join are forwarded to the central location to compute the overall join result. There are several problems with these two-phase approaches: First, the efficiency of these approaches is experimentally evaluated by counting the number of bytes that must be exchanged between nodes to compute the query result. This assumes that reducing the message size also reduces the energy consumption. This assumption does not hold if energy-aware MAC protocols are employed as discussed in Section 2.1.3 and experimentally shown in Appendix A. Using MAC protocols that are not energy-aware for sensor networks is not an option [27, 83], because radio chips waste energy due to idle listening. Second, two-phase approaches are only viable if the selectivity of the join is high, i.e., only a small portion of the nodes store tuples that contribute to the overall join result. The number of nodes detecting an arbitrary number of query-relevant objects over time can be arbitrarily high, i.e., selectivity of joins for spatio-temporal queries is low.

Summing up, mainly due to the join operators, using existing relational query processors for sensor networks would result in data on object detections being collected at the base station. As our evaluation shows, this is inefficient compared to our approaches which use in-network computation as shown in Chapter 5.

2.4 Summary

This chapter has reviewed the three major areas of related work for this dissertation: (1) the state-of-the-art regarding sensor networking technology as well as future trends, (2) the fundamentals of processing spatio-temporal queries and (3) existing approaches for processing declarative queries in sensor networks.

Our review of sensor network technology has shown why energy is and will stay the most important aspect regarding the efficiency of query processors. Specifically, reducing the number of messages that are sent and received is important. Furthermore, there exists a large number of promising approaches for the detection of various kinds of objects for sensor nodes. All of these approaches use different hardware and protocols to determine the location of an object at different degrees of accuracy. But to our knowledge, there does not exist any work on accessing the data acquired by these detection techniques declaratively using spatio-temporal queries.

Declarative access to sensor networks is a promising approach, because it frees the user from the intricacies of programming sensor nodes. This has been shown by a plethora of work aimed at processing relational queries in sensor networks. Applying these relational approaches to process spatio-temporal queries in object-tracking sensor networks is not feasible, because expressing spatio-temporal queries using relational operators results in complex queries that are inefficient to process, as research on moving object databases has shown. The review of the fundamental concepts of moving object databases has shown that applying them to sensor networks is also not feasible due to the properties of sensor networks and the aforementioned object detection mechanisms. The following chapters provide semantics for spatio-temporal queries in sensor networks and show how to process these queries efficiently with regard to communication.

2.4. SUMMARY

Chapter 3

Semantics of Spatio-Temporal Queries

This chapter develops the fundamental concepts and semantics for processing spatio-temporal queries in sensor networks, i.e., contribution **C.1**. As illustrated in the previous chapter, there exist numerous detection mechanisms for sensor networks with various properties, particularly regarding their precision. To allow the application of our semantics, we provide a node and network model which also provides an abstraction from the details of object detection. This abstraction is defined in such a way that it allows the definition of spatio-temporal semantics for all kinds of detection mechanisms without diminishing the information obtained by a specific detection mechanism.

The semantics of the spatio-temporal predicates and developments for regions as well as zones are based on the aforementioned abstraction. Most sensor networks cannot determine for all objects if they are outside, on the border or inside of a region due to limitations of the sensing hardware. Considering these limitations, we show how to obtain meaningful results for predicates expressing the relationship between an object and a region based on incomplete, imprecise object detections. Three kinds of results are distinguished: For some objects **O**, the sensor network can determine that the topological relationship to a region **R** conforms to a given predicate $P(\mathbf{O},\mathbf{R})$ despite the inaccuracy of object detection for sure. In the second case, object detection is not sufficiently accurate to yield a definite answer. The third case is that the sensor network can rule out that the topological relationship of **O** and **R** conforms to $P(\mathbf{O},\mathbf{R})$. Most important, we formally prove for our results regarding regions that they are optimal considering the limitations of sensor networks.

Contrary to regions, the concept of a zone is unknown in moving object databases. Thus, we formally introduce this concept first and provide an integration into the 9-intersection model. This allows the definition of semantics for predicates that express the spatial and spatio-temporal relationship between an object and a zone.

Using the semantics for spatio-temporal predicates, we address the semantics of spatio-temporal developments for both, zones and regions. We introduce a new concatenation operator which allows users to express spatio-temporal developments in such a way that undetected areas are taken into account. The chapter concludes with a study of the semantical depth of our approach in comparison to moving object databases. Summing up, an answer to the question "What are the semantics of spatio-temporal queries?" is provided in this chapter. The follow-up question "How can sensor networks efficiently derive results for spatio-temporal queries using these semantics?" will be addressed by chapters 4 and 5.

3.1 Node and Detection Model

The main notion introduced in this section is an abstract detection mechanism. We also illustrate how to apply this abstract detection mechanism to concrete examples of existing detection mechanisms and how to formalize the information acquired by object detection.
Notation (Sensor Network): A *sensor network* is a set $\mathcal{N} = \{\mathcal{S}_1, \mathcal{S}_2, \ldots, \mathcal{S}_n\}$ of sensor nodes. Every node has a position $\mathsf{POS}_i \in \mathbb{E}^d$ ($1 \leq i \leq n$) after the deployment is finished.

Processing spatio-temporal predicates requires detection of objects moving in the area where the sensor network has been deployed. We keep our approach independent from various existing detection mechanisms by abstracting from the details and characteristics of these mechanisms. First, we define the area that is observed by a node:

Definition 11 (Detection Area): The *detection area* $\mathbf{DA}_i$ of a node $\mathcal{S}_i$ is the set of points $\mathbf{DA}_i \subseteq \mathbb{E}^d$ where $\mathcal{S}_i$ can detect an object. □

As shown in Section 2.1.1, the detection area of a node may have any shape or size and may change over time due to external influences like rain or objects that reduce the detection area. Figure 3.1 illustrates this for node[1] $\mathcal{S}_1$ where a rock limits the detection area $\mathbf{DA}_1$. Thus, objects behind the rock remain undetected. A *node $\mathcal{S}_i$ detects the object* $\mathbf{O}$ *at time* t if the position p of $\mathbf{O}$ is in $\mathbf{DA}_i$ at t, i.e., $\mathsf{p} \in \mathbf{DA}_i$. The detection function formalizes this:

Definition 12 (Detection Function): The *detection function* $detect(\mathcal{S}_i, \mathbf{O}, t)$ is defined as follows:

$$detect(\mathcal{S}_i, \mathbf{O}, t) = \begin{cases} \mathcal{T} & \text{iff } \mathbf{O} \in \mathbf{DA}_i \text{ at } t \\ \mathcal{F} & \text{otherwise} \end{cases} \quad (3.1)$$

An *object* $\mathbf{O}$ *is detected at time* t if $detect(\mathcal{S}_i, \mathbf{O}, t) = \mathcal{T}$ for at least one $i \in \{1, \ldots, n\}$. Depending on the deployment, it is possible that detection areas overlap. If an object moves into this overlap, it is detected by more than one node simultaneously.
Definition 13 (Detection Set): The *detection set* $\mathcal{D}_t^\mathbf{O} \subseteq \mathcal{N}$ is the set of all nodes that detect an object $\mathbf{O}$ at some time t.

$$\mathcal{D}_t^\mathbf{O} = \{\mathcal{S}_i \in \mathcal{N} \mid detect(\mathcal{S}_i, \mathbf{O}, t) = \mathcal{T}\} \quad (3.2)$$

---
[1] To make node numbers in figures more discernible, we denote nodes in figures without indices, i.e., nodes $\mathcal{S}_1, \mathcal{S}_2, \ldots$ are illustrated in figures by S1, S2,....

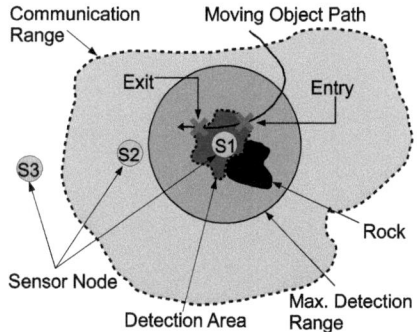

Figure 3.1: Illustration of the node model

While there exist detection mechanisms that can determine the detection area, most detection mechanisms cannot (cf. Section 2.1.1). However, the maximum detection range is typically available prior to the deployment of the nodes.

Definition 14 (Maximum Detection Range): The *maximum detection range* $\mathcal{D}_{max}$ is the maximum distance of an object to a node to be detected. □

Example 4 illustrates the difference between the detection area of a node and the maximum detection range.

Example 4: For passive infrared (PIR) motion detectors, $\mathcal{D}_{max} \approx 30$ meters. The sensor node in Figure 3.1 has been deployed close to a rock and cannot detect any object behind it. Thus, the area observed is much smaller than a circle with center POS_1 and radius $\mathcal{D}_{max}$. Next, if there is an object in front of the lens of such a sensor, the range may be only a few centimeters. Nodes typically cannot detect this. ♦

For processing spatio-temporal queries, the instants of time when objects enter or leave detection areas are important.

Definition 15 (Entry Time): The *entry time* $t_{entry} \in \mathbb{T}$ is the instant of time when an object enters the detection area of a node. □

Definition 16 (Exit Time): The *exit time* $t_{exit} \in \mathbb{T}$ is the instant of time when an object leaves the detection area of a node. □

For non-continuous detection mechanisms nodes can determine t_{entry} and t_{exit} by temporal interpolation: Suppose $\mathcal{S}_i$ checks periodically at $t_0, t_1, \ldots$ for objects. An entry occurs at t_j if $\mathcal{S}_i$

3.1. NODE AND DETECTION MODEL

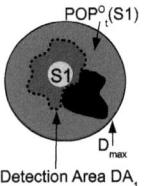
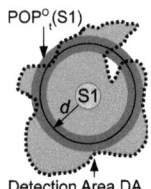
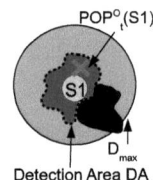

Figure 3.2: $\mathbf{PE}_t^O(\mathcal{S}_1)$ based on $\mathcal{D}_{max}$

Figure 3.3: $\mathbf{PE}_t^O(\mathcal{S}_1)$ with a distance estimating detection mechanism

Figure 3.4: $\mathbf{PE}_t^O(\mathcal{S}_1)$ with a position-precise detection mechanism

did not detect an object at t_{j-1} but detects it at t_j, i.e., $t_{entry} = t_j$. An exit occurs at t_j if $\mathcal{S}_i$ detected an object at t_j and does not detect it at t_{j+1}, i.e., $t_{exit} = t_{j+1}$. The frequency at which nodes must check for objects obviously depends on the properties of the used hardware and the object it is intended for. An example of such a property is the expected maximum speed of the objects observed. Research on detection mechanisms reviewed in Section 2.1.1 provides promising approaches to detect continuously moving objects using non-continuous detection mechanisms with limited temporal resolution.

Detection mechanisms are used to localize objects detected as accurately as possible. It depends on the used hardware and several other properties how accurate such a detection is. To allow the application of our approach to any kind of detection mechanism, we model the result of an object detection as a point set.

Definition 17 (Position Estimate): The *position estimate for an object* **O** *detected by* $\mathcal{S}_i$ *at time* $t \in \mathbb{T}$ is a set $\mathbf{PE}_t^O(\mathcal{S}_i) \subseteq \mathbb{E}^d$ containing all possible points $\mathsf{p} \in \mathbb{E}^d$ where **O** could be based on the information provided by the detection mechanism of $\mathcal{S}_i$. □

The shape and size of $\mathbf{PE}_t^O(\mathcal{S}_i)$ depends on the detection mechanism as Example 5 illustrates.

Example 5: Simple mechanisms like acoustic vehicle detection [18, 119] or PIR-based motion detectors cannot determine their detection area. Furthermore, these detection mechanisms only determine whether an object **O** is in the vicinity, i.e., in the detection area $\mathbf{DA}_1$, of a node $\mathcal{S}_1$ or not. In these cases, $\mathbf{PE}_t^O(\mathcal{S}_1)$ equals the circle with center POS$_1$ and radius $\mathcal{D}_{max}$ as shown in Figure 3.2. More sophisticated mechanisms, e.g., laser scanners, determine the distance d from the node to the detected object. Taking into account a certain deviation ϵ, $\mathbf{PE}_t^O(\mathcal{S}_1)$ is ring-shaped, see Figure 3.3. Note that some parts of $\mathbf{PE}_t^O(\mathcal{S}_1)$ in Figure 3.3 are not part of the detection area $\mathbf{DA}_1$ of $\mathcal{S}_1$. If $\mathcal{S}_1$ cannot determine its detection area, it cannot distinguish between points in $\mathbf{PE}_t^O(\mathcal{S}_1)$ that are in its detection area and those that are not. Figure 3.4 illustrates $\mathbf{PE}_t^O(\mathcal{S}_i)$ for mechanisms which precisely determine the position of **O**. ♦

If several nodes detect an object simultaneously, the sensor network can refine the information on the object position by intersecting the position estimates acquired by different nodes.

Definition 18 (Possible Object Positions): The *set of possible object positions* $\mathbf{POP}_t^O \subseteq \mathbb{E}^d$ at time $t \in \mathbb{T}$ is the intersection of all position estimates $\mathbf{PE}_t^O(\mathcal{S}_i)$ of nodes $\mathcal{S}_i \in \mathcal{D}_t^O$.

$$\mathbf{POP}_t^O = \begin{cases} \bigcap_{\mathcal{S}_i \in \mathcal{D}_t^O} \mathbf{PE}_t^O(\mathcal{S}_i) & \text{iff } \mathcal{D}_t^O \neq \varnothing \\ \varnothing & \text{otherwise} \end{cases} \quad (3.3)$$

Summing up, the information acquired by object detection in a sensor network is modeled as a point set.

Definition 19 (Communication Area): The *communication area* $\mathbf{CA}_i \subseteq \mathbb{E}^d$ of node $\mathcal{S}_i$ is the set of points where a node $\mathcal{S}_j$ with $i \neq j$ can receive messages sent by $\mathcal{S}_i$. □

A node $\mathcal{S}_i$ can directly communicate with another node $\mathcal{S}_j$ if $\mathrm{POS}_j \in \mathbf{CA}_i$. Communication areas may change over time and can have any shape or size. Furthermore, nodes typically cannot determine their communication area. As discussed in Section 2.1.2, there exist several routing protocols that determine the set of nodes that a node $\mathcal{S}_i$ can directly communicate with. These protocols allow forwarding of messages via multiple hops, e.g., to send results to the base station. To accomplish this, each node must store a short list of nodes it can communicate directly with and some routing information about the connectivity of each neighbor to the rest of the network.

Definition 20 (Communication Neighbors): The *communication neighbors* $\mathcal{CN}_i$ of a node $\mathcal{S}_i$ are the nodes that $\mathcal{S}_i$ can directly communicate with. □

3.2 Point-Set Topology for Sensor Networks

The semantics of spatio-temporal queries in moving object databases are based on the point-set topology as shown in Section 2.2.1. We inherit the concept of a region and its partitioning of space into exterior, border and interior from moving object databases. Hence, the semantics of predicates that express the relationship of a region and an object detected by sensor nodes are equal to those of moving object databases.

Section 1.1.2 has shown that there exist applications where it is advantageous to observe object movement in relation to a set of nodes, i.e., a zone. A zone $\mathcal{Z}$ is a set of nodes where every node satisfies a set of conditions $\mathbf{C}_\mathcal{Z}$, e.g., all nodes inside the swamp area that is covered by trees on the south-western side of the river of Figure 1.2. Similar to the notation for regions, we refer to the function that checks for a given node $\mathcal{S}_i$ if it satisfies $\mathbf{C}_\mathcal{Z}$ as $\mathbf{C}_\mathcal{Z}(\mathcal{S}_i)$:

$$\mathbf{C}_\mathcal{Z}(\mathcal{S}_i) = \begin{cases} \mathcal{T} & \text{iff } \mathcal{S}_i \text{ satisfies } \mathbf{C}_\mathcal{Z} \\ \mathcal{F} & \text{Otherwise} \end{cases} \quad (3.4)$$

3.2. POINT-SET TOPOLOGY FOR SENSOR NETWORKS

Definition 21 (Zone): A *zone* $\mathcal{Z}$ is a set of nodes which satisfy a set of conditions $\mathbf{C}_\mathcal{Z}$:

$$\mathcal{Z} = \{\mathcal{S}_i \in \mathcal{N} \mid \mathbf{C}_\mathcal{Z}(\mathcal{S}_i) = \mathcal{T}\} \tag{3.5}$$

A *node* $\mathcal{S}_i$ *is inside of* $\mathcal{Z}$ if $\mathcal{S}_i \in \mathcal{Z}$. Otherwise, $\mathcal{S}_i$ *is outside of* $\mathcal{Z}$. In the context of a zone $\mathcal{Z}$, we refer to the set of nodes that are outside of the zone as $\overline{\mathcal{Z}}$:

$$\overline{\mathcal{Z}} = \{\mathcal{S}_i \in \mathcal{N} \mid \mathbf{C}_\mathcal{Z}(\mathcal{S}_i) = \mathcal{F}\} \tag{3.6}$$

To define the semantics of zones and predicates that express the topological relationship between objects and zones, it is necessary to define a partitioning of space for zones. This partitioning must fulfill two requirements:

1. The partitioning must be complete and unambiguous, i.e., it must assign exactly one partition to every $\mathsf{p} \in \mathbb{E}^d$.
2. Sensor nodes must be able to derive based on $\mathbf{POP}_t^O$ in which partition of space a detected object is.

The core idea to meet these two requirements is as follows: Any point $\mathsf{p} \in \mathbb{E}^d$ can be either in no detection area, only in detection areas of nodes in $\mathcal{Z}$, only detection areas of nodes in $\overline{\mathcal{Z}}$ and in detection areas of nodes in $\mathcal{Z}$ and $\overline{\mathcal{Z}}$. Thus, every zone partitions space as follows:

Definition 22 (Unobserved Partition): The *unobserved partition* $\mathcal{Z}^\emptyset$ of a zone $\mathcal{Z}$ contains all points not contained in any detection area:

$$\mathcal{Z}^\emptyset = \{\mathsf{p} \in \mathbb{E}^d \mid \nexists \mathcal{S}_i \in \mathcal{N} : \mathsf{p} \in \mathbf{DA}_i\} \tag{3.7}$$

Definition 23 (Interior of a Zone): The *interior* $\mathcal{Z}^I$ of a zone $\mathcal{Z}$ contains all points exclusively observed by nodes in $\mathcal{Z}$:

$$\mathcal{Z}^I = \{\mathsf{p} \in \mathbb{E}^d \mid \mathsf{p} \notin \mathcal{Z}^\emptyset \wedge \nexists \mathcal{S}_i \in \overline{\mathcal{Z}} : \mathsf{p} \in \mathbf{DA}_i\} \tag{3.8}$$

Definition 24 (Exterior of a Zone): The *exterior* $\mathcal{Z}^E$ of a zone $\mathcal{Z}$ contains all points exclusively observed by nodes in $\overline{\mathcal{Z}}$:

$$\mathcal{Z}^E = \{\mathsf{p} \in \mathbb{E}^d \mid \mathsf{p} \notin \mathcal{Z}^\emptyset \wedge \nexists \mathcal{S}_i \in \mathcal{Z} : \mathsf{p} \in \mathbf{DA}_i\} \tag{3.9}$$

Definition 25 (Border of a Zone): The *border* $\mathcal{Z}^B$ of a zone $\mathcal{Z}$ contains all points of space observed by nodes from $\mathcal{Z}$ and $\overline{\mathcal{Z}}$:

$$\mathcal{Z}^B = \left\{ \mathsf{p} \in \mathbb{E}^d \mid \exists \mathcal{S}_i \in \mathcal{Z}, \exists \mathcal{S}_j \in \overline{\mathcal{Z}} : \mathsf{p} \in \mathbf{DA}_i \wedge \mathsf{p} \in \mathbf{DA}_j \right\} \quad (3.10)$$

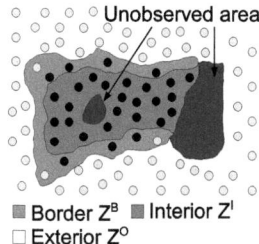

Figure 3.5: Illustration of the space partitions for a zone $\mathcal{Z}$

Figure 3.5 illustrates the partitioning of space for a zone: Circles represent nodes and every node has a detection area of a certain shape. The partitions are based on these detection areas and can change over time.

Lemma 3.1. *The point sets $\mathcal{Z}^\varnothing$, $\mathcal{Z}^I$, $\mathcal{Z}^E$ and $\mathcal{Z}^B$ partition the space, i.e., every $\mathsf{p} \in \mathbb{E}^d$ is only in one partition.*

Proof. A point $\mathsf{p} \in \mathbb{E}^d$ is either included in at least one detection area or unobserved. $\mathcal{Z}^\varnothing$ covers all points $\mathbb{E}^d \setminus \bigcup_{1 \leq i \leq n} \mathbf{DA}_i$. The observed points $\bigcup_{1 \leq i \leq n} \mathbf{DA}_i$ are covered by one of the remaining partitions: All points exclusively observed by nodes outside of $\mathcal{Z}$ are covered by $\mathcal{Z}^E$. Similarly, $\mathcal{Z}^I$ covers all points solely observed by nodes in $\mathcal{Z}$. All points observed by nodes inside and outside of $\mathcal{Z}$ are covered by $\mathcal{Z}^B$. Since each of these point sets is pair-wise disjoint with the others, we conclude that the partitioning is *complete and unambiguous*. ∎

Table 3.1 summarizes the different types of zones and regions, their formal definition and provides and example for each type. Note that regions do not consider detection areas and do not have a partition that contains unobserved areas. This is a major challenge for processing developments with regions, because the sensor network must determine if the trajectory of an object conforms to a development even if the object was not detected for some time. For example, an object conforms to Enter $(\mathbf{O}, \mathbf{R})$ (cf. Equation 2.5) even if the object was not detected while crossing the border of $\mathbf{R}$. Section 3.4 addresses this issue.

3.3. DERIVING PREDICATE RESULTS FROM OBJECT DETECTIONS

Formula Partitions	Zone Node Set $\mathcal{Z} = \{\mathcal{S}_i \in \mathcal{N} \mid C_\mathcal{Z}(\mathcal{S}_i) = \mathcal{T}\}$ $\mathcal{Z}^\varnothing, \mathcal{Z}^E, \mathcal{Z}^I, \mathcal{Z}^B$		Region Point set $\mathbf{R} = \{p \in \mathbb{E}^d \mid C_\mathbf{R}(p) = \mathcal{T}\}$ $\mathbf{R}^E, \mathbf{R}^I, \mathbf{R}^B$	
Type	static	dynamic	static	dynamic
Example	A set of unique node identifiers	Nodes measuring a temperature greater than $0°C$	All points inside a polygon defined by GPS-coordinates	All points where the temperature is greater than $0°C$

Table 3.1: Summary of region and zone types

3.3 Deriving Predicate Results from Object Detections

This section shows how to derive predicate results from information acquired by object detection. When one or more nodes detect an object **O** at time t, the actual position of **O** is somewhere in the set of possible object positions $\mathbf{POP}_t^\mathbf{O}$. To derive predicate results from $\mathbf{POP}_t^\mathbf{O}$, one has to determine how $\mathbf{POP}_t^\mathbf{O}$ intersects with a region or a zone. We formalize different types of intersections between $\mathbf{POP}_t^\mathbf{O}$ and regions or zones as *detection scenarios*.

Definition 26 (Detection Scenario): A *detection scenario* describes the intersection between the set of possible object positions $\mathbf{POP}_t^\mathbf{O}$ and the partitions of a zone or a region. □

The detection scenarios abstract from the details of the object detection or other details like the node deployment. They also take into account simultaneous detection of an object by more than one node since they are based on $\mathbf{POP}_t^\mathbf{O}$. Next, we define the set of detection scenarios that occur in sensor networks and prove that this set is complete, i.e., covers all possible cases of object detections. For each detection scenario, a formal expression that defines the detection scenario in the context of a zone $\mathcal{Z}$ and a region $\mathbf{R}$ is provided.

Definition 27 ($\mathtt{DS}^\varnothing$): The *detection scenario* $\mathtt{DS}^\varnothing$ occurs if $\mathbf{POP}_t^\mathbf{O} = \varnothing$, i.e., **O** is undetected and thus, $\mathbf{POP}_t^\mathbf{O}$ does not intersect with any (observed) partition of the region or zone.

$$\left(\mathcal{Z}^E \cup \mathcal{Z}^B \cup \mathcal{Z}^I\right) \cap \mathbf{POP}_t^\mathbf{O} = \varnothing \qquad \left(\mathbf{R}^E \cup \mathbf{R}^B \cup \mathbf{R}^I\right) \cap \mathbf{POP}_t^\mathbf{O} = \varnothing \qquad (3.11)$$

Definition 28 ($\mathtt{DS}^E$): The *detection scenario* $\mathtt{DS}^E$ occurs if $\mathbf{POP}_t^\mathbf{O}$ is a subset of the exterior of the region or zone.

$$\mathbf{POP}_t^\mathbf{O} \subseteq \mathcal{Z}^E \qquad \mathbf{POP}_t^\mathbf{O} \subseteq \mathbf{R}^E \qquad (3.12)$$

Definition 29 (DS^I): The *detection scenario* DS^I occurs if $\textbf{POP}^O_t$ is a subset of the interior of the region or zone.

$$\textbf{POP}^O_t \subseteq \mathcal{Z}^I \qquad\qquad \textbf{POP}^O_t \subseteq \textbf{R}^I \qquad (3.13)$$

Definition 30 (DS^B): The *detection scenario* DS^B occurs if $\textbf{POP}^O_t$ is a subset of the border of the region or zone.

$$\textbf{POP}^O_t \subseteq \mathcal{Z}^B \qquad\qquad \textbf{POP}^O_t \subseteq \textbf{R}^B \qquad (3.14)$$

Definition 31 ($\widetilde{\text{DS}^B}$): The *detection scenario* $\widetilde{\text{DS}^B}$ occurs if $\textbf{POP}^O_t$ intersects with all partitions of the region or zone, i.e., the detection mechanism cannot determine if **O** is inside, on the border or outside of a region or zone.

$$\textbf{POP}^O_t \cap \mathcal{Z}^E \neq \varnothing \land \textbf{POP}^O_t \cap \mathcal{Z}^B \neq \varnothing \land \textbf{POP}^O_t \cap \mathcal{Z}^I \neq \varnothing$$
$$\textbf{POP}^O_t \cap \textbf{R}^E \neq \varnothing \land \textbf{POP}^O_t \cap \textbf{R}^B \neq \varnothing \land \textbf{POP}^O_t \cap \textbf{R}^I \neq \varnothing \qquad (3.15)$$

According to the point-set topology for regions introduced in Section 2.2.1, the border of a region is a line. Most detection mechanisms used in sensor networks (cf. Section 2.1.1) cannot determine if an object is exactly on such a line, i.e., the border. Thus, $\widetilde{\text{DS}^B}$ typically occurs in sensor networks if the object detected is somewhere near the border and only few detection mechanisms are sufficiently accurate to distinguish such an object from one on the border. Example 6 illustrates this and how to derive detection scenarios from object detections.

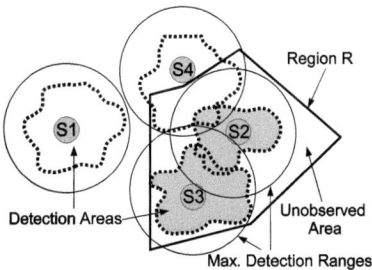

Figure 3.6: Example of detection areas, detection ranges and a region

3.3. DERIVING PREDICATE RESULTS FROM OBJECT DETECTIONS

Example 6: Let $\mathcal{N} = \{\mathcal{S}_1, \mathcal{S}_2, \mathcal{S}_3, \mathcal{S}_4\}$, and the node positions are as illustrated in Figure 3.6. Each node only detects objects in its vicinity, e.g., using a PIR-based mechanism. Thus, if $\mathcal{S}_i$ detects an object $\mathbf{O}$, $\mathbf{PE}_t^\mathbf{O}(\mathcal{S}_i)$ contains all points in the circle with radius $\mathcal{D}_{max}$ and center POS_i. If each $\mathcal{S}_i$ detects a vehicle $\mathbf{V}_i$, $1 \leq i \leq 4$, the following scenarios occur:

- $\mathbf{V}_1$: $\mathbf{PE}_t^{\mathbf{V}_1}(\mathcal{S}_1)$ contains only points from $\mathbf{R}^E$. Since $\mathcal{S}_1$ is the only node that detects $\mathbf{V}_1$, $\mathbf{POP}_t^{\mathbf{V}_1} = \mathbf{PE}_t^{\mathbf{V}_1}(\mathcal{S}_1)$ and thus DS^E occurs.
- $\mathbf{V}_2$: $\mathbf{PE}_t^{\mathbf{V}_2}(\mathcal{S}_2)$ contains only points from $\mathbf{R}^I$. Analogous to the detection of $\mathcal{S}_1$, we derive DS^I from this.
- $\mathbf{V}_3$: $\mathbf{PE}_t^{\mathbf{V}_3}(\mathcal{S}_3)$ contains points from all three partitions of $\mathbb{E}^d$. This means that the detection mechanism is not sufficiently accurate to determine on which side of the border of $\mathbf{R}$ the vehicle $\mathbf{V}_3$ is. Thus, $\widetilde{\mathsf{DS}^B}$ occurs.
- $\mathbf{V}_4$: Analogous to $\mathbf{V}_3$.

In case of simultaneous detection of $\mathbf{V}_4$ by $\mathcal{S}_4$ and $\mathcal{S}_2$, $\mathbf{POP}_t^{\mathbf{V}_4}$ is the intersection of $\mathbf{PE}_t^{\mathbf{V}_4}(\mathcal{S}_4)$ and $\mathbf{PE}_t^{\mathbf{V}_4}(\mathcal{S}_2)$. It is a subset of $\mathbf{R}^I$ and results in DS^I.

The detection scenarios for these vehicles obviously change if more sophisticated detection mechanisms are used. If $\mathcal{S}_3$ could determine its detection area $\mathbf{DA}_3$, $\mathbf{PE}_t^{\mathbf{V}_3}(\mathcal{S}_3) = \mathbf{POP}_t^{\mathbf{V}_3}$ does not overlap with $\mathbf{R}^B$ anymore, as illustrated in Figure 3.6. This increased accuracy changes the detection scenario for $\mathbf{V}_3$ from $\widetilde{\mathsf{DS}^B}$ to DS^I. ♦

The intersection of two sets A and B is empty, if $A = \emptyset$ or $B = \emptyset$. Thus, the detection scenario $\mathsf{DS}^\emptyset$ only occurs if $\mathbf{POP}_t^\mathbf{O} = \emptyset$ or if all partitions of the zone or region are empty.

Lemma 3.2. *The detection scenario $\mathsf{DS}^\emptyset$ implies that $\mathbf{POP}_t^\mathbf{O} = \emptyset$.*

Proof. As shown in Section 2.2.1, the partitioning of space by regions is complete and unambiguous for regions. Hence, there always exists at least one partition that is non-empty. According to Lemma 3.1, the partitioning for zones is complete as well. Thus, $\mathsf{DS}^\emptyset$ implies $\mathbf{POP}_t^\mathbf{O} = \emptyset$. ∎

Lemma 3.3. *For any object $\mathbf{O}$ and point of time t, exactly one of the detection scenarios $\mathsf{DS}^\emptyset$, DS^E, DS^I, DS^B or $\widetilde{\mathsf{DS}^B}$ holds.*

Proof. The lemma holds if the partitions of space where $\mathbf{O}$ could be at t based on the information provided by one of the detection scenarios are pair-wise disjoint. If $\mathsf{DS}^\emptyset$ occurs, the object is undetected at time t. A point $\mathsf{p} \in \mathbb{E}^d$ is either in at least one detection area or unobserved. $\mathsf{DS}^\emptyset$ covers all points $\mathbb{E}^d \setminus \bigcup_{1 \leq i \leq n} \mathbf{DA}_i$. Thus, only those parts of space that are observed must be considered in the following, i.e., $\bigcup_{1 \leq i \leq n} \mathbf{DA}_i$. We prove the lemma for the observed part of space in the context of zones and regions separately.

In the context of a region $\mathbf{R}$, the detection scenario DS^I covers all points from $\mathbf{R}^I$. Similarly, DS^E covers all points from $\mathbf{R}^E$. DS^B occurs if the sensor network can determine that $\mathbf{O}$ is on the border for sure. Contrary to that, $\widetilde{\mathsf{DS}^B}$ occurs if the accuracy of the object detection is insufficient to provide a definite statement if **O** is on the border, or close to it on either side. In this case an area around $\mathbf{R}^B$ is not part of $\mathbf{R}^I$ and $\mathbf{R}^E$. All of these point sets are pair-wise disjoint.

For a zone $\mathcal{Z}$, the points covered by the respective detection scenarios are analogous to those described above. The only difference is that $\widetilde{\mathsf{DS}^B}$ cannot occur, because the border $\mathcal{Z}^B$ is explicitly defined as those parts of space where objects are detected by nodes in $\mathcal{Z}$ and $\overline{\mathcal{Z}}$. Hence, the lemma holds, because all parts of space are covered by the respective detection scenarios. ∎

3.3.1 Predicate Results for Regions

This section shows how to derive results from detection scenarios for predicates that describe the topological relationship between a region and an object. DS^E, DS^B and DS^I guarantee that the object detected is in a certain partition. Thus, objects detected with these detection scenarios conform to a predicate $P(\mathbf{O}, \mathbf{R})$ in question or not. As illustrated in Example 6, this is not true for $\widetilde{\mathsf{DS}^B}$, because $\mathbf{POP}_t^\mathbf{O}$ overlaps with more than one partition of the region. Objects detected according to $\widetilde{\mathsf{DS}^B}$ could fulfill $P(\mathbf{O}, \mathbf{R})$, but this is not certain. We take this disparity regarding the certainty of the object positions into account by adding a third value $\mathcal{M}$ (Maybe) to the possible results of $P(\mathbf{O}, \mathbf{R})$:

$\mathcal{T}$: $P(\mathbf{O}, \mathbf{R})$ returns $\mathcal{T}$ if the sensor network can guarantee that **O** fulfills $P(\mathbf{O}, \mathbf{R})$.
$\mathcal{F}$: $P(\mathbf{O}, \mathbf{R})$ returns $\mathcal{F}$ if the sensor network can guarantee that **O** does not fulfill $P(\mathbf{O}, \mathbf{R})$.
$\mathcal{M}$: $P(\mathbf{O}, \mathbf{R})$ returns $\mathcal{M}$ otherwise.

Example 7: Continuing Example 6, we assume that a user interested in all vehicles inside the region, i.e., $Inside(\mathbf{V}_i, \mathbf{R})$. Recall that the sensor network can only narrow down the actual position of a detected vehicle $\mathbf{V}_i$: $\mathbf{PE}_t^{\mathbf{V}_i}(\mathcal{S}_i)$ is the circle with radius $\mathcal{D}_{max}$ around the position POS_i of the detecting node $\mathcal{S}_i$. If node $\mathcal{S}_i$ in Figure 3.6 detects $\mathbf{V}_i$, $1 \leq i \leq 4$, the results are as follows:

$\mathbf{V}_1$: The distance between $\mathcal{S}_1$ and $\mathbf{R}$ is greater than $\mathcal{D}_{max}$. Thus, it is certain that $\mathbf{V}_1$ is outside of $\mathbf{R}$. This yields $Inside(\mathbf{V}_1, \mathbf{R}) = \mathcal{F}$.
$\mathbf{V}_2$: $\mathbf{PE}_t^{\mathbf{V}_2}(\mathcal{S}_2)$ and thus $\mathbf{POP}_t^{\mathbf{V}_2} \subseteq \mathbf{R}^I$. Hence, $Inside(\mathbf{V}_2, \mathbf{R}) = \mathcal{T}$.
$\mathbf{V}_3$: Since the distance between $\mathcal{S}_3$ and the border of $\mathbf{R}$ is less than $\mathcal{D}_{max}$, the detection area could overlap the border. If a vehicle is detected only by $\mathcal{S}_3$, the sensor networks cannot determine on which side of the border it is. Thus, $Inside(\mathbf{V}_3, \mathbf{R}) = \mathcal{M}$.
$\mathbf{V}_4$: Analogously to $\mathbf{V}_3$.

Summing this up, the user knows for sure that $\mathbf{V}_2$ is in $\mathbf{R}$ and that $\mathbf{V}_3$ and $\mathbf{V}_4$ are possibly in $\mathbf{R}$ as well. ♦

The mapping of each detection scenario to a result for any predicate is specified in the following. We prove for each predicate that the result obtained this way is optimal. This mapping is the foundation for meaningful results for spatio-temporal developments in Section 3.4.

3.3. DERIVING PREDICATE RESULTS FROM OBJECT DETECTIONS

Deriving Results for $Inside(\mathbf{O}, \mathbf{R})$

Considering the five detection scenarios, there are two scenarios where an object could be in a region $\mathbf{R}$ and one where this is certain:

- DS^I: $\mathbf{POP}_t^\mathbf{O}$ only intersects with $\mathbf{R}^I$, i.e., $\mathbf{POP}_t^\mathbf{O} \subseteq \mathbf{R}^I$. Hence, $\mathbf{O}$ is in $\mathbf{R}$ for sure.
- $\widetilde{\mathsf{DS}^B}$: $\mathbf{POP}_t^\mathbf{O}$ overlaps with $\mathbf{R}^I$ but also overlaps with other partitions of $\mathbf{R}$. Thus, it is possible that $\mathbf{O}$ fulfills $Inside(\mathbf{O}, \mathbf{R})$ but is not guaranteed.
- $\mathsf{DS}^\varnothing$: Objects may be in $\mathbf{R}$ without being detected, i.e., $\mathbf{O}$ might fulfill $Inside(\mathbf{O}, \mathbf{R})$ while being undetected.

Equation 3.16 summarizes the mapping of detection scenarios to predicate results for $Inside(\mathbf{O}, \mathbf{R})$:

$$Inside(\mathbf{O}, \mathbf{R}) = \begin{cases} \mathcal{T} & \text{iff } \mathsf{DS}^I \\ \mathcal{F} & \text{iff } \mathsf{DS}^E, \mathsf{DS}^B \\ \mathcal{M} & \text{iff } \widetilde{\mathsf{DS}^B}, \mathsf{DS}^\varnothing \end{cases} \quad (3.16)$$

Lemma 3.4. *Let $\Omega_{Inside}^\mathbf{R}$ be the set of objects in $\mathbf{R}$. The set of objects where $Inside(\mathbf{O}, \mathbf{R})$ yields $\mathcal{T}$ or $\mathcal{M}$ is the smallest superset of $\Omega_{Inside}^\mathbf{R}$ that the sensor network can derive from detection scenarios.*

Proof. The lemma is true if the objects detected with DS^E and DS^B do not fulfill $Inside(\mathbf{O}, \mathbf{R})$ for sure. DS^E means that $\mathbf{POP}_t^\mathbf{O}$ is a subset of $\mathbf{R}^E$, i.e., $\mathbf{POP}_t^\mathbf{O}$ does not intersect with $\mathbf{R}^I$. The detection scenario DS^B occurs for objects that are on the border, i.e., $\mathbf{POP}_t^\mathbf{O}$ is a subset of $\mathbf{R}^B$. Hence, the object is not in $\mathbf{R}$ in both cases for sure. ∎

Lemma 3.5. *The set of objects where $Inside(\mathbf{O}, \mathbf{R}) = \mathcal{T}$ is the largest subset of $\Omega_{Inside}^\mathbf{R}$ that the sensor network can derive from the detection scenarios.*

Proof. Only DS^I corresponds to objects that fulfill $Inside(\mathbf{O}, \mathbf{R})$ for sure. The remaining detection scenarios cannot guarantee that the detected object is in $\mathbf{R}$. $\mathsf{DS}^\varnothing$ and $\widetilde{\mathsf{DS}^B}$ may occur for objects outside of $\mathbf{R}$ as well. Objects detected according to DS^E or DS^B are not in $\mathbf{R}$ for sure. Thus, there does not exist a detection scenario of $\mathbf{O}$ that guarantees $Inside(\mathbf{O}, \mathbf{R})$ except DS^I. ∎

We conclude for $Inside(\mathbf{O}, \mathbf{R})$ that the result in (3.16) is as accurate as possible considering the limitations of sensor networks, e.g., unobserved areas and imprecise detection mechanisms.

Deriving Results for $Meet(\mathbf{O}, \mathbf{R})$

The predicate $Meet(\mathbf{O}, \mathbf{R})$ is true if $\mathbf{O}$ is on the border $\mathbf{R}^B$ of the region $\mathbf{R}$. Considering the set of detection scenarios, there is one that guarantees that $\mathbf{O}$ is on the border and two others were it is possible:

DS^B: In this case $\mathbf{POP}_t^\mathbf{O} \subseteq \mathbf{R}^B$ and thus $\mathit{Meet}\,(\mathbf{O},\mathbf{R}) = \mathcal{T}$.
$\widetilde{\mathsf{DS}^B}$: Contrary to the previous case, $\mathbf{POP}_t^\mathbf{O}$ also contains points that are not part of the border. Thus, the object could be on the border, but the limited accuracy of the detection mechanism does not allow a definitive answer, i.e., $\mathit{Meet}\,(\mathbf{O},\mathbf{R}) = \mathcal{M}$ in this case.
$\mathsf{DS}^\varnothing$: The object could be on the border while not being detected by any sensor node and therefore $\mathit{Meet}\,(\mathbf{O},\mathbf{R}) = \mathcal{M}$ in this case.

Equation (3.17) summarizes this:

$$\mathit{Meet}\,(\mathbf{O},\mathbf{R}) = \begin{cases} \mathcal{T} & \text{iff } \mathsf{DS}^B \\ \mathcal{F} & \text{iff } \mathsf{DS}^I, \mathsf{DS}^E \\ \mathcal{M} & \text{iff } \widetilde{\mathsf{DS}^B}, \mathsf{DS}^\varnothing \end{cases} \qquad (3.17)$$

Lemma 3.6. *Let $\Omega_{Meet}^\mathbf{R}$ be the set of objects on the border $\mathbf{R}^B$ of $\mathbf{R}$. The set of objects where $\mathit{Meet}(\mathbf{O},\mathbf{R})$ yields $\mathcal{T}$ or $\mathcal{M}$ is the smallest superset of $\Omega_{Meet}^\mathbf{R}$ that a sensor network can derive from the detection scenarios.*

Proof. Analogous to Lemma 3.4, we prove this by considering DS^I and DS^E: DS^I ensures that $\mathbf{POP}_t^\mathbf{O}$ only contains points from $\mathbf{R}^I$, i.e., $\mathbf{O}$ is not on the border $\mathbf{R}^B$. Similarly, we derive from DS^E that $\mathbf{POP}_t^\mathbf{O}$ is a subset of $\mathbf{R}^E$ and thus does not intersect with $\mathbf{R}^B$. Thus, the set of objects where $\mathit{Meet}\,(\mathbf{O},\mathbf{R})$ yields $\mathcal{T}$ or $\mathcal{M}$ is the smallest superset of $\Omega_{Meet}^\mathbf{R}$ the sensor network can compute. ∎

Lemma 3.7. *The set of objects where $\mathit{Meet}\,(\mathbf{O},\mathbf{R}) = \mathcal{T}$ is the largest subset of $\Omega_{Meet}^\mathbf{R}$ identifiable by a sensor network.*

Proof. Only DS^B yields $\mathit{Meet}\,(\mathbf{O},\mathbf{R}) = \mathcal{T}$. Objects $\mathbf{O}$ detected according to $\widetilde{\mathsf{DS}^B}$ could be on $\mathbf{R}^B$, but it is not sure, because $\mathbf{POP}_t^\mathbf{O}$ also contains points from other partitions. Undetected objects could be on the border as well, but since they are not detected, it is not certain. For the other two detection scenarios, it is sure that the detected object is not on the border because $\mathbf{POP}_t^\mathbf{O} \cap \mathbf{R}^B = \varnothing$. Thus, a sensor network cannot compute a larger subset of $\Omega_{Meet}^\mathbf{R}$. ∎

As stated above, most detection mechanisms used in sensor networks cannot determine that some object $\mathbf{O}$ is on $\mathbf{R}^B$. Thus, once the distance of an object $\mathbf{O}$ to $\mathbf{R}^B$ falls below a certain limit, the detection mechanism cannot determine if the object is on the border or just close to it. Hence, the set of objects detected according to DS^B is typically empty.

Even if the sensor nodes are equipped with hardware that allows precise localization of an object, the result of the detection would be $\widetilde{\mathsf{DS}^B}$ in most cases instead of DS^B: Since $\mathbf{R}^B$ is a line, the time it takes for an object to move over this line is infinitely short. Capturing this moment reliably, i.e., whenever an object crosses the border, would require detection hardware with infinitely high temporal resolution. Thus, even with very sophisticated detection mechanisms, sensor networks cannot detect objects on the border reliably.

3.3. DERIVING PREDICATE RESULTS FROM OBJECT DETECTIONS

Summing up, the set of objects detected with DS^B is typically very small or empty. According to Lemma 3.7, sensor networks cannot determine a larger set of objects for which $Meet\,(\mathbf{O},\mathbf{R})$ is guaranteed. One might consider removing $Meet\,(\mathbf{O},\mathbf{R})$ from the set of predicates now since the only case where $Meet\,(\mathbf{O},\mathbf{R}) = \mathcal{T}$ will not occur or occurs rarely. However, removing $Meet\,(\mathbf{O},\mathbf{R})$ is problematic as it would reduce the set of spatio-temporal queries expressible in sensor networks significantly. For example, without $Meet\,(\mathbf{O},\mathbf{R})$ one cannot express the development Touch $(\mathbf{O},\mathbf{R})$ defined in (2.6). We show in Section 3.4 that there exist spatio-temporal developments containing $Meet\,(\mathbf{O},\mathbf{R})$ whose meaning can be guaranteed despite these problems. We conclude that the mapping in (3.17) for $Meet\,(\mathbf{O},\mathbf{R})$ is as accurate as the detection mechanisms allow even if most object detections around the border lead to $Meet\,(\mathbf{O},\mathbf{R}) = \mathcal{M}$.

Deriving Results for $Disjoint\,(\mathbf{O},\mathbf{R})$

To conform to $Disjoint\,(\mathbf{O},\mathbf{R})$, object $\mathbf{O}$ must be in $\mathbf{R}^E$. The mapping to detection scenarios is analogous to $Inside\,(\mathbf{O},\mathbf{R})$:

$$Disjoint\,(\mathbf{O},\mathbf{R}) = \begin{cases} \mathcal{T} & \text{iff } \mathsf{DS}^E \\ \mathcal{F} & \text{iff } \mathsf{DS}^I, \mathsf{DS}^B \\ \mathcal{M} & \text{iff } \widetilde{\mathsf{DS}^B}, \mathsf{DS}^\varnothing \end{cases} \quad (3.18)$$

Obviously, there are lemmas analogous to Lemmas 3.4 and 3.5 for $Disjoint\,(\mathbf{O},\mathbf{R})$. Hence, we conclude that the result in (3.18) is as accurate as possible as well.

Static and Dynamic Regions

Moving object databases model regions as (regular) point sets (cf. Definition 5). The application scenarios in Section 1.1 illustrated that there are two types of regions one must consider: Users define a *static region* $\mathbf{R}$ using a set of conditions $\mathbf{C_R}$ that does not change $\mathbf{R}$ over time. An example of such a $\mathbf{C_R}$ is a polygon that describes the border of the region and every point inside the polygon is part of the region. The second type are *dynamic regions* which are based on a $\mathbf{C_R}$ that may change the points in $\mathbf{R}$ over time. For example, a user might define a $\mathbf{C_R}$ that describes an oil spill or an area of low temperature. The points of space that are in such a region changes over time because the spatial extend of the oil spill or the area of low temperature changes.

The predicate results defined above apply to static and dynamic regions. Computing the detection scenario to obtain a predicate result for an object detection implicitly assumes that the point set representing the region is known. Thus, prior to computing a detection scenario at some time $t \in \mathbb{T}$, it is necessary to check for every $\mathsf{p} \in \mathbb{E}^d$ if it is in the region $\mathbf{R}$, i.e., $\mathbf{C_R}\,(\mathsf{p}) = \mathcal{T}$.

For static regions, this requirement is easy to meet because the region does not change over time. Thus, one can derive polygons for any static region $\mathbf{R}$ that encompass the interior of the region prior to processing a query or computing detection scenarios. Each node can store the corners of the polygon that describes $\mathbf{R}$ and given a $\mathbf{POP}_t^O$ compute the intersection $\mathbf{POP}_t^O \cap \mathbf{R}$, i.e., derive a detection scenario.

Checking if a point p is inside or outside of $\mathbf{R}$ becomes problematic if $\mathbf{R}$ is dynamic, i.e., changes over time, because computing a polygon beforehand is not possible. The problem is illustrated in Example 8.

Example 8: Suppose a user is interested in object movement in relation to a region $\mathbf{R}$ that contains all points with a temperature below $0°C$. If $\mathcal{S}_i$ detects an object $\mathbf{O}$ at time t and computes $\mathbf{POP}_t^O$, it is not possible to make any statement regarding the intersection of $\mathbf{POP}_t^O$ with the partitions of $\mathbf{R}$. Even if $\mathcal{S}_i$ measures a temperature of less than $0°C$, it is not certain that $\mathbf{O}$ is also at a position where the temperature is below $0°C$. At the same time, $\mathcal{S}_i$ cannot foreclose that $\mathbf{O}$ is at a position where the temperature is below $0°C$. ♦

There are two ways to solve this problem:

1. Deploy a node at any $\mathsf{p} \in \mathbb{E}^d$.
2. Equip sensor nodes with sophisticated sensing hardware that allows checking $C_\mathbf{R}(\mathsf{p})$ for points p where no sensor node is deployed. As a side condition, nodes must be deployed in such a way that at least one node can check every point $\mathsf{p} \in \mathbb{E}^d$.

A deployment where a node is deployed at every $\mathsf{p} \in \mathbb{E}^d$ is not viable. The second option assumes nodes equipped with sophisticated sensing hardware, e.g., infra-red cameras, which determine the temperature for the area around a sensor node. It must be noted for this case that the nodes using these cameras must have considerably more computational power than those available today to process the images taken by the cameras. Summing up, processing spatio-temporal queries interested in the relation of an object and a dynamic region requires restrictive assumptions about sensor nodes and the deployment. Instead of making such assumptions, for most sensor networks it is sufficient if the movement of an object is observed in relation to a set of nodes, i.e., a zone. We define the semantics of predicates that express the topological relationship between an object and a zone next. Since the movement is observed in relation to a set of nodes, this concept allows processing queries interested in the relationship of a moving object and another moving entity that covers more than one point in space.

3.3.2 Predicate Results for Zones

Section 3.2 has defined the space partitioning for zones. The partitioning is based on detection areas. Even if detection areas are not determinable, we can derive the partition of the zone that contains an object detected by using the following idea: If a node $\mathcal{S}_i \in \mathcal{Z}$ detects $\mathbf{O}$ at time t, the position estimate $\mathbf{PE}_t^O(\mathcal{S}_i)$ intersects with $\mathcal{Z}^I$, i.e., $\mathbf{PE}_t^O(\mathcal{S}_i) \cap \mathcal{Z}^I \neq \emptyset$. The actual position $\mathsf{p} \in \mathbb{E}^d$ of $\mathbf{O}$ is either exclusively observed by nodes in $\mathcal{Z}$ or nodes inside and outside of $\mathcal{Z}$ observe it. Thus, the object is either in $\mathcal{Z}^I$ or in $\mathcal{Z}^B$. To determine whether $\mathbf{O}$ is in $\mathcal{Z}^I$ or in $\mathcal{Z}^B$, one must consider simultaneous detections by other nodes, i.e., $\mathbf{POP}_t^O$: If there exists another $\mathcal{S}_j \in \overline{\mathcal{Z}}$ that detects

3.3. DERIVING PREDICATE RESULTS FROM OBJECT DETECTIONS

O at t, **O** is at a position p that is observed by nodes in $\mathcal{Z}$ as well as nodes in $\overline{\mathcal{Z}}$. According to the definitions of the border of a zone, this means that $\mathbf{POP}_t^{\mathbf{O}} \subseteq \mathcal{Z}^B$, i.e., DS^B. If there is no node outside of $\mathcal{Z}$ that detects **O** at t, the actual position of **O** is exclusively observed by nodes in $\mathcal{Z}$. Hence, $\mathbf{POP}_t^{\mathbf{O}} \subseteq \mathcal{Z}^I$, i.e., **O** is detected according to DS^I. Summing up, one has to consider how the detection set $\mathcal{D}_t^{\mathbf{O}}$ (cf. Definition 13) intersects with $\mathcal{Z}$ and $\overline{\mathcal{Z}}$ to determine how $\mathbf{POP}_t^{\mathbf{O}}$ intersects with the partitions of the zone, i.e., compute the corresponding detection scenario.

Lemma 3.8. *The detection scenario DS^E occurs if only nodes in $\overline{\mathcal{Z}}$ detect an object* **O**:

$$\mathcal{D}_t^{\mathbf{O}} \subseteq \overline{\mathcal{Z}} \Rightarrow \mathbf{POP}_t^{\mathbf{O}} \subseteq \mathcal{Z}^E$$

Proof. We prove this implication by contradiction[2], i.e., we have to prove that if $\mathbf{POP}_t^{\mathbf{O}}$ is not a subset of $\mathcal{Z}^E$ then $\mathcal{D}_t^{\mathbf{O}}$ is not a subset of $\overline{\mathcal{Z}}$. Let $\mathcal{S}_i \in \mathcal{Z}$ detect **O** at t, i.e., $detect(\mathcal{S}_i, \mathbf{O}, t) = \mathcal{T}$. Thus, **O** is somewhere in $\mathbf{DA}_i$. Since $\mathbf{POP}_t^{\mathbf{O}}$ is the intersection of the detection areas of all nodes that detect **O** at t, $\mathbf{POP}_t^{\mathbf{O}}$ must contain at least one $\mathsf{p} \in \mathbf{DA}_i$. Hence, $\mathbf{POP}_t^{\mathbf{O}}$ is not a subset of $\mathcal{Z}^E$, because $\mathcal{Z}^E$ contains only points exclusively observed by nodes in $\overline{\mathcal{Z}}$. If $\mathbf{POP}_t^{\mathbf{O}}$ would not contain at least one $\mathsf{p} \in \mathbf{DA}_i$ then $detect(\mathcal{S}_i, \mathbf{O}, t) = \mathcal{F}$. Summing up, $\mathcal{D}_t^{\mathbf{O}} \subseteq \overline{\mathcal{Z}}$ implies $\mathbf{POP}_t^{\mathbf{O}} \subseteq \mathcal{Z}^E$. ∎

Lemma 3.9. *The detection scenario DS^I occurs if only nodes in $\mathcal{Z}$ detect an object* **O**:

$$\mathcal{D}_t^{\mathbf{O}} \subseteq \mathcal{Z} \Rightarrow \mathbf{POP}_t^{\mathbf{O}} \subseteq \mathcal{Z}^I$$

Proof. Analogous to Lemma 3.8, one can prove this by contradiction: The lemma holds if $\overline{\mathbf{POP}_t^{\mathbf{O}} \subseteq \mathcal{Z}^I}$ implies $\overline{\mathcal{D}_t^{\mathbf{O}} \subseteq \mathcal{Z}}$. Let $\mathcal{S}_i \in \overline{\mathcal{Z}}$ detect **O** at t, i.e., $\overline{\mathcal{D}_t^{\mathbf{O}} \subseteq \mathcal{Z}}$ is true. Since $detect(\mathcal{S}_i, \mathbf{O}, t) = \mathcal{T}$, **O** is somewhere in $\mathbf{DA}_i$. This implies that there is at least one point $\mathsf{p} \in \mathbf{POP}_t^{\mathbf{O}}$ that is also in $\mathbf{DA}_i$. The partition $\mathcal{Z}^I$ is the set of points exclusively observed by nodes in $\mathcal{Z}$. Since p must exist because $\mathcal{S}_i$ detects **O** at least p is not in $\mathcal{Z}^I$ and therefore $\mathbf{POP}_t^{\mathbf{O}} \subseteq \mathcal{Z}^I$ is not true. ∎

Lemma 3.10. *The detection scenario DS^B occurs if there exists a pair of nodes $(\mathcal{S}_i, \mathcal{S}_j)$ with $\mathcal{S}_i \in \mathcal{Z}$ and $\mathcal{S}_j \in \overline{\mathcal{Z}}$ that detect* **O** *at time t:*

$$\mathcal{D}_t^{\mathbf{O}} \cap \mathcal{Z} \neq \emptyset \wedge \mathcal{D}_t^{\mathbf{O}} \cap \overline{\mathcal{Z}} \neq \emptyset \Rightarrow \mathbf{POP}_t^{\mathbf{O}} \subseteq \mathcal{Z}^B$$

Proof. $\mathcal{D}_t^{\mathbf{O}} \cap \mathcal{Z} \neq \emptyset$ implies that **O** is at some point $\mathsf{p} \in \mathbb{E}^d$ that is observed by nodes from $\mathcal{Z}$. Similarly, $\mathcal{D}_t^{\mathbf{O}} \cap \overline{\mathcal{Z}} \neq \emptyset$ means that nodes from $\overline{\mathcal{Z}}$ detect the object as well. This implies that p is observed by nodes inside and outside of $\mathcal{Z}$ which is the border of the zone (cf. Definition 25). Hence, the lemma holds. ∎

---
[2]To prove $A \Rightarrow B$ by contradiction, it is sufficient to prove $\overline{B} \Rightarrow \overline{A}$.

Lemma 3.11.
$$\mathbf{POP}^O_t \cap \mathcal{Z}^E \neq \emptyset \Rightarrow \mathbf{POP}^O_t \subseteq \mathcal{Z}^E$$
$$\mathbf{POP}^O_t \cap \mathcal{Z}^I \neq \emptyset \Rightarrow \mathbf{POP}^O_t \subseteq \mathcal{Z}^I$$
$$\mathbf{POP}^O_t \cap \mathcal{Z}^B \neq \emptyset \Rightarrow \mathbf{POP}^O_t \subseteq \mathcal{Z}^B$$

Proof. We prove $\mathbf{POP}^O_t \cap \mathcal{Z}^E \neq \emptyset \Rightarrow \mathbf{POP}^O_t \subseteq \mathcal{Z}^E$: According to Definition 24, $\mathcal{Z}^E$ only contains points that are exclusively observed by nodes in $\overline{\mathcal{Z}}$. Hence, if $\mathbf{POP}^O_t$ contains points from $\mathcal{Z}^E$, the object is at a position that is exclusively observed by nodes in $\overline{\mathcal{Z}}$. If there exists a node $S_i \in \mathcal{Z}$ that detects **O**, $\mathbf{POP}^O_t$ does not intersect with $\mathcal{Z}^E$ anymore. The proofs for the remaining two implications are analogous. ∎

Lemma 3.11 implies that in the context of a zone $\mathcal{Z}$, $\mathbf{POP}^O_t$ can never intersect with more than one partition of $\mathcal{Z}$. Thus, we can omit $\widehat{\mathsf{DS}^B}$ for the definition of predicates that express the relationship between an object and a zone. This allows the definition of predicates for zones as well as their semantics.

Definition 32 (*Disjoint*(O, Z)): The object **O** conforms to *Disjoint*(**O**, $\mathcal{Z}$) if **O** is exclusively detected by nodes in $\overline{\mathcal{Z}}$, i.e., if DS^E occurs (cf. Lemma 3.8):

$$Disjoint(\mathbf{O}, \mathcal{Z}) = \begin{cases} \mathcal{T} & \text{iff } \mathsf{DS}^E \\ \mathcal{F} & \text{Otherwise} \end{cases} \quad (3.19)$$

Other detection scenarios yield $\mathcal{F}$, because it is certain that **O** is not in the exterior $\mathcal{Z}^E$ according to Lemma 3.11. □

Definition 33 (*Inside*(O, Z)): The object **O** conforms to *Inside*(**O**, $\mathcal{Z}$) if **O** is exclusively detected by nodes in $\mathcal{Z}$, i.e., if DS^I occurs (cf. Lemma 3.9):

$$Inside(\mathbf{O}, \mathcal{Z}) = \begin{cases} \mathcal{T} & \text{iff } \mathsf{DS}^I \\ \mathcal{F} & \text{Otherwise} \end{cases} \quad (3.20)$$

Other detection scenarios yield $\mathcal{F}$, because it is certain that **O** is not in the interior $\mathcal{Z}^I$ according to Lemma 3.11. □

Definition 34 (*Meet*(O, Z)): The object **O** conforms to *Meet*(**O**, $\mathcal{Z}$) if **O** is detected by nodes in $\mathcal{Z}$ and $\overline{\mathcal{Z}}$ simultaneously, i.e., if DS^B occurs (cf. Lemma 3.10):

$$Meet(\mathbf{O}, \mathcal{Z}) = \begin{cases} \mathcal{T} & \text{iff } \mathsf{DS}^B \\ \mathcal{F} & \text{Otherwise} \end{cases} \quad (3.21)$$

3.3. DERIVING PREDICATE RESULTS FROM OBJECT DETECTIONS

Other detection scenarios yield $\mathcal{F}$, because it is certain that $\mathbf{O}$ is not in the border partition $\mathcal{Z}^B$ according to Lemma 3.11. □

Assuming $\Omega_{Disjoint}^{\mathcal{Z}}$ is the set of objects in $\mathcal{Z}^E$ of $\mathcal{Z}$. Since there is no detection scenario where $Disjoint(\mathbf{O}, \mathcal{Z}) = \mathcal{M}$, we conclude that the set of objects where $Disjoint(\mathbf{O}, \mathcal{Z})$ yields $\mathcal{T}$ equals $\Omega_{Disjoint}^{\mathcal{Z}}$. Similarly, the sets of objects where $Meet(\mathbf{O}, \mathcal{Z})$ and $Inside(\mathbf{O}, \mathcal{Z})$ yield $\mathcal{T}$ equal $\Omega_{Meet}^{\mathcal{Z}}$ and $\Omega_{Inside}^{\mathcal{Z}}$ respectively.

Note that concepts like concatenation or lifting (cf. Definition 10) are applicable to these predicates as well. Thus, one can construct developments that query the spatio-temporal relationship of objects and zones. For instance, one could define:

$$Enter(\mathbf{O}, \mathcal{Z}) = Disjoint(\mathbf{O}, \mathcal{Z}) \triangleright Meet(\mathbf{O}, \mathcal{Z}) \triangleright Inside(\mathbf{O}, \mathcal{Z}) \quad (3.22)$$

The space partitioning for regions divides all points of space into three partitions and the resulting three predicates describe in which partition an object is. In the context of zones, we introduced a fourth partition $\mathcal{Z}^\emptyset$ which contains all points that are unobserved. To allow users to express that an object movement they are interested in includes that the object is unobserved at some point in time, we define a corresponding fourth predicate:

Definition 35 (*Undetected*($\mathbf{O}$)): An object $\mathbf{O}$ conforms to $Undetected(\mathbf{O})$ if there is no node $\mathcal{S}_i \in \mathcal{N}$ that detects $\mathbf{O}$, i.e., if $\text{DS}^\emptyset$ occurs:

$$Undetected(\mathbf{O}, \mathcal{Z}) = Undetected(\mathbf{O}) = \begin{cases} \mathcal{T} & \text{iff } \text{DS}^\emptyset \\ \mathcal{F} & \text{Otherwise} \end{cases} \quad (3.23)$$

Note that we abbreviate $Undetected(\mathbf{O}, \mathcal{Z})$ to $Undetected(\mathbf{O})$ because the object is not only undetected in relation to $\mathcal{Z}$ but also in relation to any other zone. □

This predicate is particularly useful in the context of spatio-temporal developments. For example, a user could be interested in objects that fulfill $Inside(\mathbf{O}, \mathcal{Z})$ first and then move into an unobserved area:

$$Disappear(\mathbf{O}, \mathcal{Z}) = Inside(\mathbf{O}, \mathcal{Z}) \triangleright Undetected(\mathbf{O}) \quad (3.24)$$

Further examples for the use of this predicate are provided in Section 3.4 where spatio-temporal developments in sensor networks are discussed.

3.3.3 Static and Dynamic Zones

As with regions, there are two variants of zones: dynamic and static zones. As shown in Table 3.1, users define a static zone $\mathcal{Z}$ by providing a $\mathsf{C}_\mathcal{Z}$ where the set of nodes inside $\mathcal{Z}$ does not change over time. Such a $\mathsf{C}_\mathcal{Z}$ could enumerate all nodes in the zones, e.g., using the unique identifier of a node. A dynamic zone changes over time, i.e., the $\mathsf{C}_\mathcal{Z}$ contains a condition that refers to a measurable value like the temperature. As with regions, the semantics of the predicates defined above are applicable to both versions of the zone.

Contrary to dynamic regions, dynamic zones do not require sophisticated hardware like infra-red cameras, because every node only has to determine if it is inside the zone or not. For example, a dynamic zone in Table 3.1 requires each node to determine from time to time if it measures a temperature below or above $0°C$. Contrary to the infra-red camera that would be required for a dynamic region, an appropriate temperature sensor is typically available by default on sensor nodes available today (cf. Section 2.1). Thus, dynamic zones do not require any further assumptions regarding the capabilities of the nodes or the deployment.

3.3.4 Summary

Table 3.2 summarizes the mapping of detection scenarios to results of predicates expressing the relation between objects and regions in sensor networks. Each row corresponds to a predicate and every column to a detection scenario that describes how $\mathbf{POP}_t^O$ overlaps with the partitions of the region $\mathbf{R}$.

$P(\mathbf{O},\mathbf{R})$	$DS^\emptyset$	DS^E	DS^I	DS^B	$\widetilde{DS^B}$
$Inside(\mathbf{O},\mathbf{R})$	$\mathcal{M}$	$\mathcal{F}$	$\mathcal{T}$	$\mathcal{F}$	$\mathcal{M}$
$Meet(\mathbf{O},\mathbf{R})$	$\mathcal{M}$	$\mathcal{F}$	$\mathcal{F}$	$\mathcal{T}$	$\mathcal{M}$
$Disjoint(\mathbf{O},\mathbf{R})$	$\mathcal{M}$	$\mathcal{T}$	$\mathcal{F}$	$\mathcal{F}$	$\mathcal{M}$

Table 3.2: Predicate result mapping for an object $\mathbf{O}$ and a region $\mathbf{R}$

The results of predicates that describe the relation between an object and a zone are summarized similarly in Table 3.3. Due to the fact that $\widetilde{DS^B}$ cannot occur in the context of zones, the corresponding column contains '-' entries. Based on these results, we focus on spatio-temporal developments, i.e., sequences of predicates that describe an object movement in relation to a zone or region that the user is interested in.

$P(\mathbf{O},\mathcal{Z})$	$DS^\emptyset$	DS^E	DS^I	DS^B	$\widetilde{DS^B}$
$Inside(\mathbf{O},\mathcal{Z})$	$\mathcal{F}$	$\mathcal{F}$	$\mathcal{T}$	$\mathcal{F}$	-
$Meet(\mathbf{O},\mathcal{Z})$	$\mathcal{F}$	$\mathcal{F}$	$\mathcal{F}$	$\mathcal{T}$	-
$Disjoint(\mathbf{O},\mathcal{Z})$	$\mathcal{F}$	$\mathcal{T}$	$\mathcal{F}$	$\mathcal{F}$	-
$Undetected(\mathbf{O},\mathcal{Z})$	$\mathcal{T}$	$\mathcal{F}$	$\mathcal{F}$	$\mathcal{F}$	-

Table 3.3: Predicate result mapping for an object $\mathbf{O}$ and a zone $\mathcal{Z}$

3.4 Spatio-Temporal Developments

As illustrated in Section 2.2.3, users express spatio-temporal queries by concatenating predicates. By concatenating predicates, users describe the movement they are interested in declaratively. The core contribution of this chapter is the translation of sequences of object detections to results for spatio-temporal developments.

To provide such a translation, some preliminary steps are required: First, we show that the concatenation operator $\triangleright$ (cf. Definition 10) is insufficient to express certain queries in sensor networks. We solve this by introducing a new concatenation operator $\widetilde{\triangleright}$. Second, we develop a canonical collection of spatio-temporal developments for sensor networks similar to the existing collection for moving object databases. We need this collection to obtain a finite set of developments which must be translated. The last step is the actual translation of each element of the canonical collection and the proof that this translation is correct.

3.4.1 Irregularity of Zones and Concatenation

The difference between the partitioning of space for regions and the partitioning for zones is that regularity [122] cannot be assumed for zones: As stated in Section 2.2.1, regions in moving object databases are regular. Among other things, this ensures that the border $\mathbf{R}^B$ always encompasses the interior $\mathbf{R}^I$ completely. This is different with zones, as illustrated in Figure 3.5: The border $\mathcal{Z}^B$ of the illustrated zone $\mathcal{Z}$ partly encompasses the interior $\mathcal{Z}^I$ and other parts of $\mathcal{Z}^I$ adjoin to $\mathcal{Z}^\varnothing$.

This has an impact on spatio-temporal developments, as we illustrate with Enter$(\mathbf{O}, \mathbf{R})$: Assume a user is interested in all objects $\mathbf{O}$ that move into the zone $\mathcal{Z}$. For regions, the space partitions are regular, i.e., an object $\mathbf{O}$ must cross the border $\mathbf{R}^B$. In the context of a zone, a user could express an interest similar to Enter$(\mathbf{O}, \mathbf{R})$ with Enter$(\mathbf{O}, \mathcal{Z})$ as defined in (3.22). This is problematic, because Enter$(\mathbf{O}, \mathcal{Z})$ implicitly restricts the set of objects that are part of the result to those that are observed while crossing the border. For example, an object $\mathbf{O}$ might fulfill Disjoint$(\mathbf{O}, \mathcal{Z})$ at some point, then move through an unobserved area and fulfill Inside$(\mathbf{O}, \mathcal{Z})$ afterwards. From a semantical perspective, $\mathbf{O}$ also has "entered" the zone, i.e., fulfills the users query, but since Meet$(\mathbf{O}, \mathcal{Z})$ was not true, it does not fulfill Enter$(\mathbf{O}, \mathcal{Z})$.

One might consider solving this by querying for all objects that either fulfill Enter$(\mathbf{O}, \mathcal{Z})$ or HiddenEnter$(\mathbf{O}, \mathcal{Z})$ which is defined in (3.25):

$$\text{HiddenEnter}(\mathbf{O}, \mathcal{Z}) = \textit{Disjoint}(\mathbf{O}, \mathcal{Z}) \triangleright \textit{Undetected}(\mathbf{O}) \triangleright \textit{Inside}(\mathbf{O}, \mathcal{Z}) \qquad (3.25)$$

But HiddenEnter$(\mathbf{O}, \mathcal{Z})$ is not sufficient as well, because $\mathbf{O}$ could fulfill Disjoint$(\mathbf{O}, \mathcal{Z})$ first, then Undetected$(\mathbf{O})$ followed by Meet$(\mathbf{O}, \mathcal{Z})$ and finally Inside$(\mathbf{O}, \mathcal{Z})$. In this case, $\mathbf{O}$ neither fulfills Enter$(\mathbf{O}, \mathcal{Z})$ nor HiddenEnter$(\mathbf{O}, \mathcal{Z})$. A user interested in objects $\mathbf{O}$ that enter a zone $\mathcal{Z}$, but does not care if the object is detected or not while crossing the border would have to provide an infinite number of predicate sequences. This is because an object can move an arbitrary number of times between *Undetected* (**O**) and *Meet* (**O**, $\mathcal{Z}$) before fulfilling *Inside* (**O**, $\mathcal{Z}$). Furthermore, users cannot express this as follows:

$$\textit{Disjoint}\,(\mathbf{O}, \mathcal{Z}) \triangleright \textit{Inside}\,(\mathbf{O}, \mathcal{Z}) \tag{3.26}$$

The sequence in (3.26) never occurs, because $\triangleright$ requires *Inside* (**O**, $\mathcal{Z}$) to follow *Disjoint* (**O**, $\mathcal{Z}$) immediately. Summing up, users cannot express such a query given the four predicates *Disjoint* (**O**, $\mathcal{Z}$), *Meet* (**O**, $\mathcal{Z}$), *Inside* (**O**, $\mathcal{Z}$), *Undetected* (**O**) and $\triangleright$.

Definition 36 (Relaxed Concatenation): The *relaxed concatenation of two predicates*, $P \,\widetilde{\triangleright}\, Q$, is true if P is true for some time interval $[t_0; t_1[$, and Q is true at $t_2 \geq t_1$. □

Equation (3.27) defines a development that expresses the query discussed above:

$$\textit{WSNEnter}\,(\mathbf{O}, \mathcal{Z}) = \textit{Disjoint}\,(\mathbf{O}, \mathcal{Z}) \,\widetilde{\triangleright}\, \textit{Inside}\,(\mathbf{O}, \mathcal{Z}) \tag{3.27}$$

In combination with the predicate *Undetected* (**O**), this new concatenation operator increases the semantical depth because users can explicitly define if the object must be observed or not while moving as illustrated by Example 9.

Example 9: The area where the sensor network in Figure 1.2 is deployed contains a river with several bridges. Suppose that due to the controlled deployment (cf. Section 1.1.2) nodes are deployed so that caribous moving over a bridge are detected, but caribous swimming are not, i.e., the river itself is unobserved. A user only interested in caribous $\mathbf{C}_i$ entering $\mathcal{Z}$ by crossing bridges can use Enter ($\mathbf{C}_i$, $\mathcal{Z}$). If only caribous that enter $\mathcal{Z}$ by swimming are of interest, the user can express this with the development HiddenEnter (**O**, $\mathcal{Z}$) defined in (3.25). A user interested in all caribous entering $\mathcal{Z}$ can use WSNEnter ($\mathbf{C}_i$, $\mathcal{Z}$) as defined in (3.27) to express this interest. ♦

Next, we study some important properties of the $\widetilde{\triangleright}$ operator like associativity and combinability with the $\triangleright$ operator.

Lemma 3.12. $P_1 \triangleright P_2 \Rightarrow P_1 \,\widetilde{\triangleright}\, P_2$

Proof. According to Definition 36, the right-hand side is true if P_1 is true for some interval $[t_0, t_1[$ and P_2 is true at $t_2 \geq t_1$. The left-hand side of the implication states that P_1 is true for some interval $[t_0, t_1[$ and P_2 is true at $t_2 = t_1$. Hence, if the left-hand side is true, the right-hand side is true as well. ∎

Lemma 3.13. $P_1 \,\widetilde{\triangleright}\, (P_2 \,\widetilde{\triangleright}\, P_3) = (P_1 \,\widetilde{\triangleright}\, P_2) \,\widetilde{\triangleright}\, P_3$.

Proof. The left-hand side means $\exists\, [t_0, t_1[: P_1$ and $\exists\, t_2 \geq t_1 : (P_2 \,\widetilde{\triangleright}\, P_3)$. Furthermore, $\exists\, [t_2, t_3[: P_2$ and $\exists\, t_4 \geq t_3 : P_3$. The right-hand side expresses that $\exists\, [t'_0, t'_3[: (P_1 \,\widetilde{\triangleright}\, P_2)$ and $\exists\, t'_4 \geq t'_3 : P_3$. Additionally, $\exists\, [t'_0, t'_1[, t'_1 \leq t'_3 : P_1$ and $\exists\, t'_2 \geq t'_1 \wedge t'_2 \leq t'_3 : P_2$. If the left-hand side is true for $t'_0 = t_0, t'_1 = t_1, t'_2 = t_2, t'_3 = t_3$ the right-hand side is fulfilled also (and vice versa). ∎

3.4. SPATIO-TEMPORAL DEVELOPMENTS

Lemma 3.14. $P_1 \triangleright (P_2 \widetilde{\triangleright} P_3) = (P_1 \triangleright P_2) \widetilde{\triangleright} P_3$

Proof. $P_1 \triangleright (P_2 \widetilde{\triangleright} P_3)$ implies $P_1 \widetilde{\triangleright} (P_2 \widetilde{\triangleright} P_3)$ based on Lemma 3.12. Similarly, $(P_1 \triangleright P_2) \widetilde{\triangleright} P_3$ implies $(P_1 \widetilde{\triangleright} P_2) \widetilde{\triangleright} P_3$. Hence, we get $P_1 \widetilde{\triangleright} (P_2 \widetilde{\triangleright} P_3) = (P_1 \widetilde{\triangleright} P_2) \widetilde{\triangleright} P_3$ which is true according to Lemma 3.13. ∎

Summing up, users can express spatio-temporal queries using both concatenation operators in spatio-temporal developments. Thus, we define spatio-temporal developments in the context of sensor networks as follows:

Definition 37 (Spatio-Temporal Development): A *spatio-temporal development* $\mathbb{P}$ is a sequence of predicates $\mathbb{P} = P_1 \theta P_2 \theta \ldots \theta P_q$ with $\theta \in \{\triangleright, \widetilde{\triangleright}\}$ that describes the movement of an object in relation to a zone or a region.

The movement of an object **O** conforms to $\mathbb{P}$ if each pair $P_{i-1} \theta P_i$ with $2 \leq i \leq q$ is true in the order defined by $\mathbb{P}$. □

In the following, we denote developments that describe the relation of an object **O** and a region **R** with $\mathbb{P}(\mathbf{O}, \mathbf{R})$. In this case, all predicates refer to **O** and **R** as well, i.e., $P_i = P_i(\mathbf{O}, \mathbf{R})$ with $1 \leq i \leq q$. Since $\widetilde{\triangleright}$ is only required in the context of zones due to their non-regular space partitioning, $\mathbb{P}(\mathbf{O}, \mathbf{R}) = P_1(\mathbf{O}, \mathbf{R}) \triangleright \ldots \triangleright P_q(\mathbf{O}, \mathbf{R})$. For zones, we use a similar notation: $\mathbb{P}(\mathbf{O}, \mathcal{Z})$ describes the spatio-temporal relationship between an object **O** and a zone $\mathcal{Z}$. Each predicate in $\mathbb{P}(\mathbf{O}, \mathcal{Z})$ refers to **O** and $\mathcal{Z}$, i.e., $\mathbb{P}(\mathbf{O}, \mathcal{Z}) = P_1(\mathbf{O}, \mathcal{Z}) \theta \ldots \theta P_q(\mathbf{O}, \mathcal{Z})$ with $1 \leq i \leq q$ and $\theta \in \{\triangleright, \widetilde{\triangleright}\}$.

Based on this definition, we can investigate the semantical depth of our approach and derive a canonical collection of spatio-temporal developments. This allows us to limit the spatio-temporal developments which must be translated into sequences of object detections.

3.4.2 A Canonical Collection of Spatio-Temporal Developments

To obtain a canonical collection of spatio-temporal developments, [39] construct a *development graph* (cf. Section 2.2.3) which expresses possible spatio-temporal developments. A development is possible, if an object can move in such a way that the corresponding sequence of predicates $P_1 \theta P_2 \theta \ldots \theta P_q$ is satisfied.

Definition 38 (Development Graph): A *development graph* is a graph DG = (V, E) that expresses every possible predicate sequence:

V: The set of vertexes contains an element for every possible predicate.
E: The set of edges contains an element (P_i, P_j) if an object can move in such a way that $P_i \theta P_j$ is satisfied. □

As shown above, the set of predicates applicable to regions and objects differs from the set for zones and objects. Thus, we construct development graphs for zones and regions separately. Based on both graphs, we finally enumerate the possible developments.

The Object/Region Development Graph

There are three predicates that express the relationship between an object and a region. Thus, the set of vertexes V^R for the object/region development graph $DG^R = (V^R, E^R)$ contains three elements as well, i.e., $V^R = \{\mathit{Inside}\,(O, R), \mathit{Meet}\,(O, R), \mathit{Disjoint}\,(O, R)\}$.

Lemma 3.15. *For any object O and a region R, there does not exist a movement that fulfills the predicate sequences $\mathit{Inside}\,(O, R) \triangleright \mathit{Disjoint}\,(O, R)$ or $\mathit{Disjoint}\,(O, R) \triangleright \mathit{Inside}\,(O, R)$.*

Proof. According to Definition 10, the movement of an object O in relation to a region R satisfies $\mathit{Inside}\,(O, R) \triangleright \mathit{Disjoint}\,(O, R)$ if $\mathit{Inside}\,(O, R) = \mathcal{T}$ for some interval $[t_0, t_1[$ and $\mathit{Disjoint}\,(O, R) = \mathcal{T}$ at t_1. Due to the partitioning of space defined for regions (cf. Section 2.2.1), to satisfy $\mathit{Inside}\,(O, R)$ at t_i and $\mathit{Disjoint}\,(O, R)$ later at t_j, the object must cross the border at $t_i < t < t_j$. Thus, if $\mathit{Inside}\,(O, R) = \mathcal{T}$ for $[t_0, t_1[$, $\mathit{Meet}\,(O, R) = \mathcal{T}$ at t_1. Hence, $\mathit{Disjoint}\,(O, R)$ is not possible at t_1. The proof for $\mathit{Disjoint}\,(O, R) \triangleright \mathit{Inside}\,(O, R)$ is analogous. ∎

Lemma 3.15 implies that there does not exist an edge from $\mathit{Disjoint}\,(O, R)$ to $\mathit{Inside}\,(O, R)$ and vice versa. Figure 3.7 shows the object/region development graph.

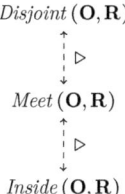

Figure 3.7: Development graph for an object O and a region R

Comparing this graph to the development graph in Figure 2.7 for objects and regions in moving object databases shows that they only differ in one vertex: As mentioned before, [39] distinguishes between $\mathit{meet}\,(o, r)$ and $\mathit{Meet}\,(O, R)$. Using their semantics, $\mathit{meet}\,(o, r) = \mathcal{T}$ if o is on the border of R for exactly one instant of time. Contrary to that, $\mathit{Meet}\,(O, R) = \mathcal{T}$ if O is on the border of R for a time interval. We omit developments with $\mathit{meet}\,(o, r)$ here, since this would assume detection mechanisms with infinite temporal resolution.

The Object/Zone Development Graph

As shown in Section 3.3, there are four predicates that express the relationship between an object and a zone. Thus, for the object/zone development graph $DG^Z = (V^Z, E^Z)$, the set of vertexes is defined as follows: $V^Z = \{\mathit{Inside}\,(O, Z), \mathit{Meet}\,(O, Z), \mathit{Disjoint}\,(O, Z), \mathit{Undetected}\,(O)\}$.

3.4. SPATIO-TEMPORAL DEVELOPMENTS

Contrary to regions, zones are not regular (cf. Section 3.4.1). As we have shown, this irregularity necessitates the usage of two different concatenation operators. Lemma 3.12 has shown that $P_1 \triangleright P_2 \Rightarrow P_1 \widetilde{\triangleright} P_2$. Thus, for each edge in E^R there must be a corresponding edge in E^Z. Furthermore, if there exists an edge for $P_1 \triangleright P_2$, there must be another edge to represent $P_1 \widetilde{\triangleright} P_2$. In addition, an object can move into or out of an undetected area at any time, i.e., the vertex representing *Undetected* (**O**) must have an edge to any other vertex and vice versa.

As with regions, the predicate sequences *Inside* (**O**, $\mathcal{Z}$) $\triangleright$ *Disjoint* (**O**, $\mathcal{Z}$) or *Disjoint* (**O**, $\mathcal{Z}$) $\triangleright$ *Inside* (**O**, $\mathcal{Z}$) are not possible. Thus, E^Z does not contain corresponding edges. Contrary to that, the sequences *Inside* (**O**, $\mathcal{Z}$) $\widetilde{\triangleright}$ *Disjoint* (**O**, $\mathcal{Z}$) and *Disjoint* (**O**, $\mathcal{Z}$) $\widetilde{\triangleright}$ *Inside* (**O**, $\mathcal{Z}$) must be part of E^Z.

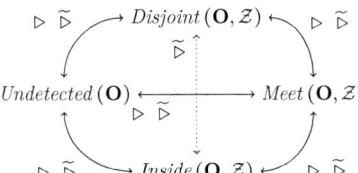

Figure 3.8: Development Graph for an object **O** and a zone $\mathcal{Z}$

Figure 3.8 summarizes the object/zone development graph. Solid lines represent concatenations that exist for both concatenation operators, namely $\triangleright$ and $\widetilde{\triangleright}$. The dotted line between *Inside* (**O**, $\mathcal{Z}$) and *Disjoint* (**O**, $\mathcal{Z}$) represents the fact that this concatenation is only possible with $\widetilde{\triangleright}$.

Enumeration of Possible Developments

Every path through a development graph represents a possible spatio-temporal development. Considering the structure of the development graphs above, the number of these paths is infinite due to cycles. As shown in [39], it is sufficient to restrict the set of developments by constructing development trees with the following approach:

1. Pick each element in V as the root of a the development tree.
2. From this root element, generate a child node in the tree for every vertex connected to this root in the development graph.
3. For each child node, construct a set of child nodes – the vertexes connected to it in the development graph.
4. A node is a leaf node, i.e., the node generation stops, if
   (a) representatives of every predicate are on the path from the root to the current node.

(b) the predicate corresponding to the current node already appears on the path from the root to the current node, i.e., in case of a cycle.

To obtain the canonical collection, we generate such a tree for every element of V based on the respective development graphs for regions and zones. Every node in such a tree represents a spatio-temporal development.

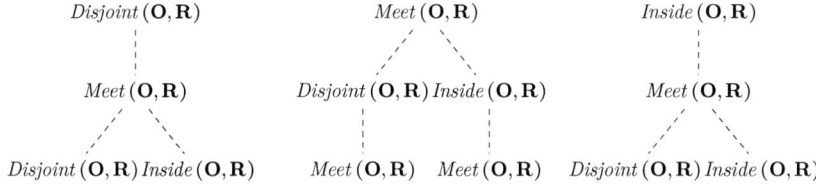

Figure 3.9: Development tree with root $Disjoint\,(\mathbf{O},\mathbf{R})$

Figure 3.10: Development tree with root $Meet\,(\mathbf{O},\mathbf{R})$

Figure 3.11: Development tree with root $Inside\,(\mathbf{O},\mathbf{R})$

Figures 3.9-3.11 show the development trees starting with $Disjoint\,(\mathbf{O},\mathbf{R})$, $Meet\,(\mathbf{O},\mathbf{R})$ and $Inside\,(\mathbf{O},\mathbf{R})$ respectively. There are 13 nodes, i.e., there are 13 unique spatio-temporal developments that describe the relationship of an object and a region in a sensor network over time. These 13 developments include three developments consisting of a single predicate. Since semantics for single predicates have been the focus of Section 3.3 already, there are 10 developments consisting of two or more predicates for which semantics have yet to be defined. Table 3.4 contains these 10 missing developments for objects and regions.

$Disjoint\,(\mathbf{O},\mathbf{R}) \triangleright Meet\,(\mathbf{O},\mathbf{R})$	$Inside\,(\mathbf{O},\mathbf{R}) \triangleright Meet\,(\mathbf{O},\mathbf{R})$
$Meet\,(\mathbf{O},\mathbf{R}) \triangleright Disjoint\,(\mathbf{O},\mathbf{R})$	$Meet\,(\mathbf{O},\mathbf{R}) \triangleright Inside\,(\mathbf{O},\mathbf{R})$
$Disjoint\,(\mathbf{O},\mathbf{R}) \triangleright Meet\,(\mathbf{O},\mathbf{R}) \triangleright Disjoint\,(\mathbf{O},\mathbf{R})$	$Disjoint\,(\mathbf{O},\mathbf{R}) \triangleright Meet\,(\mathbf{O},\mathbf{R}) \triangleright Inside\,(\mathbf{O},\mathbf{R})$
$Meet\,(\mathbf{O},\mathbf{R}) \triangleright Disjoint\,(\mathbf{O},\mathbf{R}) \triangleright Meet\,(\mathbf{O},\mathbf{R})$	$Meet\,(\mathbf{O},\mathbf{R}) \triangleright Inside\,(\mathbf{O},\mathbf{R}) \triangleright Meet\,(\mathbf{O},\mathbf{R})$
$Inside\,(\mathbf{O},\mathbf{R}) \triangleright Meet\,(\mathbf{O},\mathbf{R}) \triangleright Disjoint\,(\mathbf{O},\mathbf{R})$	$Inside\,(\mathbf{O},\mathbf{R}) \triangleright Meet\,(\mathbf{O},\mathbf{R}) \triangleright Inside\,(\mathbf{O},\mathbf{R})$

Table 3.4: Canonical collection of developments with two or more predicates for objects and regions

We translate each of these developments into a sequence of detection scenarios in Section 3.4.4. For each development there is a proof that the translation is correct.

Figures 3.12-3.15 contain the development trees starting with $Disjoint\,(\mathbf{O},\mathcal{Z})$, $Meet\,(\mathbf{O},\mathcal{Z})$, $Undetected\,(\mathbf{O})$ and $Inside\,(\mathbf{O},\mathcal{Z})$ respectively. Note that there are two types edges to reflect the different types of concatenations: A solid line indicates that the two predicates may be concatenated by either $\triangleright$ or $\widetilde{\triangleright}$. The dotted line occurring between $Disjoint\,(\mathbf{O},\mathcal{Z})$ and $Inside\,(\mathbf{O},\mathcal{Z})$ indicates that both predicates only allow the use of $\widetilde{\triangleright}$ for concatenation.

3.4. SPATIO-TEMPORAL DEVELOPMENTS

Each tree contains 31 nodes, i.e., the total number of nodes in all trees is $4 \cdot 31 = 124$. Contrary to the object/region development tree, each node represents more than one unique development because solid lines may be either $\triangleright$ or $\widetilde{\triangleright}$. The value above each node indicates the number of developments this node represents. We explain how to derive these values in the following using Figure 3.12: The root node $Disjoint\,(\mathbf{O},\mathcal{Z})$ in Figure 3.12 has edges to three predicates $Meet\,(\mathbf{O},\mathcal{Z})$, $Undetected\,(\mathbf{O})$ and $Inside\,(\mathbf{O},\mathcal{Z})$. The edge between $Disjoint\,(\mathbf{O},\mathcal{Z})$ and $Meet\,(\mathbf{O},\mathcal{Z})$ is solid, i.e., both predicates may be concatenated using $\triangleright$ and $\widetilde{\triangleright}$. Thus, there are two developments represented by this path:

1. $Disjoint\,(\mathbf{O},\mathcal{Z}) \triangleright Meet\,(\mathbf{O},\mathcal{Z})$
2. $Disjoint\,(\mathbf{O},\mathcal{Z}) \widetilde{\triangleright} Meet\,(\mathbf{O},\mathcal{Z})$.

Similarly, the path from $Disjoint\,(\mathbf{O},\mathcal{Z})$ to $Undetected\,(\mathbf{O})$ via $Meet\,(\mathbf{O},\mathcal{Z})$ represents four developments. This is because one can "append" $Undetected\,(\mathbf{O})$ to each of the two developments above using either $\triangleright$ or $\widetilde{\triangleright}$.

Since one cannot concatenate $Disjoint\,(\mathbf{O},\mathcal{Z})$ and $Inside\,(\mathbf{O},\mathcal{Z})$ using $\triangleright$ (cf. Lemma 3.15), the corresponding dotted edges only represent $\widetilde{\triangleright}$. For instance, in Figure 3.12 this occurs between the root node $Disjoint\,(\mathbf{O},\mathcal{Z})$ and $Inside\,(\mathbf{O},\mathcal{Z})$, i.e., this path only represents a single spatio-temporal development: $Disjoint\,(\mathbf{O},\mathcal{Z}) \widetilde{\triangleright} Inside\,(\mathbf{O},\mathcal{Z})$. Since it is possible to "append" $Meet\,(\mathbf{O},\mathcal{Z})$ to $Disjoint\,(\mathbf{O},\mathcal{Z}) \widetilde{\triangleright} Inside\,(\mathbf{O},\mathcal{Z})$ using $\widetilde{\triangleright}$ and $\triangleright$, the corresponding path represents two unique developments:

1. $Disjoint\,(\mathbf{O},\mathcal{Z}) \widetilde{\triangleright} Inside\,(\mathbf{O},\mathcal{Z}) \triangleright Meet\,(\mathbf{O},\mathcal{Z})$
2. $Disjoint\,(\mathbf{O},\mathcal{Z}) \widetilde{\triangleright} Inside\,(\mathbf{O},\mathcal{Z}) \widetilde{\triangleright} Meet\,(\mathbf{O},\mathcal{Z})$

By applying the scheme above to all nodes in the development trees starting with $Disjoint\,(\mathbf{O},\mathcal{Z})$, we derive that there are 146 unique developments that start with $Disjoint\,(\mathbf{O},\mathcal{Z})$. Even though the structure of the trees starting with $Meet\,(\mathbf{O},\mathcal{Z})$, $Undetected\,(\mathbf{O})$ and $Inside\,(\mathbf{O},\mathcal{Z})$ varies slightly, the number of unique spatio-temporal developments is always 146. Hence, users can express $4 \cdot 146 = 584$ unique spatio-temporal developments that describe the relationship between an object and a zone over time.

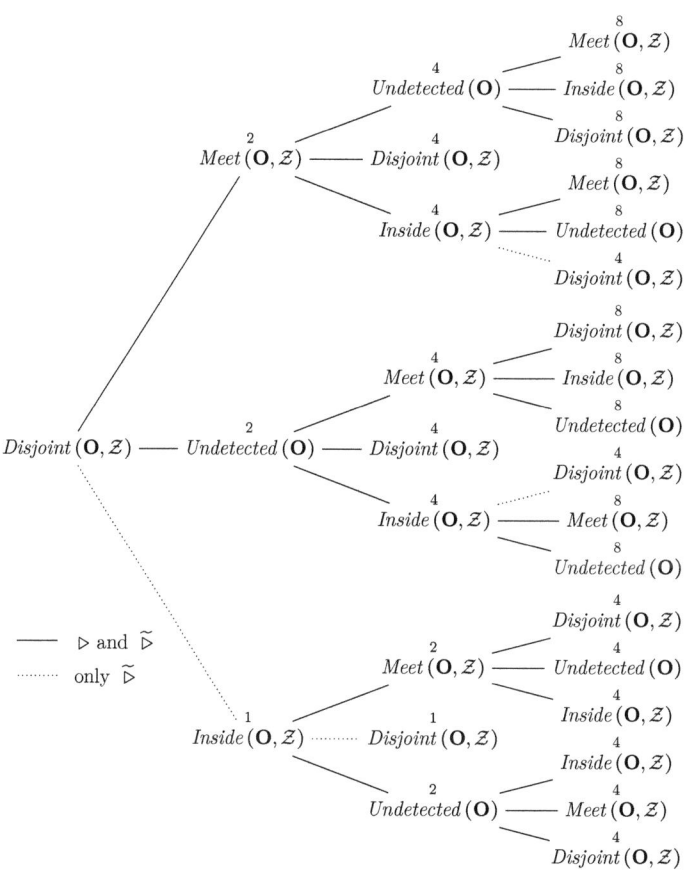

Figure 3.12: Development tree with root $Disjoint(\mathbf{O}, \mathcal{Z})$

3.4. SPATIO-TEMPORAL DEVELOPMENTS

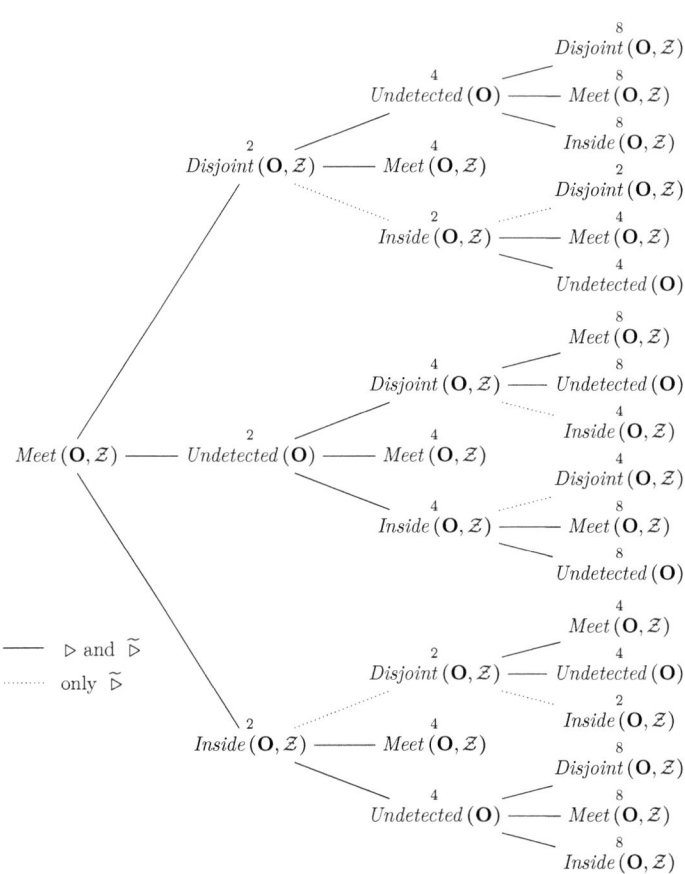

Figure 3.13: Development tree with root $Meet(\mathbf{O}, \mathcal{Z})$

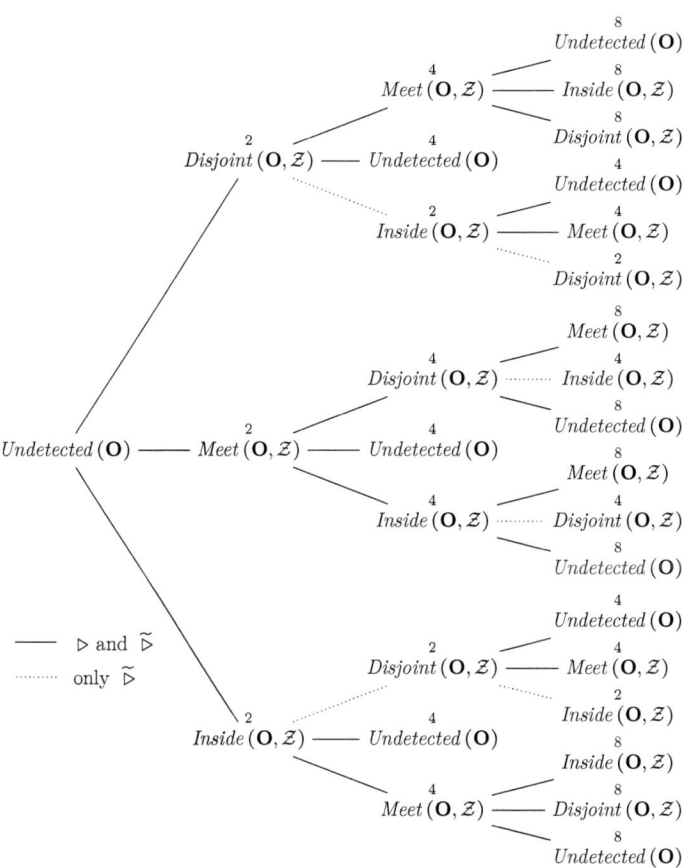

Figure 3.14: Development tree with root $Undetected\,(\mathbf{O})$

3.4. SPATIO-TEMPORAL DEVELOPMENTS

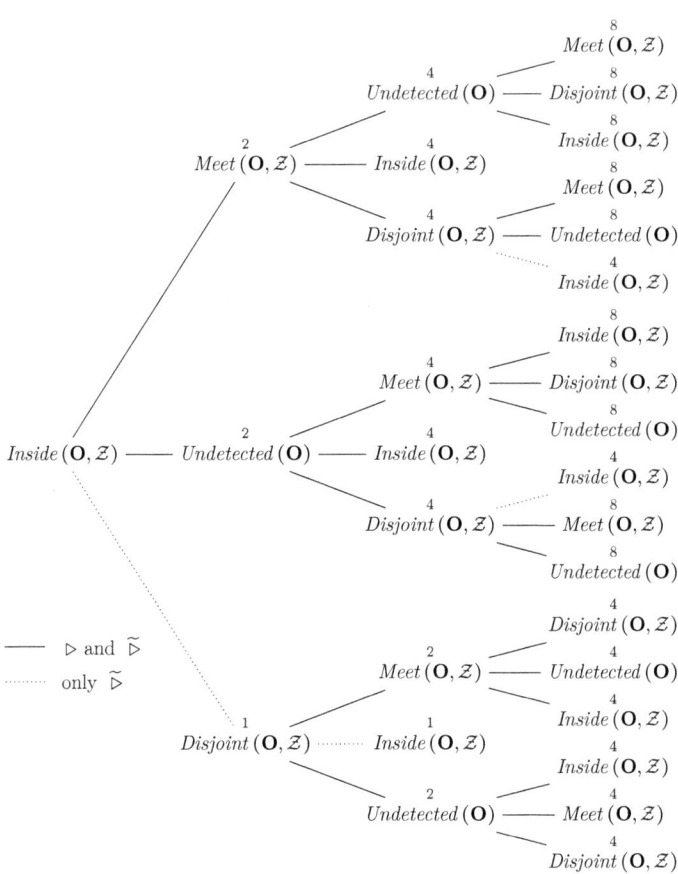

Figure 3.15: Development tree with root $Inside\,(\mathbf{O}, \mathcal{Z})$

3.4.3 Formal Description of Object Detection Sequences

According to Definition 37, a spatio-temporal development $\mathbb{P}$ is a sequence of predicates which describes the movement of an object in relation to a region or zone. The trajectory of on object matches such a development if the object fulfills the predicates in the order specified by the development. To describe trajectories formally, we define a concatenation operator for detection scenarios first:

Definition 39 (Detection Concatenation): The *concatenation of two detection scenarios*, $DS_1 \succ DS_2$, expresses that an object was detected according to DS_1 for the interval[3] $[t_1, t_2[$ and detected according to DS_2 at t_2. □

Lemma 3.16. $DS_1 \succ DS_1 = DS_1$

Proof. The left-hand side means that there is an interval $[t_1, t_2[$ where an object is detected according to DS_1 and another interval $[t_2, t_3[$ where the object is detected according to DS_1 as well. This means that the object is detected according to DS_1 during $[t_1, t_3[$ which equals the right-hand side. ∎

Definition 40 (Detection Sequence): The *detection sequence* $\mathbb{D} = DS_1 \succ \ldots \succ DS_k$ describes the trajectory of an object in relation to a region or zone. $\mathbb{D}$ means that for some time interval $[t_1, t_2[$ the detection scenario is DS_1, DS_2 for some time interval $[t_2, t_3[$ etc. □

Based on Lemma 3.16, we assume that any detection sequence has been summarized by applying $DS_1 \succ DS_1 = DS_1$. We use $\mathbb{D}_\mathbf{O}^\mathbf{R}$ to denote that the detection sequence refers to the movement of an object $\mathbf{O}$ in relation to a region $\mathbf{R}$. Analogously, $\mathbb{D}_\mathbf{O}^\mathcal{Z}$ describes the movement of $\mathbf{O}$ in the context of a zone $\mathcal{Z}$.

Lemma 3.17. *For any object $\mathbf{O}$, there exists exactly one detection sequence $\mathbb{D}_\mathbf{O}$ that represents the information on the movement of $\mathbf{O}$ acquired by the sensor network.*

Proof. According to Lemma 3.3, at each $t \in \mathbb{T}$ exactly one detection scenario holds. The detection sequence $\mathbb{D}_\mathbf{O}$ is the concatenation of these detection scenarios and hence there can be only one. ∎

Given a development $\mathbb{P}$, there exists an infinite number of detection sequences that conform to this development. This is because an object may move arbitrarily before or after conforming to the development, e.g., before conforming to Enter$(\mathbf{O}, \mathbf{R})$, the object $\mathbf{O}$ could alternate between DS^E and $DS^\emptyset$ arbitrary times. To summarize detection sequences that contain a certain pattern, we introduce the notion of a *detection term*.

Definition 41 (Detection Term): A *detection term* defines a pattern that represents a (possibly infinite) set of detection sequences. The pattern adheres to the following syntax[4]:

---

[3] We have chosen right-open intervals here to be in line with the definition of predicate sequences and the concatenation operator ▷ (cf. Definition 10). This does not cause any problems since the temporal resolution of any detection mechanism is limited in any case.

[4] The syntax is borrowed from the *Extended Backus-Naur Form* [67, 129].

3.4. SPATIO-TEMPORAL DEVELOPMENTS

$t_1|t_2$: The operator | means an alternative, e.g., $t_1|t_2$ denotes that either the detection term t_1 occurs or the detection term t_2.

$\{d\}$: The detection term t occurs an arbitrary number of times, i.e., $\{t\} = \epsilon|t|t \succ t|....$

A detection sequence is a detection term as well and the operator $\succ$ may be used to link detection terms as well with the same semantical meaning. □

Example 10: Consider the development $\text{Enter}(\mathbf{O}, \mathbf{R})$. The detection sequences $\text{DS}^E \succ \widetilde{\text{DS}^B} \succ \text{DS}^I$ as well as $\text{DS}^E \succ \text{DS}^\varnothing \succ \text{DS}^I$ describe object trajectories that conform to $\text{Enter}(\mathbf{O}, \mathbf{R})$. The latter does so because we can infer from the fact that object $\mathbf{O}$ has been detected outside of $\mathbf{R}$ and inside of it afterwards that $\mathbf{O}$ has crossed the border at some point. Additionally, there exists an infinite number of detection scenarios that conform to $\text{Enter}(\mathbf{O}, \mathbf{R})$ as well, such as $\text{DS}^E \succ \widetilde{\text{DS}^B} \succ \text{DS}^\varnothing \succ \text{DS}^I$. The following detection term reflects this and defines a pattern occuring in all detection sequences conforming to $\text{Enter}(\mathbf{O}, \mathbf{R})$:

$$\text{DS}^E \succ \left\{ \text{DS}^B | \widetilde{\text{DS}^B} | \text{DS}^\varnothing \right\} \succ \text{DS}^I \qquad (3.28)$$

All detection sequences that contain DS^E once, directly followed by an infinite number of repetitions of either $\text{DS}^\varnothing$, DS^B or $\widetilde{\text{DS}^B}$ and a concluding DS^I conform to this detection term and at the same time to $\text{Enter}(\mathbf{O}, \mathbf{R})$. Section 3.4.4 proves the correctness of this term. ♦

Definition 42 (Detection-Term Conformance): A detection sequence $\mathbb{D}$ conforms to a detection term t if $\mathbb{D}$ contains a substring of detection scenarios that is represented by t. □

To conform to a development, it is sufficient that a substring of a detection sequence conforms to the detection term. This is because objects may move in arbitrary patters before or after conforming to the term.

Example 11: Continuing Example 10, suppose that the object $\mathbf{O}$ crosses $\mathbf{R}$. This results in $\mathbb{D}_\mathbf{O}^\mathbf{R} = \text{DS}^E \succ \widetilde{\text{DS}^B} \succ \text{DS}^I \succ \widetilde{\text{DS}^B} \succ \text{DS}^E$. The substring $\text{DS}^E \succ \widetilde{\text{DS}^B} \succ \text{DS}^I$, and thus $\mathbf{O}$, conforms to the detection term in (3.28) for $\text{Enter}(\mathbf{O}, \mathbf{R})$. ♦

There exist various standard algorithms to find a substring conforming to a given pattern in a string [73]. Thus, these algorithms are sufficient to find a substring in a detection sequence which conforms to a detection term. We now provide *detection terms* for every possible detection sequence that conforms to a given spatio-temporal development.

Considering the detection term for $\text{Enter}(\mathbf{O}, \mathbf{R})$ in (3.28), we summarize that any $\mathbf{O}$ detected with DS^E at some time and later with DS^I conforms to $\text{Enter}(\mathbf{O}, \mathbf{R})$. It is not important which detection scenarios occur between DS^E and DS^I for $\mathbf{O}$ as long as the order described above is maintained. For a more concise presentation, we summarize these terms with a relaxed version of the concatenation operator for detection scenarios:

Definition 43 (Relaxed Detection Concatenation): The relaxed concatenation of two detection scenarios $\text{DS}_1 \widetilde{\succ} \text{DS}_2$, expresses that an object was detected according to DS_1 at t_1 and later according to DS_2 at t_2 with $t_1 < t_2$. □

Lemma 3.18. *Let* $\mathbb{DS} = \{\mathsf{DS}_1, \mathsf{DS}_2, \mathsf{DS}_3 \ldots, \mathsf{DS}_k\}$ *be the domain of detection scenarios. If* $d = \mathsf{DS}_3 | \ldots | \mathsf{DS}_k$ *for* $\mathsf{DS}_i \neq \mathsf{DS}_j$ *with* $i \neq j$, *then* $\mathsf{DS}_1 \succ \{d\} \succ \mathsf{DS}_2 = \mathsf{DS}_1 \widetilde{\succ} \mathsf{DS}_2$.

Proof. Follows directly from Lemma 3.3. ∎

We apply Lemma 3.18 to (3.28): In this case, $d = \mathsf{DS}^B | \widetilde{\mathsf{DS}^B} | \mathsf{DS}^\varnothing$, $\mathsf{DS}_1 = \mathsf{DS}^E$ and $\mathsf{DS}_2 = \mathsf{DS}^I$. Thus, we rewrite the term in (3.28) to $\mathsf{DS}^E \widetilde{\succ} \mathsf{DS}^I$.

Lemma 3.19. $\mathsf{DS}_1 \succ \mathsf{DS}_2 \Rightarrow \mathsf{DS}_1 \widetilde{\succ} \mathsf{DS}_2$

Proof. According to Definition 43, the right-hand side is true if DS_1 occurs for some interval $[t_0, t_1[$ and DS_2 occurs at $t_2 \geq t_1$. The left-hand side of the implication states that DS_1 occurs for some interval $[t_0, t_1[$ and DS_2 occurs at $t_2 = t_1$. Hence, if the left-hand side is true, the right-hand side is also true. ∎

3.4.4 Detection Terms

To obtain semantics for spatio-temporal developments, we derive a detection term $\mathbb{D}$ for every element $\mathbb{P}$ in the canonical collection of developments. A predicate sequence $\mathbb{P}$ returns $\mathcal{T}$ if the trajectory of an object in question conforms to the detection term $\mathbb{D}$ for sure. Similarly, we provide a detection term $\mathbb{D}$ which allows the sensor network to determine that $\mathbb{P} = \mathcal{F}$ for every development. Objects whose trajectory neither allows the sensor network to derive $\mathbb{P} = \mathcal{T}$ or $\mathbb{P} = \mathcal{F}$ are those where the inaccuracy prevents a definite answer, i.e., $\mathbb{P} = \mathcal{M}$.

Detection Terms for Regions

Table 3.5 provides a detection term $\mathbb{D}_\mathbf{O}^\mathbf{R}$ that describes a trajectory for each predicate sequence $\mathbb{P}(\mathbf{O}, \mathbf{R})$ in Table 3.4 such that $\mathbb{P}(\mathbf{O}, \mathbf{R}) = \mathcal{T}$. For each of these terms we provide a proof that the term is correct. Given a detection term d related to a development $\mathbb{P}(\mathbf{O}, \mathbf{R})$, we consider d to be correct for $\mathbb{P}(\mathbf{O}, \mathbf{R})$ if the following conditions are met:

- There does not exist a detection sequence $\mathbb{D}_\mathbf{O}^\mathbf{R}$ of an object $\mathbf{O}$ whose movement conforms to $\mathbb{P}(\mathbf{O}, \mathbf{R})$ where $\mathbb{D}_\mathbf{O}^\mathbf{R}$ does not conform to the term d.
- There does not exist a detection sequence $\mathbb{D}_\mathbf{O}^\mathbf{R}$ of an object $\mathbf{O}$ whose movement does not conform to $\mathbb{P}(\mathbf{O}, \mathbf{R})$ where $\mathbb{D}_\mathbf{O}^\mathbf{R}$ conforms to d.

3.4. SPATIO-TEMPORAL DEVELOPMENTS

$\mathbb{P}(\mathbf{O},\mathbf{R})$	Detection Term
$Disjoint(\mathbf{O},\mathbf{R}) \triangleright Meet(\mathbf{O},\mathbf{R})$	$DS^E \succ \{\widetilde{DS^B}|DS^\emptyset\} \succ (DS^B|DS^I)$
$Inside(\mathbf{O},\mathbf{R}) \triangleright Meet(\mathbf{O},\mathbf{R})$	$DS^I \succ \{\widetilde{DS^B}|DS^\emptyset\} \succ (DS^B|DS^E)$
$Meet(\mathbf{O},\mathbf{R}) \triangleright Disjoint(\mathbf{O},\mathbf{R})$	$(DS^B|DS^I) \succ \{\widetilde{DS^B}|DS^\emptyset\} \succ DS^E$
$Meet(\mathbf{O},\mathbf{R}) \triangleright Inside(\mathbf{O},\mathbf{R})$	$(DS^B|DS^E) \succ \{\widetilde{DS^B}|DS^\emptyset\} \succ DS^I$
$Disjoint(\mathbf{O},\mathbf{R}) \triangleright Meet(\mathbf{O},\mathbf{R}) \triangleright Inside(\mathbf{O},\mathbf{R})$	$DS^E \succ \{DS^B|\widetilde{DS^B}|DS^\emptyset\} \succ DS^I$
$Disjoint(\mathbf{O},\mathbf{R}) \triangleright Meet(\mathbf{O},\mathbf{R}) \triangleright Disjoint(\mathbf{O},\mathbf{R})$	$DS^E \succ DS^B \succ DS^E$
$Inside(\mathbf{O},\mathbf{R}) \triangleright Meet(\mathbf{O},\mathbf{R}) \triangleright Disjoint(\mathbf{O},\mathbf{R})$	$DS^I \succ \{DS^B|\widetilde{DS^B}|DS^\emptyset\} \succ DS^E$
$Inside(\mathbf{O},\mathbf{R}) \triangleright Meet(\mathbf{O},\mathbf{R}) \triangleright Inside(\mathbf{O},\mathbf{R})$	$DS^I \succ DS^B \succ DS^I$
$Meet(\mathbf{O},\mathbf{R}) \triangleright Disjoint(\mathbf{O},\mathbf{R}) \triangleright Meet(\mathbf{O},\mathbf{R})$	$(DS^I|DS^B) \succ \{\widetilde{DS^B}|DS^\emptyset\} \succ DS^E \succ \{DS^E|\widetilde{DS^B}|DS^\emptyset\} \succ (DS^I|DS^B)$
$Meet(\mathbf{O},\mathbf{R}) \triangleright Inside(\mathbf{O},\mathbf{R}) \triangleright Meet(\mathbf{O},\mathbf{R})$	$(DS^E|DS^B) \succ \{\widetilde{DS^B}|DS^\emptyset\} \succ DS^I \succ \{DS^I|\widetilde{DS^B}|DS^\emptyset\} \succ (DS^E|DS^B)$

Table 3.5: Detection terms $\mathbb{D}_\mathbf{O}^\mathbf{R}$ where $\mathbb{P}(\mathbf{O},\mathbf{R}) = \mathcal{T}$

Determining whether $\mathbb{P}(\mathbf{O},\mathbf{R}) = \mathcal{T}$

Lemma 3.20. *To ensure that* $Meet(\mathbf{O},\mathbf{R}) = \mathcal{T}$, *the detection sequence* $\mathbb{D}_\mathbf{O}^\mathbf{R}$ *of an object* $\mathbf{O}$ *must meet one of the following requirements:*

1. $\mathbb{D}_\mathbf{O}^\mathbf{R}$ *contains* DS^B.
2. $\mathbb{D}_\mathbf{O}^\mathbf{R}$ *conforms to* $\mathsf{DS}^I \widetilde{\succ} \mathsf{DS}^E$.
3. $\mathbb{D}_\mathbf{O}^\mathbf{R}$ *conforms to* $\mathsf{DS}^E \widetilde{\succ} \mathsf{DS}^I$.

For any other sequence, $Meet(\mathbf{O},\mathbf{R})$ *yields* $\mathcal{M}$ *or* $\mathcal{F}$.

Proof. According to (3.17), DS^B guarantees $Meet(\mathbf{O},\mathbf{R}) = \mathcal{T}$. The other two cases imply that $\mathbf{O}$ has been detected on both sides of the border $\mathbf{R}^B$. Hence, between these detections there was a time when $\mathbf{O}$ was on $\mathbf{R}^B$ even if DS^B did not occur, e.g., because the object crossed the border while not being detected by any node. Detection sequences that do not meet either of these requirements conform to $\{\mathsf{DS}^E|\widetilde{\mathsf{DS}^B}|\mathsf{DS}^\varnothing\}|\{\mathsf{DS}^I|\widetilde{\mathsf{DS}^B}|\mathsf{DS}^\varnothing\}$. According to (3.17), neither $\{\mathsf{DS}^E|\widetilde{\mathsf{DS}^B}|\mathsf{DS}^\varnothing\}$ nor $\{\mathsf{DS}^I|\widetilde{\mathsf{DS}^B}|\mathsf{DS}^\varnothing\}$ guarantee $Meet(\mathbf{O},\mathbf{R}) = \mathcal{T}$. ∎

Due to Lemma 3.20, developments consisting of two predicates require either DS^B or detection of the object in question on both sides of the border. This is reflected by the detection terms for these developments in Table 3.5. In any other case, $Meet(\mathbf{O},\mathbf{R})$ must yield either $\mathcal{M}$ or $\mathcal{F}$.

Lemma 3.21. *If* $\mathbb{D}_\mathbf{O}^\mathbf{R}$ *conforms to* $\mathsf{DS}^E \succ \{\widetilde{\mathsf{DS}^B}|\mathsf{DS}^\varnothing\} \succ (\mathsf{DS}^B|\mathsf{DS}^I)$ *the sensor network can guarantee that* $\mathbb{P}(\mathbf{O},\mathbf{R}) = Disjoint(\mathbf{O},\mathbf{R}) \triangleright Meet(\mathbf{O},\mathbf{R}) = \mathcal{T}$.

Proof. Since $\mathbb{P}(\mathbf{O},\mathbf{R})$ starts with $Disjoint(\mathbf{O},\mathbf{R})$, the start of the detection sequence must guarantee $Disjoint(\mathbf{O},\mathbf{R}) = \mathcal{T}$. According to (3.18), the only detection scenario where $Disjoint(\mathbf{O},\mathbf{R}) = \mathcal{T}$ is DS^E. After DS^E occurred, the object may move arbitrarily and $\mathbb{P}(\mathbf{O},\mathbf{R}) = \mathcal{T}$ if either DS^B occurs or DS^I guarantees that $\mathbf{O}$ crosses the border. ∎

A proof for the correctness of the entry related to $Inside(\mathbf{O},\mathbf{R}) \triangleright Meet(\mathbf{O},\mathbf{R})$ is analogous and thus omitted here.

Lemma 3.22. *If* $\mathbb{D}_\mathbf{O}^\mathbf{R}$ *conforms to* $(\mathsf{DS}^B|\mathsf{DS}^I) \succ \{\widetilde{\mathsf{DS}^B}|\mathsf{DS}^\varnothing\} \succ \mathsf{DS}^E$ *the sensor network can guarantee that* $\mathbb{P}(\mathbf{O},\mathbf{R}) = Meet(\mathbf{O},\mathbf{R}) \triangleright Disjoint(\mathbf{O},\mathbf{R}) = \mathcal{T}$.

Proof. According to Lemma 3.20, $Meet(\mathbf{O},\mathbf{R}) = \mathcal{T}$ requires either detection on both sides of the border or DS^B. For the first case, the object must be detected with DS^I first and then move arbitrarily until it is detected with DS^E. Since DS^E also yields $Disjoint(\mathbf{O},\mathbf{R}) = \mathcal{T}$, the sensor network can guarantee $\mathbb{P}(\mathbf{O},\mathbf{R}) = \mathcal{T}$ as well. The latter case above indicates that the object is on the border at first, i.e., $Meet(\mathbf{O},\mathbf{R}) = \mathcal{T}$. Hence, the object only has to fulfill $Disjoint(\mathbf{O},\mathbf{R})$ afterwards which is the case if $\{\widetilde{\mathsf{DS}^B}|\mathsf{DS}^\varnothing\} \succ \mathsf{DS}^E$. ∎

3.4. SPATIO-TEMPORAL DEVELOPMENTS

The principle of the proof for Lemma 3.22 is applicable to prove that $\left(\mathsf{DS}^B|\mathsf{DS}^E\right) \succ \left\{\widetilde{\mathsf{DS}^B}|\mathsf{DS}^\varnothing\right\} \succ \mathsf{DS}^I$ ensures that $Meet\,(\mathbf{O},\mathbf{R}) \triangleright Inside\,(\mathbf{O},\mathbf{R}) = \mathcal{T}$, because $\mathbf{O}$ only moves in the "opposite" direction. This concludes our discussion of the detection terms for developments consisting of two predicates.

Lemma 3.23. *To derive that* $Enter\,(\mathbf{O},\mathbf{R}) = \mathcal{T}$ *or* $Leave\,(\mathbf{O},\mathbf{R}) = \mathcal{T}$, *the object* $\mathbf{O}$ *must be detected according to* $\mathsf{DS}^E \widetilde{\succ} \mathsf{DS}^I$ *and* $\mathsf{DS}^I \widetilde{\succ} \mathsf{DS}^E$ *respectively.*

Proof. $\mathsf{DS}^E \widetilde{\succ} \mathsf{DS}^I$ summarizes $\mathsf{DS}^E \succ \left\{\mathsf{DS}^B|\widetilde{\mathsf{DS}^B}|\mathsf{DS}^\varnothing\right\} \succ \mathsf{DS}^I$. The sensor network derives from DS^E that $Disjoint\,(\mathbf{O},\mathbf{R}) = \mathcal{T}$ and since DS^I occurs some time afterwards, it is sure that $Meet\,(\mathbf{O},\mathbf{R}) \triangleright Inside\,(\mathbf{O},\mathbf{R}) = \mathcal{T}$ as well. The proof for the opposite direction for $Leave\,(\mathbf{O},\mathbf{R})$ and the term $\mathsf{DS}^I \succ \left\{\mathsf{DS}^B|\widetilde{\mathsf{DS}^B}|\mathsf{DS}^\varnothing\right\} \succ \mathsf{DS}^E$ is analogous. ∎

Lemma 3.24. *If* $\mathbb{P}\,(\mathbf{O},\mathbf{R}) = Disjoint\,(\mathbf{O},\mathbf{R}) \triangleright Meet\,(\mathbf{O},\mathbf{R}) \triangleright Disjoint\,(\mathbf{O},\mathbf{R})$, *the trajectory must conform to* $\mathsf{DS}^E \succ \mathsf{DS}^B \succ \mathsf{DS}^E$ *to guarantee that* $\mathbf{O}$ *fulfills* $\mathbb{P}\,(\mathbf{O},\mathbf{R})$.

Proof. The first part of the detection term, i.e., $\mathsf{DS}^E \succ \mathsf{DS}^B$ guarantees $Disjoint\,(\mathbf{O},\mathbf{R}) \triangleright Meet\,(\mathbf{O},\mathbf{R})$. The term must not contain $\mathsf{DS}^\varnothing$ or $\widetilde{\mathsf{DS}^B}$, because in both cases the object could be inside the region. If the object could be inside $\mathbf{R}$, the sensor network cannot guarantee that $Meet\,(\mathbf{O},\mathbf{R}) \triangleright Disjoint\,(\mathbf{O},\mathbf{R})$. Hence, the term must exclude all objects that could be in $\mathbf{R}$ between DS^E and DS^B. ∎

The term for $Inside\,(\mathbf{O},\mathbf{R}) \triangleright Meet\,(\mathbf{O},\mathbf{R}) \triangleright Inside\,(\mathbf{O},\mathbf{R})$ is similar to the term for $Disjoint\,(\mathbf{O},\mathbf{R}) \triangleright Meet\,(\mathbf{O},\mathbf{R}) \triangleright Disjoint\,(\mathbf{O},\mathbf{R})$: The only difference is that the term for $Inside\,(\mathbf{O},\mathbf{R}) \triangleright Meet\,(\mathbf{O},\mathbf{R}) \triangleright Inside\,(\mathbf{O},\mathbf{R})$ must exclude all objects that could have been outside of $\mathbf{R}$.

Lemma 3.25. *The term* $\left(\mathsf{DS}^I|\mathsf{DS}^B\right) \succ \left\{\widetilde{\mathsf{DS}^B}|\mathsf{DS}^\varnothing\right\} \succ \mathsf{DS}^E \succ \left\{\mathsf{DS}^E|\widetilde{\mathsf{DS}^B}|\mathsf{DS}^\varnothing\right\} \succ \left(\mathsf{DS}^I|\mathsf{DS}^B\right)$ *guarantees that* $\mathbf{O}$ *conforms to* $Meet\,(\mathbf{O},\mathbf{R}) \triangleright Disjoint\,(\mathbf{O},\mathbf{R}) \triangleright Meet\,(\mathbf{O},\mathbf{R})$.

Proof. The first part of the detection term, $\left(\mathsf{DS}^I|\mathsf{DS}^B\right) \succ \left\{\widetilde{\mathsf{DS}^B}|\mathsf{DS}^\varnothing\right\} \succ \mathsf{DS}^E$, already guarantees that $Meet\,(\mathbf{O},\mathbf{R}) \triangleright Disjoint\,(\mathbf{O},\mathbf{R})$. This is because the result of the object detection either conforms to DS^B and then DS^E, or the object is detected on both sides of the border. Afterwards, $\mathbf{O}$ may move arbitrarily outside of $\mathbf{R}$ as reflected by $\left\{\mathsf{DS}^E|\widetilde{\mathsf{DS}^B}|\mathsf{DS}^\varnothing\right\}$. To conform to $Disjoint\,(\mathbf{O},\mathbf{R}) \triangleright Meet\,(\mathbf{O},\mathbf{R})$, the object must either cross the border again or DS^B must occur. This is expressed by the second part of the term, i.e., $\mathsf{DS}^E \succ \left\{\mathsf{DS}^E|\widetilde{\mathsf{DS}^B}|\mathsf{DS}^\varnothing\right\} \succ \left(\mathsf{DS}^I|\mathsf{DS}^B\right)$. ∎

Since the proof for $Meet\,(\mathbf{O},\mathbf{R}) \triangleright Inside\,(\mathbf{O},\mathbf{R}) \triangleright Meet\,(\mathbf{O},\mathbf{R})$ is analogous, we omit it here. Summing up, we have proved the correctness of all detection terms in Table 3.5.

Determining whether $\mathbb{P}(\mathbf{O},\mathbf{R}) = \mathcal{F}$ Now we show how sensor networks derive $\mathbb{P}(\mathbf{O},\mathbf{R}) = \mathcal{F}$. The most important difference to the previous study regarding $\mathbb{P}(\mathbf{O},\mathbf{R}) = \mathcal{T}$ is that one must consider the whole detection sequence instead of a substring: While it is sufficient to find a substring in the detection sequence that conforms to a detection term to determine that $\mathbb{P}(\mathbf{O},\mathbf{R}) = \mathcal{T}$, to compute $\mathbb{P}(\mathbf{O},\mathbf{R}) = \mathcal{F}$ the sensor network must rule out that any part of the detection sequence could possibly conform to $\mathbb{P}(\mathbf{O},\mathbf{R})$.

Lemma 3.26. *Any object detected according to $\widetilde{\mathsf{DS}^B}$ could possibly conform to any spatio-temporal development $\mathbb{P}(\mathbf{O},\mathbf{R})$ that describes the relationship of an object $\mathbf{O}$ and a region $\mathbf{R}$ over time.*

Proof. According to Definition 31, $\widetilde{\mathsf{DS}^B}$ means that $\mathbf{POP}_t^\mathbf{O}$ intersects with all partitions of $\mathbf{R}$. This means that the position of $\mathbf{O}$ is so "close" to the border that the sensor network cannot provide a definite answer on which side of the border $\mathbf{O}$ is. Thus, an object could repeatedly move around and over the border of $\mathbf{R}$ in any way while the sensor network can only determine $\widetilde{\mathsf{DS}^B}$. During this time, $\mathbf{O}$ could fulfill any development that describes the relationship between $\mathbf{O}$ and $\mathbf{R}$. ∎

Lemma 3.26 implies that detection sequences that definitely do not conform to a development must not contain $\widetilde{\mathsf{DS}^B}$. Looking at Table 3.2, this also applies to $\mathsf{DS}^\varnothing$. This is because detection areas typically may have any shape or size and undetected objects can cross the border of a region in arbitrary ways unless assumptions regarding the coverage of space with detection areas are made. For controlled deployments (cf. Section 1.1), making such assumptions is sometimes viable and thus we discuss three of these so called *coverage assumptions* in the following:

- $\mathrm{CA}^\varnothing$: We assume nodes have been deployed randomly and it is not fixed a priori which parts of space are observed.
- CA^B: Nodes have been deployed in such a way that a complete coverage of the border $\mathbf{R}^B$ can be assumed for query processing.

$$\mathbf{R}^B \subseteq \bigcup_{i=1}^{n} \mathbf{DA}_i \qquad (3.29)$$

Thus, objects cannot cross the border without being detected.

- CA^{BI}: The deployment guarantees that objects inside as well as objects on the border are detected.

$$\mathbf{R}^B \cup \mathbf{R}^I \subseteq \bigcup_{i=1}^{n} \mathbf{DA}_i \qquad (3.30)$$

This means, that $\mathsf{DS}^\varnothing$ may only occur for objects that are in the exterior of $\mathbf{R}$.

We show how to determine $\mathbb{P}(\mathbf{O},\mathbf{R}) = \mathcal{F}$ in case of $\mathsf{DS}^\varnothing$ with respect to different coverage assumptions in the following.

Lemma 3.27. *In case of $CA^\varnothing$, an object $\mathbf{O}$ that is temporarily undetected, i.e., $\mathsf{DS}^\varnothing$ occurs at least once in $\mathbb{D}_\mathbf{O}^\mathbf{R}$, could conform to any development $\mathbb{P}(\mathbf{O},\mathbf{R})$.*

3.4. SPATIO-TEMPORAL DEVELOPMENTS

$$\mathbb{P}_{CA^\varnothing}(\mathbf{O}, \mathbf{R}) = \begin{cases} \mathcal{T} & \text{iff } \mathbb{D}_\mathbf{O}^\mathbf{R} \text{ conforms to } d \\ \mathcal{F} & \text{iff } \left(\mathbb{D}_\mathbf{O}^\mathbf{R} = \{\mathsf{DS}^I\}\right) \vee \left(\mathbb{D}_\mathbf{O}^\mathbf{R} = \{\mathsf{DS}^E\}\right) \\ \mathcal{M} & \text{Otherwise} \end{cases} \qquad (3.31)$$

$$\mathbb{P}_{CA^B}(\mathbf{O}, \mathbf{R}) = \begin{cases} \mathcal{T} & \text{iff } \mathbb{D}_\mathbf{O}^\mathbf{R} \text{ conforms to } d \\ \mathcal{F} & \text{iff } \mathbb{D}_\mathbf{O}^\mathbf{R} \text{ does not conform to } d \text{ and } \mathbb{D}_\mathbf{O}^\mathbf{R} = \{\mathsf{DS}^I|\mathsf{DS}^E|\mathsf{DS}^\varnothing|\mathsf{DS}^B\} \\ \mathcal{M} & \text{Otherwise} \end{cases} \qquad (3.32)$$

$$\mathbb{P}_{CA^{BI}}(\mathbf{O}, \mathbf{R}) = \begin{cases} \mathcal{T} & \text{iff } \mathbb{D}_\mathbf{O}^\mathbf{R} \text{ conforms to } d \text{ with } \mathsf{DS}^\varnothing \text{ replaced by } \mathsf{DS}^E \\ \mathcal{F} & \text{iff } \mathbb{D}_\mathbf{O}^\mathbf{R} \text{ does not conform to } d \text{ and } \mathbb{D}_\mathbf{O}^\mathbf{R} = \{\mathsf{DS}^I|\mathsf{DS}^E|\mathsf{DS}^B\} \\ \mathcal{M} & \text{Otherwise} \end{cases} \qquad (3.33)$$

Proof. As stated above, detection areas may have any size or shape and thus the set of points that is unobserved could intersect with any partition of $\mathbf{R}$. An undetected object $\mathbf{O}$ could be at any of these unobserved points in space and thus in any partition of $\mathbf{R}$. Hence, $\mathbf{O}$ may conform to any development that describes the relation between $\mathbf{O}$ and $\mathbf{R}$. ∎

Summing up, if assumptions about the coverage of space, i.e., the area observed, are unfeasible, any occurrence of $\mathsf{DS}^\varnothing$ or $\widetilde{\mathsf{DS}^B}$ in the detection sequence rules out $\mathbb{P}(\mathbf{O}, \mathbf{R}) = \mathcal{F}$. Therefore, $\mathbb{P}(\mathbf{O}, \mathbf{R}) = \mathcal{F}$ only if the object is detected according to either DS^I or DS^E at all times.

This changes if one of the other coverage assumptions is taken into account: Assuming CA^B, the sensor network can derive that objects do not cross the border while being undetected. Thus, any detection sequence that does not conform to the development $\mathbb{P}(\mathbf{O}, \mathbf{R})$ in question and whose detection sequence contains any detection scenarios except $\widetilde{\mathsf{DS}^B}$ definitely does not conform to the development, i.e, $\mathbb{P}(\mathbf{O}, \mathbf{R}) = \mathcal{F}$. The case with CA^{BI} is similar: Objects cannot cross the border without being detected. Thus, the rule above regarding the question if $\mathbb{P}(\mathbf{O}, \mathbf{R}) = \mathcal{F}$ applies as well. Additionally, any undetected object must be outside of the region $\mathbf{R}$, i.e., in $\mathbf{R}^E$. Thus, prior to determining if the detection sequence of $\mathbf{O}$ conforms to the term in Table 3.4 associated with $\mathbb{P}(\mathbf{O}, \mathbf{R})$, we can replace any occurrence of $\mathsf{DS}^\varnothing$ with DS^E.

Summary – Development results for queries with regions This concludes our study regarding results of spatio-temporal developments in the context of objects and regions. Given a detection term d associated with a development $\mathbb{P}(\mathbf{O}, \mathbf{R})$, Equations 3.31-3.33 summarize how the result of $\mathbb{P}(\mathbf{O}, \mathbf{R})$ is determined in a sensor network.

Theorem 1. *The results for spatio-temporal developments which describe the relationship between an object and a region are optimal considering the limitations of detection mechanisms in sensor networks.*

Proof. Let $\Omega_{\mathbb{P}(\mathbf{O}, \mathbf{R})}$ be the set of objects that conform to a development $\mathbb{P}(\mathbf{O}, \mathbf{R})$ in question. The set of objects where $\mathbb{P}(\mathbf{O},\mathbf{R}) = \mathcal{T}$ is the largest subset of $\Omega_{\mathbb{P}(\mathbf{O},\mathbf{R})}$ a sensor network can derive according to the lemmas in Section 3.4.4. Similarly, the set of objects where $\mathbb{P}(\mathbf{O},\mathbf{R}) = \mathcal{F}$ is the largest superset of $\Omega_{\mathbb{P}(\mathbf{O},\mathbf{R})}$ the sensor network can derive. Therefore, the set of objects where $\mathbb{P}(\mathbf{O},\mathbf{R}) = \mathcal{M}$ is minimal, i.e., contains only objects where the accuracy of the object detection prevents a definitive answer. ∎

Detection Terms for Zones

According to Table 3.3, all predicates that express the relation between an object $\mathbf{O}$ and a zone $\mathcal{Z}$ either yield $\mathcal{T}$ or $\mathcal{F}$, but never $\mathcal{M}$. Furthermore, the table shows also that for any predicate $P(\mathbf{O},\mathcal{Z})$, there exists exactly one detection scenario DS_i which yields $P(\mathbf{O},\mathcal{Z}) = \mathcal{T}$ and all other detection scenarios $\mathsf{DS}_j \neq \mathsf{DS}_i$ yield $P(\mathbf{O},\mathcal{Z}) = \mathcal{F}$. Compared to regions, this eases the translation of detection sequences to development results considerably.

Lemma 3.28. *Suppose DS_i is the detection scenario which yields $P_i(\mathbf{O},\mathcal{Z}) = \mathcal{T}$ and DS_j is the detection scenario which yields $P_j(\mathbf{O},\mathcal{Z}) = \mathcal{T}$. If $\mathbb{D}_\mathbf{O}^\mathcal{Z}$ conforms to $\mathsf{DS}_i \succ \mathsf{DS}_j$, then $P_i(\mathbf{O},\mathcal{Z}) \triangleright P_j(\mathbf{O},\mathcal{Z}) = \mathcal{T}$. If $\mathbb{D}_\mathbf{O}^\mathcal{Z}$ does not conform to $\mathsf{DS}_i \succ \mathsf{DS}_j$, then $P_i(\mathbf{O},\mathcal{Z}) \triangleright P_j(\mathbf{O},\mathcal{Z}) = \mathcal{F}$.*

Proof. We prove $P_i(\mathbf{O},\mathcal{Z}) \triangleright P_j(\mathbf{O},\mathcal{Z}) = \mathcal{T}$ first: According to Definitions 39 and 42, conformance of $\mathbb{D}_\mathbf{O}^\mathcal{Z}$ to $\mathsf{DS}_i \succ \mathsf{DS}_j$ means that the object $\mathbf{O}$ was detected with DS_i during $[t_1, t_2[$ and then with DS_j at t_2. Since DS_i yields $P_i(\mathbf{O},\mathcal{Z}) = \mathcal{T}$, we derive that $P_i(\mathbf{O},\mathcal{Z}) = \mathcal{T}$ for the interval $[t_1, t_2[$ and $P_i(\mathbf{O},\mathcal{Z}) = \mathcal{T}$ at t_2. Hence, $P_i(\mathbf{O},\mathcal{Z}) \triangleright P_j(\mathbf{O},\mathcal{Z}) = \mathcal{T}$.

If $\mathbb{D}_\mathbf{O}^\mathcal{Z}$ does not conform to $\mathsf{DS}_i \succ \mathsf{DS}_j$, there is no substring in $\mathbb{D}_\mathbf{O}^\mathcal{Z}$ where DS_i is followed by DS_j. This means that either DS_j never follows DS_i, or DS_i or DS_j never occur. For all of these cases, the sensor network can guarantee that $\mathbf{O}$ does not fulfill $P_i(\mathbf{O},\mathcal{Z}) \triangleright P_j(\mathbf{O},\mathcal{Z})$ and thus return $\mathcal{F}$. ∎

Lemma 3.29. *Suppose DS_i is the detection scenario which yields $P_i(\mathbf{O},\mathcal{Z}) = \mathcal{T}$ and DS_j is the detection scenario which yields $P_j(\mathbf{O},\mathcal{Z}) = \mathcal{T}$. If $\mathbb{D}_\mathbf{O}^\mathcal{Z}$ conforms to $\mathsf{DS}_i \widetilde{\succ} \mathsf{DS}_j$, then $P_i(\mathbf{O},\mathcal{Z}) \widetilde{\triangleright} P_j(\mathbf{O},\mathcal{Z}) = \mathcal{T}$.*

Proof. Analogous to the proof for Lemma 3.28. ∎

Lemmas 3.28 and 3.29 imply the detection terms for any of the developments for zones defined in Section 3.4.2 are simply obtained by iteratively concatenating detection scenarios. Assuming a development $\mathbb{P}(\mathbf{O},\mathcal{Z}) = P_1(\mathbf{O},\mathcal{Z}) \; \theta \; P_2(\mathbf{O},\mathcal{Z}) \; \theta \; \ldots \; \theta \; P_q(\mathbf{O},\mathcal{Z})$ this works as follows: DS_i is the detection scenario where $P_i(\mathbf{O},\mathcal{Z}) = \mathcal{T}$ according to Table 3.3. Thus, the detection term starts with DS_1 and the second detection scenario in the term is DS_2. If the concatenation operator between $P_1(\mathbf{O},\mathcal{Z})$ and $P_2(\mathbf{O},\mathcal{Z})$ is $\triangleright$, then the detection term starts with $\mathsf{DS}_1 \succ \mathsf{DS}_2$. Otherwise, the detection terms starts with $\mathsf{DS}_1 \widetilde{\succ} \mathsf{DS}_2$. Next, we consider $P_3(\mathbf{O},\mathcal{Z})$ and how it is concatenated to $P_2(\mathbf{O},\mathcal{Z})$. This continues until a detection scenario corresponding to $P_q(\mathbf{O},\mathcal{Z})$ terminates the detection term. For example, the development $\mathrm{Enter}(\mathbf{O},\mathcal{Z})$ defined in (3.22) has the detection term $\mathsf{DS}^E \succ \mathsf{DS}^B \succ \mathsf{DS}^I$.

3.5. SUMMARY

This approach is applicable to any of the 584 developments of the canonical collection of spatio-temporal developments developed in Section 3.4.2. Since deriving these detection terms is straightforward and due to the large number of developments, we do not list them in this dissertation.

Theorem 2. *Suppose $\Omega_{\mathbb{P}(\mathbf{O},\mathcal{Z})}$ is the set of objects that conform to a development $\mathbb{P}(\mathbf{O},\mathcal{Z})$. The set of objects $\mathbf{O}$ determined by the sensor network where $\mathbb{P}(\mathbf{O},\mathcal{Z}) = \mathcal{T}$ equals $\Omega_{\mathbb{P}(\mathbf{O},\mathcal{Z})}$.*

Proof. Directly follows from Lemmas 3.28 and 3.29 and the fact that there does not exist a predicate $P(\mathbf{O},\mathcal{Z})$ which yields $\mathcal{M}$ for any detection scenario. ∎

3.5 Summary

This chapter developed the fundamental concepts regarding spatio-temporal queries in sensor networks. First, we have introduced a space partitioning for zones similar to the one existing for regions from moving object databases. The space partitioning is important, because it allows the application of the 9-intersection model which is also the foundation for moving object databases. We also investigated the differences between the space partitioning for regions and the space partitioning for zones. Most importantly, the latter partitioning is not regular which is problematic because users cannot express certain queries given the set of predicates and operators known from moving object databases. To solve this problem, we introduced predicates and operators specifically aimed at sensor networks. Second, we have shown how to abstract from the details of object detection and how to apply our approach to any kind of sensor network deployed with the intent to track moving objects. Using these two first steps, we introduced the notion of detection scenarios which formalize the information obtained through object detection.

Based on the detection scenarios, we defined the semantics of spatio-temporal predicates that describe the relation between an object and a region or a zone over time. For regions, we have shown that the inaccuracy of object detection mechanisms and other properties of sensor networks, e.g. unobserved areas, sometimes prevent a definitive answer if some predicate or development is true or not. This problem has been solved by classifying objects into three categories: The first category contains objects that conform to a given predicate or development, the second one contains objects that do not conform for sure and the third category consists of objects that possibly conform but where it is not sure. We studied the semantical depth of spatio-temporal queries in sensor networks in the context of regions and zones by obtaining a canonical collection of spatio-temporal developments for both cases. Most importantly, we have proved for every element in these collections that the aforementioned classes are optimal taking the properties of sensor networks and detection mechanisms into account. This concludes our study regarding Contribution **C.1** and the remainder of this dissertation focused on deriving the results defined here efficiently, i.e., with a minimal amount of communication.

Chapter 4
Query Dissemination in Sensor Networks

Processing any kind of query, i.e., relational or spatio-temporal, consists of four steps:

1. Dissemination of the query from the base station to the nodes of the sensor network.
2. Capturing sensor values depending on the query.
3. Processing the query based on values sensed.
4. Returning intermediate or overall results to the base station.

The dissemination of queries, i.e., contribution **C.2**, is the subject of this chapter. We address the steps 2-4 for spatio-temporal queries in chapter 5. Despite the focus on spatio-temporal queries in this dissertation, the dissemination approach presented in the following is applicable to relational queries which require tuples from all nodes as well.

4.1 Problem Statement

While the result of a query may be based on the sensor data of a few nodes, the number of nodes, that must receive the query to ensure a correct result, is typically much larger. As we show in this chapter, spatio-temporal queries require that all nodes receive the query. Thus, while the number of nodes that detect an object may be arbitrarily small, the query dissemination always requires communication with all nodes. Considering that communication has a major impact on the lifetime of sensor nodes (cf. Appendix A), reducing the number of messages for query dissemination is a priority. Hence, this chapter focuses on the dissemination of a query to all nodes while sending and receiving a minimum number of messages.

The simplest form of query dissemination to reach all nodes is *flooding*: The base station broadcasts the query to all nodes it can reach directly. Following this initial broadcast, each node receiving the query rebroadcasts the query once. Flooding wastes a lot of energy, because a large number of

4.1. PROBLEM STATEMENT

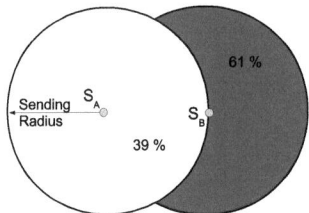
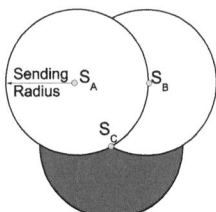

Figure 4.1: Additional area covered by a rebroadcast of node S_B after receiving a query from S_A

Figure 4.2: Additional area covered by a rebroadcast of node S_C after S_A and S_B received the query

rebroadcasts do not result in additional nodes being reached. As illustrated in Figure 4.1, whenever a node rebroadcasts a query, at most 61% additional area are reached by this rebroadcast. This is a theoretical optimum that only occurs if circular sending ranges are assumed[1] and nodes are placed in such a way that the distance between nodes equals the sending range. If there are more than two nodes, the additional area is further reduced as illustrated in Figure 4.2 and drops to less than 20% for average networks [98]. The main difficulty for energy-efficient query dissemination is choosing a minimal set of nodes that rebroadcast the query while reaching all nodes. Finding this minimal set is equivalent to the Dominating Set Problem, which is NP-complete [48].

Since finding an optimal set of rebroadcast nodes is not viable, a large number of heuristic approaches for query dissemination have been proposed (cf. [117, 128] for an overview). However, these algorithms have not been tested in real sensor networks and evaluations so far have been limited to simulations. Thus, comparing them with the goal of using an existing approach for dissemination of spatio-temporal queries is problematic due to different evaluation setups and assumptions used with different simulators. We conducted a study to evaluate existing approaches in a sensor network consisting of Sun SPOTs. The results of this study are presented in Section 4.3 and show that most sophisticated broadcast algorithms do not work in sensor networks or require excessive overhead to cope with the reality of sensor networks. Contrary to this, relatively simple algorithms like *probabilistic* or *counter-based dissemination* are well-suited for our purpose.

With probabilistic dissemination, whenever a node receives a query for the first time, the node rebroadcasts with a probability of $0 < P < 1$. The core problem of this approach is the value of the constant P: If P is too low, many nodes do not receive the query and if P is close to 1, the energy is wasted due to unnecessary broadcasts. We provide an optimization approach that allows finding a value for P so that all nodes are reached while avoiding unnecessary broadcasts. With counter-based dissemination, after receiving a query, each node waits a timeout of random length

---
[1]While this assumption is frequently made, it is unrealistic and highly misleading. We use this assumption here just for illustration purposes.

before it determines if the query must be rebroadcasted. While waiting for the timeout, the node counts the number of additional rebroadcasts of the query by its neighbors. If this number exceeds a threshold T_{CBD}, the node does not rebroadcast and otherwise the node rebroadcasts. As with probabilistic dissemination, the core problem is the value for T_{CBD}.

Summing up, we address the following issues in this chapter; the numbers are in line with the corresponding sections:

- **4.2:** This section shows that the evaluation of spatio-temporal queries requires that all nodes receive the query.
- **4.3:** Instead of simulations, we use data on reachability and efficiency acquired using Sun SPOT deployments to compare existing query dissemination approaches. This shows that probabilistic dissemination is the most promising approach for our purpose.
- **4.4:** For probabilistic dissemination, the rebroadcast probability is the most important optimization parameter. However, setting this parameter for different network topologies has not been investigated so far. We are the first to provide an optimization approach that finds a minimal value for the rebroadcast probability while reaching all nodes.
- **4.5:** This section investigates the effectiveness regarding the number of reached nodes and efficiency regarding the number of messages sent or received of our optimization approach. We also study the general impact of the rebroadcast probability on reachability.

It must be noted that the optimization approach for the rebroadcast probability could be used for the dissemination of any kind of message in a sensor network. Thus, while this dissertation is aimed at spatio-temporal queries, the results on query dissemination are also applicable to relational query processing in sensor networks.

4.2 Dissemination of Spatio-Temporal Queries

Prior to the dissemination of a query, one must answer which nodes must receive the query to warrant that all nodes, which could possibly contribute to the result of the query, receive the query. While determining the set of nodes that could possibly contribute to a query result for "What is the average temperature on the third floor?" is straightforward, spatio-temporal queries are more complicated: Consider the case of a static region $\mathbf{R}$ and a development $\mathbb{P}(\mathbf{O},\mathbf{R}) =$ *Disjoint*$(\mathbf{O},\mathbf{R}) \triangleright Meet(\mathbf{O},\mathbf{R})$. According to Table 3.5, to determine the result for this query, we must be able to determine for the detection sequence $\mathbb{D}_{\mathbf{O}}^{\mathbf{R}}$ of any object $\mathbf{O}$, if it conforms to the following detection term:

$$\mathsf{DS}^E \succ \left\{ \widetilde{\mathsf{DS}^B} | \mathsf{DS}^\varnothing \right\} \succ \left(\mathsf{DS}^B | \mathsf{DS}^I \right)$$

To determine DS^E, the nodes outside of the region $\mathbf{R}$ must know that $\mathbf{O}$ is of interest, i.e., receive the query. Similarly, the regions in $\mathbf{R}$ must receive the query, because DS^I is part of the detection term. Looking at the detection terms in Table 3.5, this applies to all spatio-temporal developments.

Thus, only queries that contain a single predicate would allow a reduction of the number of nodes that must receive the query.

For queries interested in the relationship of a zone and an object, the situation is similar: Any development that contains the three predicates $Disjoint(\mathbf{O},\mathcal{Z})$, $Meet(\mathbf{O},\mathcal{Z})$ and $Inside(\mathbf{O},\mathcal{Z})$ requires that all nodes receive the query. If the zone is dynamic, i.e., the nodes inside the zone change over time, the query must be disseminated to all nodes because nodes must determine if they are in the zone or outside of it. Thus, only queries with one or two predicates would be possible candidates for a reduction of the number of nodes that must receive a query.

Assuming one of the above cases occurs where it is sufficient if a subset of all nodes receives the query, actually reducing this number is difficult, because it requires knowledge about the topology of the sensor network: Assuming a node $\mathcal{S}_i$ has received a query. To determine that $\mathcal{S}_i$ does not have to forward the query, $\mathcal{S}_i$ must ensure that suppressing the query does not prevent the query from being received at some node $\mathcal{S}_j$ which must receive the query. To make this decision, knowledge on the network topology is required because $\mathcal{S}_i$ must know that $\mathcal{S}_j$ will be reached via another node if $\mathcal{S}_i$ does not forward the query. Amongst other things, this chapter illustrates that acquiring information on the topology of the network that would allow this decision is costly in terms of communication and energy consumption. Hence, we conclude that spatio-temporal queries should be disseminated to all nodes.

4.3 Performance Study on Existing Dissemination Approaches

There has been a plethora of research related to broadcasting techniques and query dissemination in ad-hoc networks (see [117, 128] for an overview). To choose an approach that disseminates a query to all nodes of a sensor network most efficiently, we conducted a study to compare these existing approaches. While there exist comparisons and each approach has been evaluated separately as well, to our knowledge these evaluations are solely based on simulations. It has been noted that simulations tend to make simplified assumptions that often do not hold well in practice [57]. In particular, real-world phenomena that impact the wireless communication between sensor nodes are usually not considered in simulations. Thus, we carefully selected a set of dissemination algorithms and evaluated them in different sensor networks consisting of Sun SPOTs. This study considers the following two aspects to measure the efficiency and effectiveness of existing dissemination approaches:

Efficiency: Communication is of utmost importance in sensor networks as discussed in Section 2.1.3. We measure the efficiency for dissemination approaches by counting the messages sent and received. As shown in Appendix A, counting the number of messages sent or received is a sufficiently accurate measure to evaluate the energy consumption of mechanisms at application level like query dissemination and processing.

Effectiveness: In our case, reaching all nodes is important regarding the correctness of query results. We refer to the ratio between the nodes reached and the total number of nodes as *reachability*. Maintaining high reachability while reducing the communication for query dissemination is our goal.

Our results differ significantly from those obtained through simulations previously. We discuss the reasons for these differences.

4.3.1 Existing Dissemination Approaches

In this section we describe the dissemination approaches we used for our evaluation in detail. There exist two classes of dissemination approaches: *topology-based dissemination* and *epidemic dissemination*. Topology-based approaches, e.g., [79, 101, 102, 107], use detailed information on the network topology to choose the nodes that rebroadcast a message. The *scalable broadcast algorithm (SBA)* [102] requires knowledge about all nodes reachable via two hops. While the procedure to choose the set of nodes that rebroadcasts varies between the topology-based algorithms, all of them have in common that the maintenance of the topology information incurs significant overhead. As our evaluation shows, this overhead is larger than the total number of messages used by epidemic approaches and therefore SBA is the only representative of this class in our study.

Epidemic approaches do not use information on the nodes in their vicinity to determine the nodes that should rebroadcast the query. For example *counter-based dissemination* [92, 93] uses a threshold value T_{CBD} to determine if a node should rebroadcast: If a node receives T_{CBD} broadcasts in a certain period of time after receiving the query for the first time, it does not rebroadcast. Similarly, probabilistic approaches assign a probability P to each node to determine the probability of a rebroadcast. We evaluated different variations of counter-based and probabilistic dissemination.

Flooding

Flooding [99] is the simplest query dissemination algorithm as illustrated by Algorithm 1: The base station broadcasts the query initially and each receiver S_i of the query rebroadcasts it once. To ensure that the query is rebroadcasted only once, each S_i stores an identifier of the query or a hash value. This is necessary, because each node typically receives the same query multiple times.

Algorithm 1: Flooding for query dissemination

Input: OldQueries — Set of queries stored at S_i that have been rebroadcasted previously
1 **When** S_i *receives the query q* **do**
2   **if** $q \notin$ OldQueries **then**   // Was the query rebroadcasted previously?
3   Insert identifier of q into OldQueries
4   Rebroadcast q
5   **end**
6 **end**

4.3. PERFORMANCE STUDY ON EXISTING DISSEMINATION APPROACHES

Flooding has significant drawbacks: Most importantly, in networks with a high node density, i.e., each node has multiple 1-hop neighbors, it results in a large number of broadcasts even though a small number would be sufficient. Another drawback is the so called "broadcast storm problem" [98] due to the contention between nodes rebroadcasting simultaneously: The CSMA/CA (cf. Section 2.1.2) used by the MAC layer checks if the medium is busy before rebroadcasting the query. If the medium is busy for an extended period of time, the broadcast is aborted which could result in nodes not being reached by the query. The nature of flooding is conductive to contention, because a node rebroadcasts a query, all receivers will try to rebroadcast simultaneously. Furthermore, in combination with the lack of collision detection at the MAC layer level, the simultaneous rebroadcast is likely to result in collisions. As our evaluation shows, these possible reasons for message losses result in the fact that flooding sometimes does not reach all nodes of the sensor network.

Counter-Based Dissemination

The core idea of the *counter-based dissemination (CBD)* [92, 93] shown in Algorithm 2 is as follows: When a node receives a query and waits for a random time, it will receive rebroadcasts of the same query. The number of rebroadcasts of the same query this node receives while waiting is indirectly proportional to the additional area/nodes reached by a rebroadcast. The random wait time is called *Random Access Delay (RAD)* and it serves two purposes: First, it avoids collisions and contention because rebroadcasts of nodes that received the query from the same node are spread over time. Second, it allows nodes to count the number of redundant query rebroadcasts by neighbor nodes and estimate probability that additional nodes are reached by its own rebroadcast. After the RAD expired, the node compares the number of redundant query rebroadcasts it received with a threshold value T_{CBD}: If T_{CBD} is greater (see Line 9), the node rebroadcasts. Otherwise, the rebroadcast is suppressed.

The approach is based on two parameters: the length of the RAD and T_{CBD}. The RAD can be any random value from a given interval $[t_{min}, t_{max}]$. The length of this interval must be sufficiently large to spread the rebroadcasts and avoid collisions. The main optimization parameter is T_{CBD}, as it controls how many rebroadcasts are suppressed. If T_{CBD} is too small, the query may not reach all nodes, particularly in areas of the network with low node density. On the other hand, a high value for T_{CBD} results in a large number of redundant query rebroadcasts.

The main drawback of CBD is the fact that it requires redundant query rebroadcasts to determine if a node should rebroadcast the query. Thus, once a node decides to suppress a rebroadcast, energy has already been wasted for sending and receiving these redundant messages.

Probabilistic Dissemination

Algorithm 3 illustrates *probabilistic dissemination*: Whenever a node $\mathcal{S}_i$ receives a query, $\mathcal{S}_i$ rebroadcasts this query only with a probability of $0 < P \leq 1$. Similar to CBD, our implementation of the probabilistic dissemination uses a RAD to avoid collisions and contention.

Algorithm 2: Counter-based query dissemination (CBD)

Input: OldQueries — Set of queries stored at S_i that have been rebroadcasted previously
Input: T_{CBD} — CBD threshold value

1 **When** S_i *receives the query q* **do**
2   **if** $q \notin$ OldQueries **then**   // Check if query was rebroadcasted previously
3   **if** *Counter for q exists* **then**   // Has q been received by S_i previously?
4   Increment counter for q by 1
5   Exit   // Another thread has already started the RAD for q
6   **else**
7   Create a counter for q with initial value of 1
8   Start the Random Access Delay (RAD) and sleep until it expires
9   **if** T_{CBD} *is greater than the counter value for q* **then**
10   Rebroadcast query q
11   Insert identifier of q into OldQueries
12   **end**
13   **end**
14   **end**
15 **end**

Regarding communication and reachability, the rebroadcast probability P must be optimized: If P is too high, the approach degenerates into flooding resulting in the aforementioned drawbacks. Contrary to this, a low P results in a large number of nodes not receiving the query. The tradeoff between reachability and communication overhead is not well understood. We investigate this tradeoff and provide an optimization approach to find a minimal value for P where all nodes are reached in Section 4.4.

Probabilistic Counter-based Dissemination

According to simulation results [92, 94], efficiency of CBD can be improved by introducing a rebroadcast probability P_{PCBD}. We refer to this variant CBD as *probabilistic counter-based dissemination (PCBD)*. This approach is a combination of CBD and the probabilistic dissemination approach, i.e., it counts the number of rebroadcasts and then rebroadcasts with a predefined probability P_{PCBD}.

Algorithm 4 outlines this dissemination approach: When a node S_i receives a query, it checks if the query has been received before. If it is the first time that q has been received, S_i starts a RAD and counts duplicates of q it receives in the meantime. If the number of duplicates received during the RAD is greater than T_{PCBD}, S_i does not rebroadcast q. In any other case, S_i generates a random number as shown in Line 10. By comparing the random value with P_{PCBD}, S_i determines if q must

4.3. PERFORMANCE STUDY ON EXISTING DISSEMINATION APPROACHES

Algorithm 3: Probabilistic query dissemination
Input: OldQueries — Set of queries stored at $\mathcal{S}_i$ that have been rebroadcasted previously
Input: P — rebroadcast probability between 0 and 1
1 **When** $\mathcal{S}_i$ *receives the query* q **do**
2   **if** $q \notin$ OldQueries **then**   // Check if query was rebroadcasted previously
3      $randomNumber \leftarrow$ random value between 0 and 1
4   **if** $randomNumber \leq P$ **then**
5   Start the Random Access Delay (RAD) and sleep until it expires
6   Rebroadcast query
7   Insert identifier of q into OldQueries
8   **end**
9   **end**
10 **end**

---

be rebroadcasted or not. Summing up, the approach has two optimization parameters inherited from CBD and probabilistic dissemination. The properties of these parameters are analogous to the respective algorithm described above.

SBA: Scalable Broadcast Algorithm

The *Scalable Broadcast Algorithm (SBA)* [102] uses knowledge on the local network topology to determine the set of nodes that rebroadcast the query. The topology knowledge is stored on each node $\mathcal{S}_i$ in a list that contains an entry for each 1-hop neighbor of $\mathcal{S}_i$. Each entry corresponding to a 1-hop neighbor $\mathcal{S}_j$ of $\mathcal{S}_i$ is a list that contains the 1-hop neighbors of $\mathcal{S}_j$, i.e., 2-hop neighbors (via $\mathcal{S}_j$) of $\mathcal{S}_i$. The core idea of SBA is that a node can determine if there are neighbors that did not receive the query yet based on the topology information and the rebroadcasts of a query.

As illustrated in Algorithm 5, whenever a node $\mathcal{S}_i$ receives a query for the first time, it copies the list containing the topology information (cf. Line 4). Since the query was broadcasted by a 1-hop neighbor $\mathcal{S}_j$, $\mathcal{S}_j$ and all of its 1-hop neighbors can be removed from the list. This is because, at the time when $\mathcal{S}_j$ rebroadcasts, it reaches its 1-hop neighbors as well. Similar to CBD, a RAD is used to delay the rebroadcast and allow other neighbors to rebroadcast first. Each time another copy of the query arrives at $\mathcal{S}_i$, the sender and its 1-hop neighbors are removed from the list of remaining nodes (cf. Line 12). After the RAD expired, $\mathcal{S}_i$ can determine if a sufficient number of neighbors did not receive the query yet. The parameter T_{SBA} determines how many nodes must be left in the list of remaining nodes to require a rebroadcast of the query by $\mathcal{S}_i$.

To acquire the topology information stored in **RemainingNodes**, each node $\mathcal{S}_i$ broadcasts a *Hello-Packet* periodically. This message contains a list of the 1-hop neighbors of $\mathcal{S}_i$. Each node receiving this list creates or updates the entry corresponding to $\mathcal{S}_i$ stored locally. The *Hello-Packet Rate*

Algorithm 4: Probabilistic Counter-based query dissemination (PCBD)

Input: OldQueries — Set of queries stored at $\mathcal{S}_i$ that have been rebroadcasted previously
Input: T_{CBD} — CBD threshold value

1 **When** $\mathcal{S}_i$ *receives the query q* **do**
2   **if** $q \notin$ OldQueries **then**   // Check if query was rebroadcasted previously
3   **if** *Counter for q exists* **then**   // Did $\mathcal{S}_i$ receive q previously?
4   Increment counter for q by 1
5   Exit   // Another thread has already started the RAD for q
6   **else**
7   Create a counter for q with initial value of 1
8   Start the Random Access Delay (RAD) and sleep until it expires
9   **if** T_{PCBD} *is greater than the counter value for q* **then**
10             $randomNumber \leftarrow$ random value between 0 and 1
11   **if** $randomNumber \leq P_{PCBD}$ **then**
12   Rebroadcast query q
13   Insert identifier of q into OldQueries
14   **end**
15   **end**
16   **end**
17   **end**
18 **end**

(HPR) controls the length of the periods between Hello-Packets. Setting the HPR is difficult: If the HPR is too short, the overhead for maintaining topology information increases drastically. The reason for this is that broadcasting a Hello-Packet from each node in the network equals the communication for flooding the complete network once with a message. Furthermore, a short HPR results in contention and collisions, e.g., query messages are lost due to collisions with Hello-Packets. If the HPR is too long, the topology information of sensor nodes becomes outdated resulting in nodes being missed by the query. Even if the nodes are not moved, external influences continuously change the topology of the network, e.g., because doors are opened and closed.

In addition to the HPR, the parameters for T_{SBA} and the length of the RAD are important. The characteristics of the RAD have been discussed in the context of CBD previously and apply here as well. With the default implementation, T_{SBA} equals 1. Increasing T_{SBA} obviously comes at the risk of nodes not receiving the query.

4.3. PERFORMANCE STUDY ON EXISTING DISSEMINATION APPROACHES

Algorithm 5: Scalable Broadcast Algorithm

Input: OldQueries — Set of queries stored at $\mathcal{S}_i$ that have been rebroadcasted previously
Input: T_{SBA} — SBA threshold value
Input: 2HopNeighbors — List of all communication neighbors and their communication neighbors

1 **When** $\mathcal{S}_i$ *receives the query* q **do**
2   **if** $q \notin$ OldQueries **then**   // Check if query was rebroadcasted previously
3   **if** *This is the first time* $\mathcal{S}_i$ *received* q **then**
4   RemainingNodes ← Copy of 2HopNeighbors
5   Remove the sender of q and its 1-hop neighbors from RemainingNodes
6   Start the Random Access Delay (RAD) and sleep until it expires
7   **if** *Length of* RemainingNodes $\geq T_{SBA}$ **then**
8   Rebroadcast query   // This is executed after the RAD
9   Insert identifier of q into OldQueries
10   end
11   **else**
12   Remove the sender of q and its 1-hop neighbors from RemainingNodes
13   end
14   end
15 end

4.3.2 Experimental Setup

We implemented the aforementioned dissemination approaches for Sun SPOTs using KSN software modules (cf. Appendix C for further information). In the following, we describe the different node setups and values we measured during the evaluation.

Node Setups

We used two different deployments of Sun SPOTs [120]: the *Grid-Setup* and the *IPD-Setup*. For the Grid-Setup we deployed 24 Sun SPOTs as illustrated in Figure 4.4. The distance between the nodes was 2.5 cm and the sending range of each Sun SPOT was reduced to minimum (Output Power −30). This ensures, that each node can only communicate directly with the nodes next to it. We also varied the position of the node that starts the query dissemination, i.e., the base station. There are two possible start positions, *center* and *periphery*, for the dissemination which are marked by black circles.

The IPD-Setup consists of 24 nodes as illustrated in Figure 4.3 and partly overlaps with the KSN Testbed (cf. Appendix C.1). Contrary to the Grid-Setup, the output power of the radio chip was not reduced. The IPD-Setup is more challenging than the Grid-Setup, because nodes do not

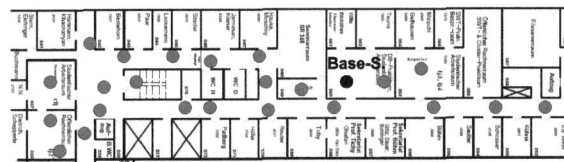 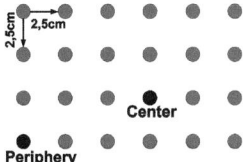

Figure 4.3: IPD-Setup for the evaluation of existing dissemination algorithms

Figure 4.4: Grid-Setup

have a uniform distance between each other and communication ranges vary, e.g., because doors are opened and closed.

Parameters and Measurands

For all dissemination approaches evaluated, we varied the following parameters:

Query rate: The query rate determines the time between queries. For the Grid-Setup, we used query rates from 5 to 120 seconds. In the IPD-Setup, the query rate was constant at 3 minutes.

Base station position: As illustrated in Figure 4.4, the position of the base station was varied in the Grid-Setup between a node at the periphery and one in the center.

Number of queries: This is the number of queries disseminated into the sensor network with regard to the query rate. For the Grid-Setup, we used 10 queries and for the IPD-Setup, we disseminated between 12 and 20 queries.

To compare effectiveness and efficiency of the different approaches, we measured the following values:

Number of Hello-Packets: This is the number of messages sent and received for acquiring topology information required for SBA. For all other dissemination approaches, this measurand is 0.

Number of query messages: This measurand counts communication required for the dissemination of the query.

Sum of all messages: By summing up the number of Hello-Packets and the number of messages for the dissemination of the query, we measure the total communication required for query dissemination.

Average number of queries received: To measure reachability, we count the number of queries received at each node and compute the average over all nodes. By taking into account the total number of queries disseminated, this allows us to determine the relative reachability.

Rebroadcast rejections: Each dissemination approach tries to reduce the number of rebroadcasts. This value counts the number of nodes that rejected the rebroadcast because it was

4.3. PERFORMANCE STUDY ON EXISTING DISSEMINATION APPROACHES

determined to be redundant. By taking into account the total number of nodes, we can derive the percentage of nodes that rebroadcasted a query.

Recall that our main focus is reachability, i.e., the ratio between the nodes reached and the total number of nodes in the sensor network. The performance of a dissemination approach is the ratio between reachability and the amount of communication required.

4.3.3 Results and Analysis

This section analyzes and compares the results of the dissemination approaches introduced above for both setups. We present the results for the Grid-Setup for each approach separately first and then provide the results for the IPD-Setup. We used query rates of 5, 15, 30 and 90 seconds and for each query rate 10 queries were disseminated. If applicable, the RAD was in an interval of 0 to 25 seconds, i.e., the rebroadcast was delayed by 25 seconds at most for each node.

Flooding

Tables 4.1 and 4.2 show the number of messages and the reachability for flooding in the Grid-Setup with query rates from 5 to 90 seconds. Since there are 24 nodes and 10 queries, the theoretical expectation is that the number of messages sent is always $24 \cdot 10 = 240$ and the reachability equals 100%.

With the base station at the center, the reachability across all query rates is always well above 90%, but never 100%. This means that in every run there were one or two nodes that did not receive the query even with flooding. The reason for this are collisions resulting in disrupted messages and the general unreliability of the wireless medium. Despite the efforts of CSMA/CA (cf. Section 2.1.2), these collisions occur because of the hidden terminal problem [45, 109].

In contrast to the results for the base station at the center, placing the base station at the periphery of the network affects the results significantly: With low query rates, the reachability is close to the optimum and even a little bit better than those obtained with the base station at the center. The reason for this is that the dissemination runs "one directional", i.e., from the bottom left to the upper right corner. This reduces the probability for the hidden terminal problem to occur. With high query rates, a relatively large number of the queries are lost because nodes repeatedly try to access the wireless medium but cannot because the medium "is busy". These timeouts when accessing the medium also occurred with the base station at the center, but with the base station at the center the nodes were reached before the medium was busy permanently.

Summing up, even with flooding the reachability is never 100% due to the unreliability of the medium and collisions. All other approaches try to achieve the reachability of flooding while requiring less messages.

Query Rate	Query rebroadcasts	Reachability
90	239	99.5%
30	235	98%
15	175	73%
5	156	65%
Average	201	84%

Table 4.1: Results for flooding with a peripheral base station

Query Rate	Query rebroadcasts	Reachability
90	222	93%
30	226	94%
15	230	96%
5	223	93%
Average	225	94%

Table 4.2: Results for flooding with base station at the center

Counter-Based Dissemination

The results for CBD with the Grid-Setup averaged over query rates of 5, 15, 30 and 90 seconds are shown in Table 4.3. For the Grid-Layout we tested different values for T_{CBD} between 2 and 5. A look at the number of rejected rebroadcasts shows that values above 4 for T_{CBD} are not viable, since at 5 there are no rebroadcast rejections. This means that CBD with $T_{CBD} = 5$ performs like flooding for this setup except for the delay due to the RAD.

As expected, increasing T_{CBD} results in an increase of the number of query broadcasts, i.e., messages sent. For the setup with the base station at the center, this increase only results in a marginal increase of reachability. It is noteworthy, that $T_{CBD} = 2$ already achieves a reachability above 90% while reducing the number of messages by 41%. As with flooding, the reachability is reduced significantly if the dissemination starts at the periphery of the network. Particularly at high query rates, a large number of queries is lost due to collisions and unreliability of the medium.

The average number of messages across all experiments with CBD achieving a reachability of more than 90% is 203. Thus, compared to flooding, CBD requires 40 messages ($\approx 17\%$) less. A more detailed look reveals that most of the disseminations, that achieved a reachability above 90%, had a query rate of 90 or 30 seconds: Only 3 disseminations at 15 second and none at 5 second query rates reached more than 90% of the nodes. Summing up, CBD is a very efficient and effective

4.3. PERFORMANCE STUDY ON EXISTING DISSEMINATION APPROACHES

Base Station Position	T_{CBD}	Query rebroadcasts	Reachability
Center	2	160	91%
Center	3	204	94%
Center	4	216	94%
Center	5	227	95%
Periphery	2	116	67%
Periphery	3	146	70%
Periphery	4	180	80%
Periphery	5	205	86%

Table 4.3: Result for CBD averaged over query rates from 5 to 90 seconds

approach for query dissemination at low query rates and if query are not disseminated from the periphery of the network.

Probabilistic Counter-Based Dissemination (PCBD) [92, 94] reports, that the efficiency of CBD can be improved by introducing a rebroadcast probability P_{PCBD} as described above. We tested values of 50%, 65% and 90% for P_{PCBD} with the same setup we used for CBD. It has been reported that P_{PCBD} = 65% is optimal for the average scenario. The results in Table 4.4 are averaged across all query rates (5, 15, 30, 90) and base station positions (center, periphery).

P_{PCBD}	Query rebroadcasts	Avg. Reachability
50%	37	27%
65%	86	57%
90%	135	70%

Table 4.4: Average number of messages and reachability for PCBD

A general look at the results shows that the reachability achieved with PCBD is much lower than with CBD or flooding. The reason for this is obviously that required rebroadcasts (according to CBD) are suppressed due to the probability parameter. A detailed look at the result shows that the ratio between the actual number of rebroadcasts and the number of rebroadcasts that CBD would have made corresponds to the probability used. For example, while CBD would have rebroadcasted the query 108 times, PCBD with P_{PCBD} = 65% rebroadcasted 69 times, which equals 64%. Due to the low reachability, we did not conduct any further experiments with PCBD in the IPD-Setup.

Probabilistic Dissemination

Similar to the previous experiments, we used different query rates for the experiments with probabilistic query dissemination. Table 4.5 shows some of the results averaged across all query rates. The rebroadcast probability P was increased in steps of 5% from 15% to 95% and for each value of P, we disseminated 10 queries.

Base Station Position	P	Query rebroadcasts	Avg. Reachability
Center	15%	12	27%
...	...	...	...
Center	65%	118	83%
Center	70%	143	95%
Center	75%	161	95%
Center	80%	175	96%
...	...	...	...
Center	95%	216	98%
Periphery	15%	7	17%
...	...	...	...
Periphery	65%	106	62%
Periphery	70%	113	71%
Periphery	75%	147	86%
Periphery	80%	162	87%
...	...	...	...
Periphery	95%	191	89%

Table 4.5: Average number of messages and reachability for probabilistic dissemination

The result shows two important points: First, the increase in reachability is not linear compared to the increase of the rebroadcast probability P. At some value of $P < 1$, the reachability is "saturated" and further increases do not result in higher reachability. This is expected as the analysis in [75] has shown. For example with the base station at the center, this "saturation point" is reached somewhere between a rebroadcast probability of 65% and 70%. At this point, the reachability is equal to the reachability offered by flooding or CBD. In some cases the reachability is even higher than with flooding, because the amount of rebroadcasts is significantly lower reducing the probability for collisions.

The second important point is the fact that the probabilistic dissemination at an optimal value for P is more effective and efficient than CBD with an optimal value for T_{CBD}: With the base station at the periphery of the network, CBD reaches 86% of the nodes with more than 200 rebroadcasts, the same number of nodes is reached with more than 50 rebroadcasts less with probabilistic dissemination. Similarly, with the base station at the center, the probabilistic approach requires

4.3. PERFORMANCE STUDY ON EXISTING DISSEMINATION APPROACHES

significantly less messages to reach 95% of the nodes.

Summing up, probabilistic dissemination is promising and offers a huge potential for energy savings compared to both, CBD and flooding at no cost regarding reachability. The only drawback is that finding an optimal value for P is more difficult than with CBD where basically $T_{CBD} = 2$ or $T_{CBD} = 3$ is always a good choice.

Scalable Broadcast Algorithm

For the experiments with SBA we varied the length of the RAD, the Hello-Packet Rate (HPR) and T_{SBA}. Before we analyze results, we discuss two important problems that our initial experiments with SBA revealed: At first, we started the experiment by initiating a Hello-Packet broadcast on each node, waited for a constant time interval and then started the query dissemination. This resulted reachability values of less then 20% most of the time and never more than 40%. The reason for this, even though we carefully initiated the Hello-Packet broadcasts to avoid collisions, was that the topology information stored on each node was incomplete, i.e., nodes missed Hello-Packets from 1-hop neighbors. This is because broadcasts are not acknowledged and a broadcast of S_i in the setup illustrated in Figure 4.5 rarely reaches eight nodes as expected by theory. As shown in Table 4.6, from a total of 100 broadcasts consisting of one packet, most of the times four to six of the surrounding eight nodes received the broadcast. In some cases, only three and in less than 10% of the cases seven or eight nodes are reached. To solve this problem for our experiments, we had to conduct an initialization phase consisting of two or three Hello-Packet broadcasts for each node. While this solves the problem, it also shows that the efficiency of SBA degrades significantly if external influences frequently result in topology changes and require frequent updates of the topology information for SBA.

The second problem were the Hello-Packets themselves: When a query dissemination was started by the base station and other nodes were in the process of broadcasting Hello-Packets, the amount of collisions was high. This resulted in low reachabilities for these experiments of less than 50% on average. Particularly with query rates of 5 or 15 seconds, the problem was serious and leads to the conclusion that SBA is not viable with high query rates. We solved this, by stopping the broadcasting of Hello-Packets before the dissemination of the query started. Summing up, before the dissemination of the queries started at the given rate, each node sent two or three Hello-Packets and then waited for the dissemination to start.

Table 4.7 shows the result of our experiment with SBA for query rates of 30 and 90 seconds with $T_{SBA} = 1$. Initial tests with $T_{SBA} > 1$ resulted reachabilities of less than 20% which is the reason why this parameter was kept constant for our experiments. Other parameters like the length of the RAD were also varied and the results showed that their impact on the reachability is negligible. Since each of the 24 nodes sent two or three Hello-Packets during initialization, the values in the second column are always multiples of 24.

The most important fact regarding the results is that SBA performs worse than flooding or CBD regarding the amount of messages as well as the reachability. We did not encounter a case

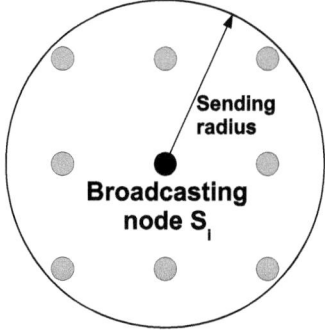

Figure 4.5: Setup for broadcast reachability study

Nodes reached (out of 8)	Occurrences
1	0
2	2
3	7
4	21
5	38
6	27
7	4
8	1
Total Number of Broadcasts	100

Table 4.6: Results of the broadcast reachability study

Query Rate	Hello-Packets	Query rebroadcasts	Total Messages sent	Reachability
30	48	152	200	67%
30	72	161	233	82%
90	48	181	229	82%
90	72	184	256	85%

Table 4.7: Results for SBA for query rates of 30 and 90 seconds

4.3. PERFORMANCE STUDY ON EXISTING DISSEMINATION APPROACHES

Dissemination approach	Broadcasts	Reachability
Flooding	378	79%
CBD with T_{CBD} = 3	335	76%
Probabilistic with P = 0.75	307	84%
SBA	577	85%

Table 4.8: Query dissemination results for the IPD-Setup

where more than 90% of the nodes were reached, even for low query rates. In most cases, the sum of Hello-Packets and queries is higher than with flooding. The reason for this behaviour can be deducted from the results regarding broadcast reachability in Table 4.6: SBA is based on the assumption that broadcasts are perfect, i.e., all surrounding nodes are reached. In addition to this, SBA heavily depends on the correctness of the topology information stored on a node. This is problematic as our initial attempts to use SBA have shown.

IPD-Setup

For all experiments using the IPD-Setup, we disseminated 20 queries at a rate of one query every three minutes into the network. Table 4.8 shows the results.

Compared to the Grid-Setup, the reachabilities of all approaches were significantly lower. This must be attributed to the characteristics of indoor deployments with doors, walls and other obstacles that influence sending ranges permanently or temporary. For further details regarding the difficulties associated with this setup refer to Section C.1.

For CBD, we used the threshold value of 3 which resulted in a reduced number of messages compared to flooding with a comparable reachability. For the dissemination with SBA, we adapted the process we used for the Grid: During the initialization phase, each node broadcasted two Hello-Packets and afterwards each node broadcasted another Hello-Packet every 10 minutes for the duration of the 60 minute experiment. Thus, each node had to send 8 Hello-Packets resulting in 192 broadcasts of Hello-Packets throughout the experiment. Considering the 577 broadcasts of SBA overall, this leaves 385 rebroadcasts of queries which is a little bit more than the other approaches required altogether. It must be noted though that the reachability of the other approaches compared to SBA is a little bit lower. As with the Grid-Setup, sending Hello-Packets does not pay off.

The best result was observed with the probabilistic dissemination at a rebroadcast probability of 75%. Since setting P = 75% was a guess, we also tested P = 80%. This resulted in a similar reachability (85%) so it must be assumed that the aforementioned saturation point is at or below 75%. Even with this possibly sub-optimal value for P, the reachability is similar to SBA while reducing the communication required significantly, particularly compared to SBA. This shows that probabilistic dissemination is the most promising approach of those studied and finding an approach to determine an optimal P has a great potential to reduce energy consumption.

4.3.4 Discussion

Most of the topology-based, sophisticated mechanisms do not work or do not disseminate the query efficiently compared to flooding even for small networks. While all of them determine rebroadcast nodes differently, their main problem is acquiring topology information and the overhead associated with it. Typically the topology information requires so called Hello-Packets which must be sent periodically and thus cause contention as well as collisions when disseminating a query. Each period of sending Hello-Packets equals the flooding of a message through the network and this overhead can only pay off if several queries have to be disseminated per Hello-Packet period. Our experiments have shown that particularly with high query rates, topology-based mechanisms like SBA show a low reachability. Simple approaches dominate and typically are more robust regarding incomplete or partially incomplete topology information.

The results justify our decision to further investigate probabilistic query dissemination and the optimization of the rebroadcast probability parameter instead of CBD or SBA: SBA does not increase reachability significantly, but drastically increases the amount of messages required for query dissemination, particularly due to Hello-Packets. Thus, SBA and other algorithms using Hello-Packets to obtain network topology information are not viable options for our purpose. CBD obtains reasonable reachability at values of 2-3 for T_{CBD} and further increases do not increase reachability but only increase its communication overhead. Probabilistic dissemination with a well-chosen rebroadcast probability can achieve a high reachability and significantly reduce communication compared to CBD. The main drawback with probabilistic dissemination is that finding such a rebroadcast probability in sensor networks is difficult and has not been investigated yet. We address this issue in Section 4.4.

Another important fact regarding the processing of spatio-temporal queries is that none of the dissemination algorithms can reliably provide a reachability of 100%. Since this also occurs with flooding, the reasons for these losses of queries must be attributed to the characteristics of the wireless medium. Hence, it is unlikely that other dissemination protocols could be able to provide a reachability of 100% at reasonable costs in terms of energy consumption. Thus, it must be expected that there are some nodes that did not receive the query and therefore do not participate in query processing.

4.4 Optimizing Probabilistic Query Dissemination

In this section we focus on probabilistic dissemination where each node rebroadcasts queries with a fixed probability P. Parameter P allows to fine-tune the tradeoff between energy spent for query dissemination and the number of nodes reached. Moreover, our performance study as well as the analysis in [75] have shown that in sensor networks there exists a *saturation point* for the rebroadcast probability. This means that there exists a rebroadcast probability $P_{Sat} < 1$ such that increasing P beyond P_{Sat} does not increase the number of nodes reached significantly. Thus, the query dissemination can save energy by using P_{Sat} as rebroadcast probability. Our goal is to

4.4. OPTIMIZING PROBABILISTIC QUERY DISSEMINATION

develop a model to predict for every value of P the number of nodes R reached and the energy E consumed by the query-dissemination process. Knowing the dependencies between P, R and E allows the base station to estimate how many nodes can be reached using a fixed amount of energy, or at which P improving the reachability means spending a huge amount of energy to reach only a few nodes more.

Our energy-usage prediction depends on reachability prediction, which in turn depends on the network topology. The more the base station knows about network topology, the more precise the predictions can be. However, gathering topology information consumes energy as shown for SBA in Section 4.3. We are interested in making predictions using topological information which can be obtained without exhausting potential energy savings due to gathering fine-grained topology information.

In the following we develop two functions: The *reachability function* $R(P)$ estimates the dependency between the number of nodes reached R and the rebroadcast probability P. Similarly, the energy consumption function $E(P)$ predicts the energy consumption for the dissemination of a query with rebroadcast probability P. More specifically, $E(P)$ estimates the energy consumption based on the number of messages sent and received.

4.4.1 Topology Information

Our predictions regarding reachability and energy consumption are based on topological information. This section defines the underlying network model of our approach and formalizes the information regarding network topology. We outline several different ways to collect this information and Appendix D provides a detailed description of the implementation we used for our experiments. The overhead associated with acquiring the information on the network topology will be investigated in our evaluation in Section 4.5.

It is important to note that information required by our approach differs significantly from the information required by SBA and other topology-based approaches: For SBA, the required information was relatively fine-grained and had to be updated whenever small changes or external influences had an impact on the connectivity of the nodes among each other. Thus, each node must broadcast Hello-Packets frequently which resulted in a large overhead. Our approach uses topology information that provides a very coarse view of the network and the connectivity of the nodes. Thus, external influences rarely change the topology information which reduces the overhead associated with acquiring this information drastically. Even though the information is not fine-grained, it allows relatively accurate predictions regarding reachability and energy consumption as the evaluation shows.

The Hop-Set Model

Our estimation of the reachability and energy consumption is based on a *Hop-Set model*. We use this model to abstract from the details of the sensor network topology.

When the base station broadcasts a message to disseminate it to all nodes of the sensor network, the message disperses through the network in several steps, beginning at the base station. We refer to these steps as *hops*. If a node S_B receives a broadcast from node S_A, S_B *is reached by* S_A. If S_B rebroadcasts the message it received from S_A and reaches S_C, S_C *was reached via 2 hops*.

Definition 44 (Message Path): The *path of a message* $P = [S_{send}, S_i, \ldots, S_j, S_{recv}]$ is the sequence of nodes the message travelled from the sender S_{send} via an arbitrary sequence of intermediate nodes $S_i, \ldots, S_j$ to the receiver S_{recv}. The *path length* equals $|P| - 1$ if $|P|$ is the number of elements in P. □

For example, the path of the message above received at S_C is $[S_A, S_B, S_C]$ with length 2. Whenever a node S_i receives a message that is being disseminated, this message has travelled h hops over the path from the base station to S_i. An arbitrary node may receive several instances of the same message via different paths during dissemination.

Definition 45 (Minimal Path Length): If S_i receives n instances of the same message via the paths $P_1, \ldots, P_n$, the *minimal path* P_{min} is the path with the fewest elements/nodes. The *minimal path length* is the length of P_{min}, i.e., $|P_{min}|$. □

Since each node rebroadcasts a message once at most (cf. Section 4.3.1), rebroadcasting stops after all nodes that are connected to the network have received the query. Implicitly, this assigns a distance h to every node S_i which equals the minimal path length from the base station to S_i.

Definition 46 (Hop Set): Hop Set The *hop set* $\mathcal{HS}_h$ is the set of all nodes with a minimal path length of h hops to the base station. □

The Hop-Set model classifies nodes by their distance in terms of hops from the base station. Figure 4.9 shows an example where the hop set $\mathcal{HS}_{i-1}$ contains 2 nodes and $\mathcal{HS}_i$ contains 3.

Hop-Set Connectivity

Using the abstraction of the hop-set model, a node S_{recv} can receive a message broadcasted by S_{send} in three different ways:

Direct: The broadcast from S_{send} reaches S_{recv} *directly* if $S_{send} \in \mathcal{HS}_{i-1}$ and $S_{recv} \in \mathcal{HS}_i$. Figure 4.6 illustrates this.

Indirect: The broadcast from S_{send} reaches S_{recv} *indirectly* if S_{send} and S_{recv} are in the same hop set as illustrated by Figure 4.7.

Reverse: The broadcast from S_{send} reaches S_{recv} *reversely* if $S_{recv} \in \mathcal{HS}_i$ and $S_{send} \in \mathcal{HS}_j$ with $i < j$. See Figure 4.8 for an illustration of reverse broadcasts.

It is important to note that the sender S_{send} of a reverse broadcast is not necessarily from $\mathcal{HS}_{i+1}$ if the receiver S_{recv} is in $\mathcal{HS}_i$. Broadcast[2] communication between sensor nodes is not bi-directional,

---

[2] Unicasts typically require bi-directional communication since the receiver of a unicast message must acknowledge the message with the sender as defined by 802.15.4. Broadcasts do not use acknowledgements.

4.4. OPTIMIZING PROBABILISTIC QUERY DISSEMINATION

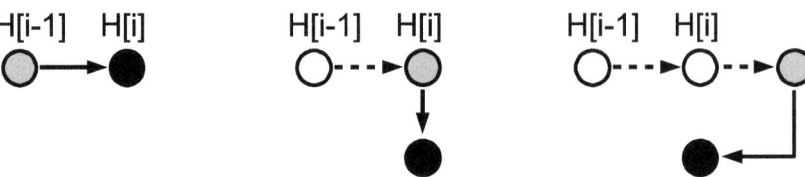

Figure 4.6: Direct broadcast   Figure 4.7: Indirect broadcast   Figure 4.8: Reverse broadcast

i.e., if $\mathcal{S}_{send}$ can communicate with $\mathcal{S}_{recv}$ this does not imply that $\mathcal{S}_{recv}$ can also communicate directly with $\mathcal{S}_{send}$. Thus, it is possible that $\mathcal{S}_{recv} \in \mathcal{HS}_i$ receives reverse broadcasts from $\mathcal{S}_{send}$ even if $\mathcal{S}_{send}$ is not in $\mathcal{HS}_{i+1}$.

The hop-set model only considers messages that disperse from the base station, but not the opposite direction. Taking reverse broadcasts into account for reachability prediction would require more detailed topology information. Acquiring and maintaining this information would increase the overhead associated with topology information. Hence, we will not consider reverse broadcasts to predict the reachability of probabilistic query dissemination. We will show in Section 4.5, that our predictions are sufficiently accurate to determine a probability where (almost) all nodes are reached, but only a fraction of nodes forwards the queries.

To predict how the query disperses through the hop sets by direct and indirect broadcasts, we need the following information for each hop set $\mathcal{HS}_h$:

Hop-Set size: The hop set size $|\mathcal{HS}_h|$, i.e., the number of nodes in $\mathcal{HS}_h$.

Inter-Connectivity: Inter[h] equals the average number of nodes in $\mathcal{HS}_h$ that will receive a broadcast by an arbitrary node from $\mathcal{HS}_{h-1}$. We need this value to predict the number of nodes reached by direct broadcasts.

Intra-Connectivity: Intra[h] is the average number of nodes in $\mathcal{HS}_h$ that an arbitrary node from the same hop set can reach. This value is required to predict how many nodes will be reached by indirect broadcasts.

Example 12 illustrates these values for the topology in Figure 4.9. Note that both connectivity values are averages. This is important, because external influences that reduce or increase the communication range of a few nodes typically do not have a significant impact on these averages. Thus, frequent updates are avoided. For example, a test with the KSN Testbed (cf. Appendix C) has shown that both connectivity values did not change significantly over the course of 24 hours while SBA required updates in the order of minutes.

Example 12: Figure 4.9 contains a cut-out of a sensor network topology. Vertexes represent sensor nodes aligned as hops sets and edges correspond to uni-directional links between nodes. Table 4.9 shows the hop set sizes and connectivity information for the topology in Figure 4.9.

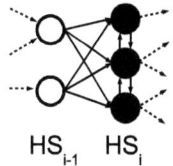

	$\mathcal{HS}_{i-1}$	$\mathcal{HS}_i$	$\mathcal{HS}_{i+1}$
Hop Set Size	2	3	
Interconnectivity		3	$\frac{5}{3}$
Intraconnectivity	0	$\frac{4}{3}$	

Figure 4.9: Illustration of the Hop-Set model

Table 4.9: Topology information for Figure 4.9

Empty cells represent values that would require information not contained in Figure 4.9. $\mathcal{HS}_i$ consists of 3 nodes and $\mathcal{HS}_{i-1}$ of 2 nodes. Hence, $|\mathcal{HS}_i| = 3$ and $|\mathcal{HS}_{i-1}| = 2$. $\mathcal{HS}_{i+1}$ is not shown in Figure 4.9.

Since the nodes of $\mathcal{HS}_{i-1}$ cannot communicate with each other, the intra-connectivity for $\mathcal{HS}_{i-1}$ equals 0. The intra-connectivity of $\mathcal{HS}_i$ is computed as follows: The node on top has a link to the node in the middle, the node in the middle a link to the node on top and to the bottom one, and the node at the bottom a connection the node in the middle. Thus, there are 4 connections within $\mathcal{HS}_i$ and 3 nodes resulting in $\text{Intra}[i] = \frac{4}{3}$. Inter-connectivity for $\mathcal{HS}_i$ equals 3 because there are two nodes in $\mathcal{HS}_{i-1}$ and each one of them reaches 3 nodes in $\mathcal{HS}_i$ with a broadcast. $\text{Inter}[i+1] = \frac{5}{3}$ is computed similarly. ♦

Topology Information Discovery

As stated above, to predict reachability, we require for each hop set $\mathcal{HS}_h$ the size $|\mathcal{HS}_h|$, the inter-connectivity $\text{Inter}[h]$ and the intra-connectivity $\text{Intra}[h]$. Topology discovery has received a lot of attention resulting in multiple approaches applicable to a wide range of node types and usage scenarios [4, 71, 90, 112]. All of these approaches acquire information on the topology of a sensor network at a granularity that would be sufficient for our purpose. Another source for required information are the data structures of routing protocols commonly used for sensor networks, e.g., CTP [44] or AODV [103]. These protocols must acquire topology information and store it in routing tables to allow the forwarding of messages over multiple hops (cf. Section 2.1.2).

It strongly depends on the underlying communication protocols, hardware and the system architecture which one of these existing approaches is applicable to a concrete deployment. To avoid such dependencies, particularly for our evaluation, we implemented a very simple topology discovery protocol based on the echo-algorithm [23]. The main steps of this topology discovery protocol are as follows:

1. The base station broadcasts a *topology request message* to all nearby nodes. This topology request contains a hop counter whose initial value is 0 and an address field which identifies the last node that broadcasted this message.

4.4. OPTIMIZING PROBABILISTIC QUERY DISSEMINATION

2. Whenever a node S_i receives the topology request for the first time, it stores the hop counter value, the marks the last rebroadcaster as its parent node, increments the hop counter, replaces the address of the topology request with its own and rebroadcasts it. Afterwards, S_i creates three empty lists: Uncles, Siblings and Children.
3. After the first topology request has been received, S_i waits a limited amount of time for other instances of the same topology request. When such a copy arrives at S_i, the node modifies the aforementioned lists and parent node pointers according to the hop count value in the topology request copy. For example, if the hop counter value in the received topology request is equal to the hop counter value the node stored initially, the node is stored in Siblings as it has the same distance from the base station, i.e., it is in the same hop set.
4. Based on the three lists and the hop count value, each node can compute its own connectivity values and its distance from the base station in hops. After the wait time has ended, each node forwards these connectivity values to its parent. Each parent aggregates the values of its children and forwards these towards the base station.

Appendix D provides a detailed description of the data structures and implementation of this protocol. Obviously, flooding the whole sensor network with the topology request requires a large number of messages and is less efficient than the sophisticated topology discovery protocols mentioned above. Despite this inefficiency, our evaluation shows that the overhead associated with this topology discovery protocol pays off after a few probabilistic query disseminations. Recall that the average values regarding connectivity of the hop sets remain relatively constant over time even if the sending ranges of a nodes change over time.

4.4.2 Reachability Prediction

In the following, we predict total reachability $R(P)$ for a given rebroadcast probability P by considering the nodes reached directly and those reached indirectly separately: Let $R_{direct}(h, P)$ be the number of nodes in hop set $\mathcal{HS}_h$ which have been reached directly, and let $R_{indirect}(h, P)$ denote the number of nodes which are reached indirectly. Since reverse broadcasts are left aside, the number of nodes $R(h, P)$ reached at the h-th hop can be computed as follows:

$$R(h, P) = min\left(R_{direct}(h, P) + R_{indirect}(h, P), |\mathcal{HS}_h|\right) \quad (4.1)$$

The minimum function is necessary to ensure that the maximum number of nodes returned is not greater than the actual number of nodes in the hop set. This can occur, because direct and indirect reachability are estimated separately and a node can receive multiple instances of the same query from surrounding nodes. Thus, $R_{direct}(h, P) + R_{indirect}(h, P)$ could be larger than the number of nodes in the hop set $\mathcal{HS}_h$.

The total reachability for a given P is the sum over all hops:

$$R(P) = \sum_h R(h, P) \quad (4.2)$$

In the following we will show how the functions $R_{direct}(h,P)$ and $R_{indirect}(h,P)$ can be computed to predict $R(h,P)$. Based on these predictions, we compute the reachability for different values of P before the dissemination of a query using the topology information described above. Thus, we determine a minimal value for P where $R(P)$ equals the number of nodes in the sensor network and disseminate the query using this rebroadcast probability.

Predicting direct reachability

Independently of the value for P the query dissemination always starts with a broadcast of the query by the base station. Thus, all nodes in the first hop set $\mathcal{HS}_1$ are reached directly (the base station corresponds to $\mathcal{HS}_0$), i.e., $R_{direct}(1,P) = |\mathcal{HS}_1|$. The core idea based on recursion for the prediction of the number of nodes reached for all hop sets $\mathcal{HS}_h$ with $h > 1$ is as follows: A node in the hop set $\mathcal{HS}_{h-1}$ can only rebroadcast after it has been reached directly or indirectly. Therefore, the number of nodes that could potentially rebroadcast the query from $\mathcal{HS}_{h-1}$ to $\mathcal{HS}_h$ is equal to the number of nodes reached in $\mathcal{HS}_{h-1}$, i.e., $R(h-1,P)$. Of these $R(h-1,P)$ nodes, only $B_{h-1} = R(h-1,P) \cdot P$ rebroadcast. We predict the number of nodes reached by these B_{h-1} rebroadcasts based on the links from $\mathcal{HS}_{h-1}$ to $\mathcal{HS}_h$, i.e., the interconnectivity $\texttt{Inter}[h]$. Summing up, we estimate the number of nodes reached directly for $\mathcal{HS}_h$ based on the total number of nodes reached in the previous hop set $\mathcal{HS}_{h-1}$. This recursion stops at $\mathcal{HS}_1$ where we know that $|\mathcal{HS}_h|$ nodes have been reached by the broadcast of the base station.

The prediction of the number of nodes reached by the aforementioned B rebroadcasts is based on an urn model which we explain in the following: Let P(event) denote the probability of a certain event. We need the probability of the event "A node from $\mathcal{HS}_h$ is reached directly", i.e., a node in $\mathcal{HS}_h$ receives its message from a node in $\mathcal{HS}_{h-1}$. The probability of this event is:

$$P(\text{A node from } \mathcal{HS}_h \text{ is reached directly}) = 1 - P(\text{not reached directly}) \quad (4.3)$$

We compute the counter-event "not reached directly" by considering the nodes in $\mathcal{HS}_{h-1}$ which have not received the query previously. If $B_{h-1} = R(h-1,P) \cdot P$, then the number of nodes that do not rebroadcast is $\overline{B_{h-1}} = |\mathcal{HS}_{h-1}| - B_{h-1}$. Thus, the hop set $\mathcal{HS}_{h-1}$ is partitioned into a set of B_{h-1} broadcasters and $\overline{B_{h-1}}$ non-broadcasters.

Equation 4.4 computes the probability of the counter-event, and its fundamental idea is as follows: The counter-event corresponds to randomly choosing $\texttt{Inter}[h]$ nodes out of hop set $\mathcal{HS}_{h-1}$ and choosing non-broadcasters only. When randomly choosing the first node, the probability to choose one of the $\overline{B_{h-1}}$ non-broadcasters is $\frac{\overline{B_{h-1}}}{|\mathcal{HS}_{h-1}|}$. For every node chosen, the total number of nodes remaining is reduced by 1. Therefore, assuming that the first node chosen was a non-broadcaster, the probability that the next randomly chosen node is also a non-broadcaster is $\frac{\overline{B_{h-1}}-1}{|\mathcal{HS}_{h-1}|-1}$. Thus, the probability that the first $\texttt{Inter}[h]$ randomly chosen nodes are non-broadcasters is computed

4.4. OPTIMIZING PROBABILISTIC QUERY DISSEMINATION

by Equation 4.4:

$$P(\text{not reached directly}) = \prod_{l=0}^{\lceil \texttt{Inter}[h] \rceil - 1} \frac{\overline{B}_{h-1} - l}{|\mathcal{HS}_{h-1}| - l} \quad (4.4)$$

We predict the number of nodes from $\mathcal{HS}_h$ receiving the query directly by multiplying the probability $P(\text{A node from } \mathcal{HS}_h \text{ is reached directly})$ with the size of the hop set $|\mathcal{HS}_h|$:

$$R_{direct}(h, P) = P(\text{A node from } \mathcal{HS}_h \text{ is reached directly}) \cdot |\mathcal{HS}_h| \text{ if } h > 1 \quad (4.5)$$

Due to the fact that $P(\text{A node from } \mathcal{HS}_h \text{ is reached directly})$ is computed using $\overline{B}_{h-1} = R(h-1, P) \cdot P$, this results in the following recursive function:

$$R_{direct}(h, P) = \begin{cases} |\mathcal{HS}_1| & \text{if } h = 1 \\ P(\text{A node from } \mathcal{HS}_h \text{ is reached directly}) \cdot |\mathcal{HS}_h| & \text{if } h > 1 \end{cases} \quad (4.6)$$

Nodes in hop set $\mathcal{HS}_h$ that are not reached directly can still be reached indirectly, i.e., by a subsequent broadcast by nodes from the same hop set. We predict the number of nodes reached in this way next.

Predicting indirect reachability

To calculate the number of nodes reached indirectly, we assume that the nodes which have received the query, are equally distributed over the hop set. Thus, if $R_{direct}(h, P)$ out of $|\mathcal{HS}_h|$ nodes are reached directly, each node in $\mathcal{HS}_h$ has obtained the message with probability $\frac{R_{direct}(h,P)}{|\mathcal{HS}_h|}$. Our experimental evaluation will show that this simplification is legitimate, i.e., it is not necessary to collect topological information in more detail.

To estimate the number of nodes reached indirectly, we re-use the approach from above: If there are $R_{direct}(h, P)$ nodes that were reached directly, then $R_{direct}(h, P) \cdot P$ rebroadcast the query. It depends on the intraconnectivity $\texttt{Intra}[h]$ of the hop set $\mathcal{HS}_h$ how many nodes receive these $R_{direct}(h, P) \cdot P$ rebroadcasts:

$$R_{indirect}(h, P) = R_{direct}(h, P) \cdot P \cdot \texttt{Intra}[h] \quad (4.7)$$

4.4.3 Estimating Energy Consumption

Based on the prediction of the number of nodes reached, we can estimate the number of messages sent and received. As shown in Appendix A, counting the messages sent and received provides an estimation of the energy consumption for probabilistic dissemination. The number of messages sent in hop set $\mathcal{HS}_h$ is as follows:

$$MSG_{send}(h, P) = R(h, P) \cdot P \quad (4.8)$$

A node in hop set $\mathcal{HS}_h$ might receive messages from nodes in many other hop sets. As we have explained in Section 4.4.1, modeling reverse broadcasts (cf. Figure 4.8) would require topological information with a very high level of detail. To avoid this, we estimate the number of received messages $MSG_{recv}(h, P)$ by considering nodes in the previous ($\mathcal{HS}_{h-1}$), current ($\mathcal{HS}_h$) and next ($\mathcal{HS}_{h+1}$) hop set, because the majority of broadcasts are received from these nodes. Equations 4.9 and 4.10 estimate how many messages sent by nodes in $\mathcal{HS}_h$ are received from nodes in the previous/current hop set respectively:

$$MSG_{recv}^{previous}(h, P) = \mathbf{E}_{send}(h, P) \cdot \text{Inter}[h] \qquad (4.9)$$

$$MSG_{recv}^{current}(h, P) = \mathbf{E}_{send}(h, P) \cdot \text{Intra}[h] \qquad (4.10)$$

Since topology information to estimate reverse broadcasts is not available, we estimate the number of links from $\mathcal{HS}_{h+1}$ to $\mathcal{HS}_h$ based on the average connectivity of nodes in $\mathcal{HS}_h$ to nodes of $\mathcal{HS}_{h+1}$. This implies bi-directional links which generally cannot be assumed, but our evaluation shows that this is sufficiently accurate to estimate the number of messages received. We multiply this number with the number of sent messages to estimate the number of received messages in the next hop set $MSG_{recv}^{next}(h, P)$:

$$MSG_{recv}^{next}(h, P) = \mathbf{E}_{send}(h, P) \cdot \frac{\text{Inter}[h+1] \cdot |\mathcal{HS}_{h+1}|}{|\mathcal{HS}_{h+1}|} \qquad (4.11)$$

Finally, we estimate the total number of messages received as follows:

$$MSG_{recv}(h, P) = \mathbf{E}_{recv}^{previous}(h, P) + \mathbf{E}_{recv}^{current}(h, P) + \mathbf{E}_{recv}^{next}(h, P) \qquad (4.12)$$

To convert these values for the messages sent and received, it is sufficiently accurate to multiply them with average energy consumption constants for sending e_{send} and receiving e_{recv}. Typically, these constants can be obtained from the data sheet of the sensor nodes used or determined by experiments similar to those in Appendix A. The total energy cost of the probabilistic flooding is calculated by multiplying the messages sent and received with the vector of energy consumption constants, and adding them up for every hop set:

$$\mathbf{E}(P) = \sum_h (MSG_{send}(h, P), MSG_{recv}(h, P)) \cdot \begin{pmatrix} e_{send} \\ e_{recv} \end{pmatrix} \qquad (4.13)$$

For most sensor node platforms, sending and receiving consumes a similar amount of energy (cf. Appendix A), i.e., $e_{send} \approx e_{recv}$.

4.5 Evaluation

In this section we evaluate the prediction model with different node setups using simulations and a deployment of 17 Sun SPOT sensor nodes [120]. We compare the predictions to the query dissemination in simulated networks of up to 425 nodes and in a real sensor network. Specifically, we investigate the following hypotheses:

4.5. EVALUATION

H.1 Spending energy to obtain the topology information required for our reachability prediction for probabilistic query dissemination pays off after a few queries.

H.2 The accuracy of the reachability prediction based on the topology information is high.

H.3 Compared to other existing approaches, our approach for optimizing probabilistic dissemination reduces communication.

H.4 In particular, the number of messages received during query dissemination is reduced significantly by our approach.

H.5 Probabilistic query dissemination is appropriate for sensor networks of a wide range of characteristics regarding node distribution or density.

H.6 The topology information required for the reachability prediction does not require frequent updates.

Our model produces stochastic results for the average case, i.e., it works well for sufficiently dense networks or for large numbers of trials. Thus, we expect a small deviation between the predicted values and experimental results.

4.5.1 Simulation

For the simulation we used our *Karlsruhe Sensor Networking Simulator* (cf. Appendix C), which is interface-compatible to Sun SPOT sensor nodes. This enables us to deploy the prediction model and the topology-discovery protocol in both the simulated environment and the real deployment.

Simulation setup

To evaluate our approach with a wide range of parameters, we generated networks of varying node densities and two different topologies.

Uniform: This topology is an example for a sensor deployment that has been carefully planned to provide a defined coverage of a region. The nodes are distributed uniformly in a circular area with a radius of 30 units around the base station, as illustrated in Figure 4.10. We used a fixed radius and varied the average number of neighbors (the *average node degree*) for every node from 4 to 16 to create topologies ranging from sparse to dense.

Gaussian: This topology corresponds to a "smart-dust scenario" where the nodes are arbitrarily deployed over an area of interest, e.g., from an airplane. The placement of nodes follows a Gaussian distribution. In particular, we use Gaussian sampling with the center of the environment as mean and a standard deviation of 18 units to place the nodes. Again, the area covered has a size of 30 units. For our simulations, we vary the number of nodes from 125 to 425. As shown in in Figure 4.11, most nodes are located close to the center, and the further away from the base station, the lower the node density. Because some of the nodes close to the edge of the area are disconnected from the network, even a rebroadcast probability of $P = 1.0$ will not deliver the query to all nodes.

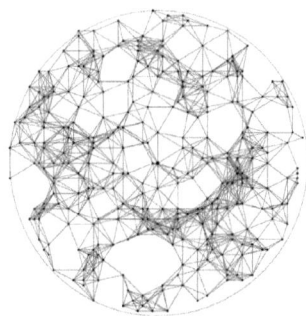 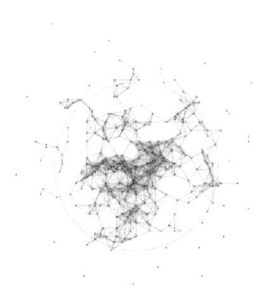

Figure 4.10: Example: Uniform Topology (Node Degree 12)

Figure 4.11: Example: Gaussian Topology (325 Nodes)

We generated 40 instances for each parameter setup to exclude stochastic errors, i.e., 320 different topologies. To enable a comparison between both topology types, Table 4.10 shows which node degree in uniform node distributions equals which number of nodes.

Average Node Degree	Used Sensors
4	125
8	225
12	325
16	425

Table 4.10: Average node degree in Uniform scenario and number of nodes

Energy consumption constants In order to determine the energy consumption for (1) a simulated query dissemination and (2) the energy-consumption prediction, the energy consumption constants e_{send} and e_{recv} must be determined. We obtained these values from experiments with MicaZ [131] described in Appendix A.

$$e_{send} = 0.0691 \; mAs \quad (4.14)$$

$$e_{recv} = 0.0583 \; mAs \quad (4.15)$$

Similar values have been obtained in [83].

4.5. EVALUATION

Experiment execution

We evaluated each of the 320 different topologies in four steps:

Step 1 Fetch the required topology information using the topology-discovery protocol of outlined in Section 4.4.1.
Step 2 Predict the total reachability $R(P)$ for rebroadcast probabilities $P \in \{0, 0.05, \cdots, 1\}$.
Step 3 For each rebroadcast probability, simulate 120 query disseminations and count the number of messages sent and received.
Step 4 Compute the energy consumption using Equation 4.13.

Since we conducted 120 query disseminations for each of the 320 topologies, the experimental results in the following are based on more than 38.000 simulation runs. This is a sufficiently high number to foreclose a significant impact on the results due to stochastic errors or anomalies.

Results and Analysis

Figures 4.12–4.15 show the simulation results for uniform node distributions and Figures 4.16–4.19 those of Gaussian node distributions. On each diagram, the x-axis shows the rebroadcast probability P used to disseminate the query. The relative reachability for this value of P, i.e., the percentage of nodes reached, is plotted on the left side and the energy consumption based on e_{send} and e_{recv} on the right side of each diagram.

For all simulations, the predicted number of nodes is relatively close to the actual number of nodes reached, but always below it, i.e., the model never overestimates reachability. While there is some deviation between the prediction and the actual number of nodes reached, e.g., in Figure 4.15 at $P = 0.3$, this deviation is very small at the point where reachability is close to 100%. Since it is important for processing spatio-temporal queries that all nodes are reached, this is the point where we need the accuracy. An in-depth look at the results reveals the reason for this deviation: If the reachability is significantly below 100%, the portion of nodes that are reached by reverse broadcasts only increases. Since our model does not take into account reverse broadcasts, the prediction always underestimates the reachability in these cases. The slight underestimation of the reachability in all cases is also advantageous considering the fact that the actual reachability in real deployments will be lower than the reachability computed by the simulator. Summing up, the results support **H.2**, in particular for values of P that achieve a reachability close to 100%.

Our results also provide an insight regarding the applicability of probabilistic query dissemination and its limitations: Except for relatively sparse networks, i.e., networks where the average node has 4 nodes or less it can reach with wireless communication, reachabilities of more than 90% were observed. Generally, the higher the density of the nodes, the higher are the possible energy savings. In those cases, where the actual reachability was below 90%, it is still possible to reduce energy consumption by missing some nodes: For example, with networks of 325 or 425 nodes with Gaussian distribution, the results in Figures 4.18 and 4.19 show that there exists a rebroadcast probability

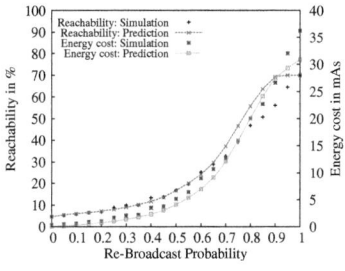

Figure 4.12: Simulation result for uniform distribution with average node degree 4 (125 nodes)

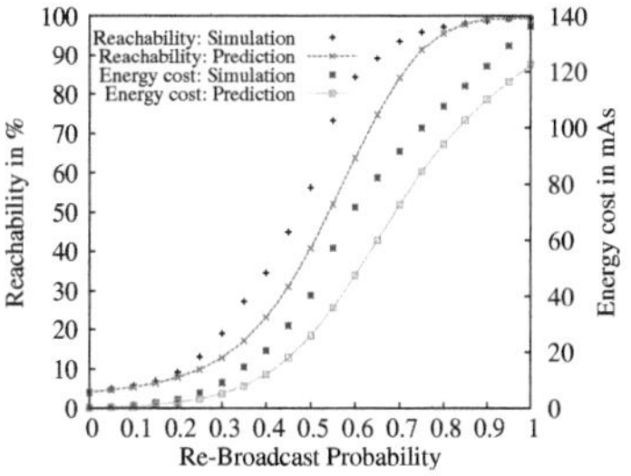

Figure 4.13: Simulation result for uniform distribution with average node degree 8 (225 nodes)

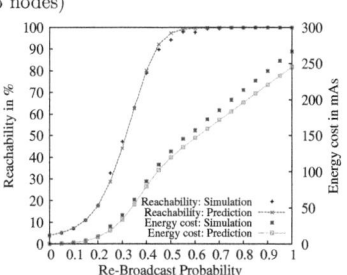
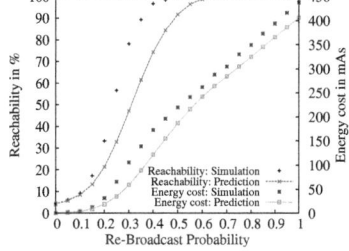

Figure 4.14: Simulation result for uniform distribution with average node degree 12 (325 nodes)

Figure 4.15: Simulation result for uniform distribution with average node degree 16 (425 nodes)

$0.65 \leq P_{Sat} \leq 1$ at which the reachability stagnates. Further increases of the rebroadcast probability beyond this point increase energy consumption linearly while only increasing reachability marginally or not at all. The only cases where probabilistic query dissemination is not advantageous are those where the average node density is 4 or less. In these scenarios, a significant part, e.g., in Figure 4.16 about 40% of the nodes, of the network is completely unreachable. It is questionable if such networks occur in reality and other dissemination approaches would not achieve better results. At least for moderately dense networks, probabilistic query dissemination achieves high reachabilities at relatively low costs, and for these networks our results support **H.5**.

Table 4.11 shows the average number of messages sent/received for the uniform topologies with 425 nodes for $P \geq 0.5$, i.e., some of the absolute values for the diagram in Figure 4.15. Based on

4.5. EVALUATION

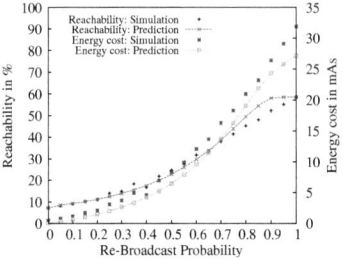

Figure 4.16: Simulation result for Gaussian distribution with 125 nodes

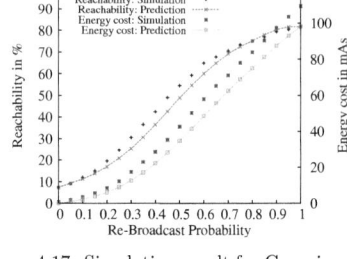

Figure 4.17: Simulation result for Gaussian distribution with 225 nodes

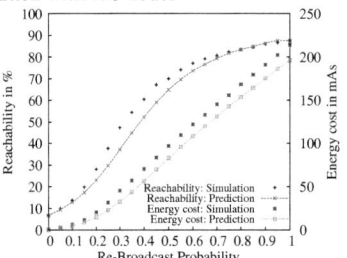

Figure 4.18: Simulation result for Gaussian distribution with 325 nodes

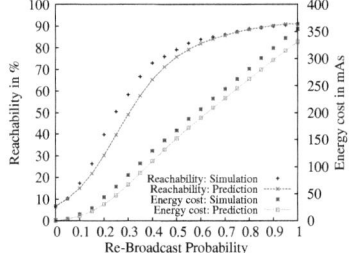

Figure 4.19: Simulation result for Gaussian distribution with 425 nodes

these message counts, the energy consumed by sending or receiving is computed using (4.13) in combination with the constants e_{send} and e_{recv}.

The energy savings compared to flooding are large. With flooding ($P = 1$), the dissemination of a query to all 425 nodes would require $29.37 + 408.71 = 438.09$ mAs on average. According to our model, all nodes are reached with $P = P_{Sat} = 0.6$. The simulation shows that this prediction is accurate since all nodes are reached, but the energy consumption is considerably lower with about $17.52 + 244.29 = 261.81$ mAs on average. Except for topologies with a low node density, the energy savings are similar. Additional experiments using CBD with $T_{CBD} = 2$ to disseminate a query in the same scenarios (uniform, 425 nodes) resulted in an average energy consumption of more than 310 mAs. Hence, we conclude that our results confirm **H.3**.

Table 4.11 also provides an insight regarding the composition of these energy savings: For the uniform topologies with 425 nodes, probabilistic query dissemination with $P = 0.6$ reduces average energy consumption by $438.09 - 261.81 = 176.28$. The energy saved due to messages that are not

Rebroadcast	Sending		Receiving	
Probability	Messages	Energy in mAs	Messages	Energy in mAs
0.5	211.9	14.64	3516.0	204.98
0.6	253.6	17.52	4190.2	244.29
0.7	295.8	20.44	4882.0	284.62
0.8	339.1	23.43	5600.3	326.50
0.9	382.1	26.40	6306.9	367.70
1.0	425.0	29.37	7010.6	408.71

Table 4.11: Avg. messages sent/received for uniform node distribution with 425 nodes

sent is 29.37 − 17.52 = 11.85 mAs. Thus, most of the energy savings must be attributed to messages that are not received, i.e., **H.4** is confirmed.

4.5.2 Break-Even Analysis

This section investigates **H.1** and shows that that the topology-discovery pays off after a few probabilistic query disseminations with an optimized rebroadcast probability P. In the following, we assume a uniform scenario with 425 nodes and an average node degree of 16. As shown above, using a rebroadcast probability of $P = 0.6$, query dissemination requires 261.81 mAs. In comparison, flooding ($P = 1$) requires 438.09 mAs, i.e., 176.28 mAs more than probabilistic query dissemination. However, our reachability prediction requires topology information which must be obtained prior to probabilistic query dissemination while flooding does not require any topology information. Thus, these costs must be taken into account when comparing flooding with probabilistic query dissemination.

Computing the energy consumption of the topology discovery protocol for this scenario is straight-forward. Each of the 425 nodes broadcasts a topology request once to its neighbors. Since each node has 16 communication neighbors on average, this results in $425 \cdot 16$ messages that are received during the phase where the topology request is flooded into the network. Equation (4.16) estimates the energy consumption for this:

$$\begin{aligned} E_{TopDisc}^{Expansion} &= 0.0691 \frac{mAs}{Send} \cdot 425 \\ &+ 0.0583 \frac{mAs}{Receive} \cdot 425 \cdot 16 \frac{Receives}{Send} \\ &= 425.8075 \text{ mAs} \end{aligned} \qquad (4.16)$$

After each node has broadcasted a topology request once, the topology information must be aggregated and transported back to the base station. For this, each node collects the topology information from 16 nodes on average and forwards it towards the base station. According to (4.17), this

4.5. EVALUATION

part of the topology discovery protocol also consumes 425.8075 mAs for our example of 425 nodes:

$$\begin{aligned}
E_{TopDisc}^{Contraction} &= 0.0583 \frac{mAs}{Receive} \cdot 425 \cdot 16 \frac{Receives}{Send} \\
&+ 0.0691 \frac{mAs}{Send} \cdot 425 \\
&= 425.8075 \text{ mAs}
\end{aligned} \qquad (4.17)$$

Summing up, acquiring the topology information to predict the reachability and determine P_{Sat} consumes 811.615 mAs in this particular scenario. Considering the energy savings of 176.28 mAs per probabilistic query dissemination, we compute $4 \cdot 176.28 < 811.615 < 5 \cdot 176.28$. Hence, after the dissemination of five queries, this initial energy consumption has paid off and each query disseminated afterwards further increases the energy saved by our approach.

A calculation for the Gaussian topology yields similar results. As the analysis in [75] has shown, there exists a $P_{Sat} < 1$ for any densely connected sensor network such that probabilistic flooding reaches all nodes. Our prediction model allows for precomputation of P_{Sat} prior to the dissemination of the query. Afterwards we use a rebroadcast probability close or equal to P_{Sat}, thus saving energy. Thus, compared to flooding, the topology discovery will pay off for any of these sensor networks after a few query disseminations.

In addition to this, it must be noted that there are several other topology discovery protocols [4, 71, 90, 112] that are more efficient but require assumptions on node hardware, software or system architecture. If one of these protocols is applicable, they should be used to further reduce the number of query disseminations until the probabilistic approach pays off. Summing up, this confirms **H.1**.

4.5.3 Sun SPOT Case Study

We have tested our model and the topology-discovery protocol in a real environment. Figure 4.20 shows 17 Sun SPOT sensor nodes (circles) and a base station (square) deployed in our offices. Each node counts and stores the number of incoming and outgoing messages locally. We have repeated the following experiment 10 times:

1. Disseminate a query using flooding ($P = 1.0$) to determine the number of nodes that can be reached. This is necessary, because in real deployments external factors such as metal doors or electrical devices can prevent nodes from being reached in any case.
2. Fetch the topology data using the topology-discovery protocol.
3. Predict the number of nodes reached with different values for the rebroadcast probability P based on the topology information collected. Determine P_{Sat}, the lowest value for P where reaching all 17 nodes is predicted.
4. Disseminate a query message into the network using probabilistic flooding with a rebroadcast probability of P_{Sat}.

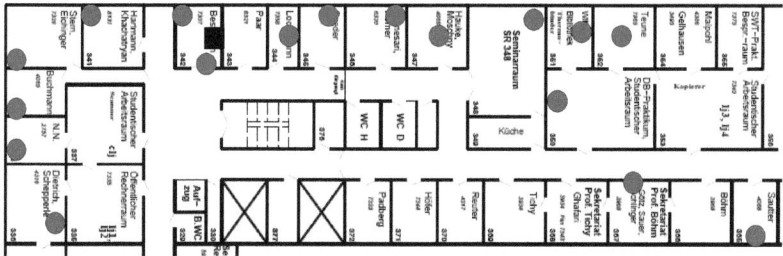

Figure 4.20: Map of 17 Sun SPOTs and a Base Station deployed at the IPD

Table 4.12 shows the average results for the 10 query disseminations with flooding and probabilistic dissemination: Generally, the accuracy of the prediction and thereby the number of nodes reached with P_{Sat} is good, even though there is a small difference between the 16.3 nodes reached by simple flooding compared to the probabilistic flooding with 15.4 nodes reached on average. This confirms our simulation results and **H.2**.

	Avg. Reached Nodes (of 17)	Messages Sent	Messages Received
Flooding	16.3	16.3	63.8
Probabilistic	15.4	10.2	34

Table 4.12: Result of the flooding experiment using the Sun SPOT deployment

The nodes that were not reached were always the two nodes at the bottom-right corner of Figure 4.20. Further analysis of their routing tables shows that both of them only have a single node that connects them to the rest of the network. With simple flooding, external factors like metal doors or electric devices might prevent these nodes from obtaining the query. Probabilistic flooding further decreases the probability that these nodes receive the query by $(1-P)$. Hence, probabilistic flooding should not be used in sparse networks or areas of the network that are sparsely connected. Sensor nodes can detect this, e.g., by looking at their routing tables, and use flooding in these areas of the network by default.

Furthermore, Table 4.12 confirms that the number of messages sent and received with probabilistic flooding is much lower than the one with the simple flooding. The amount of energy saved due to reduced communication clearly outweighs the small inaccuracy of the prediction. Thus, the results of the case study support **H.4** and **H.3**. Since wireless sensor networks cannot guarantee 100% reachability anyway, a small deviation in the prediction of the number of nodes reached does not limit the applicability of our approach.

4.6. SUMMARY

After the 10 disseminations of the query, we continued to collect topology information every 10 minutes for 24 hours using the topology discovery protocol outlined in Section 4.4.1. After the topology discovery was completed, we computed P_{Sat} and recorded it. Analogous to the 10 times where the query was disseminated afterwards, the result of this computation was always $P_{Sat} \approx 0.63$. Thus, despite humans moving throughout the building, lifts, fire doors and other obstacles, the topology information was relatively unaffected. This confirms that the structure of our topology information does not require a lot of maintenance contrary to the topology information required by SBA and other topology-based approaches. With this, we conclude that **H.6** as well as all of our other hypotheses have been confirmed by our evaluation results.

4.6 Summary

This chapter focused on the first step towards the efficient processing of spatio-temporal queries whose semantics have been defined in Chapter 3: The dissemination such a query into the sensor network. First, we have shown that spatio-temporal queries require that all nodes receive the query, i.e., a large number of nodes must communicate with each other. Since communication is expensive in terms of energy, it is of utmost importance that this communication-intensive part of the query processing is completed efficiently.

Dissemination of messages in sensor networks has received a lot of attention from the networking community. With the aim of finding an existing approach for our case, we have evaluated a set of state-of-the-art dissemination approaches in different sensor networks consisting of Sun SPOTs. The evaluation showed that probabilistic query dissemination is a promising approach. The main challenge of probabilistic dissemination is finding P_{Sat}, i.e., a minimal rebroadcast probability P where all nodes receive the query. We developed an analytical model that predicts the number of nodes reached for a given value of P and connectivity information. Our evaluation shows that our predictions are sufficiently accurate to determine P_{Sat} before the query dissemination starts and then disseminate the query efficiently. This concludes our discussion regarding Contribution **C.2**. In the following, we assume that the query has been disseminated using this approach before the processing of the spatio-temporal query starts.

Chapter 5
Energy-Efficient Processing of Spatio-Temporal Queries

As illustrated in Section 2.1, energy is and will be a valuable resource in sensor networks. Thus, query processing must avoid excessive energy consumption. While Chapter 4 focused on the dissemination of the query, this chapter will assume that the query has been disseminated to all nodes and try to compute results for spatio-temporal queries with minimal energy consumption, i.e., Contribution **C.3**.

Processing a spatio-temporal query requires the collection of all query-relevant information, e.g., on objects detected or changes of a dynamic zone, from the nodes of the sensor network and derive detection scenarios from this information. A straightforward approach for this is sending all of this information to the base station. Our evaluation shows that this approach is prohibitively inefficient for sufficiently large sensor networks, e.g., more than 40 nodes. The core contribution of this chapter are two strategies which allow in-network processing of spatio-temporal queries and only send results to the base station. These strategies reduce the number of messages required to collect the necessary information significantly.

This chapter concludes with an extensive evaluation of our measures using simulations as well as Sun SPOTs. Our results show that the two in-network strategies reduce communication by 45% to 89% compared to collecting all information at the base station. Recall that existing relational query processors for sensor networks would collect the information on object detections at the base station. As illustrated using WSNEnter $(\mathbf{O}, \mathcal{Z})$ as an example in Appendix B, this is due to the join operations required to express spatio-temporal semantics using relational operators.

5.1 Preface

For the remainder of the chapter, we assume that the following steps have been completed before the sensor network starts to process a query:

5.2. DATA STRUCTURES AND ALGORITHMS

1. Definition of a condition $C_{\mathcal{Z}}$ (see 3.4).
2. Specification of the movement of interest as a spatio-temporal development $\mathbb{P}(\mathbf{O}, \mathcal{Z})$.
3. Dissemination of a pair $[\mathbb{P}(\mathbf{O}, \mathcal{Z}), C_{\mathcal{Z}}]$ to all nodes of the sensor network.

The last step is important, because it allows each node determine if it is in the zone or outside of it. Furthermore, every node can determine which predicate or detection scenarios are of interest.

The query result returned to the base station, i.e., to the user, includes every element whose movement conforms to $\mathbb{P}(\mathbf{O}, \mathcal{Z})$ as defined by Chapter 3. To accomplish this, the sensor nodes must compute the detection scenario whenever an object $\mathbf{O}$ is detected. This results in a sequence of detection scenarios $\mathbb{D}_\mathbf{O}$ (cf. Definition 40). Based on $\mathbb{D}_\mathbf{O}$, the sensor network can use the detection term associated with $\mathbb{P}(\mathbf{O}, \mathcal{Z})$ derived in Section 3.4 to determine if $\mathbf{O}$ conforms to $\mathbb{P}(\mathbf{O}, \mathcal{Z})$. We describe our approach in the following steps; the numbers are in line with the ones of the respective sections:

5.2 Data Structures and Algorithms: We describe the data structures where we store information on object detections by different nodes, and whether a node is in the zone or outside of it. Based on this, we describe algorithms that compute detection scenarios based on these data structures.

5.3 Centralized Data Collection: A straightforward strategy to acquire the information necessary to compute detection scenarios collects all data at the base station. This is our base-line strategy.

5.4 Distributed Data Collection: We propose two strategies that exploit the spatial correlation of object detections to allow in-network computation of detection scenarios. The evaluation in Section 5.5 shows that this reduces communication significantly.

The chapter concludes with an evaluation of our measures using simulations as well as Sun SPOT deployments.

Since nodes may fail at any time, we also address failure detection and handling for the distributed data strategies proposed in Section 5.4. If the result of a detection scenario computation could be affected by a node failure, we notify the base station of this problem and mark the respective detection scenario. This allows users to dismiss certain results or at least consider that the result is potentially incorrect because a node failed.

5.2 Data Structures and Algorithms

To store the information on objects detected, we use a list **Detections**. It depends on the strategy where **Detections** is stored: For the centralized strategy, we store **Detections** at the base station. Contrary to that, the distributed strategies share and replicate the elements of **Detections** in such a way that sensor nodes can compute detection scenarios based on it. Every element of **Detections** represents the detection of an object $\mathbf{O}$ by a node $\mathcal{S}_i$ during a time interval $[t_{entry}, t_{exit}]$. Thus, every element of **Detections** has the following structure:

NodeID: Identifier of the node $\mathcal{S}_i$ detecting **O**.
ObjectID: An identifier of the object **O** that has been detected by $\mathcal{S}_i$.
t^O_{entry}: The entry time (cf. Definition 15) at which **O** entered the detection area of $\mathcal{S}_i$.
t^O_{exit}: This value either equals ∅ or a time $t > t_{entry}$. If it equals ∅, this indicates that $\mathcal{S}_i$ is still detecting **O**. Otherwise, this value equals the exit time t_{exit} (cf. Definition 16) at which **O** left the detection area of $\mathcal{S}_i$.

We say *an element E originates from node* $\mathcal{S}_i$ *if* $E.NodeID = \mathcal{S}_i$. Note that an object that repeatedly enters and leaves the detection area of a node may result in several list elements originating from the same node.

In the following, we assume that standard methods like add(E) for adding elements to Detections as well as mechanisms which allow iteration over all elements of Detections are supported. The data stored in ObjectID depends on the properties of the objects and how they are detected: For RFID-tagged objects, the attribute of a list entry is the identifier associated with the RFID-tag. Similarly, radio-collars for animal tracking (cf. Section 1.1.2) always correspond to some kind of identifier which is stored in this field. Even in cases where identifiers are not assigned a-priori to objects, there are cases where generating a unique identifier from detections is possible. For example in [18], vehicles are detected and identified using microphones and according to their results one can generate so called signatures based on the data acquired by the microphones. Their approach uses these signatures generated by engines and propulsion gear to identify different vehicles. In this case, ObjectID would be this signature or a hash value generated from such an approach.

According to Definition 15, the moment an object **O** moves into the detection area of a node $\mathcal{S}_i$ is the entry time. When such an entry occurs at time t_1, an entry E = $[\mathcal{S}_i, \mathbf{O}, t_1, \emptyset]$ is added to Detections by calling Detections.add(E). Afterwards, **O** may be in the detection area of $\mathcal{S}_i$ for an arbitrary time. This entry E must be updated when **O** leaves the detection area at t_2, i.e., the entry E is modified and becomes $[\mathcal{S}_i, \mathbf{O}, t_1, t_2]$. As discussed in Section 3.1, our approach is applicable to non-continuous detection mechanisms by temporal interpolation as well.

Similarly, the information which nodes are inside of the zone $\mathcal{Z}$ is stored in a list called Zones. Again, we assume a list implementation that supports standard list operations and supports iteration. Every element of the list has the following attributes:

NodeID: Identifier of the node $\mathcal{S}_i$ that is in the zone $\mathcal{Z}$ for some time.
$t^{\mathcal{Z}}_{entry}$: This value marks the start of the time interval during which $\mathcal{S}_i$ was in $\mathcal{Z}$.
$t^{\mathcal{Z}}_{exit}$: This value marks the end of the time interval during which $\mathcal{S}_i$ was in $\mathcal{Z}$. As with objects, $t^{\mathcal{Z}}_{exit}$ either equals ∅ or $t > t^{\mathcal{Z}}_{exit}$. The first case indicates that $\mathcal{S}_i$ is still in $\mathcal{Z}$ and the latter case that $\mathcal{S}_i$ has been in $\mathcal{Z}$ during $\left[t^{\mathcal{Z}}_{entry}, t^{\mathcal{Z}}_{exit}\right]$.

Modeling zones in this way assumes that there is only one zone. To support multiple zones, a list element in Zones would require an additional field for a "zone identifier". We omit this additional attribute to ease our presentation.

5.2. DATA STRUCTURES AND ALGORITHMS

As with Detections above, modifications of the list occur if S_i enters or leaves a Z. Whenever a node S_i determines that $C_Z(S_i) = T$ at t_1 while $C_Z(S_i) = F$ at the last test before t_1, it generates an entry $E = [S_i, t_1, \emptyset]$ and calls Zones.add(E). For static zones, This occurs only at the time when S_i receives the query for the first time. Afterwards S_i is either in Z or in $\overline{Z}$ for all times. Thus, $t_{exit}^Z = \emptyset$ for all times in the context of static zones. With dynamic zones, nodes may enter and leave a zone multiple times. When S_i leaves Z at time $t_2 > t_1$, the element $[S_i, t_1, \emptyset]$ mentioned above is updated to $[S_i, t_1, t_2]$.

5.2.1 Detection Scenario Computation

According to Section 3.3.2, the sensor network must compute how the detection set $\mathcal{D}_t^O$ intersects with Z and $\overline{Z}$ to compute a detection scenario at time t for a given object O. We refer to this computation as isDetecting(S^*, t, O), which is defined as follows:

$$\text{isDetecting}(S^*, t, O) = \begin{cases} T & \text{iff } \exists S_i \in S^* : detect(S_i, O, t) = T \\ F & \text{Otherwise} \end{cases} \quad (5.1)$$

Algorithm 6: Implementation of isDetecting(S^*, t, O)

Input: The lists Detections and Zones
Input: An object identifier ObjectID of O, a set of nodes S^* and a value $t \in \mathbb{T}$
Output: T if a node in S^* detected O at t, otherwise F

1 **for** *each node* $S_i \in S^*$ **do**
2   **for** *each entry* E *in* Detections **do**
3   **if** $E.NodeID = S_i.NodeID$ AND $E.ObjectID = O.ObjectID$ AND $E.t_{entry}^O \le t \le E.t_{exit}^O$
       then
4   **return** T // Node in S^* detects O at t
5   **end**
6   **end**
7 **end**
8 **return** F

The input parameter S^* is either Z or $\overline{Z}$. Determining Z and $\overline{Z}$ for some time t is straightforward and only requires a single iteration over Zones. Algorithm 6 provides an implementation for isDetecting(S^*, t, O): The algorithm consists of two nested loops. The outer loop runs through the nodes of S^* and the inner loop tests for each $S_i \in S^*$ if it detects O at time t.

To compute a detection scenario in the context of a zone Z, we use isDetecting(S^*, t, O) twice: First, we compute isDetecting(Z, t, O) and then isDetecting$(\overline{Z}, t, O)$. According to Lemmas 3.8-3.10, one can determine the detection scenario according to Table 5.1: Each cell

	isDetecting$(\overline{\mathcal{Z}}, t, \mathbf{O})$	
	$\mathcal{T}$	$\mathcal{F}$
isDetecting$(\mathcal{Z}, t, \mathbf{O})$ $\mathcal{T}$	DS^B	DS^I
$\mathcal{F}$	DS^E	DS$^\emptyset$

Table 5.1: Deriving detection scenarios using isDetecting$(\mathcal{S}^*, t, \mathbf{O})$

corresponds to a pair of booleans that represent the result of the calls to isDetecting$(\mathcal{Z}, t, \mathbf{O})$ and isDetecting$(\overline{\mathcal{Z}}, t, \mathbf{O})$ and contains the corresponding detection scenario.

In the following, we address the collection of the elements in **Detections** and **Zones** to ensure that the result of the detection scenario computation according to Table 5.1 is correct.

Definition 47 (Correctness): The *computation of a detection scenario* DS* *is correct* if the space partition that corresponds to DS* (cf. Definitions 32-34) contains the position $\mathbf{p} \in \mathbb{E}^d$ of the object detected. □

Definition 48 (Completeness): A *lists* Detections *and* Zones *are complete regarding an object* **O** *and a time t* if they meet the following requirements:

- Detections must contain all elements $[\mathcal{S}_i, \mathbf{O}, t_1, t_2]$ with $t_1 \le t$ and $t \le t_2$ or $t_2 = \emptyset$.
- Zones must contain all elements $[\mathcal{S}_i, t_3, t_4]$ with $t_3 \le t$ and $t \le t_4$ or $t_4 = \emptyset$. □

Lemma 5.1. *If* Detections *and* Zones *are complete, the detection scenario computed according to Table 5.1 is correct.*

Proof. Without loss of generality, assume the computed detection scenario regarding an object **O** and a time t is DS^E, i.e., **O** is in $\mathcal{Z}^E$ according to Definition 24. Considering Lemma 3.8, this implies that there is at least one node $\mathcal{S}_i \in \overline{\mathcal{Z}}$ that detects **O**. The computed detection scenario would be incorrect, if there existed another node $\mathcal{S}_j \in \mathcal{Z}$ which detects **O** at t as well. Such a node cannot exist since **Detections** and **Zones** are complete. For the other detection scenarios, the proof is similar. ∎

Summing up, the base station or an arbitrary sensor node must store complete lists **Detections** and **Zones** locally to compute a detection scenario for a given object **O** and a time t. Acquiring the elements for both lists to keep them complete while minimizing the amount of messages is our goal in the following.

5.2.2 Memory Requirements and Management

While future developments are likely to lift memory restrictions of sensor nodes, we briefly investigate the memory footprint of both lists. This shows that even with current, memory-restricted sensor nodes storing these lists on sensor nodes is viable.

5.3. CENTRALIZED STRATEGY

The Sun SPOT sensor nodes we used for our reference implementation are uniquely identified by a so called IEEE address which are 16 bytes long. Thus, the attribute NodeID requires 16 bytes. This could be reduced to 8 bytes, because IEEE addresses contain a prefix and a postfix where the prefix identifies Sun as the manufacturer of the devices. This prefix is equal for all nodes and thus could be omitted, but since memory was never an issue for our reference implementation, we stored the complete IEEE address. The timestamps in both lists, i.e., t_{entry} and t_{exit}, require 16 bytes each as well, since they are time values obtained through the standard java clock interface.

We analyze the memory footprint of a single element in **Zones** first: Every element takes $16 \cdot 3 = 48$ bytes of memory. An element is created whenever a node enters a zone. Note that leaving a zone does not result in another element, because the element is only modified.

The amount of memory required per element in **Detections** depends on the properties of the object: As with **Zones**, we need 48 bytes per element for NodeID and the two timestamps. As mentioned above, the size of the object identifier depends on the object. Our reference implementation used another 16 bytes for ObjectID which lead to a total size of 64 bytes per element in **Zones**.

Considering the 512 kilobytes of RAM that are available on Sun SPOT sensor nodes, we conclude that a single node could store thousands of elements in both lists before memory becomes an issue. Therefore, we assume in the following that nodes always have sufficient amounts of memory to store list elements required to compute a detection scenario. On platforms that are more memory restricted, it would be advisable to treat both lists like queues and remove old items whenever new items must be added.

5.3 Centralized Strategy

A straightforward approach to collect information on objects detected and zones is that every node notifies the base station whenever an object enters or leaves a detection area or a node joins or leaves a zone. Based on these notifications, the base station can generate elements for **Detections** and **Zones** and compute detection scenarios according to Table 5.1.

Algorithm 7 illustrates this strategy in two parts: Arbitrary nodes that detect objects or join/leave $\mathcal{Z}$ execute Lines 1-5. Transmitting such a notification from a node $\mathcal{S}_i$ to the base station requires routing protocols (cf. Section 2.1.2). These protocols forward messages via multiple hops if $\mathcal{S}_i$ is not a communication neighbor of the base station.

The base station executes the second part starting at Line 7: First, the information contained in the notification received by the base station is integrated into one of the lists **Detections** or **Zones**. Afterwards, the base station must wait a timeout t_{delay} before the computation of the detection scenario can start. The timeout ensures that notifications of other nodes which simultaneously detect the same object or join/leave a zone have arrived before the computation of the detection scenario starts. The actual value of t_{delay} depends on factors such as communication hardware, distance of the notifying node $\mathcal{S}_i$ to the base station, the routing protocol etc. For our reference implementation we used a delay of 30 seconds.

Algorithm 7: Centralized data collection
---
1 **When** O *enters/leaves* **DA**$_i$ *of* S_i *at* t **do**
2   S_i sends enter/exit notification [S_i, O, t] to base station
3 **end**
4 **When** S_i *joins/leaves* $\mathcal{Z}$ *at* t **do**
5   S_i sends join/leave notification [S_i, t] to base station
6 **end**
7 **When** *base station receives notification from* S_i **do**
8   Modify **Detections** or **Zones** at base station
9   Wait t_{delay}
10   **if** *Detections has to be modified* **then**
11   Derive Detection Scenario DS* using Table 5.1
12        $\mathbb{D}_O^{\mathcal{Z}} \leftarrow \mathbb{D}_O^{\mathcal{Z}} \succ$ DS* // Append DS* to detection term
13   **else**
14   **for** *each object* O *in Detections* **do**
15   Derive Detection Scenario DS* using Table 5.1
16            $\mathbb{D}_O^{\mathcal{Z}} \leftarrow \mathbb{D}_O^{\mathcal{Z}} \succ$ DS*
17   **end**
18   **end**
19   Check if there is an object O whose detection term conforms to $\mathbb{P}(O, \mathcal{Z})$
20 **end**

Lemma 5.2. *Suppose S_i sends a notification about object detection or zone change at $t \in \mathbb{T}$. If t_{delay} is the maximum time a notification needs to travel from a node S_i to the base station, Detections stored at the base station is complete at $t + t_{delay}$.*

Proof. We produce the proof of the contrary: If the notification from S_i has not arrived at $t + t_{delay}$, then t_{delay} was not the maximum time a notification may need to reach the base station. ∎

After the timeout expired, the base station can assume that **Detections** and **Zones** are complete. Hence, the base station can compute the detection scenario and check if any objects fulfill the users query $\mathbb{P}(O, \mathcal{Z})$.

5.4 Distributed Object-Information Collection

In the following, we propose two strategies which distribute the both lists among the nodes of the sensor network, i.e., each node stores only a part of both lists. The distribution is done in such a way that any node S_i detecting an object O can compute the detection scenario. As we show, this reduces communication for two reasons:

5.4. DISTRIBUTED OBJECT-INFORMATION COLLECTION

- Nodes only notify the base station of objects that possibly fulfill the query, i.e., those that at least fulfill one $P(\mathbf{O}, \mathcal{Z}) \in \mathbb{P}(\mathbf{O}, \mathcal{Z})$.
- There are fewer nodes from which data must be collected, i.e., only some nodes communicate.

The latter point stems from the following idea: When a node $\mathcal{S}_i$ detects an object $\mathbf{O}$, only nodes in its vicinity can detect the object simultaneously. This is because $\mathbf{O}$ at position $\mathsf{p} \in \mathbb{E}^d$ can be detected only by nodes whose detection area contains p. The problem is that detection mechanisms in sensor networks typically do not allow precise localization of the object detected, i.e., p is unknown. But in turn, $\mathcal{S}_i$ can derive that only nodes that are close-by could possibly detect $\mathbf{O}$ at the same time. More formally, only nodes whose detection area overlaps with $\mathbf{DA}_i$ of $\mathcal{S}_i$ could possibly detect $\mathbf{O}$ simultaneously, i.e., contain p.

Definition 49 (Detection Neighbor): Node $\mathcal{S}_j$ is a *detection neighbor of* $\mathcal{S}_i$ if the detection areas of both nodes overlap, i.e., $\mathbf{DA}_i \cap \mathbf{DA}_j \neq \emptyset$. $\mathcal{DN}_i$ is the set of detection neighbors of $\mathcal{S}_i$. □

Recall that the detection area is indeterminable as well for most detection mechanisms but we show in Section 5.4.4 how sensor nodes can approximate their set of detection neighbors.

Notation (Detection Neighbor Subsets): We refer to the subset of detection neighbors of a node $\mathcal{S}_i$ that are in $\mathcal{Z}$ as $\mathcal{DN}_i^{\mathcal{Z}}$. Similarly, $\mathcal{DN}_i^{\overline{\mathcal{Z}}}$ contains all detection neighbors of $\mathcal{S}_i$ that are outside of $\mathcal{Z}$, i.e., in $\overline{\mathcal{Z}}$. Note that $\mathcal{DN}_i^{\mathcal{Z}} \cap \mathcal{DN}_i^{\overline{\mathcal{Z}}} = \emptyset$.

For static zones, every node $\mathcal{S}_i$ can derive for each detection neighbor $\mathcal{S}_j \in \mathcal{DN}_i$ if it is in $\mathcal{Z}$ or not since the query has been disseminated to all nodes previously. In case of dynamic zones, we develop a light-weight protocol in Section 5.4.4 which allows each node to determine which of its detection neighbors are inside or outside of the zone. Thus, we assume in the following that Zones at least contains the information which of its detection neighbors are in $\mathcal{Z}$ and which are in $\overline{\mathcal{Z}}$.

Lemma 5.3. *Detections stored at $\mathcal{S}_i$ is complete regarding the object $\mathbf{O}$ and time t if $\mathcal{S}_i$ detects $\mathbf{O}$ at t and obtains all list elements for Detections regarding $\mathbf{O}$ originating from its detection neighbors $\mathcal{DN}_i$.*

Proof. We prove this by showing that there cannot exist a node $\mathcal{S}_j \notin \mathcal{DN}_i$ that detects $\mathbf{O}$ at t. $\mathcal{S}_j \notin \mathcal{DN}_i$ implies that the detection areas of $\mathcal{S}_i$ and $\mathcal{S}_j$ do not overlap, i.e., $\mathbf{DA}_i \cap \mathbf{DA}_j = \emptyset$. Thus, there does not exist a $\mathsf{p} \in \mathbb{E}^d$ where $\mathcal{S}_i$ and $\mathcal{S}_j$ can detect $\mathbf{O}$ simultaneously. Hence, $\mathcal{S}_j$ cannot detect $\mathbf{O}$ at t. ∎

Lemma 5.3 limits the nodes from which $\mathcal{S}_i$ must acquire list elements for Detections to the detection neighbors $\mathcal{DN}_i$. By taking into account that $\mathcal{S}_i$ is either in $\mathcal{Z}$ or $\overline{\mathcal{Z}}$ we actually can compute a correct detection scenario without Detections being complete.

Definition 50 (Semi-Completeness): *Detections regarding $\mathbf{O}$ and t stored at a node $\mathcal{S}_i \in \mathcal{Z}$ is semi-complete if it contains all list elements $[\mathcal{S}_j, \mathbf{O}, t_1, t_2]$ with $t_1 \leq t \leq t_2$ where $\mathcal{S}_j \in \mathcal{DN}_i^{\overline{\mathcal{Z}}}$.*

Detections regarding $\mathbf{O}$ and t stored at a node $\mathcal{S}_i \in \overline{\mathcal{Z}}$ is semi-complete if it contains all list elements $[\mathcal{S}_j, \mathbf{O}, t_1, t_2]$ with $t_1 \leq t \leq t_2$ where $\mathcal{S}_j \in \mathcal{DN}_i^{\mathcal{Z}}$. □

The notion of semi-completeness is important, because it allows for a significant reduction of the number of nodes which must exchange list elements from **Detections** to determine a detection scenario.

Lemma 5.4. *Let S_i detect $\mathbf{O}$ at t. Without loss of generality, let $S_i \in \mathcal{Z}$. If Detections stored at S_i is semi-complete regarding $\mathbf{O}$ and t, the computation of the detection scenario at S_i according to Table 5.1 is correct.*

Proof. Since S_i detects $\mathbf{O}$, $\texttt{isDetecting}(\mathcal{Z}, t, \mathbf{O}) = \mathcal{T}$. Thus, only $\texttt{isDetecting}(\overline{\mathcal{Z}}, t, \mathbf{O})$ remains to be computed by S_i. This only requires list elements from nodes in $\overline{\mathcal{Z}}$ as shown in Algorithm 6, i.e., $\mathcal{S}^* = \overline{\mathcal{Z}}$. ∎

Lemma 5.4 implies that the detection scenario computation is still correct if **Detections** contains only list elements from a subset of certain detection neighbors. This reduces the communication, because this set is empty for most nodes.

Definition 51 (Border Node): S_i is a *border node* if

- $S_i \in \mathcal{Z}$ and $\mathcal{DN}_i^{\overline{\mathcal{Z}}} \neq \varnothing$, or
- $S_i \in \overline{\mathcal{Z}}$ and $\mathcal{DN}_i^{\mathcal{Z}} \neq \varnothing$. □

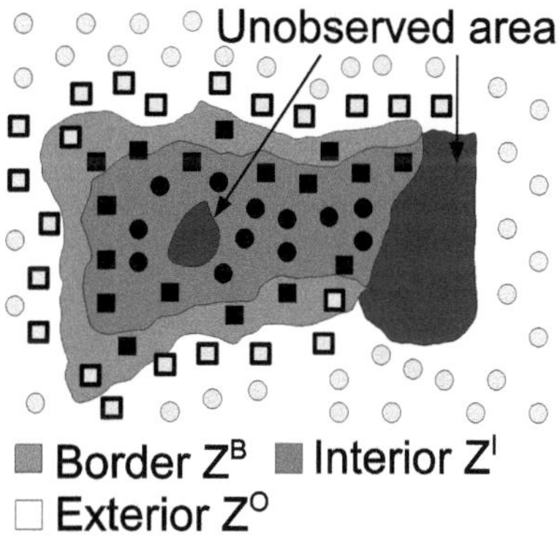

Figure 5.1: Border Nodes

Figure 5.1 illustrates the concept of border nodes using the deployment and zone partitioning for zone $\mathcal{Z}$ in Figure 3.5: Non-border nodes inside $\mathcal{Z}$ are represented by black-colored circles. Black-colored squares correspond to border nodes inside $\mathcal{Z}$. Similarly, grey-colored squares and

5.4. DISTRIBUTED OBJECT-INFORMATION COLLECTION

circles correspond to border and non-border nodes outside of $\mathcal{Z}$, respectively. A significant share of the nodes in this scenario are non-border nodes. According to Lemma 5.5, non-border nodes can compute detection scenarios without obtaining elements for **Detections** originating from any detection neighbor. This reduces the amount of communication and thus conserves energy.

Lemma 5.5. *If a non-border node $\mathcal{S}_i$ detects $\mathbf{O}$ at t and modifies* **Detections** *accordingly,* **Detections** *stored at $\mathcal{S}_i$ is semi-complete.*

Proof. Without loss of generality let $\mathcal{S}_i \in \mathcal{Z}$ and $\mathcal{DN}_i^{\overline{\mathcal{Z}}} = \emptyset$, i.e., $\mathcal{S}_i$ is not a border node. $\mathcal{DN}_i^{\overline{\mathcal{Z}}} = \emptyset$ implies that there does not exist a node $\mathcal{S}_j \in \overline{\mathcal{Z}}$ whose detection area overlaps with the detection area of $\mathcal{S}_i$. Thus, simultaneous detection of an object by $\mathcal{S}_i$ and some $\mathcal{S}_j \in \overline{\mathcal{Z}}$ is not possible by definition. Hence, detection of an object $\mathbf{O}$ by $\mathcal{S}_i$ implies $\texttt{isDetecting}\left(\overline{\mathcal{Z}}, t, \mathbf{O}\right) = \mathcal{F}$ and $\texttt{isDetecting}\left(\mathcal{Z}, t, \mathbf{O}\right) = \mathcal{T}$. ∎

Summing up, non-border nodes do not exchange any elements stored in **Detections** with detection neighbors to compute a detection scenario. As illustrated by Figure 5.1, the portion of border nodes is relatively small compared to the number of non-border nodes.

Depending on the structure of the development $\mathbb{P}(\mathbf{O}, \mathcal{Z})$ queried, the concept of border nodes allows for further reduction of communication as shown by Lemma 5.6:

Lemma 5.6. *Let $\mathbb{P}(\mathbf{O}, \mathcal{Z}) = P_1(\mathbf{O}, \mathcal{Z}) \triangleright P_2(\mathbf{O}, \mathcal{Z})$.* **Detections** *and the resulting list elements stored in* **Detections** *originating from non-border nodes are not necessary to process $\mathbb{P}(\mathbf{O}, \mathcal{Z})$.*

Proof. Without loss of generality, assume the non-border node $\mathcal{S}_i$ detects $\mathbf{O}$ at time t_1 and derives a detection scenario DS^* that yields $P_1(\mathbf{O}, \mathcal{Z}) = \mathcal{T}$ according to Table 3.3. If $\mathbf{O}$ fulfills $\mathbb{P}(\mathbf{O}, \mathcal{Z})$ at some time $t_2 > t_1$, there will be a border node $\mathcal{S}_j$ that detects $\mathbf{O}$ and computes DS^*. Thus, $\mathcal{S}_j$ derives $P_1(\mathbf{O}, \mathcal{Z}) = \mathcal{T}$ as well and if $\mathbf{O}$ fulfills $\mathbb{P}(\mathbf{O}, \mathcal{Z})$ this must be followed directly by $P_2(\mathbf{O}, \mathcal{Z}) = \mathcal{T}$. If no such border node exists, $\mathbf{O}$ does not fulfill $\mathbb{P}(\mathbf{O}, \mathcal{Z})$ and therefore $\mathbf{O}$ is irrelevant regarding the users interest. Hence, the detection of a non-border node is irrelevant for developments like $\mathbb{P}(\mathbf{O}, \mathcal{Z})$. ∎

Lemma 5.6 refers to developments constructed using $\triangleright$ exclusively. Sensor nodes typically have a *deep-sleep mode* [113] which reduces their energy consumption significantly. Recall from Section 2.1 that most sensor nodes support different sleep modes which reduce power consumption by order of magnitude by switching off unused hardware components. Appendix A provides a comparison of the energy consumption of Sun SPOTs using different sleep modes. According to Lemma 5.6, non-border nodes can employ such a deep-sleep mode to conserve energy while developments like Enter$(\mathbf{O}, \mathcal{Z})$ are processed. These non-border nodes only have to wake up occasionally to forward results to the base station. Next, we propose two strategies which allow a node $\mathcal{S}_i$ that detects $\mathbf{O}$ to efficiently obtain list elements for **Detections** originating from detection neighbors to compute the detection scenario.

5.4.1 Reactive Strategy

The core idea of the *reactive strategy* is as follows: At query-dissemination time, each node has received $\mathbb{P}(\mathbf{O}, \mathcal{Z})$. Each predicate of the development is related to a detection scenario according to Table 3.3. For instance, for WSNEnter$(\mathbf{O}, \mathcal{Z})$ each node knows that only DS^E and DS^I are relevant. When an object $\mathbf{O}$ enters or leaves the detection area of $\mathcal{S}_i$ at time t, $\mathcal{S}_i$ checks if this possibly results in a predicate $P(\mathbf{O}, \mathcal{Z})$ of $\mathbb{P}(\mathbf{O}, \mathcal{Z})$ being true. If so, $\mathcal{S}_i$ requests list elements for **Detections** regarding $\mathbf{O}$ from some or all of its detection neighbors. $\mathcal{S}_i$ stores each list element from the detection neighbors and computes a detection scenario DS^* after the list elements from all detection neighbors have arrived. If DS^* yields $P(\mathbf{O}, \mathcal{Z}) = \mathcal{T}$ for any $\mathbb{P}(\mathbf{O}, \mathcal{Z})$, $\mathcal{S}_i$ notifies the base station. A core question is: "When $\mathcal{S}_i$ detects $\mathbf{O}$, which detection neighbors could have elements stored in their **Detections**-list that are relevant to compute the detection scenario?" The answer to this question depends on three aspects whenever a node $\mathcal{S}_i$ detects or stops detecting an object $\mathbf{O}$:

- The predicates $P(\mathbf{O}, \mathcal{Z})$ that form $\mathbb{P}(\mathbf{O}, \mathcal{Z})$.
- Whether $\mathcal{S}_i \in \mathcal{Z}$ or $\mathcal{S}_i \in \overline{\mathcal{Z}}$.
- Whether $\mathbf{O}$ has entered or left the detection area $\mathbf{DA}_i$.

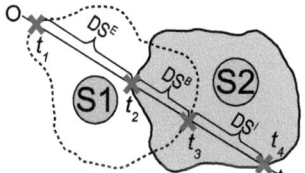
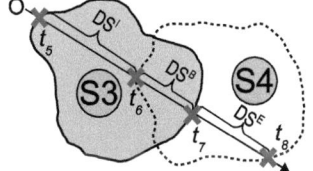

Figure 5.2: Detection events when $\mathbf{O}$ moves into $\mathcal{Z}$ ($\mathcal{S}_1 \in \mathcal{Z}$, $\mathcal{S}_2 \in \overline{\mathcal{Z}}$)

Figure 5.3: Detection events when $\mathbf{O}$ leaves $\mathcal{Z}$ ($\mathcal{S}_3 \in \mathcal{Z}$, $\mathcal{S}_4 \in \overline{\mathcal{Z}}$)

Table 5.2 summarizes from which detection neighbors $\mathcal{S}_i$ has to request list elements for **Detections** from to check if a given detection scenario has occurred when $\mathcal{S}_i$ detects $\mathbf{O}$. In the following, we explain these cells, using Figures 5.2 and 5.3 as an illustration. Figure 5.2 shows two nodes $\mathcal{S}_1$ and $\mathcal{S}_2$, their respective detection areas and the trajectory of an object $\mathbf{O}$. $\mathcal{S}_2$ is in $\mathcal{Z}$ and $\mathcal{S}_1$ is not in $\mathcal{Z}$, i.e., $\mathcal{S}_1 \in \overline{\mathcal{Z}}$. The trajectory of $\mathbf{O}$ shows that the object moves into $\mathcal{Z}$ and the instants of time where $\mathbf{O}$ either enters or leaves a detection area are marked t_i with $1 \le i \le 4$. Similarly, Figure 5.3 shows an object that leaves $\mathcal{Z}$. To ease presentation, we use nodes $\mathcal{S}_3$ and $\mathcal{S}_4$ as well as time instants marked t_i with $5 \le i \le 8$ to discuss this case.

The first row of Table 5.2 is related to DS^I, i.e., $\mathbb{P}(\mathbf{O}, \mathcal{Z})$ contains *Inside*$(\mathbf{O}, \mathcal{Z})$. There are two cases that can lead to DS^I:

(1) An object enters the detection area $\mathbf{DA}_i$ of a node $\mathcal{S}_i \in \mathcal{Z}$.

5.4. DISTRIBUTED OBJECT-INFORMATION COLLECTION

(2) An object leaves $\mathbf{DA}_j$ of $\mathcal{S}_j \in \overline{\mathcal{Z}}$.

For all other detection events, no communication is required, as reflected by the '∅' entries.

	Reactive	$\mathcal{S}_i \in \mathcal{Z}$	$\mathcal{S}_i \in \overline{\mathcal{Z}}$
DS^I	Entry	$\mathcal{DN}_i^{\overline{\mathcal{Z}}}$	∅
	Exit	∅	$\mathcal{DN}_i$
DS^B	Entry	$\mathcal{DN}_i^{\overline{\mathcal{Z}}}$	$\mathcal{DN}_i^{\mathcal{Z}}$
	Exit	∅	∅
DS^E	Entry	∅	$\mathcal{DN}_i^{\mathcal{Z}}$
	Exit	$\mathcal{DN}_i$	∅

Table 5.2: Detection-neighbor partitions for the reactive strategy

Case **(1)** occurs at t_2 in Figure 5.2 and t_5 in Figure 5.3. Applying Lemma 5.4, $\mathcal{S}_2$ only requires list elements for **Detections** from its detection neighbors outside of $\mathcal{Z}$, i.e., $\mathcal{DN}_2^{\overline{\mathcal{Z}}}$, to compute the detection scenario at t_2. The corresponding $\mathcal{DN}_i^{\overline{\mathcal{Z}}}$ entry in Table 5.2 reflects this. At t_2, $\mathcal{S}_1 \in \mathcal{DN}_2^{\overline{\mathcal{Z}}}$ returns a list element $[\mathcal{S}_1, \mathbf{O}, t_1, \emptyset]$. From this, $\mathcal{S}_2$ can derive that $\mathcal{S}_1$ and $\mathcal{S}_2$ detect $\mathbf{O}$ simultaneously, i.e., DS^I did not occur. Contrary to this, $\mathcal{S}_3$ derives DS^I for $\mathbf{O}$ for t_5 because its only detection neighbor $\mathcal{S}_4$ does not detect $\mathbf{O}$ at this time.

Case **(2)** is different, because objects leave $\mathbf{DA}_{i,}j$ of $\mathcal{S}_j \in \overline{\mathcal{Z}}$, i.e., $\mathcal{S}_j$ does not detect the object any more and thus cannot apply Lemma 5.4. Hence, **Detections** stored at $\mathcal{S}_j$ has to be complete, i.e., $\mathcal{S}_j$ must request tuples from all detection neighbors. This is reflected by the $\mathcal{DN}_i$ entry in the first row of Table 5.2. This case occurs at t_3 in Figure 5.2 and t_8 in Figure 5.3. In both cases, the node outside of $\mathcal{Z}$ must verify that no other node outside of $\mathcal{Z}$ still detects the object, and that there is at least one node in $\mathcal{Z}$ detecting it. Hence, DS^I occurs at t_3 but not at t_8.

The second row of Table 5.2 is related to DS^B, i.e., $Meet(\mathbf{O}, \mathcal{Z})$ is part of $\mathbb{P}(\mathbf{O}, \mathcal{Z})$. DS^B requires simultaneous detection of $\mathbf{O}$ by nodes inside and outside of the zone $\mathcal{Z}$. Thus, when an object leaves a detection area, DS^B either already has occurred or does not occur at all, i.e., no communication is required. Contrary to that, objects entering a detection area can result in DS^B. This allows applying Lemma 5.4. Thus, if $\mathcal{S}_i \in \mathcal{Z}$, only tuples from $\mathcal{DN}_i^{\overline{\mathcal{Z}}}$ are required and vice versa.

The entries in Table 5.2 for DS^E, i.e., $\mathbb{P}(\mathbf{O}, \mathcal{Z})$ contains $Disjoint(\mathbf{O}, \mathcal{Z})$, are derived analogously to those for DS^I: An object detection can conform to DS^E the moment it enters the detection area of a node outside of $\mathcal{Z}$ or by leaving the detection area of a node in $\mathcal{Z}$. The first case occurs for $\mathcal{S}_1$ at t_1. Thus, $\mathcal{S}_1$ requests list elements from $\mathcal{S}_2$ at t_1 to ensure that $\mathcal{S}_2$ does not detect $\mathbf{O}$ simultaneously. In this case, $\mathcal{S}_2$ indicates that it does not detect $\mathbf{O}$ at t_1 and thus DS^E occurs which yields $Disjoint(\mathbf{O}, \mathcal{Z}) = \mathcal{T}$. Similarly, $\mathcal{S}_3 \in \mathcal{Z}$ has to request list elements from all detection neighbors at t_7, because Lemma 5.4 is inapplicable. This is because $\mathcal{S}_3$ does not detect $\mathbf{O}$ anymore. In this case, DS^E occurs because $\mathcal{S}_4 \in \mathcal{DN}_3^{\overline{\mathcal{Z}}}$ detects $\mathbf{O}$.

Algorithm 8: Reactive Strategy	
1	**When O** *enters or leaves the detection area of* $\mathcal{S}_i$ **do**
2	Modify **Detections** as described in Section 5.2;
3	$\mathcal{DN}_i^* \leftarrow$ Set of detection neighbors that must be queried according to Table 5.2 ;
4	Request list elements regarding **O** from every node in $\mathcal{DN}_i^*$;
5	Wait for response from every node in $\mathcal{DN}_i^*$;
6	Determine detection scenario DS* according to Table 5.1;
7	Notify base station if DS* yields $P(\mathbf{O}, \mathcal{Z}) = \mathcal{T}$ for any $P(\mathbf{O}, \mathcal{Z})$ in $\mathbb{P}(\mathbf{O}, \mathcal{Z})$;
8	**end**

Algorithm 8 summarizes the reactive strategy. When **O** enters or leaves the detection area of $\mathcal{S}_i$ at t, $\mathcal{S}_i$ modifies **Detections** accordingly. Afterwards, $\mathcal{S}_i$ requests tuples on **O** from a set $\mathcal{DN}_i^*$ of detection neighbors. Each response from a detection neighbor is inserted into **Detections** stored at $\mathcal{S}_i$. We address node failures, i.e., cases where nodes in $\mathcal{DN}_i^*$ fail to respond to the request sent by $\mathcal{S}_i$ in Section 5.4.5.

After all detection neighbors have responded, $\mathcal{S}_i$ determines the detection scenario DS*. The base station is notified if DS* yields $P(\mathbf{O}, \mathcal{Z}) = \mathcal{T}$ for any $P(\mathbf{O}, \mathcal{Z})$ in $\mathbb{P}(\mathbf{O}, \mathcal{Z})$. This is necessary, because for example with Enter$(\mathbf{O}, \mathcal{Z})$, an arbitrary node that determines *Inside*$(\mathbf{O}, \mathcal{Z})$ for some object **O** cannot determine if **O** has conformed to *Disjoint*$(\mathbf{O}, \mathcal{Z})$ or *Meet*$(\mathbf{O}, \mathcal{Z})$ previously. Since objects may enter and leave the detection area of a node $\mathcal{S}_i$ repeatedly, this can result in sending multiple notifications regarding the same object and predicate to the base station. It depends on the query, if such a notification is redundant or required for query processing: For $\mathbb{P}(\mathbf{O}, \mathcal{Z})$ = Enter$(\mathbf{O}, \mathcal{Z})$, multiple notifications on a single predicate are obviously redundant because every predicate occurs once in Enter$(\mathbf{O}, \mathcal{Z})$. Contrary to that, developments like Touch$(\mathbf{O}, \mathcal{Z})$ possibly require multiple notifications regarding a single predicate, e.g., *Disjoint*$(\mathbf{O}, \mathcal{Z})$, and these may originate from the same node:

$$\text{Touch}(\mathbf{O}, \mathcal{Z}) = \textit{Disjoint}(\mathbf{O}, \mathcal{Z}) \triangleright \textit{Meet}(\mathbf{O}, \mathcal{Z}) \triangleright \textit{Disjoint}(\mathbf{O}, \mathcal{Z}) \tag{5.2}$$

Section 5.4.6 addresses this problem.

5.4.2 Proactive Strategy

As illustrated in Algorithm 8, the reactive strategy requires communication for requesting tuples and for responding to these requests. The proactive strategy tries to avoid responses. Algorithm 9 outlines the proactive strategy, and the core idea is as follows: When **O** enters or leaves the detection area of $\mathcal{S}_i$ at t, $\mathcal{S}_i$ modifies the **Detections**-list it stores. This modification is either an insertion or an update of a list element in **Detections**. In case of an insertion, $\mathcal{S}_i$ adds an element E = $[\mathcal{S}_i, \mathbf{O}, t, \emptyset]$ with Detections.add(E). An update indicates that **O** left $\mathbf{DA}_i$, i.e., some element $[\mathcal{S}_i, \mathbf{O}, t_1, \emptyset]$ is changed to $[\mathcal{S}_i, \mathbf{O}, t_1, t_2]$ (cf. Section 5.2). Afterwards, $\mathcal{S}_i$ immediately sends the modified list

5.4. DISTRIBUTED OBJECT-INFORMATION COLLECTION

element to a subset $\mathcal{DN}_i^*$ of its detection neighbors. Each detection neighbor $\mathcal{S}_j \in \mathcal{DN}_i^*$ stores the modified tuple. This ensures that **Detections** stored at $\mathcal{S}_i$ and each $\mathcal{S}_j$ is semi-complete as long as either node detects **O**. According to Lemma 5.4, $\mathcal{S}_i$ and any $\mathcal{S}_j \in \mathcal{DN}_i^*$ that currently detects **O** can compute the detection scenario correctly.

Algorithm 9: Proactive Strategy

1 **When O** *enters/leaves detection area of* $\mathcal{S}_i$ **do**
2   Modify **Detections** as described in Section 5.2;
3     $\mathcal{DN}_i^* \leftarrow$ Detection neighbors determined according to Table 5.3;
4   Send updated tuple(s) to every node in $\mathcal{DN}_i^*$;
5   **if O** *entered the detection area of* $\mathcal{S}_i$ **then**
6   Goto Line 12;
7   **end**
8 **end**
9 **When** $\mathcal{S}_i$ *receives updated tuples about* **O** *from a detection neighbor* $\mathcal{S}_j$ **do**
10   Insert updated tuples into **Detections**;
11   **if O** *left the detection area of* $\mathcal{S}_j$ *and* $\mathcal{S}_i$ *detects* **O** **then**
12   Wait a timeout t_{delay};
13   Determine detection scenario DS* according to Table 5.1;
14   Notify base station if DS* yields $P(\mathbf{O}, \mathcal{Z}) = \mathcal{T}$ for any $P(\mathbf{O}, \mathcal{Z})$ in $\mathbb{P}(\mathbf{O}, \mathcal{Z})$;
15   **end**
16 **end**

Algorithm 9 consists of two parts: The first part is only executed by the node $\mathcal{S}_i$ whose detection area is either entered or left by **O**. First, $\mathcal{S}_i$ must modify the locally stored version of **Detections**. Second, if $\mathcal{S}_i \in \mathcal{Z}$, the detection neighbors outside of $\mathcal{Z}$, i.e., $\mathcal{DN}_i^{\overline{\mathcal{Z}}}$, must be informed about this change. Last, $\mathcal{S}_i$ must compute a detection scenario if **O** entered $\mathbf{DA}_i$. Before $\mathcal{S}_i$ can do so it has to wait t_{delay} to ensure that nodes whose detection areas were entered simultaneously get time to report their updates. For our reference implementation this delay was 10 seconds. If the object left $\mathbf{DA}_i$, **Detections** stored at $\mathcal{S}_i$ is not semi-complete anymore.

The second part starting at Line 9 is executed by by nodes receiving the update from the node whose detection area was either entered or left by **O**. As expected, each node must update the locally stored list **Detections**. Next, the node that received the update must determine if it has to compute a detection scenario: If the update indicates that **O** entered a detection area, the node does not have to trigger the computation of a detection scenario, because the node who sent the update will compute it. If **O** left the detection area, the node receiving the update can only compute a new detection scenario if the node itself detects **O**.

As with the reactive strategy, when an object enters and leaves the detection area of a single node more than once, multiple notifications are sent to the base station. Section 5.4.6 shows how to reduce communication related to redundant notifications sent from arbitrary nodes to the base station.

Again, the important step is determining the set $\mathcal{DN}_i^*$ in Line 3 since it determines the number of messages. Analogously to the reactive strategy, Table 5.3 lists which detection neighbors must receive an update to ensure semi-completeness, for each detection scenario. Similarly to the reactive strategy, we explain each cell using the trajectories in Figures 5.2 and 5.3 as examples.

Proactive		$S_i \in \mathcal{Z}$	$S_i \in \overline{\mathcal{Z}}$
DS^I	Entry	∅	$\mathcal{DN}_i^\mathcal{Z}$i
	Exit	∅	$\mathcal{DN}_i^\mathcal{Z}$i
DS^B	Entry	$\mathcal{DN}_i^{\overline{\mathcal{Z}}}$i	$\mathcal{DN}_i^\mathcal{Z}$i
	Exit	$\mathcal{DN}_i^{\overline{\mathcal{Z}}}$i	$\mathcal{DN}_i^\mathcal{Z}$i
DS^E	Entry	$\mathcal{DN}_i^{\overline{\mathcal{Z}}}$i	∅
	Exit	$\mathcal{DN}_i^{\overline{\mathcal{Z}}}$i	∅

Table 5.3: Detection-neighbor partitions for the proactive strategy

Recall that DS^I can either occur (1) when an object enters the detection area of a node inside the zone or (2) when the detection area of a node outside of the zone is left. An object detection conforming to DS^I requires at least one node $S_i \in \mathcal{Z}$ to detect the object. If such a detection occurs, S_i must determine if there exists a simultaneous detection by another node $S_j \in \overline{\mathcal{Z}}$. Case (1) occurs at t_2 in Figure 5.2 and at t_5 in Figure 5.3. To compute the detection scenario correctly at t_2, S_2 must know that $S_1 \in \overline{\mathcal{Z}}$ currently detects $\mathbf{O}$. Case (2) occurs when $\mathbf{O}$ leaves the detection area of S_1 at t_3. In this case, the information at S_2 is updated, and S_1 then correctly determines DS^I for $\mathbf{O}$. Regarding $\mathbf{O}$ in Figure 5.3, S_3 computes DS^I at t_5, because there do not exist any relevant detections by any $S_i \in \overline{\mathcal{Z}}$. Summing up, if the query requires DS^I, nodes outside of the zone must send updates to their detection neighbors inside the zone whenever objects enter/leave their detection areas.

DS^B requires simultaneous detection by nodes in $\mathcal{Z}$ as well as $\overline{\mathcal{Z}}$. Thus, every $S_i \in \mathcal{Z}$ must be informed about detections of detection neighbors in $\overline{\mathcal{Z}}$ and vice versa. The entries in the row corresponding to DS^B in Table 5.3 reflect this.

5.4.3 ZIP – Zone Information Protocol

So far, we assumed that the entries in Zones are available and that nodes are able to partition their detection neighbors into $\mathcal{DN}_i^\mathcal{Z}$ and $\mathcal{DN}_i^{\overline{\mathcal{Z}}}$. As illustrated in Table 3.1, for static regions this assumption is valid by definition, because $\mathbf{C}_\mathcal{Z}$ resembles a list of node identifiers that are in $\mathcal{Z}$. After receiving $\mathbf{C}_\mathcal{Z}$ at time t, every node S_i inserts an element $[S_j,t,\emptyset]$ into Zones stored at S_i for every S_j in $\mathbf{C}_\mathcal{Z}$. Based on this information, S_i determines $\mathcal{DN}_i^\mathcal{Z}$ and $\mathcal{DN}_i^{\overline{\mathcal{Z}}}$ by iterating once

5.4. DISTRIBUTED OBJECT-INFORMATION COLLECTION

through Zones, i.e., detection neighbors that have no corresponding entry in Zones are in $\mathcal{DN}_i^{\overline{Z}}$. Neither Zones nor $\mathcal{DN}_i^{Z}$ and $\mathcal{DN}_i^{\overline{Z}}$ needs to be updated at any time afterwards, because the zone is static.

With dynamic zones, this is different because nodes may join or leave $\mathcal{Z}$ at any time. To ensure that spatio-temporal query processing derives correct results after a node $\mathcal{S}_i$ joins or leaves $\mathcal{Z}$ the following steps must be completed:

1. $\mathcal{S}_i$ must notify all of its detection neighbors $\mathcal{DN}_i$ that it joined or left $\mathcal{Z}$ at time $t \in \mathbb{T}$.
2. If $\mathcal{S}_i$ detects an object **O** while joining/leaving $\mathcal{Z}$, $\mathcal{S}_i$ must compute a new detection scenario for **O**. This requires collecting information on **O** from detection neighbors that were irrelevant for detection-scenario computation previously.

The reasoning behind the second step is illustrated by Example 13:

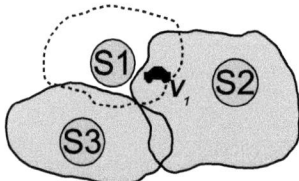
Figure 5.4: Sensor network before $\mathcal{S}_2$ leaves the zone $\mathcal{Z}$ ($\mathcal{S}_2, \mathcal{S}_3 \in \mathcal{Z}$)

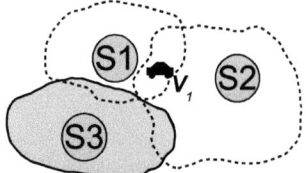
Figure 5.5: Sensor network after $\mathcal{S}_2$ left the zone $\mathcal{Z}$ ($\mathcal{S}_3 \in \mathcal{Z}$)

Example 13: Figure 5.4 shows three detection neighbors $\mathcal{S}_1$, $\mathcal{S}_2$ and $\mathcal{S}_3$ and a vehicle **V**$_1$ at some time t_i. At this time, $\mathcal{S}_2$ and $\mathcal{S}_3$ are in a dynamic zone $\mathcal{Z}$. The vehicle **V**$_1$ is detected by $\mathcal{S}_1$ and $\mathcal{S}_2$, but not by $\mathcal{S}_3$. Thus, **V**$_1$ is detected with DS^B. At t_{i+1}, $\mathcal{S}_2$ determines that $\mathsf{C}_\mathcal{Z}(\mathcal{S}_2) = \mathcal{F}$, i.e., $\mathcal{S}_2$ leaves $\mathcal{Z}$ at t_{i+1}, as illustrated by Figure 5.5. This change also affects the detection scenario of **V**$_1$ even if it has not moved at all because it is detected exclusively by nodes outside of $\mathcal{Z}$ at t_{i+1}, i.e., DS^E occurs which yields $Disjoint\,(\mathbf{O}, \mathcal{Z}) = \mathcal{T}$. ♦

A straightforward approach to accomplish both steps would be sending the notification first, sending the list of objects detected by $\mathcal{S}_i$ next and then sending all **Detections**-lists stored at detection neighbors of $\mathcal{S}_i$ back to $\mathcal{S}_i$. In the following, we show that this is inefficient and provide a better approach that exploits the characteristics of the data collection strategies described above. The Zone Information Protocol ensures semi-completeness after $\mathcal{S}_i$ joins/leaves $\mathcal{Z}$ while reducing communication and thus reducing energy consumption. To ease the presentation, we present ZIP in three algorithms that represent the three phases of ZIP:

P.1 Notify all detection neighbors $\mathcal{DN}_i$ of the node $\mathcal{S}_i$ that joined/left $\mathcal{Z}$.

P.2 Collect object-detection information from detection neighbors of S_i to ensure semi-completeness for correct detection scenario computation.

P.3 Recompute the detection scenario for every object detected while S_i joined/left $\mathcal{Z}$.

Algorithm 10: P.1 of ZIP – Notifying detection neighbors
1   **When** S_i *joins or leaves* $\mathcal{Z}$ *at* t_i **do**
2   List L ← ∅
3   **for** *all elements E in* **Detections** *where* $E.\text{NodeID} = S_i$ *and* $E.t_{exit}^O = \emptyset$ **do**
4   L.add(E)
5   **end**
6   Send notification containing L to every $S_j \in \mathcal{DN}_i$
7       $\mathcal{DN}_i^* \leftarrow$ Set of detection neighbors from which responses to the notification are expected
8   Wait until all nodes in $\mathcal{DN}_i^*$ have responded and continue in Algorithm 12
9   **end**

Phase **P.1** of ZIP is illustrated in Algorithm 10 After S_i joins or leaves $\mathcal{Z}$, it generates a list L of all objects that are currently in the detection area **DA**$_i$. This list is attached to the notification that S_i either left or joined $\mathcal{Z}$. S_i sends this notification to all $S_j \in \mathcal{DN}_i$, i.e., all detection neighbors of S_i.

In Line 7, S_i computes a set $\mathcal{DN}_i^*$ of detection neighbors from which it expects a response regarding the notification it just sent. The core idea to compute $\mathcal{DN}_i^*$ at this point is as follows: According to Lemma 5.4, it is sufficient for correct detection scenario computation of a node $S_i \in \mathcal{Z}$ that detects **O** at t requests list elements from $\mathcal{DN}_i^{\overline{\mathcal{Z}}}$ and vice versa. This is applicable to detection-scenario computation for the time t when S_i joined or left $\mathcal{Z}$ as well. Thus, if $S_i \in \mathcal{Z}$ after t, i.e., after S_i joined $\mathcal{Z}$, all nodes $S_j \in \mathcal{DN}_i^{\overline{\mathcal{Z}}}$ must respond by sending a list of all objects detected at t. Analogously, if S_i left $\mathcal{Z}$ at t, i.e., $S_i \in \overline{\mathcal{Z}}$ at t, all nodes $S_j \in \mathcal{DN}_i^{\mathcal{Z}}$ must inform S_i about objects they detected at t. Example 14 illustrates this idea.

Example 14: Continuing Example 13, S_2 left $\mathcal{Z}$, i.e., $S_2 \in \overline{\mathcal{Z}}$ at t_{i+1}. To determine the detection scenario for t_{i+1}, S_2 requires list elements from $\mathcal{DN}_2^{\mathcal{Z}}$. Thus, S_2 only expects a response from $\mathcal{DN}_2^{\mathcal{Z}}$, i.e., S_3, but not from $\mathcal{DN}_2^{\overline{\mathcal{Z}}} = \{S_1\}$. ◆

Note that any detection neighbor S_j can determine if it must reply to the notification sent by S_i by using the same idea: If $S_i \in \mathcal{Z}$ and $S_j \in \overline{\mathcal{Z}}$ or if $S_i \in \overline{\mathcal{Z}}$ and $S_j \in \mathcal{Z}$, the recipient of the notification must send a response to S_i that contains all objects currently detected by S_j. Algorithm 11 illustrates this. As shown in Algorithm 12, every response that the node which joined or left $\mathcal{Z}$ receives, results in new elements in **Detections** stored at S_i. After all responses have arrived, i.e., S_i received replies from all nodes in $\mathcal{DN}_i^*$ computed in Line 7 of Algorithm 10, the computation of detection scenarios as described in Section 5.2 starts. With this we conclude our discussion regarding distributed processing of spatio-temporal queries in the context of dynamic

5.4. DISTRIBUTED OBJECT-INFORMATION COLLECTION

Algorithm 11: P.2 of ZIP – Responding to Notifications

1 **When** $\mathcal{S}_j$ *receives notification that* $\mathcal{S}_i$ *joined/left* $\mathcal{Z}$ *at* t_i **do**
2   Modify the element corresponding to $\mathcal{S}_i$ in Zones (cf. Section 5.2)
3   **if** *($\mathcal{S}_i \in \mathcal{Z}$ and $\mathcal{S}_j \in \overline{\mathcal{Z}}$) or ($\mathcal{S}_i \in \overline{\mathcal{Z}}$ and $\mathcal{S}_j \in \mathcal{Z}$)* **then**
4   List $\mathsf{L}_{\mathcal{S}_j} \leftarrow \emptyset$
5   **for** *all elements E in Detections where* $E.\mathtt{NodeID} = \mathcal{S}_j$ *and* $E.t_{exit}^O = \emptyset$ **do**
6              $\mathsf{L}_{\mathcal{S}_j}.\mathtt{add}(E)$
7   **end**
8   Send $\mathsf{L}_{\mathcal{S}_j}$ to $\mathcal{S}_i$;
9   **end**
10 **end**

Algorithm 12: P.3 of ZIP – Recomputing detection scenarios

1 **When** $\mathcal{S}_i$ *receives response regarding zone change at* t_i *from* $\mathcal{S}_j$ **do**
2   Insert all elements from $\mathsf{L}_{\mathcal{S}_j}$ into Detections stored at $\mathcal{S}_i$
3 **end**
4 **When** $\mathcal{S}_i$ *has received responses from all nodes in* $\mathcal{S}^*$ *computed in Algorithm 10* **do**
5   **for** *Objects* $\mathbf{O}$ *detected by* $\mathcal{S}_i$ *at* t_i **do**
6   Determine detection scenario $\mathtt{DS}^*$ according to Table 5.1
7   Notify base station if $\mathtt{DS}^*$ yields $P(\mathbf{O}, \mathcal{Z}) = \mathcal{T}$ for any $P(\mathbf{O}, \mathcal{Z})$ in $\mathbb{P}(\mathbf{O}, \mathcal{Z})$
8   **end**
9 **end**

zones. The evaluation shows that ZIP reduces communication significantly compared to sending all list elements to the base station.

5.4.4 Detection Neighbor Approximation

As stated in Section 3.1, there exist detection mechanisms where the detection area is indeterminable. In this case, nodes cannot determine their detection neighbors. To solve this problem, we use a superset $\widetilde{\mathcal{DN}}_i$ which contains at least all detection neighbors $\mathcal{DN}_i$, i.e., $\mathcal{DN}_i \subseteq \widetilde{\mathcal{DN}}_i$. Using $\widetilde{\mathcal{DN}}_i$ instead of $\mathcal{DN}_i$ obviously still yields a correct result, because those nodes in $\widetilde{\mathcal{DN}}_i$ that are not detection neighbors of $\mathcal{S}_i$ cannot detect an object simultaneously. Several approaches to derive such a superset are conceivable, and we outline two of them:

Communication Neighbors: If the communication range can be assumed to be much larger than the maximum detection range, a valid superset is $\mathcal{CN}_i$ (cf. Definition 20), i.e., $\widetilde{\mathcal{DN}}_i = \mathcal{CN}_i$.

In this case, all detection neighbors are communication neighbors as well. This approach is applicable to most detection mechanisms used in WSN, and we use it for our evaluation.

Node Positions: Another approach is applicable if nodes know their position: The set $\widetilde{\mathcal{DN}}_i$ contains all nodes with a distance of at most $2 \cdot \mathcal{D}_{max}$ to $\mathcal{S}_i$.

The evaluation in Section 5.5 uses the approximation $\widetilde{\mathcal{DN}}_i = \mathcal{CN}_i$ and investigates the associated overhead. More sophisticated approaches to determine detection neighbors are a subject for future work as we discuss in Section 6.2.4.

5.4.5 Failure Handling

When a node fails, there are two possible consequences:

1. An object **O** that would have been detected is not detected.
2. Some nodes detect **O**, but the detection-scenario computation is possibly incorrect because it is based on an incomplete list **Detections**.

We have shown how users can express queries if they are interested in objects that are temporarily unobserved in Section 3.4.1. Therefore we focus on (2), i.e., we notify the user if query results returned could be incorrect due to node failures. We discuss the detection of failures first and continue with failure handling.

Failure Detection

It depends on the strategy used for data collection how failures are detected. A node $\mathcal{S}_i$ using the reactive strategy requests tuples from its detection neighbors $\mathcal{DN}_i^*$ and expects a response from each of them. If no such response has been received after a timeout, $\mathcal{S}_i$ derives that the detection neighbors whose responses are missing have failed.

The drawback of the proactive strategy is that nodes cannot detect failures of detection neighbors using missing responses. Without further measures, a failed node might not send updates to detection neighbors and thus affect query results. A practical approach to solve this is sending beacon messages periodically to detection neighbors. If beacon messages are missing from a detection neighbor, nodes will assume a failure. Our evaluation includes the additional messages induced by this. Note that this problem also occurs with the centralized strategy, i.e., additional messages are required to detect node failures if the centralized strategy is used.

Failure Handling

The user must be notified of a node failure if it could have an impact on the query result, i.e., if the computation of the detection scenario is incorrect. In the following, we refer to the node whose failure has been detected as $\mathcal{S}_f$. When $\mathcal{S}_i$ detects the failure of $\mathcal{S}_f \in \mathcal{DN}_i$ and computes a detection scenario later, the result is possibly incorrect. We denote the detection scenario computed based on an incomplete relation **Detections** with DS_{err}.

5.4. DISTRIBUTED OBJECT-INFORMATION COLLECTION

Lemma 5.7. *If $DS_{err} = DS^B$, the failure of S_f did not affect the computation of the detection scenario.*

Proof. According to Table 5.1, DS^B occurs if there exists at least one node in $\mathcal{Z}$ and one node from $\overline{\mathcal{Z}}$ that detect the object. This is independent from the potential detection of S_f and thus the detection scenario computation is not affected by the failure of S_f. ∎

Lemma 5.8. *If $DS_{err} = DS^I$ and $S_f \in \mathcal{Z}$ or $DS_{err} = DS^E$ and $S_f \in \overline{\mathcal{Z}}$, the failure of S_f did not affect the computation of the detection scenario.*

Proof. We prove this only for the case of $DS_{err} = DS^I$. The reasoning for $DS_{err} = DS^E$ is analogous. $DS_{err} = DS^I$ implies that there exists a node $S_j \in \mathcal{Z}$ that currently detects **O**. Since $S_f \in \mathcal{Z}$, an additional tuple originating from S_f would not change the result of the detection scenario computation. Hence, the failure of S_f cannot affect the result. ∎

Summing up, the base station must be notified of node failures in the following two cases:

- $DS_{err} = DS^I$, and $S_f \in \overline{\mathcal{Z}}$
- $DS_{err} = DS^E$, and $S_f \in \mathcal{Z}$

This notification is a message that contains DS_{err}, the identifier of the object detected and an identifier of S_f.

5.4.6 Distributed Notification Filtering

According to Algorithms 8, 9 and 12, nodes that compute a detection scenario DS^* which yields $P(\mathbf{O}, \mathcal{Z}) = \mathcal{T}$ for any predicate $P(\mathbf{O}, \mathcal{Z})$ in the query $\mathbb{P}(\mathbf{O}, \mathcal{Z})$ send a notification to the base station. Each of these notifications consists of an object identifier `ObjectID` and the predicate $P(\mathbf{O}, \mathcal{Z})$.

On the one hand, these notifications are necessary to determine if the trajectory of **O** conforms to the predicates in the order defined by $\mathbb{P}(\mathbf{O}, \mathcal{Z})$. On the other hand, objects could move repeatedly in and out of the same detection area. This would generate an arbitrary number of *redundant* notifications. We call a notification redundant, if the notification is related to a predicate $P(\mathbf{O}, \mathcal{Z})$ of $\mathbb{P}(\mathbf{O}, \mathcal{Z})$ for which another notification has been sent to the base station previously. Preventing these redundant notifications completely is problematic, because it would require coordination among many nodes of the sensor network which would require more communication than sending the redundant notifications. This problem is illustrated by Example 15.

Example 15: The sensor network in Figure 5.6 consists of 29 sensor nodes deployed as a grid and a base station $\mathcal{BS}$. Of these 29 nodes, there are four, specifically S_{22}, S_{23}, S_{28} and S_{29}, that form a static zone $\mathcal{Z}$. The solid, black edges between nodes indicate that the connected nodes are communication neighbors (cf. Definition 20). Assuming the user is interested in WSNEnter $(\mathbf{O}, \mathcal{Z})$, the base station must be notified if *Inside* $(\mathbf{O}, \mathcal{Z})$ or *Disjoint* $(\mathbf{O}, \mathcal{Z})$ occurs.

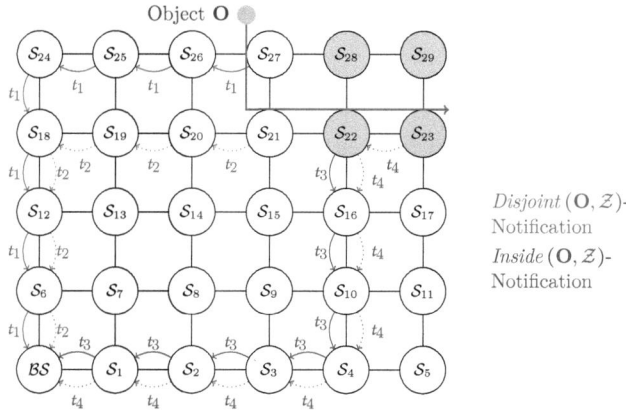

Figure 5.6: Example for redundant notifications

The blue line represents the trajectory of the object **O** and $\mathcal{S}_{27}$ is the first to detect **O** at t_1. Assuming the detection-scenario computation at $\mathcal{S}_{27}$ results in DS^E, $\mathcal{S}_{27}$ must send a notification regarding $Disjoint(\mathbf{O}, \mathcal{Z}) = \mathcal{T}$ to the base station via 7 hops (solid, red lines). Next, $\mathcal{S}_{21}$ detects **O** and resulting in another notification regarding $Disjoint(\mathbf{O}, \mathcal{Z}) = \mathcal{T}$ at t_2 via 6 hops (red, dotted lines). Obviously, this notification is redundant, because $\mathcal{S}_{27}$ has previously sent the same notification at t_1. To prevent this and future notifications about $Disjoint(\mathbf{O}, \mathcal{Z})$, $\mathcal{S}_{27}$ would have to inform all other nodes where $Disjoint(\mathbf{O}, \mathcal{Z}) = \mathcal{T}$ could occur, i.e., all nodes outside of $\mathcal{Z}$, that further notifications regarding $Disjoint(\mathbf{O}, \mathcal{Z}) = \mathcal{T}$ are redundant. There are 29 − 4 = 25 such nodes in $\overline{\mathcal{Z}}$, i.e., the communication required to send this notification is much larger than just forwarding the notification. Note that informing 25 nodes does not equate 25 hops, but a much larger number of hops, because $\mathcal{S}_{27}$ cannot communicate with all of these nodes directly. This would change, if **O** would "visit" a sufficient number of nodes outside of $\mathcal{Z}$ resulting in a higher number of notifications.

At t_3, $\mathcal{S}_{22}$ detects **O** which results in DS^I and yields $Inside(\mathbf{O}, \mathcal{Z}) = \mathcal{T}$. This requires a notification to the base station which travels 7 hops. The following notification at t_4 is redundant, because the base station was notified about $Inside(\mathbf{O}, \mathcal{Z}) = \mathcal{T}$ previously. In this case, all nodes in $\mathcal{Z}$ would have to be informed after t_3 that $Inside(\mathbf{O}, \mathcal{Z})$ is not of interest anymore. Thus, informing these four nodes would pay off because it saves 8 hops for transmitting the second, redundant notification at t_4 (green, dotted line). This must be attributed to the small number of nodes inside $\mathcal{Z}$, i.e., with a larger zone it would not pay off.

Summing up, even with the small example in Figure 5.6, informing other nodes to prevent

5.4. DISTRIBUTED OBJECT-INFORMATION COLLECTION

redundant notifications is communication intensive and only pays of if the number of nodes which must be informed is very small. ◆

Note that the problem above is mainly relevant for queries with relaxed concatenation $\widetilde{\triangleright}$, because according to Lemma 5.6, only border nodes are active for queries with $\triangleright$. Thus, in the following, we focus on queries constructed using $\widetilde{\triangleright}$.

We conducted an in-depth performance study for networks with 100-400 nodes where redundant notifications are prevented completely. As illustrated by Example 15, preventing the redundant notifications is problematic, because in most cases the communication required for this coordination is larger then sending redundant notifications. Omitting the details, in general, these approaches only pay off in two cases: The first case occurs if the zone is very small, i.e., consists of few nodes, $\mathbb{P}(\mathbf{O}, \mathcal{Z})$ does not contain $Disjoint(\mathbf{O}, \mathcal{Z})$ and the objects move in repeating patterns through the same detection areas. This case is illustrated in Example 15. The second case is just the opposite, i.e., the zone almost covers the whole sensor network, $\mathbb{P}(\mathbf{O}, \mathcal{Z})$ does not contain $Inside(\mathbf{O}, \mathcal{Z})$ and objects move repeatedly through the same detection areas. Therefore, we provide a filtering approach that does not require any coordination among sensor nodes, but filters redundant notifications.

The core idea to filter notifications on the way between sensor nodes and the base station is illustrated in Figure 5.7: A sensor network can be viewed as a tree where the root is the base station and edges represent links to the base station over which notifications are forwarded. To filter out redundant notifications, each node $\mathcal{S}_i$ keeps a list of previously forwarded notifications. Whenever a notification must be forwarded by $\mathcal{S}_i$, this list is used to check if forwarding the notification is redundant. The notification is suppressed in this case. The actual route that a notification travels to reach the base station is determined by the routing protocol that is in use (cf. Section 2.1.2). As previously stated, choosing the route is complicated and the networking community has developed several promising routing protocols that solve this problem. We do not interfere with the routing decisions of these protocols and just use the approach outlined above to stop messages from being routed/forwarded at all.

When a node $\mathcal{S}_i$ receives a query, $\mathcal{S}_i$ generates a list **ForwardedPredicates** which represents the query $\mathbb{P}(\mathbf{O}, \mathcal{Z})$ and associates each predicate $P(\mathbf{O}, \mathcal{Z})$ with a list of object identifiers for which notifications regarding $P(\mathbf{O}, \mathcal{Z})$ have been forwarded previously by $\mathcal{S}_i$. Thus, every element in **ForwardedPredicates** has the following two attributes:

$P(\mathbf{O}, \mathcal{Z})$: The predicate $P(\mathbf{O}, \mathcal{Z})$ from $\mathbb{P}(\mathbf{O}, \mathcal{Z})$ this list entry corresponds to.

ForwardedObjID: A list of object identifiers. The node $\mathcal{S}_i$ storing **ForwardedPredicates** adds an object identifier ObjectID to this list, when it forwards a notification regarding $P(\mathbf{O}, \mathcal{Z}) = \mathcal{T}$ for an object identified by ObjectID towards the base station.

Algorithm 13 describes the initialization of **ForwardedPredicates**. It is important in the following that the order of the elements in **ForwardedPredicates** equals the order of the predicate in $\mathbb{P}(\mathbf{O}, \mathcal{Z})$.

As shown in Algorithm 14, whenever the node $\mathcal{S}_i$ receives a notification regarding an object **O** and a predicate $P(\mathbf{O}, \mathcal{Z})$ travelling towards the base station, it checks **ForwardedPredicates** to

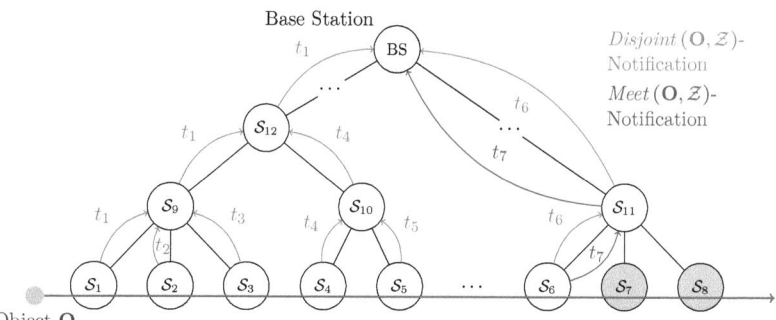

Figure 5.7: Illustration of the filter layer with a zone $\mathcal{Z} = \{\mathcal{S}_7, \mathcal{S}_8\}$

Algorithm 13: Initialization of ForwardedPredicates

1 **When** $\mathcal{S}_i$ *receives a query with* $\mathbb{P}(\mathbf{O}, \mathcal{Z})$ *for the first time* **do**
2   **for** *each* $P(\mathbf{O}, \mathcal{Z})$ *in* $\mathbb{P}(\mathbf{O}, \mathcal{Z})$ **do**
3   ForwardedPredicates ← ∅
4   Generate new list element E with E.$P(\mathbf{O}, \mathcal{Z})$ = $P(\mathbf{O}, \mathcal{Z})$ and E.ForwardedObjID = ∅
5   Add E to the end of ForwardedPredicates
6   **end**
7 **end**

---

determine, if forwarding this notification would be redundant. If the notification is not redundant, it is forwarded (Line 5). The notification is redundant, if there exists an entry in ForwardedPredicates related to $P(\mathbf{O}, \mathcal{Z})$ where the identifier of $\mathbf{O}$ is not in ForwardedObjID. After the notification has been forwarded, the node must check if it can ensure that future notifications regarding $\mathbf{O}$ and $P(\mathbf{O}, \mathcal{Z})$ are redundant. For developments that contain each predicate at most once, this is simple, i.e., when $P(\mathbf{O}, \mathcal{Z})$ occurs once, every subsequent forwarding is redundant. Example 16 illustrates this.

Example 16: Considering the routing tree displayed in Figure 5.7, i.e., every edge represents a route from a $\mathcal{S}_i$ to the base station chosen by the routing layer. The trajectory of the object $\mathbf{O}$ results in detections of $\mathbf{O}$ by nodes $\mathcal{S}_1$-$\mathcal{S}_8$. The zone $\mathcal{Z}$ contains $\mathcal{S}_7$ and $\mathcal{S}_8$ and the user is interested in $\mathbb{P}(\mathbf{O}, \mathcal{Z})$ = $Disjoint(\mathbf{O}, \mathcal{Z})$ $\widetilde{\triangleright}$ $Meet(\mathbf{O}, \mathcal{Z})$. At first, $\mathcal{S}_1$ detects $\mathbf{O}$ and notifies the base station of $Disjoint(\mathbf{O}, \mathcal{Z})$ = $\mathcal{T}$ by sending a notification message via $\mathcal{S}_9$ and $\mathcal{S}_{12}$. Next, $\mathcal{S}_2$ detects $\mathbf{O}$ and sends another – in this case redundant – notification to $\mathcal{S}_9$. Due to the fact that

5.4. DISTRIBUTED OBJECT-INFORMATION COLLECTION

Algorithm 14: Filtering redundant notifications

```
1  When S_i generated or received a notification regarding O and a predicate P(O, Z) do
2     for every element E in ForwardedPredicates (from first to last element) do
3        if E.P(O, Z) equals P(O, Z) then
4           if E.ForwardedObjID does not contain the identifier of O then
5              Forward notification using the routing layer
6              if object identifier of O is contained in every ForwardedObjID list before E then
7                 E.ForwardedObjID.add(O)
8              end
9              Exit           // Element found; notification has been forwarded
10          end
11       end
12    end
13 end
```

$\mathcal{S}_9$ has already forwarded a notification related to $Disjoint(\mathbf{O}, \mathcal{Z})$ and $\mathbf{O}$ it can derive that this notification is redundant. Similarly, $\mathcal{S}_9$ suppresses the notification of $\mathcal{S}_3$. Using the same reasoning, $\mathcal{S}_{12}$ suppresses the notifications by $\mathcal{S}_4$ and $\mathcal{S}_5$. Note that there may be an arbitrary number of hops between the base station $\mathcal{BS}$ and $\mathcal{S}_{12}$. ♦

For developments which contain at least one predicate more than once, e.g., $Touch(\mathbf{O}, \mathcal{Z})$ (cf. Equation (5.2)), suppressing notifications is not as simple: Assuming $P(\mathbf{O}, \mathcal{Z})$ occurs twice in $\mathbb{P}(\mathbf{O}, \mathcal{Z})$, $\mathcal{S}_i$ can only ensure that subsequent notifications of $P(\mathbf{O}, \mathcal{Z})$ are redundant if $\mathcal{S}_i$ already forwarded notifications for all predicates that must occur before $P(\mathbf{O}, \mathcal{Z})$, i.e., the first instance of $P(\mathbf{O}, \mathcal{Z})$ as well. Example 17 illustrates this.

Example 17: Assuming $\mathbb{P}(\mathbf{O}, \mathcal{Z}) = Disjoint(\mathbf{O}, \mathcal{Z}) \,\widetilde{\triangleright}\, Meet(\mathbf{O}, \mathcal{Z}) \,\widetilde{\triangleright}\, Disjoint(\mathbf{O}, \mathcal{Z})$ and a node $\mathcal{S}_i$ receives a notification which indicates that an object $\mathbf{O}$ conformed to $Disjoint(\mathbf{O}, \mathcal{Z})$. If such a notification $Disjoint(\mathbf{O}, \mathcal{Z})$ arrives for the first time, the node has to forward it anyways. When the same notification arrives for the second time, e.g., because $\mathbf{O}$ repeatedly moves in and out of the detection area of a single node, $\mathcal{S}_i$ cannot rule out that $Meet(\mathbf{O}, \mathcal{Z})$ has occurred in the meantime. Thus, $\mathcal{S}_i$ must forward notifications regarding $Disjoint(\mathbf{O}, \mathcal{Z})$ until it has forwarded a notification for $Meet(\mathbf{O}, \mathcal{Z})$. ♦

This filtering approach has an important property that might not be obvious: The probability that a node suppresses a notification increases as the distance to the base station decreases (in terms of hops). This is useful, because nodes that connect the base station to the sensor network are typically the nodes that are burdened the most with forwarding messages to and from the base station. If one of these nodes fails because its batteries are depleted, the base station loses one of its connections to the network and a whole part of the network might not be connected to the base station anymore. Contrary to this, nodes that are far away from the base station rarely forward messages and thus do not spend so much energy. Thus, the aforementioned approach protects the most important nodes of the sensor network.

5.5 Evaluation

We have evaluated our approach thoroughly using simulations and Sun SPOT deployments to investigate the following hypotheses:

H.1 Both distributed strategies scale better with the number of nodes and the number of detections than the centralized strategy.

H.2 The proactive strategy is the most energy-efficient for $\mathit{Inside}\,(\mathbf{O}, \mathcal{Z})$ and $\mathit{Disjoint}\,(\mathbf{O}, \mathcal{Z})$.

H.3 The reactive strategy is the most energy-efficient for $\mathit{Meet}\,(\mathbf{O}, \mathcal{Z})$.

H.4 The centralized strategy is energy-efficient for small networks and nodes around the base station.

H.5 Distributed strategies reduce communication required for processing spatio-temporal developments like $\mathit{Enter}\,(\mathbf{O}, \mathcal{Z})$ or $\mathit{WSNEnter}\,(\mathbf{O}, \mathcal{Z})$.

We present the evaluation setup for static and dynamic zones separately in the following. To run exactly the same software for simulations and the Sun SPOT deployments, we used the KSN Simulator (cf. Appendix C).

5.5.1 Static Zones – Evaluation

Each simulation run consists of the following steps:

1. Generate a WSN of 100-300 nodes that are randomly deployed over an area. The size of the area is constant to account for different node densities, i.e., varying numbers of detection and communication neighbors.
2. Define a zone of varying size. Zones contain between 2 and 30 nodes.
3. Generate 50 different object paths using a random walk model with starting points randomly chosen.
4. For each object path evaluate each detection scenario using each strategy.
5. Count the number of messages sent and received.

Overall, the results presented here are based on more than 100.000 simulation runs.

Since detection areas tend to be indeterminable, we have approximated the set of detection neighbors with the set of communication neighbors: To do so, a node sends a beacon message periodically. Each node receiving it adds the sender to the list of detection neighbors. We graph the communication required for these beacons for distributed strategies separately. For the proactive approach, these periodic beacon messages would allow the detection of failures and notification of the base station as well.

5.5. EVALUATION

Simulation Results

Figure 5.8 shows the average number of messages per simulation run for WSN of 100-300 nodes to compute DS^I. Graphs for other detection scenarios are similar and omitted here. As expected, the number of messages required by the centralized strategy increases linearly with network size. Contrary to this, network size only affects both distributed strategies marginally. The reason for this is the increasing node density, i.e., more detection neighbors per node. Even the added overhead for the approximation of detection neighbors does not change this. The large share of communication related to detection-neighbor approximation suggests that more sophisticated mechanisms for this could reduce energy-consumption even further. Thus, we conclude that **H.1** is true. Detection-neighbor approximation should be investigated in future work.

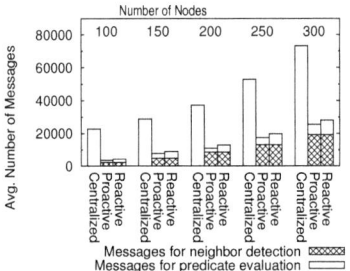

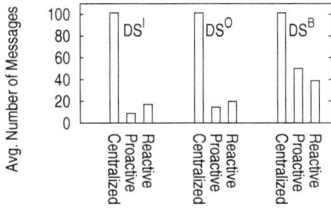

Figure 5.8: Scalability of data-collection strategies

Figure 5.9: Communication per detection-scenario

Figure 5.9 shows the average number of messages per detection-scenario computation. Since the centralized strategy sends all tuples to the base station and computes the detection scenario there, the average number of messages is constant. The result is that distributed strategies require between 45%–85% less messages than the centralized strategy. Comparing both distributed strategies shows that the proactive strategy is advantageous for DS^I and DS^E. This is expected, because $\mathcal{S}^*$ is smaller for the proactive strategy when objects leave the detection area of a node (cf. Tables 5.2 and 5.3). These roles are reversed for DS^B, because the proactive strategy is triggered more often than the reactive one. Summing up, these results confirm **H.2** and **H.3**.

The distributed strategies reduce communication to process spatio-temporal developments as well. Table 5.4 shows the average number of messages to determine that $\mathbf{O}$ conforms to $Enter(\mathbf{O}, \mathcal{Z})$ or $WSNEnter(\mathbf{O}, \mathcal{Z})$ (cf. (3.22) and (3.27)), respectively. As expected, the centralized strategy requires at least twice as much communication since every detection event must be forwarded to the base station. For $WSNEnter(\mathbf{O}, \mathcal{Z})$, the proactive strategy is most efficient. This is because this development does not contain $Meet(\mathbf{O}, \mathcal{Z})$. The difference between $Enter(\mathbf{O}, \mathcal{Z})$ and

Dissertation of Markus Bestehorn Karlsruhe Institute of Technology

Strategy	Number of Messages per Object for	
	Enter $(\mathbf{O}, \mathcal{Z})$	WSNEnter $(\mathbf{O}, \mathcal{Z})$
centralized	334	334
proactive	44,3	123,8
reactive	39,1	163,1

Table 5.4: Avg. number of messages for Enter $(\mathbf{O}, \mathcal{Z})$ and WSNEnter $(\mathbf{O}, \mathcal{Z})$

WSNEnter $(\mathbf{O}, \mathcal{Z})$ must be attributed to Lemma 5.6 because all non-border nodes are basically inactive for Enter $(\mathbf{O}, \mathcal{Z})$. Compared to the centralized strategy the savings of distributed strategies are between 51% and 89%. This confirms **H.5**.

Sun SPOT Case Study

Since simulations always abstract from certain real-world phenomena and these may impact performance, e.g., interferences or collisions, we conducted a case study using real sensor nodes. For our case study, we used two Sun SPOT deployments: The first deployment used 26 Sun SPOTs and a base station deployed on our office floors as shown in Figure 5.10. The second deployment used 50 nodes deployed outside of the computer science building of the Karlsruhe Institute of Technology. We discuss both deployments in the following separately.

Indoor deployment As shown in Figure 5.10, we deployed 26 Sun SPOT sensor nodes on the floors of the Institute of Program Structures and Data Organization. Blue dots indicate a node outside of the zone $\mathcal{Z}$, and a red dot corresponds to a node inside $\mathcal{Z}$. The object moved on the path indicated in black and the base station is represented by the black square on the right-hand side of the figure. For this setup, we only evaluated a single predicate $Inside\,(\mathbf{O}, \mathcal{Z})$.

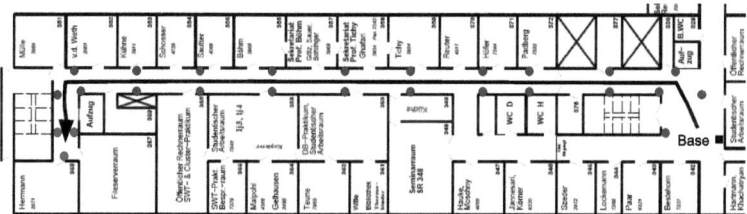

Figure 5.10: Case Study: Sun SPOT positions and object path

In analogy to the simulations, we assumed that nodes cannot determine their detection areas by themselves. Thus, a node periodically sent beacons to approximate the set of its detection

143

5.5. EVALUATION

neighbors, i.e., $\mathcal{DN}_i = \mathcal{CN}_i$.

Strategy	Number of Messages		
	Collect	Result Forward.	Total
centralized	137	0	137
proactive	115	42	157
reactive	145	33	178

Table 5.5: Case study results

Table 5.5 shows the result of the case study: The rightmost column contains the total number of messages sent, i.e., the sum of the two columns in the middle which reflect messages for data collection (left) and result forwarding (right). Since the centralized strategy computes all results at the base station, the number of messages sent to forward the result is 0. A simulation that replicated the node setup and object movement of the case study had the same results. This is important, because it indicates that real-world phenomena from which simulations have abstracted would not significantly change the previous findings based on simulations.

The centralized strategy required 137 messages, the distributed approaches 20 respectively 41 more. The result is expected due to the relatively small network: Messages required 5 hops at most to reach the base station, i.e., communicating with detection neighbors required more messages than computing detection scenarios at the base station. Considering the simulation results and the result of the case study, we conclude that **H.4** is true.

Further analysis shows that the approximation $\mathcal{DN}_i = \mathcal{CN}_i$ has resulted in an over assessment: Prior to the experiment, we determined the number of detection neighbors $|\mathcal{DN}_i|$ for every node by calibration. Approximately 50% of the communication neighbors were not detection neighbors. While this does not affect the result, it increases the number of messages sent for data collection. Thus, while the simple approximation $\mathcal{DN}_i = \mathcal{CN}_i$ yields correct results, the potential for further reduction of energy consumption by improving detection-neighbor approximation is large.

Outdoor deployment Figure 5.11 shows a bird's eye view of an outdoor deployment consisting of 50 Sun SPOTs deployed over an area of approximately 2500m^2. The L-shaped building on the left and bottom of the figure is the computer science building of the Karlsruhe Institute of Technology. As the picture in Figure 5.12 shows, every node was attached to a tree. Again, blue dots represent nodes outside of $\mathcal{Z}$, red dots nodes inside of $\mathcal{Z}$ and the black square is the base station. Note that despite the larger number of nodes compared to the indoor deployment, the distance in terms of hops from most nodes to the base station has not changed significantly: for the majority of the nodes, 1-4 hops are sufficient to reach the base station.

Out of several object paths we tested, we selected the two shown in Figure 5.11 because they offer the most important insights in combination with a given query: The green-colored trajectory belongs to the object $\mathbf{O}_1$ and we present the results for processing the query Enter($\mathbf{O}_1, \mathcal{Z}$) here.

Object O_2 moved as indicated by the red-colored trajectory and the results presented here belong to $\text{Touch}(O_2, \mathcal{Z})$ (cf. Equation (5.2)). For both trajectories, we processed the query using the centralized, reactive and proactive strategy.

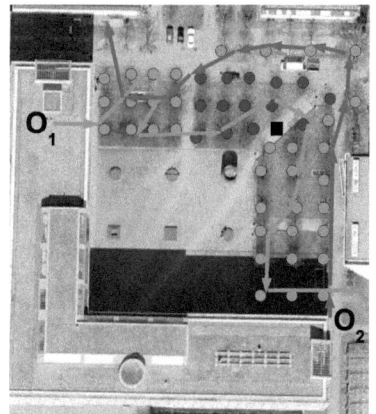 

Figure 5.11: Outdoor Deployment of 50 Sun SPOT nodes

Figure 5.12: Ground view of nodes deployed on trees

The results of $\text{Enter}(O_1, \mathcal{Z})$ are shown in Table 5.6. Compared to the indoor deployment, the most obvious difference is the increase in messages for the centralized strategy. This number increased due to the large number of nodes that detected O_1. Even though the number of hops for sending a corresponding message to the base station was similar to the indoor deployment, the increase in nodes that actually detected O_1 made the difference. Thus, the result confirms **H.1**.

A detailed study of the result reveals the reason for the difference between the reactive and the proactive approach: When objects leave the detection area of a border node $\mathcal{S}_i$, the reactive approach results in querying all detection neighbors of $\mathcal{S}_i$. With the trajectory of O_1, this occurred several times and resulted in a large number of messages for collecting the information with the reactive strategy. Since both distributed strategies require considerably less communication than the centralized strategy, **H.5** is confirmed as well for this setup.

The results of $\text{Touch}(O_2, \mathcal{Z})$ are shown in Table 5.7. Again, the centralized approach results in a large number of messages, despite the fact that the object mostly moves in the vicinity of

5.5. EVALUATION

Strategy	Number of Messages		
	Collect	Result Forward.	Total
centralized	264	0	264
proactive	147	12	159
reactive	168	16	184

Table 5.6: Results for Enter $(\mathbf{O}_1, \mathcal{Z})$

the base station. Compared to both distributed strategies, the difference regarding the number of messages is significant. For even larger networks or in deployments where the base station is not in the center of the network, it is expected that the centralized approach is completely unfeasible. Another problem that we observed with the centralized approach is the fact that the routing layer is constantly forced to find routes to the base station, because every node that detects the object requires a route to the base station. These messages are not included in the numbers provided here, because they largely depend on the routing protocol used. But they affect query processing, for example because the messages required for route discovery and maintenance collide with those for query processing.

Strategy	Number of Messages		
	Collect	Result Forward.	Total
centralized	302	0	302
proactive	144	73	217
reactive	123	55	178

Table 5.7: Results for Touch $(\mathbf{O}_2, \mathcal{Z})$

The most interesting aspect of this results is the comparison between reactive and proactive: The reactive strategy required less messages. This is because the object travels along the border of the zone for most of the time. The reason is $Meet(\mathbf{O}, \mathcal{Z})$: The reactive strategy only sends requests into the zone whenever $\mathbf{O}_2$ enters a detection area, for $Meet(\mathbf{O}, \mathcal{Z})$ and $Disjoint(\mathbf{O}, \mathcal{Z})$. Contrary to that, the proactive strategy required border nodes to send updates to detection neighbors whenever $\mathbf{O}_2$ has entered or left a detection area. Since $\mathbf{O}_2$ mostly has moved outside or in the border of $\mathcal{Z}$, the communication intensive case where a node using the reactive strategy has to request list elements from all of its detection neighbors only occurred twice. The combination these two facts results in less messages for the reactive strategy. Considering the results obtained for Enter $(\mathbf{O}_2, \mathcal{Z})$ as well as those for Touch $(\mathbf{O}_2, \mathcal{Z})$, we consider **H.3** and **H.2** to be confirmed as well.

Considering all results we obtained with different outdoor deployments (even those omitted here), object trajectories and spatio-temporal developments, we conclude:

- The proactive approach typically requires the lowest number of messages.
- The centralized strategy requires the largest number of messages of all three strategies unless the trajectory as well as the distance to the base station in term of hops is very short.
- There exist few cases, e.g., the experiment with Touch $(\mathbf{O}_2, \mathcal{Z})$ above, where the reactive approach is considerably better than the proactive strategy.

Summing up, our evaluation for static zones confirms all of our hypotheses.

5.5.2 Dynamic Zones – Evaluation

We repeated the simulations above for a dynamic zone, i.e., the same node distributions as well as object trajectories were used. The only difference between the experiments above and this experiment is that we simulated a zone that moved from the right side of the sensor network to the left side, like a wave. Thus, at first there are no nodes in the zone, then nodes join the zone over time and each node remains in the zone for a constant amount of time. After this time has elapsed, each node leaves the zone and stays out of the zone. Figure 5.13 shows the result in a similar way to Figure 5.8, i.e., the result is for DS^I which yields $\textit{Inside}\,(\mathbf{O}, \mathcal{Z}) = \mathcal{T}$. The results for the other detection scenarios/predicates is similar.

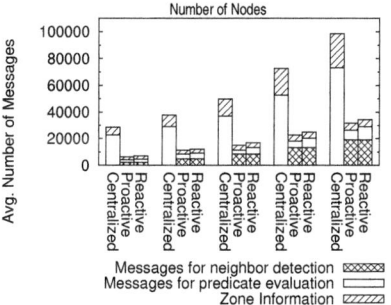

Figure 5.13: Scalability with dynamic zones

As expected, the result is similar to the result for static zones. The amount of traffic generated to determine detection neighbors in both distributed cases is unaffected by the dynamic zone. Since the predicate evaluation is integrated into ZIP, the number of messages related to collecting information on objects detected does not change significantly compared to Figure 5.8. The additional messages directly related to ZIP depends on the density of the network. The higher the density, the larger is the set of detection neighbors per node and thus the amount of messages with dynamic zones increases.

Note that the "zone movement" we used for this experiment is extreme, because all nodes join and leave the zone once. In reality, it would depend on the underlying phenomenon but it is more likely that few nodes join and leave the region over time. We conducted experiments with less nodes that joined or left the zone and in most cases, the amount of traffic related to the ZIP protocol was minor unless large numbers of nodes join/left the zone. Summing up, we conclude that the findings for static zones hold for dynamic zones as well.

5.6 Summary

This section has addressed the energy-efficient processing of spatio-temporal queries in sensor networks. Based on the semantics of Chapter 3 and the assumptions that the query has been disseminated efficiently using the approach in Chapter 4, we have shown how to process spatio-temporal predicates in-network. Processing spatio-temporal queries requires the collection of information on zones and objects detected from different nodes. Sending all of this information to the base station is a straightforward approach, but unfeasible considering the limited energy resources of sensor nodes.

By introducing the fundamental concepts of detection neighbors and border nodes, we have shown how to reduce the number of nodes that must exchange information on objects and zones significantly. As we have shown, object detections by significant parts of the sensor network cannot contribute to the query result for queries like Enter $(\mathbf{O}, \mathcal{Z})$. Thus, these nodes may use sleep modes to conserve power. For the remaining nodes, we introduced to strategies to exchange information on objects detected efficiently and only when necessary. Both strategies combine the spatial correlation of object detections and the semantics of spatio-temporal queries to reduce communication and thus energy consumption. Our evaluation using simulations as well as Sun SPOT sensor nodes shows that both strategies reduce communication and thereby energy consumption significantly: The number of messages required for processing single predicates as well as spatio-temporal developments is reduced by 45% to 90% compared to collecting all information at the base station.

Chapter 6

Conclusion and Future Work

A significant portion of sensor networks is deployed with aim of observing the movement of objects detected by sensor nodes. Database research has shown that accessing sensor networks declaratively is a promising approach. But so far, the focus of research has been relational queries. Relational queries are insufficient to express queries interested in the movement of objects, i.e., the queries occurring in the aforementioned type of sensor network. This dissertation provides the fundamental concepts for spatio-temporal semantics in sensor networks, as well as an approach to processing spatio-temporal queries efficiently. The following chapter concludes this dissertation by summarizing the most important contributions as well as interesting, related subjects for future work.

6.1 Summary

The first part of this dissertation has exclusively addressed the semantics of spatio-temporal queries in sensor networks. As the discussion of the properties of sensor networks in general and detection mechanisms in particular has shown, these semantics had to be defined in such a way that they can cope with inaccurate or incomplete information on moving objects. In addition to the concept of regions, which we inherited from moving object databases, we have also introduced the notion of a zone. Thus, users of sensor networks can express queries interested in the spatio-temporal relationship between objects detected by sensor nodes and a region, i.e., a point set, or a zone, i.e., a set of nodes. For both, regions and zones, we defined the semantics of spatio-temporal predicates as well as developments, i.e., concatenations of predicates that describe complex movement patterns the user is interested in.

Based on a flexible model of sensor networks and their detection mechanisms, we have defined five detection scenarios and shown how to map every possible detection of an object to a detection scenario. Thus, the detection scenarios formalize the information obtainable by sensor networks and any kind of detection mechanism on the objects detected. Each detection scenario describes

6.1. SUMMARY

how the region or zone overlaps with the set of points where the object could be based on the information acquired by the detection mechanism. This approach takes into account the varying degrees of accuracy of different object detection mechanisms, simultaneous detection of a single object by several nodes, unobserved areas etc.

The semantics defined in the context of regions address the problem, that most sensor networks cannot determine if a detected object is outside, on the border or inside of the region if the actual position of the object is sufficiently close to the border of the region. To solve this issue, a sensor network returns three sets of objects regarding a query interested in the spatio-temporal relationship of an object and a region: The first set contains all objects that definitely conform to the query. The second set contains objects that definitely do not conform to the query. The last set contains objects which possibly conform to the query, but the inaccuracy of object detection or unobserved areas prevent a definitive answer. We have proven that this result is optimal independently of the detection.

To process spatio-temporal queries in the context of zones, we introduced a space partitioning that allows the application of the 9-intersection model known from moving object databases. The semantics of predicates that express the relationship between an object and a zone are based on this space partitioning. Using the aforementioned detection scenarios, we have shown how to map object detections to predicate results in the context of zones. An important detail is that the space partitioning for zones is not regular. The predicates and concatenation operators for regions are based on the assumption that the space partitioning is regular. Thus, in the context of zones, there exist queries that cannot be expressed using these operators. To solve this, we introduced concatenation operators and an additional predicate that allow users to express spatio-temporal queries with non-regular space partitions.

A study of the semantical depth has shown that there exist queries in moving object database that require infinite temporal resolution of the detection mechanism and thus cannot be applied to sensor networks. All remaining spatio-temporal developments have been translated to detection terms, i.e., terms that describe sequences of object detections based on detection scenarios. The semantical depth of queries related to zones has been investigated as well: There are 584 unique spatio-temporal developments that describe the spatio-temporal relationship of an object and a zone.

Since sensor nodes have limited resources, particularly regarding energy, we addressed energy efficient processing of spatio-temporal queries as well, i.e., processing queries with a minimal amount of communication. Processing queries in sensor networks requires dissemination of the query first and then the collection of information from different sensor nodes. The second part of this dissertation studies query dissemination in sensor networks. A performance evaluation of existing mechanisms for query dissemination shows that particularly simple mechanisms are well-suited for sensor networks. In particular, probabilistic query dissemination provides a good tradeoff between reliability, i.e., disseminating the query to all nodes, and energy spent for communication. We developed an optimizer that determines a rebroadcast probability for probabilistic query dissemination that reduces communication while reaching all nodes.

The third part of this dissertation studies the energy-efficient processing of spatio-temporal queries and how to collect information on moving objects in an efficient way. Sending all information regarding on objects and zones to the base station is inefficient because most object detections are irrelevant for the query result. To solve this, we propose two strategies that exploit the spatial correlation of object detection and the semantics of spatio-temporal queries to reduce the number of noes that must communicate with each other significantly. As a result, for most queries, a large portion of the nodes does not communicate at all and if communication is required, only direct neighbors exchange messages.

All of the mechanisms have been evaluated systematically using simulations as well as Sun SPOT deployments. The simulations investigated the scalability of our measures which is important for sensor networks consisting of hundreds or thousands of sensor nodes. The various deployments of Sun SPOT sensor nodes have shown that our measures can cope with the intricacies of sensor networks. Furthermore, these deployments confirmed the results obtained through simulations.

6.2 Future Work

There are a number of interesting research questions that we did not address to limit the scope of this dissertation. We conclude with a selection research topics that either built on top of this dissertation or are related to the topic of spatio-temporal queries in sensor networks.

6.2.1 Queries with non-identifiable Objects

This dissertation has assumed that objects are uniquely identifiable. As stated in Section 1.1, this means that if S_i detects **O** at some time t_1 and S_j detects **O** at $t_2 > t_1$, the sensor network can derive that both nodes detected the same object. Despite the increasing level of sophistication of detection mechanisms and the advances of hardware used in sensor networks, there are detection mechanisms that will never allow the identification of objects. For instance, induction loops cannot identify objects detected. It remains to be investigated which concepts of this dissertation could be reused for sensor networks where identification of objects is unfeasible.

Even though queries interested in the movement of a single object are not possible if objects cannot be identified, there are spatio-temporal predicates and queries users could be interested in: Continuing the example of a network of induction loops, a user could be interested in the number k of objects that entered a region. While an accurate computation of k might not be possible, the sensor network could try to derive lower and upper bounds for k. This is useful, because users can derive how many objects have entered a region for sure and how many additional objects possibly have entered the region. Such an approach would require predicates that return lower and upper bounds for the number of objects conforming to it. Furthermore, new concatenation operators for these predicates and ultimately new ways to express queries would have to be developed.

Applications for these types of spatio-temporal queries overlap with those used to motivate this dissertation: Scientists that observe the population of different kinds of animals could analyze

6.2. FUTURE WORK

how many animals of a given population exhibit a certain behaviour/movement by expressing a declarative query. Similarly, authorities could access traffic monitoring systems to investigate the reasons or patterns that lead to traffics jams.

6.2.2 Detection Cost Optimization

As discussed in Section 2.1.1, for certain types of objects there exist various detection mechanisms. For example, there are various mechanisms that detect vehicles [6, 18, 58] using different types of sensing hardware. These different detection mechanisms also require various amounts of energy to detect an object and relatively accurate mechanisms typically require more energy than those that only determine if an object is in the vicinity of a node or not.

Considering the semantics of predicates related to regions (cf. Section 3.3.1), if nodes are equipped with various detection mechanisms, the differences regarding energy consumption could be exploited. Whenever a node detects an object according to $\widetilde{\mathsf{DS}^B}$ using the "cheap" (in terms of energy consumption) detection mechanism, one should consider applying the more expensive but more accurate mechanism. While this is straightforward for a single node, it becomes more complicated if detection neighbors are taken into account or the case where several nodes detect the object simultaneously. Selecting a subset of a set of detection neighbors which should use the more accurate mechanism and coordinating nodes after the subset has been selected is complex. The detection neighbors must be selected in such a way that the information gained by using the more accurate mechanism is maximal while keeping the number of nodes that actually use the "expensive" mechanism is minimal. This selection process should also take into account current energy levels, e.g., to avoid that a detection neighbors whose battery already is relatively low has to use the more "expensive" mechanism.

6.2.3 Object-Object, Region-Region and Region-Zone Predicates

This dissertation has focused on moving objects and their relation to regions and zones. Besides predicates that express the relation of objects and regions, moving object databases also allow users to query relations of regions and regions. These predicates allow users to express queries like "Did the oil spill overlap with the nature protection area?".

Considering the concept of zones introduced in this dissertation, users could express queries related to zones and zones or zones and regions in sensor networks. In the example above, the oil spill would be modeled by a dynamic zone and the nature protection area as a static region. It remains to be investigated if the space partitioning for zones provided in Section 3.3.2 is applicable to these queries as well. Independently of that, predicates related to the topological relationship of a point set and a node set have not been addressed previously. Additionally, the semantics of queries interested in the spatio-temporal relationship of two dynamic zones have not been addressed so far. Assuming the semantics of the two types of queries have been defined, the next question in both cases is processing these queries efficiently.

Another type of queries not addressed by this dissertation are queries interested in the relationship between trajectories of (different) objects. For example, a user might be interested which trajectories of other objects have crossed the trajectory of an object O_1. Such queries would require other concatenation operators and different mechanisms for processing them efficiently in a sensor network.

6.2.4 Approximation of Detection Neighbors

Our mechanisms in Chapter 5 are based on the concept of detection neighbors. Determining these detection neighbors is problematic in sensor networks where nodes cannot determine their detection area. We proposed two approaches for the approximation the set of detection neighbors and used the substitution with the set of communication neighbors for our evaluation. While this approximation is correct for most sensor networks, our evaluation shows that a significant communication overhead is related to messages related to this approximation. Furthermore, this approximation over-estimates the number of detection neighbors significantly, e.g., the indoor deployment (cf. Section 5.5) showed that approximately 50% of assumed detection neighbors were not detection neighbors in reality. This affects the efficiency of query processing, because nodes exchange information on object detections or zones with other nodes that are not detection neighbors. Thus, the development of such approximations for different detection mechanisms that approximate detection neighbors is a promising approach for research.

The approximation based on communication neighbors requires further investigation as well, particularly reducing the over-estimation. Figure 6.1 illustrates the problem: While S_2 is a detection neighbor of S_1, S_3 is not. But using the approach to approximate the detection area with the set of communication neighbors leads to S_1 treating S_3 as a detection neighbor and thus wasting energy. Note that communication as well as detection areas are illustrated using circles in for this example. As we pointed out earlier, they usually are not, but we use this simplification here to outline the problem and a few ideas to solve it. An optimal approach would select exactly those communication neighbors that are detection neighbors as well. Without information on the detection mechanism or the actual detection area of all nodes, getting such a selection is typically not possible.

To demonstrate the different research questions that arise from this problem, we outline several ideas regarding the selection of detection neighbors from a set of communication neighbors for an arbitrary node S_i:

Reduction of output power: Instead of selecting a subset of communication neighbors as detection neighbors, this approach would reduce the number of communication neighbors completely. Most radio chips support different radio output power modes, i.e., one could reduce the output power to remove nodes from the set of communication neighbors that are too far away to be detection neighbors. As illustrated in Figure 6.2 this can solve the problem, but might also result in detection neighbors not being identified. Furthermore, this approach could result in a partitioned network, i.e., a subset of nodes is not connected to the base station anymore.

6.2. FUTURE WORK

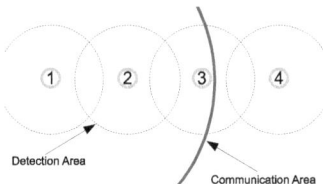

Figure 6.1: Approximating detection neighbors based on communication neighbors

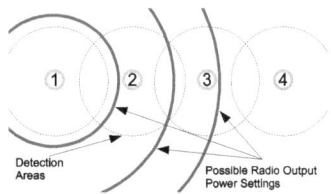

Figure 6.2: Reduction of radio output power to approximate detection neighbors

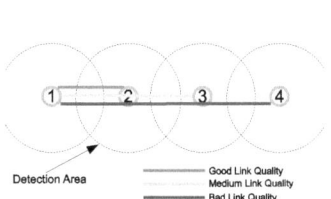

Figure 6.3: Link-quality based detection neighbor approximation

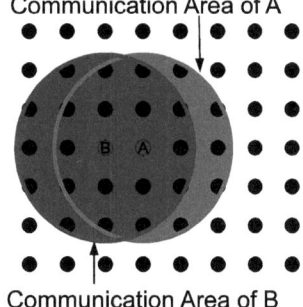

Figure 6.4: Detection neighbor approximation based on 2-hop neighbors

Link Quality: If supported by the radio stack, e.g., the KSN Radio Stack (cf. Appendix C), nodes can derive the link quality to different communication neighbors. Typically, if the link between two nodes S_i and S_j has a high quality, one can derive that both nodes are relatively close to each other. Depending on the maximum range of the detection mechanism and the radio hardware, the set of detection neighbors of S_i could be approximated by only selecting communication neighbors with a good link quality. Figure 6.3 illustrates this. This approach is problematic if external influences reduce the link quality between two nodes but do not affect the detection area.

2-Hop Neighborhood: Another approach that allows a node S_i to determine which communication neighbors are closer than others is comparing the set of communication neighbors. As illustrated in Figure 6.4, if the set of communication neighbors of S_i mostly overlaps with the set of communication neighbors of a node S_j, we can derive that both nodes are close to each other. Contrary to this, if the sets of communication neighbors from both nodes do not overlap, it is likely that both nodes are not close to each other and thus not detection neighbors. This approach is problematic because it is communication intensive because every node $\mathcal{S}_i$ must send its set of communication neighbors to all of its communication neighbors.

More fundamental research regarding the approximation of detection neighbors could improve the performance of spatio-temporal query processing significantly.

6.2.5 Advanced Concatenations and Predicates

Both, this dissertation as well as moving object databases, are based on predicates $P(\mathbf{e}_1, \mathbf{e}_2)$ that express the relationship of two spatio-temporal entities over time. While this is sufficient to express queries like Enter $(\mathbf{O}, \mathbf{R})$ that are only concerned with two entities, expressing relationships of three or more entities is difficult.

A user might be interested in objects $\mathbf{O}$ that are in $\mathbf{R}_1$ and inside of $\mathbf{R}_2$ at the same time. Defining predicates that allow three arguments, e.g, *Inside* $(\mathbf{O}, \mathbf{R}_1, \mathbf{R}_2)$ in the case above, is sufficient for queries related to three entities but not for four. Defining a new set of predicates for every number of entities would result in an infinity number of predicates that must be supported by the query processor. Thus, the approach is not viable.

A more elegant approach to express the afore mentioned query is the definition of additional concatenation operators. For the query above, it suffices to define a concatenation operator whose semantic is "and at the same time". Adding this concatenation operator would allow the user the express the query with "*Inside* $(\mathbf{O}, \mathbf{R}_1)$ and at the same time *Inside* $(\mathbf{O}, \mathbf{R}_2)$". This approach is better than the one discussed above, because it does not require any additional predicates and offering additional flexibility. For instance, queries like "*Inside* $(\mathbf{O}, \mathbf{R}_1)$ and at the same time *Disjoint* $(\mathbf{O}, \mathbf{R}_2)$" are possible as well. Further flexibility could be achieved by introducing concatenation operators allowing queries like "*Inside* $(\mathbf{O}, \mathbf{R}_1)$ and *Disjoint* $(\mathbf{O}, \mathbf{R}_2)$ at least 5 minutes before". Finding a minimal set of operators, similar to the set of relational operators for relation databases, that is complete in the context of spatio-temporal queries, allows the expression of every possible spatio-temporal query, is a challenging task.

6.2.6 Querying the Movement of Humans with Privacy-Related Position Obfuscation

Location-based services are information or entertainment services that use the geographical position of a user to enhance or personalize the service presented to the user. With the advent of handheld, GPS-enabled devices, an increasing number of such services have been created ranging from emergency services [42] to advertisement customized to the users position. Note that for certain applications, it is desirable to reveal the users position completely, e.g., emergency services, while other applications do not require an accurate position of the user.

6.2. FUTURE WORK

Revealing the users position and allowing certain entities to accurately track the user over time has been identified as a privacy threat. These privacy threats in the context of location-based services has received a lot of attention from the research community. This research tries to reach two conflicting goals: The users position must be protected by obfuscating its position or ensure that the user is sufficiently anonymous towards the provider of the service. If the users position is completely obfuscated, the quality of the service degrades to the point where it is unusable. Thus, the users position must be sufficiently obfuscated to ensure privacy while still allowing the execution of the service. For instance, to find the nearest cash terminal, it might be sufficient if the service provider knows that the user is within a certain region to determine a set of nearby cash terminals.

These location-based services require spatial or spatio-temporal queries. Due to the position obfuscation, the situation of the service is similar to sensor nodes using detection mechanisms that cannot determine the position of a detected object accurately. It remains to be investigated, how the detection model and the resulting detection scenarios as well as their translations could be applied to allow the execution of location-based services based on obfuscated position data.

Appendix A

Energy Consumption Profile of Sensor Nodes

Prior to the energy efficient implementation of the query dissemination and spatio-temporal query processor, we conducted a set of experiments to determine the important aspects of energy efficiency in sensor networks. The setup and the results of these experiments are provided in this section and justify our approach to evaluate our measures by counting the number of messages sent and received. More precisely, the following hypotheses are proven experimentally:

- **H.1** Exchanging information via wireless communication reduces the time until batteries are depleted significantly.
- **H.2** Energy consumption for sending a message is marginally higher than receiving a message.
- **H.3** The number of bytes contained in a single message has a minor impact on energy consumption, particularly if energy-efficient MAC protocols are used.

For each node type, we describe the experimental setup first and investigate aforementioned hypotheses based on the results.

A.1 Experimental Setup

To measure the energy consumption of a sensor node we used the ***Sensor Node Management Device (SNMD)*** [60]. The SNMD was attached between the battery and energy consuming components of the sensor nodes, e.g., CPU, memory, wireless communication chip and sensing board. Figure A.1 illustrates a simplified circuit diagram of the setup and Figure A.2 shows the energy measurement device with a Mica mote attached to it[1]. We measured the voltage drawn by the node at a high temporal resolution of up to 20 kHz and computed the energy consumption based on this.

---
[1]The experiments were conducted at a time when the SNMD was still in development and had a less compact appearance, but the basic features have not been changed since then.

A.2. RESULTS AND ANALYSIS

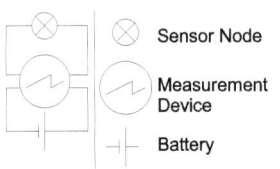

Figure A.1: Circuit diagram for energy measurements

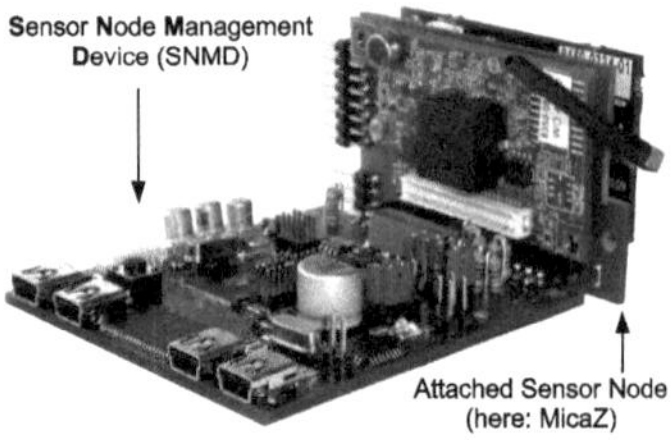

Figure A.2: Sensor Node Management Device [60] and attached Mica Mote

A.2 Results and Analysis

For each measurement, we ran different applications with different properties regarding energy consumption on the nodes. We describe these applications first and the analyze the results of the energy measurement in the context of our hypotheses.

A.2.1 Impact of Communication on node lifetime

For this experiment, we fully charged the batteries of three Sun SPOTs according to the specification of the battery. Afterwards, we assigned one of the following applications to one of the SPOTs:

High: This application prevented the usage of any power conservation features of the SPOTs. To increase power consumption, the radio and CPU were in use permanently.

Medium: This application raised an event on the SPOT every five minutes. After the event was raised, the SPOT sends data and then uses the *shallow sleep mode* to conserve energy while waiting for the next event. Note that the radio is not switched off during shallow sleep.

Low: A SPOT running this application is put into shallow sleep mode at all times.

While *shallow sleep mode* reduces energy consumption considerably, the overall power consumption is still orders of magnitude higher than in *deep sleep mode*. Table A.1 compares both power saving modes. SPOTs that run mainly in deep sleep mode can run for up to 900 days.

Figure A.3 shows the measured voltage over time (in hours). The experiment ends when the battery reaches a critical voltage at $\approx 3.3V$. If this occurs, the battery hardware shuts the SPOT down. The application "high" depleted the battery an hour while each of the other applications ran 15 hours or more. Thus, constant usage of the CPU and radio drastically reduce the lifetime of the node. Comparing the "medium" and the "low" application shows that the additional use of the radio compared to using the sleep mode continuously reduces node lifetime considerably.

Regarding the absolute values in Figure A.3 it must be noted, that in shallow sleep certain parts of the hardware are still switched on and consume energy as shown in Table A.1. Most

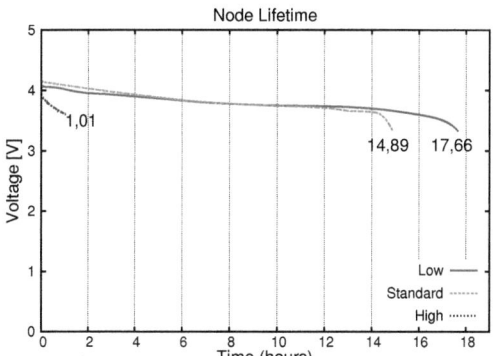

Figure A.3: Node lifetime measurement result

importantly, the radio is still switched on. Switching the radio off would require energy-aware MAC protocols, e.g., B-MAC [105], that ensure communication between nodes while switching off the radio for certain periods of time. Initial tests of the three applications with B-MAC resulted in the following: The "high" application was unaffected, since the radio is constantly in use and B-MAC cannot shut down the radio chip. Both, the "medium" and the "low" applications achieved lifetimes of more than two weeks and the experiment was stopped. While these protocols increase node lifetime by reducing energy consumption for idle listening, they increase energy consumption for sending messages due to synchronization overhead (see Section 2.1.3). We investigate this overhead in Section A.2.3 and conclude that the results of this experiment confirm **H.1**. Similar results have been obtained for Mica motes in [83].

A.2.2 Energy consumption of sending and receiving

This experiment used two nodes where a sender sends a message of varying size to a receiver. The size of the message was increased from 1 packet to 10 packets. The experiment was conducted as follows:

1. Sender and receiver are started and switch off their radio.
2. The energy measurement using the SNMD is started and both SPOTs switch their radio back on.
3. After the radio is ready at the sender, the sender tries to deliver the first packet to the receiver.
4. After receiving an acknowledgement for the first packet, the next packet is sent. This procedure continues until all packets are sent.

A.2. RESULTS AND ANALYSIS

	Shallow Sleep	Deep Sleep
CPU	On with CPU clock stopped	Off
Master System Clock	On	Off
Low-level firmware	On	On[a]
RAM	On, but inactive	Main power off, RAM content preserved with low power standby
Flash memory	On, but inactive	Off
CC2240 radio chip	On	Off
AT91 peripheral clocks	On, if in use, otherwise off	Off
External/sensor board	On	Off
Power consumption	≈ 24 mA	$\approx 32\ \mu A$

Table A.1: Energy saving modes for Sun SPOTs

[a] This is required to wake up the SPOT, e.g., at a given time.

5. After the last packet has been acknowledged by the receiver, the energy measurement is stopped.

Switching off the radio before the start of the experiment simulates the fact that before nodes can send messages the radio must be switched on. Keeping the radio on at all times is not a viable option as the experiment above has shown. Therefore the energy consumption for switching the radio on before sending a message must be taken into account to measure the energy consumed for sending a message. On both nodes, the usage of sleep modes or any other power-saving mechanism was prevented, i.e., all components of the nodes were on at any time. Both nodes used the KSN Radio Stack (see Section C.3) on top of the default Sun SPOT MAC protocol, i.e., no energy-aware MAC protocol was used.

Figure A.4 shows the result of the experiment. The difference regarding energy consumption between the sender and the receiver is marginal even for 10 packets. This confirms **H.2**. In addition to the result also shows that the size of the message has a minor impact on energy consumption even if there is no energy-aware MAC protocol. Sending a message consisting of a single packet consumed 9.14 mAs. Doubling the size to two packets leads to an energy consumption of 9.94 mAs, i.e., an increase of 8.8%. Increasing the message size by an order of magnitude only doubles the energy consumption. Thus, even without energy-aware MAC protocols **H.3** is confirmed. With energy-aware MAC protocols this relative increase becomes even smaller since these protocols induce a large constant overhead for sending and receiving. We investigate energy consumption of these protocols in the following.

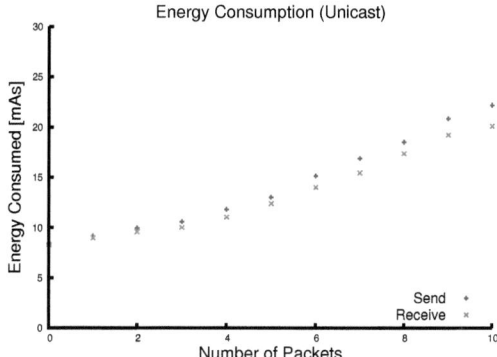

Figure A.4: Energy Consumption for communication

A.2.3 Impact of energy-aware MAC protocols

So far, all experiments used a default implementation of a 802.15.4 compatible MAC protocol which was not energy-aware, i.e., the radio chip was on at all times. This section investigates the impact of energy-aware MAC protocols such as B-MAC [105] or X-MAC [20]. Contrary to the previous experiments, we use Mica motes for this to ease presentation. This is because energy readings are difficult to interpret on Sun SPOTs because parallel processes such as garbage collection distort the readings. Experiments with SUN SPOTs had similar results which is expected since both node types use the CC2420 radio chip. Again, we used the Sensor Node Management Device (SNMD) [60] to obtain energy measurements.

We used two Mica Motes where the access to the wireless medium was controlled by a B-MAC implementation [72] provided with TinyOS [61]. One of the nodes broadcasts (sender) a single packet and the other mote (receiver) just receives the message broadcasted. Figure A.5 shows the energy readings of both nodes and Figure A.6 illustrates the schema of B-MAC as explained in Section 2.1.3. We explain the important points in time (marked with $[T_1], [T_2], [T_3], [T_4]$) for sender and receiver in the following.

The time interval t at which each node checks the medium for incoming messages is 1 second. The point in time where sender and receiver switch on the radio and check if there are incoming messages are marked with $[T_1]$. For the first two intervals, both nodes switch off the radio immediately and save energy. After 2.3 seconds (at $[T_2]$), the sender application starts the sending process by switching the radio on, listening to the medium. Since there is no other node currently sending a message, the sender starts with the preamble. Since the radio chip is packet-based, it sends short packets to indicate that a.) no other node should send at this time and b.) the intended receivers

A.2. RESULTS AND ANALYSIS

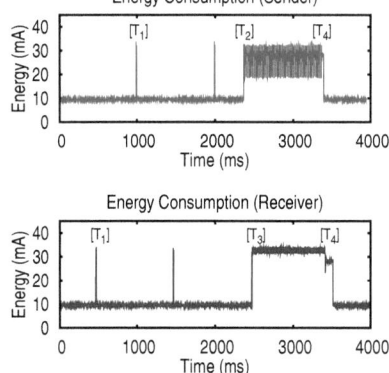

Figure A.5: Energy consumption with B-MAC [105]

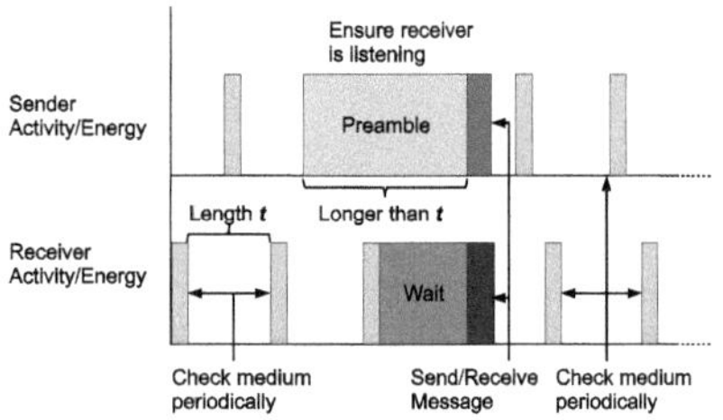

Figure A.6: Illustration of B-MAC [105]

(in this case all surrounding nodes since it is a broadcast) should keep the radio on. The length of the preamble is longer than 1 second to ensure that all receivers have time to switch their radio on. At $[T_3]$, the receiver wakes up the radio since 1 second has elapsed since the last wake up. Contrary to the last two times, this time the radio is kept on since the preamble of the sender indicates that the receiver is an intended recipient of a message. Broadcasting the actual message happens in a few milliseconds at $[T_4]$. Both nodes switch the radio off a few milliseconds after the message is broadcasted/received.

The readings from sender and receiver show two important points with regard to our hypotheses **H.2** and **H.3**: While the radio is switched on, both nodes consume an almost equal amount of energy, i.e., **H.2** is confirmed. Compared to the preamble of more than 1 second and the waiting for the actual message at the receiver, the time and energy spent for sending/receiving the message is negligible. An increase of the message size would result in a longer time spent sending the actual message. The time/energy spent previously for preamble and waiting is bigger by at least an order of magnitude unless hundreds of packets must be sent. With this we conclude that **H.3** is confirmed as well.

A.3 Lessons Learned

This section investigated the energy consumption characteristics of sensor nodes in particular with regard to communication. As expected, communication has by far the largest impact on node lifetime. More accurately, the amount of time a sensor node has to switch the radio chip on significantly reduces its lifetime. As observed by [27] and our experiments, keeping the radio on at all times is not a viable option. The networking community has taken major steps to reduce idle listening, i.e., time where the radio chip is on but there no message to receive. While these efforts reduce idle listening and thereby increase node lifetimes significantly, they come at the cost of a large overhead for sending and receiving messages. Thus, the number of messages exchanged between sensor nodes is the most important factor for the evaluation of the energy efficiency of an application. Within reasonable limits, the actual size of the messages does not affect energy consumption significantly which is a common misconception, particularly of the database community.

This confirms our approach for the evaluation of our mechanisms for query dissemination and in-network processing: We count the number of messages sent and received to measure its impact on the sensor networks lifetime.

A.3. LESSONS LEARNED

Appendix B

Spatio-temporal queries with relational operators

This portion of the appendix serves as an illustration why expressing spatio-temporal semantics with relational operators and executing them over a table is inefficient and unnecessarily complex. We use the development WSNEnter $(\mathbf{O}, \mathcal{Z})$ defined in (B.1) as an example of a simple spatio-temporal query in a sensor network:

$$\text{WSNEnter}(\mathbf{O}, \mathcal{Z}) = \textit{Disjoint}(\mathbf{O}, \mathcal{Z}) \mathbin{\widetilde{\triangleright}} \textit{Inside}(\mathbf{O}, \mathcal{Z}) \tag{B.1}$$

From a semantical point of view, the user is interested in every object $\mathbf{O}$ that is exclusively detected by nodes not in $\mathcal{Z}$ at first and later on exclusively detected by nodes in $\mathcal{Z}$ (cf. Section 3.3.2). We assume that the zone is dynamic, i.e., nodes may be in the zone at some time and leave the zone at a later time. We introduce a relational schema for storing dynamic zones and object detections at first. Afterwards, we derive the SQL statement that expresses WSNEnter $(\mathbf{O}, \mathcal{Z})$. Finally, we show that a query regarding the spatio-temporal relationship of an object and a region, e.g., Enter $(\mathbf{O}, \mathbf{R})$, is even more complex to express because SQL does not provide operators for point sets.

Since we only want to illustrate the difficulties associated with the expression of spatio-temporal queries using relational operators, we will not deal with any aspect of the implementation. Prior to the execution of the SQL statement derived in Section B.2, all data on zones and objects detected must be collected wherever the statement is executed. An approach to achieve this data collection would be the centralized strategy we introduced in Chapter 5, i.e., whenever a node detects an object, stops detecting an object, enters or leaves the zone, it sends a corresponding message to the base station.

B.1 Relational Schema

The relation **Detections** stores the detection of objects by different nodes at different times. Table B.1 illustrates the schema of **Detections**. The table contains a tuple for each time an object moves into the detection area of a node. After this entry, the object may move arbitrarily inside the detection area and leave it at some time. Whenever this leave happens, the node updates the attribute t_{exit} of the tuple created at the time of the entry.

Attribute Name	Attribute Description
NodeID	Identifier of the node S_i detecting the object identified by attribute ObjectID.
ObjectID	Identifier of the object detected by S_i.
t_{entry}	$t \in \mathbb{T}$ when S_i starts to detect the object.
t_{exit}	This value is either $\emptyset$ or a $t > t_{entry}$. If it is $\emptyset$, S_i is still detecting the object. Otherwise, S_i has detected the object during the time interval $[t_{entry}; t_{exit}[$.

Table B.1: The schema of the relation **Detections**

Note that this schema assumes continuous detection of objects. In cases where the used detection mechanism is non-continuous, one can interpolate detections: Suppose S_i checks periodically at $t_0, t_1, \ldots$ for objects. With interpolation, an arbitrary node S_i inserts a corresponding tuple whenever it did not detect an object **O** at t_{j-1} but detects it at t_j. Similarly, S_i updates t_{exit} in the tuple corresponding to the object **O** from $\emptyset$ to t_j if S_i detected **O** at time t_{j-1}, but does not detect **O** at t_j.

The relation **Zones** stores the times for each node when it was inside a given zone. The schema illustrated in Table B.2 is similar to **Detections**. The main difference is that each tuple stores an identifier of the zone instead of an object identifier. The mechanisms for maintaining the tuples in this relation are analogous to those described above: Whenever a node S_i determines that it is part of the zone $\mathcal{Z}$ at time t_i, it inserts a tuple $[S_i, \mathcal{Z}, t_i, \emptyset]$ into **Zones**. This tuple is updated to $[S_i, \mathcal{Z}, t_i, t_j]$ if S_i determines that it is not part of the zone anymore at time t_j with $t_i < t_j$.

B.2 Expressing a Spatio-Temporal Query using SQL

This section describes how to express the development WSNEnter $(\mathbf{O}, \mathcal{Z})$ using SQL based on the schema described above. The core idea for this is as follows: First, one needs to determine all objects **O** that have fulfilled *Disjoint* $(\mathbf{O}, \mathcal{Z})$ at some time t_i, i.e., have been detected by nodes outside of $\mathcal{Z}$ exclusively (cf. Definition 32). One of these objects **O** fulfills WSNEnter $(\mathbf{O}, \mathcal{Z})$ if there exists a time $t_j > t_i$ where **O** is detected exclusively by nodes in $\mathcal{Z}$, i.e., if it fulfills *Inside* $(\mathbf{O}, \mathcal{Z})$ after t_i.

To ease presentation, we decompose the development of the SQL statement into several steps:

Attribute Name	Attribute Description
NodeID	Identifier of the node S_i that this tuple is about.
ZoneID	Identifier of the zone S_i is/was in.
t_{entry}	$t \in \mathbb{T}$ when S_i "entered" the zone.
t_{exit}	This value is either $\emptyset$ or a $t > t_{entry}$. If it is $\emptyset$, S_i is still in the zone identified by ZoneID. Otherwise, S_i has been in this zone during the time interval $[t_{entry}; t_{exit}[$.

Table B.2: The schema of the relation Zones

Step 1 Obtain a set of tuples [ObjectID, iStart, iEnd] where nodes outside of $\mathcal{Z}$ detect the object identified by ObjectID during the time interval [iStart, iEnd]. We construct a view called OutsideDetected^v that contains these tuples.

Step 2 Similarly to the previous step, we generate a set of tuples [ObjectID, iStart, iEnd] where nodes inside of $\mathcal{Z}$ detect the object. As with the result from **Step 1**, we summarize the tuples computed in this step using a view called InsideDetected^v.

Step 3 Join OutsideDetected^v and InsideDetected^v to check which of the time intervals of the tuples overlap and compute tuples [ObjectID, iStart, iEnd] that correspond to intervals where only nodes outside of $\mathcal{Z}$ detect the object identified by ObjectID. The tuples obtained in this step correspond to objects and time intervals where the predicate *Disjoint*(**O**, $\mathcal{Z}$) is true. The view DisjointView^v contains the corresponding tuples.

Step 4 Similar to the previous step, we join OutsideDetected^v and InsideDetected^v again to compute those objects where *Inside*(**O**, $\mathcal{Z}$) has been true for some time. The query result of this step will be summarized in the view InsideView^v.

Step 5 By joining InsideView^v and DisjointView^v we compute those objects where *Disjoint*(**O**, $\mathcal{Z}$) has been true before *Inside*(**O**, $\mathcal{Z}$) was true.

We use views in the following to summarize intermediate results to ease our presentation. Views are marked with a 'v' superscript to clearly separate them from materialized relations, i.e., relations physically stored on sensor nodes or the base station. This is important, because views are reconstructed whenever their data is required, i.e., the underlying query is executed. For sensor networks this means that accessing the view either requires re-execution of the underlying query or storing all tuples required for the reconstruction at a central point, e.g., the base station.

B.2.1 Step 1 – Computing OutsideDetected^v

This section provides the SQL statement that constructs the view OutsideDetected^v. The SQL statement in Algorithm 15 generates a tuple [ObjectID, iStart, iEnd] for every start of a detection by node outside of $\mathcal{Z}$ of an object identified by ObjectID at some time. The values of iStart and iEnd frame the interval during which an object was detected by nodes outside of $\mathcal{Z}$.

B.2. EXPRESSING A SPATIO-TEMPORAL QUERY USING SQL

Algorithm 15: SQL statement to get all objects detected by nodes outside of $\mathcal{Z}$

1 **SELECT** ObjectID, d.t_{entry} **AS** iStart, d.t_{exit} **AS** iEnd **FROM** Detections d
2   **WHERE NOT EXISTS SELECT** * **FROM** Zones z
3   **WHERE** d.NodeID = z.NodeID **AND** z.ZoneID= $\mathcal{Z}$
4   **AND** z.t_{entry} ≤ d.t_{entry}
5   **AND** ((d.t_{entry} ≤ z.t_{exit}) **OR** (z.t_{exit} = Ø))
6   **AND NOT EXISTS SELECT** * **FROM** Zones z
7   **WHERE** d.NodeID = z.NodeID **AND** z.ZoneID= $\mathcal{Z}$
8   **AND** d.t_{entry} ≤ z.t_{entry}
9   **AND** ((z.t_{entry} ≤ d.t_{exit}) **OR** (d.t_{exit} = Ø))
10 **UNION**
11 **SELECT** ObjectID, d.t_{entry} **AS** iStart, z.t_{entry} **AS** iEnd **FROM** Detections d, Zones z
12   **WHERE** d.NodeID = z.NodeID **AND** z.ZoneID = $\mathcal{Z}$
13   **AND** d.t_{entry} ≤ z.t_{entry}
14   **AND** ((z.t_{entry} ≤ d.t_{exit}) **OR** (d.t_{exit} = Ø))
15 **UNION**
16 **SELECT** ObjectID, z.t_{exit} **AS** iStart, d.t_{exit} **AS** iEnd **FROM** Detections d, Zones z
17   **WHERE** d.NodeID = z.NodeID **AND** z.ZoneID = $\mathcal{Z}$
18   **AND NOT** (z.t_{exit} = Ø)
19   **AND** d.t_{entry} ≤ z.t_{exit}
20   **AND** ((z.t_{exit} < d.t_{exit}) **OR** (d.t_{exit} = Ø))

There are four different cases that must be taken into account to acquire these intervals and each subquery in Algorithm 15 corresponds to one of them:

1. An object was detected by a node that never joins or leaves the zone $\mathcal{Z}$. In this case, there is a node $\mathcal{S}_i$ that detected an object but there does not exist a tuple for $\mathcal{S}_i$ in Zones. This case is covered by Lines 1-9. In this case, iStart and iEnd equal the start and the end of the detection as stored in Detections.

2. A node detects an object before it joins or after has left $\mathcal{Z}$. Figures B.1 and B.2 illustrate this using time bars for two tuples from Zones and Detections. Lines 1-9 address this case as well: The EXIST statements requests tuples from Zones that indicate that the node $\mathcal{S}_i$ that detected an object according to Detections has joined or left $\mathcal{Z}$ while detecting an object. If no such tuple in Zones exists, the node detecting the object was outside of $\mathcal{Z}$ and thus, the start and the end of the interval [iStart, iEnd] equal d.t_{entry} and d.t_{exit} respectively.

3. A node joins $\mathcal{Z}$ while detecting an object (see Figure B.4). This case occurs if d.t_{entry} ≤ z.t_{entry} and z.t_{entry} ≤ d.t_{exit} (Lines 11-14). In this case, the interval returned is defined as iStart = d.t_{entry} and iEnd = z.t_{entry}.

4. A node leaves $\mathcal{Z}$ while it detects an object (see Figure B.3). This case is analogous to the case

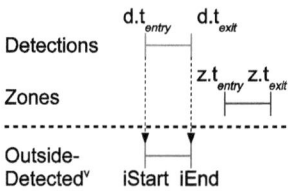

Figure B.1: `OutsideDetected`^{v} – Node detected object before joining $\mathcal{Z}$

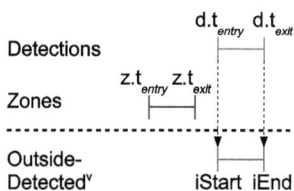

Figure B.2: `OutsideDetected`^{v} – Node detected object after joining $\mathcal{Z}$

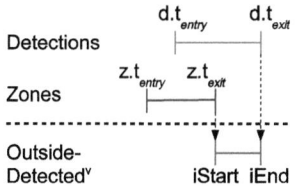

Figure B.3: `OutsideDetected`^{v} – Node detected object while joining $\mathcal{Z}$

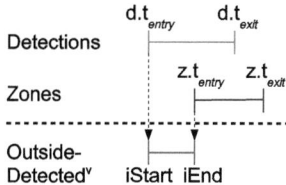

Figure B.4: `OutsideDetected`^{v} – Node detected object while leaving $\mathcal{Z}$

where the node joins the zone while detecting the object. Hence, the object must be detected after $z.t_{entry}$ and at least until the node leaves the zone, i.e., $d.t_{entry} \leq z.t_{exit}$ (cf Lines 16-20). Therefore, iStart = $z.t_{exit}$ and iEnd = $d.t_{exit}$.

Summing up, `OutsideDetected`^{v} contains a tuple [ObjectID, iStart, iEnd] for every detection of an object by a node during a time when the node was outside of $\mathcal{Z}$ at some time. Note that each of these tuples does not imply $Disjoint(\mathbf{O}, \mathcal{Z}) = \mathcal{T}$ for the corresponding object $\mathbf{O}$ because there could be nodes in $\mathcal{Z}$ that detect $\mathbf{O}$ at a time that overlaps with the time indicated by the tuple.

B.2.2 Step 2 – Computing `InsideDetected`^{v}

The SQL statement in Algorithm 16 constructs the view `InsideDetected`^{v}. Analog to `OutsideDetected`^{v}, the SQL statement generates a tuple [ObjectID, iStart, iEnd] for every start of a detection by node inside of $\mathcal{Z}$ of an object identified by ObjectID at some time.

Similar to Algorithm 15, we decompose the query into several subqueries. Each subquery corresponds to one of the following cases where a node inside $\mathcal{Z}$ detects an object; similar to `OutsideDetected`^{v}, we illustrate each case with a figure that displays time bars representing tuples from Zones and Detections:

B.2. EXPRESSING A SPATIO-TEMPORAL QUERY USING SQL

Algorithm 16: SQL statement to get all objects detected by nodes in $\mathcal{Z}$

1 **SELECT** ObjectID, d.t_{entry} **AS** iStart, d.t_{exit} **AS** iEnd **FROM** Detections d, Zones z
2 **WHERE** d.NodeID = z.NodeID **AND** z.ZoneID = $\mathcal{Z}$
3 **AND** z.t_{entry} ≤ d.t_{entry}
4 **AND** ((d.t_{exit} ≤ z.t_{exit}) **OR** (z.t_{exit} = ∅))
5 **UNION**
6 **SELECT** ObjectID, d.t_{entry} **AS** iStart, z.t_{exit} **AS** iEnd **FROM** Detections d, Zones z
7 **WHERE** d.NodeID = z.NodeID **AND** z.ZoneID = $\mathcal{Z}$
8 **AND** z.t_{entry} ≤ d.t_{entry}
9 **AND NOT** (z.t_{exit} = ∅)
10 **AND** d.t_{entry} ≤ z.t_{exit}
11 **AND** ((z.t_{exit} ≤ d.t_{exit}) **OR** (d.t_{exit} = ∅))
12 **UNION**
13 **SELECT** ObjectID, z.t_{entry} **AS** iStart, d.t_{exit} **AS** iEnd **FROM** Detections d, Zones z
14 **WHERE** d.NodeID = z.NodeID **AND** z.ZoneID = $\mathcal{Z}$
15 **AND** d.t_{entry} ≤ z.t_{entry}
16 **AND NOT** (d.t_{exit} = ∅)
17 **AND** z.t_{entry} ≤ d.t_{exit}
18 **AND** ((d.t_{exit} ≤ z.t_{exit}) **OR** (z.t_{exit} = ∅))
19 **UNION**
20 **SELECT** ObjectID, z.t_{entry} **AS** iStart, z.t_{exit} **AS** iEnd **FROM** Detections d, Zones z
21 **WHERE** d.NodeID = z.NodeID **AND** z.ZoneID = $\mathcal{Z}$
22 **AND** d.t_{entry} ≤ z.t_{entry}
23 **AND NOT** (z.t_{exit} = ∅)
24 **AND** ((z.t_{exit} ≤ d.t_{exit}) **OR** (d.t_{exit} = ∅))

1. Lines 1-4 generate a tuple [ObjectID, iStart, iEnd] for all detections where the node was in $\mathcal{Z}$ for all times while detecting an object. Figure B.5 illustrates this case using time bars. In this case, the beginning and the end of the detection frame the interval [iStart, iEnd], i.e., iStart = d.t_{entry} and iEnd = d.t_{exit}.
2. As illustrated by Figure B.6, a node $\mathcal{S}_i \in \mathcal{Z}$ may leave the zone while detecting an object. The subquery in Lines 6-11 of Algorithm 16 addresses this case. The appropriate intervals for the tuple [ObjectID, iStart, iEnd] are iStart = d.t_{entry} and iEnd = z.t_{exit}.
3. Similarly to the previous case, a node may join $\mathcal{Z}$ while detecting an object and then stop detecting the object while still being in the zone as shown by the time bars in Figure B.7. As defined by the subquery in Lines 13-18, the attribute values for the tuple [ObjectID, iStart, iEnd] are iStart = z.t_{entry} and iEnd = d.t_{exit}.
4. The counter-case to the first one is that a node detects an object while joining and leaving $\mathcal{Z}$.

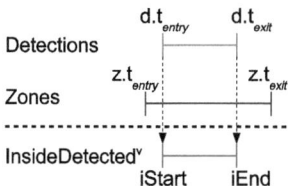

Figure B.5: InsideDetected^v – Node is in $\mathcal{Z}$ while detecting object

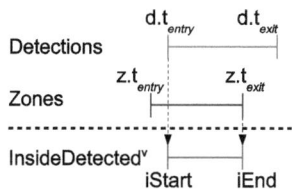

Figure B.6: InsideDetected^v – Node detects object while leaving $\mathcal{Z}$

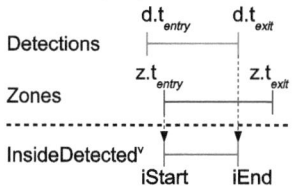

Figure B.7: InsideDetected^v – Node detects object while joining $\mathcal{Z}$

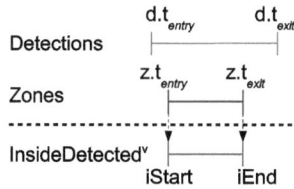

Figure B.8: InsideDetected^v – Node joins and leaves $\mathcal{Z}$ while detecting object

This is illustrated by Figure B.8. Lines 20-24 contain the subquery corresponding to this case. It results in $\text{iStart} = z.t_{entry}$ and $\text{iEnd} = z.t_{exit}$ for the tuple [ObjectID, iStart, iEnd].

Analogous to OutsideDetected^v, the set of tuples created by the SQL statement in Algorithm 16 creates a tuple for every object detection by a node $\mathcal{S}_i$ that is in $\mathcal{Z}$ at some time during the detection. Recall that these tuples do not necessarily correspond to objects $\mathbf{O}$ where $Inside(\mathbf{O}, \mathcal{Z}) = \mathcal{T}$, because the time intervals could still overlap with detections by nodes outside of $\mathcal{Z}$.

B.2.3 Step 3 – Computing DisjointView^v

The previous steps derived tuples [ObjectID, iStart, iEnd] which describe intervals where nodes inside or outside of $\mathcal{Z}$ detected objects. The results of these steps have been summarized in the two views InsideDetected^v and OutsideDetected^v respectively. Next, we provide an SQL statement that computes tuples [ObjectID, iStart, iEnd] for objects $\mathbf{O}$ where $Disjoint(\mathbf{O}, \mathcal{Z}) = \mathcal{T}$ for the interval [iStart, iEnd].
Notation (Tuple Overlap): A tuple $T_1 = [\text{ObjectID}, \text{iStart}, \text{iEnd}]$ *overlaps* with another tuple $T_2 = [\text{ObjectID}, \text{iStart}, \text{iEnd}]$ if at least one of the following conditions is true:

- $T_1.\text{iStart} \leq T_2.\text{iStart} \leq T_1.\text{iEnd}$

B.2. EXPRESSING A SPATIO-TEMPORAL QUERY USING SQL

- $T_2.\texttt{iStart} \leq T_1.\texttt{iStart} \leq T_2.\texttt{iEnd}$
- $T_2.\texttt{iStart} \leq T_1.\texttt{iEnd} \leq T_2.\texttt{iEnd}$
- $T_1.\texttt{iStart} \leq T_2.\texttt{iEnd} \leq T_1.\texttt{iEnd}$

Similarly to the previous queries, this SQL statement consists of several subqueries, but since these are a little more complex, we describe them one by one. Due to its length, we omit the complete SQL statement at this point, but to obtain it, one has to use the UNION operator to "concatenate" all of them into the view definition of $\texttt{DisjointView}^v$.

Algorithm 17: $\textit{Disjoint}\,(\mathbf{O}, \mathcal{Z})$ – Tuples without overlapping detections in $\texttt{InsideDetected}^v$

1 **SELECT** o.ObjectID, o.iStart, o.iEnd **FROM** $\texttt{OutsideDetected}^v$ o
2 **WHERE NOT EXISTS** (
3   **SELECT** * **FROM** $\texttt{InsideDetected}^v$ i
4   **WHERE** i.ObjectID = o.ObjectID
5   **AND** i.iStart $\leq$ o.iStart
6   **AND** ((o.iStart $\leq$ o.iEnd) **OR** (i.iEnd = $\emptyset$))
7) **AND NOT EXISTS** (
8   **SELECT** * **FROM** $\texttt{InsideDetected}^v$ i
9   **WHERE** i.ObjectID = o.ObjectID
10   **AND** o.iStart $\leq$ i.iStart
11   **AND** ((i.iStart $\leq$ o.iEnd) **OR** (o.iEnd = $\emptyset$))
12)

The first subquery in Algorithm 17 computes all tuples that describe a detection by a node $\mathcal{S}_i \in \overline{\mathcal{Z}}$ for an interval [iStart, iEnd] that does not overlap with any detection/tuple in $\texttt{InsideDetected}^v$. The first part of the query (Lines 2-6) checks for every tuple [ObjectID, iStart, iEnd] in $\texttt{OutsideDetected}^v$ if there is a tuple in $\texttt{InsideDetected}^v$ which overlaps with iStart. The second part (Lines 7-11) of the query performs the same check with iEnd for every tuple in $\texttt{OutsideDetected}^v$. For every tuple that fulfills both conditions, it is sure that the corresponding object $\mathbf{O}$ conforms to $\textit{Disjoint}\,(\mathbf{O}, \mathcal{Z})$ for the interval [iStart, iEnd].

The remaining cases are those where either iStart, or iEnd or both overlap with tuples from $\texttt{InsideDetected}^v$, i.e., there are detections by nodes outside of $\mathcal{Z}$ that partly or completely overlap with detections by nodes inside of $\mathcal{Z}$. We consider these three cases separately in the following.

First, we consider the case where several tuples [ObjectID, iStart, iEnd] in $\texttt{InsideDetected}^v$ describe detections which overlap with iStart of a single tuple in $T_o = [\texttt{ObjectID, iStart, iEnd}]$ from $\texttt{OutsideDetected}^v$. Algorithm 18 computes a tuple [ObjectID, iStart, iEnd] for of these tuples T_o from $\texttt{OutsideDetected}^v$ where [iStart, iEnd] describes an interval where the object is detected exclusively by nodes outside of $\mathcal{Z}$. According to Definition 32, $\textit{Disjoint}\,(\mathbf{O}, \mathcal{Z}) = \mathcal{T}$ for these intervals. As shown in Algorithm 18, the computation first requires an equi-join of

Algorithm 18: *Disjoint* $(O, \mathcal{Z})$ – Tuples where only iStart overlaps with tuples in InsideDetected^v

1 **SELECT** o.ObjectID, MAX$(i.\text{iEnd})$ **AS** iStart, o.iEnd **FROM** OutsideDetected^v o, InsideDetected^v i
2 **WHERE** o.ObjectID = i.ObjectID
3 **AND** i.iStart ≤ o.iStart
4 **AND NOT** (i.iEnd = ∅)
5 **AND** o.iStart ≤ i.iEnd
6 **AND NOT EXISTS** (
7   **SELECT** * **FROM** InsideDetected^v i2
8   **WHERE** i2.ObjectID = o.ObjectID
9   **AND** i2.iStart ≤ o.iEnd
10   **AND** ((o.iEnd ≤ i2.iEnd) **OR** (i2.iEnd = ∅))
11)
12 **GROUP BY** o.ObjectID, o.iEnd
13 **HAVING** MAX$(i.\text{iEnd})$ < o.iEnd

InsideDetected^v and OutsideDetected^v using ObjectID. Lines 3-5 select those tuples from the join result, where T_o.iStart overlaps with a detection inside of $\mathcal{Z}$. To compute the correct iStart where the object was detected exclusively outside of $\mathcal{Z}$, one has to find the detection from inside $\mathcal{Z}$ with the maximum iEnd. The HAVING in the end ensures that this maximum is not greater than T_o.iEnd, because in this case the object was never detected exclusively outside of $\mathcal{Z}$.

Similar to above, we consider tuples T_o = [ObjectID, iStart, iEnd] from OutsideDetected^v where iEnd overlaps with tuples from InsideDetected^v. To compute the interval [iStart, iEnd] for T_o where the object was detected exclusively outside of $\mathcal{Z}$, the tuple with the minimum iStart out of those tuples from InsideDetected^v that overlap with T_o must be found. Again, we use an equi-join of OutsideDetected^v and InsideDetected^v as well as a group-operator to find this tuple. Lines 2-4 selects tuples from the join result, where T_o.iEnd overlaps with tuples from InsideDetected^v. These tuples are grouped by ObjectID and T_o.iStart and then we compute the minimum iStart from detections by nodes inside of $\mathcal{Z}$.

Algorithm 20 is a combination of the two previous cases: Assuming there is a tuple T_o = [ObjectID, iStart, iEnd] where iEnd as well as iStart are overlapped by detections in InsideDetected^v. To obtain a correct result tuple [ObjectID, iStart, iEnd] that describes an interval where the object is exclusively detected by nodes outside of $\mathcal{Z}$, the steps described in Algorithms 18 and 19 must be completed for each of these tuples in OutsideDetected^v.

B.2. EXPRESSING A SPATIO-TEMPORAL QUERY USING SQL

Algorithm 19: $Disjoint(\mathbf{O}, \mathcal{Z})$ – Tuples where only iEnd overlaps with tuples in InsideDetected^v

1 **SELECT** o.ObjectID, o.iStart, MIN$(i.$iStart$)$ **AS** iEnd **FROM** OutsideDetected^v o, InsideDetected^v i
2 **WHERE** o.ObjectID = i.ObjectID
3 **AND** o.iStart ≤ i.iStart
4 **AND** ((i.iStart ≤ o.iEnd) **OR** (o.iEnd = Ø))
5 **AND NOT EXISTS** (
6   **SELECT** * **FROM** InsideDetected^v i2
7   **WHERE** o.ObjectID = i2.ObjectID
8   **AND** i2.iStart ≤ o.iStart
9   **AND** ((o.iStart ≤ i2.iEnd) **OR** (i2.iEnd = Ø))
10)
11 **GROUP BY** o.ObjectID, o.iStart
12 **HAVING** o.iStart < MIN$(i.$iEnd$)$

Algorithm 20: $Disjoint(\mathbf{O}, \mathcal{Z})$ – Tuples where iStart and iEnd overlap with tuples in InsideDetected^v

1 **SELECT** o.ObjectID, MAX$(i1.$iEnd$)$ **AS** iStart, MIN$(i2.$iStart$)$ **AS** iEnd **FROM** OutsideDetected^v o, InsideDetected^v i1, InsideDetected^v i2
2 **WHERE** o.ObjectID = i1.ObjectID **AND** o.ObjectID = i2.ObjectID
3 **AND** i1.iStart ≤ o.iStart
4 **AND NOT** (i1.iEnd = Ø)
5 **AND** o.iStart ≤ i1.iEnd
6 **AND** o.iStart ≤ i2.iStart
7 **AND** ((i2.iStart ≤ o.iEnd) **OR** (o.iEnd = Ø))
8 **GROUP BY** o.ObjectID, o.iStart, o.iEnd
9 **HAVING** MAX$(i1.$iEnd$)$ < MIN$(i2.$iStart$)$

B.2.4 Step 4 – Computing InsideView^v

This section provides SQL statements to compute tuples [ObjectID, iStart, iEnd] that describe time intervals during which an object identified by ObjectID has been detected exclusively by nodes in $\mathcal{Z}$. As with *Disjoint* $(\mathbf{O}, \mathcal{Z})$ above, this computation is based on the tuples InsideDetected^v and OutsideDetected^v and consists of four subqueries which we discuss separately in the following. To obtain the complete SQL statement for *Inside* $(\mathbf{O}, \mathcal{Z})$, the subqueries must be "concatenated" using UNION operations.

Algorithm 21: *Inside* $(\mathbf{O}, \mathcal{Z})$ – Tuples without overlapping detections in OutsideDetected^v

1   **SELECT** i.ObjectID, i.iStart, i.iEnd **FROM** InsideDetected^v i
2   **WHERE NOT EXISTS** (
3   **SELECT** * **FROM** OutsideDetected^v o
4   **WHERE** o.ObjectID = i.ObjectID
5   **AND** o.iStart ≤ i.iStart
6   **AND** ((i.iStart ≤ o.iEnd) **OR** (o.iEnd = ∅))
7   ) **AND NOT EXISTS** (
8   **SELECT** * **FROM** OutsideDetected^v o
9   **WHERE** o.ObjectID = i.ObjectID
10   **AND** i.iStart ≤ o.iStart
11   **AND** ((o.iStart ≤ i.iEnd) **OR** (i.iEnd = ∅))

The subquery in Algorithm 21 derives tuples [ObjectID, iStart, iEnd] for all tuples in InsideDetected^v which do not overlap with any tuples from InsideDetected^v. The approach is analogous to Algorithm 17: The first part (Lines 2-6) determines for a given tuple T_i from InsideDetected^v if there are tuples in OutsideDetected^v that overlap with T_i.iStart. The check if there are tuples in OutsideDetected^v performs the same check for T_i.iEnd in Lines 7- 11

Algorithms 22 and 23 are analogous to Algorithms 18 and 19 respectively: Both restrict the start or the end of the interval appropriately for tuples that partly overlap with detections by nodes outside of $\mathcal{Z}$. Based on this, Algorithm 24 combines both steps in cases where the start and the end of a detection stored in InsideDetected^v overlaps with tuples in OutsideDetected^v.

B.2. EXPRESSING A SPATIO-TEMPORAL QUERY USING SQL

Algorithm 22: $Inside(\mathbf{O}, \mathcal{Z})$ – Tuples where only iStart overlaps with tuples in OutsideDetected^v

1 **SELECT** i.ObjectID, MAX(o.iEnd) **AS** iStart, i.iEnd **FROM** InsideDetected^v i, OutsideDetected^v o
2   **WHERE** i.ObjectID = o.ObjectID
3   **AND** o.iStart ≤ i.iStart
4   **AND NOT** (o.iEnd = Ø)
5   **AND** i.iStart ≤ o.iEnd
6   **AND NOT EXISTS** (
7   **SELECT** * **FROM** OutsideDetected^v o2
8   **WHERE** o2.ObjectID = i.ObjectID
9   **AND** o2.iStart ≤ i.iEnd
10   **AND** ((i.iEnd ≤ o2.iEnd) **OR** (o2.iEnd = Ø))
11   )
12   **GROUP BY** i.ObjectID, i.iEnd
13   **HAVING** MAX(o.iEnd) < i.iEnd

Algorithm 23: $Inside(\mathbf{O}, \mathcal{Z})$ – Tuples where only iEnd overlaps with tuples in OutsideDetected^v

1 **SELECT** i.ObjectID, i.iStart, MIN(o.iStart) **FROM** InsideDetected^v i, OutsideDetected^v o
2   **WHERE** i.ObjectID = o.ObjectID
3   **AND** i.iStart ≤ o.iStart
4   **AND** ((o.iStart ≤ i.iEnd) **OR** (i.iEnd = Ø))
5   **AND NOT EXISTS** (
6   **SELECT** * **FROM** OutsideDetected^v o2
7   **WHERE** o2.ObjectID = i.ObjectID
8   **AND** o2.iStart ≤ i.iStart
9   **AND** ((i.iStart ≤ o2.iEnd) **OR** (o2.iEnd = Ø))
10   )
11   **GROUP BY** i.ObjectID, i.iStart
12   **HAVING** i.iStart < MIN(o.iStart)

Algorithm 24: $Inside(\mathbf{O}, \mathcal{Z})$ – Tuples where iStart and iEnd overlap with tuples in OutsideDetected^v

1 **SELECT** i.ObjectID, MAX(o1.iEnd) **AS** iStart, MIN(o2.iStart) **AS** iEnd **FROM** InsideDetected^v i, OutsideDetected^v o1, OutsideDetected^v o2
2 **WHERE** i.ObjectID = o1.ObjectID **AND** i.ObjectID = o2.ObjectID
3 **AND** o1.iStart ≤ i.iStart
4 **AND NOT** (o1.iEnd = ∅)
5 **AND** i.iStart ≤ o1.iEnd
6 **AND** i.iStart ≤ o2.iStart
7 **AND** ((o2.iStart ≤ i.iEnd) **OR** (i.iEnd = ∅))
8 **GROUP BY** i.ObjectID, i.iStart, i.iEnd
9 **HAVING** MAX(o1.iEnd) < MIN(o2.iStart)

B.2.5 Step 5 – Assembling the subqueries for WSNEnter $(\mathbf{O}, \mathcal{Z})$

Using the two views `InsideView`^{v} and `DisjointView`^{v} the computation of the set of objects whose movement conforms to WSNEnter $(\mathbf{O}, \mathcal{Z})$ is straightforward: As illustrated in Algorithm 25, both views are joined and the respective starts of the intervals are compared. Any object with a tuple in `DisjointView`^{v} which has a corresponding tuple in `InsideView`^{v} afterwards conforms to WSNEnter $(\mathbf{O}, \mathcal{Z})$.

Algorithm 25: SQL statement to determine objects that conform to WSNEnter $(\mathbf{O}, \mathcal{Z})$

1 **SELECT** d.ObjectID **FROM** DisjointView^v d, InsideView^v i
2 **WHERE** d.ObjectID = z.ObjectID **AND** z.ZoneID = $\mathcal{Z}$
3 **AND** d.iStart < i.iStart

We implemented the aforementioned views using an Oracle 10g DBMS. The resulting relational execution plan had a depth of 16, i.e., some tuples had to be accessed by 16 relational operators. Most importantly, the operator tree contained several joins and self-joins. This problematic considering the problems associated with join processing in sensor networks (cf. Section 2.3). Hence, we conclude that sending all tuples for Detections and Zones to the base station would be the best strategy for a relational query processor.

B.3 Relational Schemas and Regions

The query addressed in the previous section did not require any operations on point sets. Instead, we only demonstrated the complexity of expressing a sequence of detections by nodes that are either inside or outside of a given zone $\mathcal{Z}$. The resulting query is already complex and the execution requires several joins and exist operations on the given tuples.

A query that operates on point sets is even more complex. Consider the development Enter$(\mathbf{O},\mathbf{R})$ as an example: First, one would have to find a schema to model the position estimate (cf. Definition 17). Such a representation has to distribute the point set that represents the position estimation of a single detection over several tuples or relations to decompose it into the basic types supported by relational database systems. Thus, to compute the possible object position (cf. Definition 18) for some instant of time would require several (self-)joins to reconstruct the position estimation for every node detecting a given object. Once these point sets are reconstructed, computing the intersection of these point sets would finally yield the possible object positions. Since the intersection of two point sets is not an operation that is supported by database systems, this would require further subqueries with joins.

Summing up, it is reasonable to conclude that expressing Enter$(\mathbf{O},\mathbf{R})$ using SQL would be even more complex than WSNEnter$(\mathbf{O},\mathcal{Z})$ because operations on point sets are not supported by relational database systems. This also applies to the existing relational query processors for sensor networks, since they only provide an abstraction of these relational concepts for sensor networks.

B.4 Lessons Learned

This section has illustrated the difficulties that occur when users try to express queries that have spatio-temporal semantics using a relational database system. Even a relatively simple spatio-temporal query is problematic, because expressing sequences of events, temporal intervals and the relation between these intervals results in complex queries. Even more problematic are queries where point sets and their topological relation are involved: Point sets must be reconstructed through several (self-)joins and operations to check if point sets overlap are difficult to express with SQL or relational operators.

It must be noted also that the intermediate results generated by these queries are large, because tuples originating from every node of the sensor network are joined. Furthermore, the tests for non-existence tests in some of these queries require sending a confirmation from every node in the sensor network to a central point, e.g., the base station. Thus, the existing relational query processors would transport all tuples to the base station and execute joins as well as non-existence operators there.

Appendix C
The Karlsruhe Sensor Networking Project

The Karlsruhe Sensor Networking Project (KSN) served as a platform to publish general-purpose software for Sun SPOTs created for this dissertation. At the beginning of our work, the software available for Sun SPOTs was also in its infancy: Among other things, communication was problematic due to bugs in low-level layers of the default communication stack. Additionally, programming SPOTs was error-prone mainly because the missing serialization lead to unnecessarily complex code for relatively simple applications. In the meantime, some of these problems have been addressed, but since we used most of the KSN software for the evaluation of the various mechanisms presented in this dissertation, we describe it here.

The published software is not tailored towards query processing as numerous other projects have shown, e.g., in [137] the KSN Radio Stack was used for water monitoring. Before we describe the various pieces of KSN software, we describe the KSN testbed and thereby introduce several problems we encountered during our work with sensor nodes in general and Sun SPOTs in particular. This provides insight into the motivation and the most important design targets for our work.

C.1 KSN Testbed

To evaluate and test our mechanisms, we deployed 41 Sun SPOT sensors nodes at the Institute for Program Structures and Data Organization (IPD) as displayed in Figure C.1. This setup has several intricacies that influenced the design of the spatio-temporal query processor described in the main part of the dissertation as well as all components developed in the KSN project. We describe a few of them to motivate our measures, particularly regarding the development of the KSN Radio Stack and the KSN Management Application.

Deploying 41 Sun SPOT sensor nodes to test and evaluate software for sensor networks poses the unique challenge that one has to administrate sensor nodes without having physical access to

C.2. KSN SERIALIZATION AND COLLECTIONS

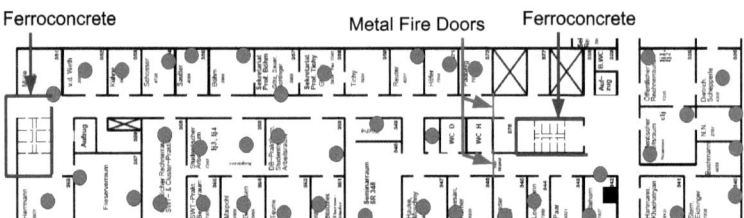

Figure C.1: The KSN Testbed: 41 Sun SPOTs deployed at the IPD

them. This is because manually walking into each office to reset nodes or update software is not an option. While the software provided with Sun SPOTs has a so called *over-the-air (OTA) command server* which allows users to access nodes using the radio, the software was not developed with a testbed of this size in mind. As we show in Section C.5, this OTA command server is relatively unreliable and inefficient regarding the time it takes to update software on up to 41 nodes.

Another problem with this setup are the external influences that interfere with radio communication: Most importantly, this testbed is deployed in a computer science building with many wireless networks and wireless devices accessing the Internet using these networks. The frequencies used by Sun SPOTs and their 802.15.4-compatible radio chip as well as the 802.11-compatible devices commonly used by wireless devices such as laptops overlap. This causes contention, collisions and reduced radio ranges. Thus, all our measures must be able to cope with such a collision-rich environment.

Another problem is the building itself: There are fire doors consisting of steel as well as ferroconcrete walls that prevent wireless communication. While the ferroconcrete walls are just constantly preventing communication, the fire doors are opened and closed by people using the building. Opening one of the fire doors changes the network topology, because nodes that previously could not communicate directly are able to exchange messages temporarily. These changes influence processes like software deployment in the testbed, because the network topology changes while the transfer is in progress. Summing up, the external conditions require that software is designed in such a way that nodes can cope with topology changes quickly even during data transmission.

C.2 KSN Serialization and Collections

Sun SPOT run Java programs, i.e., use an object-oriented approach to define data structures and operators. While this is advantageous for complex applications to maintain software quality and allow reusability of code, it is problematic when object structures must be transferred from one place to another. This includes storing objects on a disk, in flash memory or transferring them between different hosts. The reason for this is that the physical devices responsible for storage or transmission are not object-oriented, i.e., they only "understand" simple data types like bytes or integers. Serialization techniques have proven to be very useful to solve this issue.

In general, serialization techniques encapsulate the process of transferring an object from one host to another as follows: First, before the object is sent, the object is decomposed into a string of bytes, i.e., *serialized*. This string of bytes is then transferred to a remote host. After the string has been received completely at the remote host, the sent object is reconstructed from the string of bytes, i.e., *deserialized*. To serialize an object, the structure of the object and how it is organized in memory must be known. In Java, this depends on the virtual machine (VM) and therefore the serialization must be reimplemented for every virtual machine with serialization support. However, the Squawk VM used on Sun SPOTs does not support serialization.

While implementation and maintenance of small applications is possible without serialization, larger programs like query processors require it, as the following example demonstrates: Consider a query processor that has to deliver a result set from a given node to the base station. In most cases, the result set will be a complex data structure containing tuples with different attribute values of varying types. Without a serialization mechanism, the result set would require a custom implementation of the decomposition into a string of bytes for every complex data structure. Implementing these custom mechanisms is not only error-prone and time consuming, it also breaches software engineering principles. For example the principle of *locality* is breached because changing a data structure in the result set would also require modifications of the communication process. Other important aspects like *type safety* of software engineering are also neglected by this *manual serialization*: Errors during the reconstruction of an object at the receiver could result in differences between the sent object and the object reconstructed at the receiver. These errors result in exceptions that are hard to track because they are raised in a totally different part of the code.

The KSN Serialization [10] offers a general approach to solve these issues. In combination with the KSN Radio Stack (cf. Section C.3) it offers an almost desktop-like solution for programming communication intensive applications for Sun SPOTs. In addition to the serialization mechanism, we implemented a complete set of serializable collection data structures for Sun SPOTs like hash maps or array lists. More specifically, the KSN Serialization has the following main features:

1. Applicable to almost any kind of object structure. Limitations are investigated in Section C.2.1.
2. Full Java ME compatibility. This is important because it allows the use of the KSN Serialization on other devices like mobile phones or robots as well.
3. Can be applied without modification of the VM. The implementation is written completely in Java and usable by including the necessary classes and interfaces.
4. Automatically resolves object references, i.e., serializing an object that contains a reference to another object results in the serialization of the references object as well.
5. Adheres to software engineering principles like *locality*: A change of the structure of a class only leads to changes inside the class and does not affect other parts of the implementation, e.g., communication code.

C.2. KSN SERIALIZATION AND COLLECTIONS

6. Ensures type safety.
7. Complete implementation of the Java Collection API including serialization for Java ME.

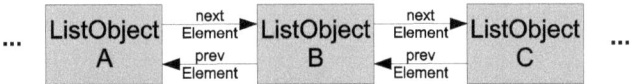

Figure C.2: Structural information requiring serialization in a double linked list

The advantages of serialization come at the cost of increased message size compared to manual serialization, i.e., writing a custom serialization routine for each type of object that is transmitted. This is because the information on the structure of the objects is contained in the source code of the application and not in the message itself. For example, if a program requires transmission of a double linked list (cf. Figure C.2), with manual serialization it is sufficient to send the elements of the list. Since the programmer knows in which order the items were sent and that the list is double linked. The complete structure of the initial list can be reconstructed at the receiver solely based on the elements in the list. Contrary to this, serialization must sent the structural information as well. In case of the double linked list, this structural information includes references to the predecessor and successor in addition to the element of the list. As we show, this overhead can be excessive preventing an application of serialization to sensor nodes. We provide a very efficient approach to reduce this overhead significantly resulting in a viable serialization approach for sensor networks.

C.2.1 The KSN Serialization Process

This section provides an in-depth look at the steps that must be performed for serialization. We use the serialization and deserialization of the double-linked list as a running example (see Figure C.2). The class that implements the double-linked list is called `DoubleLinkedList` from now on. Every element of the list is an instance of the class `ListElement`. Each of these elements contains a random integer declared as `int number` and two references to the previous and the next element, i.e., two references to other instances of `ListElement`. Listing C.1 contains a code fragment that declares this class.

In Java, the serialization and deserialization of data is accomplished through streams. In the following, we denote the stream that is responsible for serializing data into bytes as `OutputStream`. The counterpart of this stream is the `InputStream` which reconstructs a copy of the data from the bytes created by the `OutputStream`.

```
public class ListElement implements KSNSerializable {
  private ListElement next;
  private ListElement previous;
  private int number;
  public ListElement(ListElement next, ListElement previous, int number) {
    this.next = next;
    this.previous = previous;
    this.number = number;
  }
  // Remainder of this class will be illustrated in the following
  ...
}
```

Listing C.1: Declaration of the class ListElement

Serialization method	Description
writeBoolean()	Serializes boolean values
writeByte()	Serializes byte values
writeChar()	Serializes char values
writeFloat()	Serializes Float values
writeInt()	Serializes int values
writeObject()	Serializes complex objects

Table C.1: Methods of OutputStream

Serialization of primitive values OutputStream encapsulates methods that decompose primitive types like int or char or objects into bytes. As shown in Table C.1, for each primitive type[1], there is a method that serializes this type. Thus, to serialize the random integer number in an element of the list, one simply uses OutputStream.writeInt(number).

In JAVA, a variable of type int requires 4 bytes [51]. Prior to writing the four bytes that determine the value of number, the KSN Serialization must denote that these four bytes must belong to an int value. To do so, the KSN Serialization uses a *type identifier*, i.e., a byte value that uniquely identifies each primitive type. Hence, for the serialization of the number one needs 4 + 1 = 5 bytes. Other instances of primitive types are serialized similarly.

The counterpart of the OutputStream at the receiver is the InputStream. For every write-method in Table C.1 the InputStream has a corresponding read-method as shown in Table C.2. The InputStream is responsible for the reconstruction of primitive types and objects. For the aforementioned int-value, the receiver reads the first of the 5 bytes to restore the byte type iden-

---
[1] We have omitted some types in this table and the corresponding table for InputStream. The documentation of the KSN Serialization [10] presents a complete list.

C.2. KSN SERIALIZATION AND COLLECTIONS

tifier. Based on the type identifier, the receiver determines that the next four bytes belong to a `int`-value. Thus, the receiver reserves four bytes in memory, reads four bytes and stores them in the memory reserved.

Deserialization method	Description
`readBoolean()`	Reconstructs `boolean` values
`readByte()`	Reconstructs `byte` values
`readChar()`	Reconstructs `char` values
`readFloat()`	Reconstructs `Float` values
`readInt()`	Reconstructs `int` values
`readObject()`	Reconstructs complex objects

Table C.2: Methods of `InputStream`

Serialization of complex objects The serialization process is started when the method `writeObject()` of an instance of `OutputStream` is called. To allow serialization on a Sun SPOT, a class must implement the interface `KSNSerializable`. This interface requires every serializable class to implement two methods:

- `WriteObjectOnSensor()`: This method is called by the `OutputStream` to write the state of an object to the stream.
- `ReadObjectOnSensor()`: This method reads bytes from the stream and reconstructs the state of the serialized object.

Both methods are necessary because the Squawk VM used on Sun SPOT does not support serialization. Additionally, every class that implements `KSNSerializable` must also implement a *no-argument constructor*. In the following, we show how `WriteObjectOnSensor()` and `ReadObjectOnSensor()` are implemented, how references are reconstructed and the role of the no-argument constructor.

As shown in Listing C.1 implements `KSNSerializable`. The serialization of an instance of `ListElement` requires writing the `int` value as well as the references to the next and the previous element in the list to `OutputStream`. Listing C.2 shows how accomplish this in three steps: The first step in Line 8 serializes the primitive data type as described above. Afterwards, the two references to the next (Line 9) and the previous element (Line 10) in the list must be serialized.

The serialization of the reference to the next and the previous element in the list is more complicated as the serialization of a primitive value like `number`. The main reason for this is that the references must be resolved correctly in order to keep the original list consistent with the previous one. The KSN Serialization deals automatically with this problem: Whenever an object is serialized for the first time, the serialization mechanism generates a unique identifier of the object based

```
public class ListElement implements KSNSerializable {
    private ListElement next;
    private ListElement previous;
    private int number;
    // See Listing C.1 for constructor
    ...
    public void WriteObjectOnSensor(OutputStream oos) {
        oos.writeInt(number);
        oos.writeObject(next);
        oos.writeObject(previous);
    }
    // Remainder of this class will be illustrated in the following
    ...
}
```

Listing C.2: Implementation of WriteObjectOnSensor() for ListElement

on the internal address where the object is stored in memory. This identifier is stored on the SPOT during serialization. Thus, when a node serializes an object structure where the same object is referenced more than once, the node can check if the object references has been serialized already. This is important to resolve cyclic references in object structures.

If an object is serialized for the first time, the serialization starts by writing a special type identifier that mark the beginning of an object structure to the instance of OutputStream. In the following, the unique identifier mentioned above is written to the stream and the complete class name of the object that is being serialized. Afterwards, the method WriteObjectOnSensor() of the object is called and the process recurs until all elements of the list are serialized once.

The deserialization reverses the whole process: First, the special type identifier that marks the beginning of an object structure is read from the instance of InputStream. This allows the receiver of the object structure to determine that the next set of bytes is a class name to corresponds to the class of the object that was serialized. After reading this class name, the receiver creates an empty instance of this class by calling the no-argument constructor. Thus, the KSN Serialization cannot be applied to classes that do not implement a no-argument constructor. After this empty instance has been created in memory, the method ReadObjectOnSensor() is called and restores the internal state of the object. Listing C.3 illustrates the implementation of ReadObjectOnSensor() for the ListElement class.

Note that ReadObjectOnSensor() reads the values of the internal variables in the same order as they were written on the stream: Line 8 uses the process for deserialization of primitive values described above. The references to the next and the previous element of the list are resolved by reading the unique identifier, creating an empty instance and restoring their internal values first. Again, references are restored based on the unique identifier computed during the serialization.

C.2. KSN SERIALIZATION AND COLLECTIONS

```
public class ListElement implements KSNSerializable {
  private ListElement next;
  private ListElement previous;
  private int number;
  public ListElement(){} // No-argument constructor
  // deserialization
  public void ReadObjectOnSensor(InputStream ois) {
    this.number = ois.readInt();
    this.next = ois.readObject();
    this.previous = ois.readObject();
  }
}
```

Listing C.3: Implementation of `WriteObjectOnSensor()` for `ListElement`

Hence, the complete structure of the object including all references are restored in memory.

KSN Serialization vs. Java Serialization for PCs

Compared to the serialization offered by Java for personal computers, the KSN Serialization requires some additional code for every class that requires serialization support:

- No-argument constructor.
- A class specific implementation of `WriteObjectOnSensor()` and `ReadObjectOnSensor()`.

The no-argument constructor is typically a single line of code per class as illustrated in Listing C.3. The two methods for reading and writing the state of an object to the stream are typically one line per internal variable of a class. Recent, but yet unpublished work by users of the KSN Serialization have focused at automatic generation of this additional code. These additional lines of code are required until the virtual machine used on Sun SPOTs supports serialization, but in general, the overhead is relatively small. For example, the additional programming required for the serialization of the double-linked list is less than 30 lines of code. Sending the double-linked list without KSN Serialization requires significantly more than these 30 lines, mainly because references must be reconstructed even if they are not transmitted.

Even if it "feels" like Java Serialization, there are some limits to our approach which cannot be overcome without VM support:

- KSN Serialization cannot process internal variables declared with the attribute `final`. This is because these variables are protected from being written after the instantiation of an object, i.e., before `ReadObjectOnSensor()` is called.

- The requirement to have a no argument constructor can lead to difficulties if a class needs certain parameters to exist.

Reducing the Overhead of Serialization

As explained above, the complete class name is required for the deserialization of an object and thus must be written to the stream. Class names can be relatively long and increase the length of the byte array that is transmitted from one node to another significantly, particularly if the actual content of a class is relatively low. In initial versions of the KSN Serialization, this resulted in node failures, because nodes were out of memory. We address this issue by introducing two measures that reduce the overhead related to serialization.

To serialize a variable that corresponds to a primitive piece of data, e.g., an int-value, one has to decompose the byte into two pieces: The value itself which results in 4 bytes in case of an int and the structural information that these 4 bytes belong to an int. For the initial version of the KSN Serialization, this was a string of 7 bytes that identified a primitive data type. Thus, the serialization of the int value results in 11 bytes. This is clearly inefficient and we changed the encoding scheme in such a way that every primitive data type only results in a into a single additional byte for structural information. This comes at the cost of limiting the design to a maximum of 256 primitive data types but considering the fact most modern programming languages have less than 20 primitive data types, this is sufficient. Our evaluation shows that this reduces the overhead associated with serialization significantly.

With the double-linked list above, the complete class name of the class `ListElement` must be transmitted once for each reference to an instance of this class. Considering a double-linked list of n elements, this means this class name is transmitted at least $2 \cdot n$ times. This is clearly inefficient.

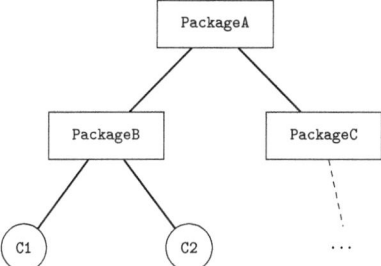

Figure C.3: Hierarchical class names in Java

We solve this problem using an online tree-compression that transfers each class name only once at most. Its core idea is as follows: As illustrated in Figure C.3, Java class names are hierarchic, i.e., represent a tree. For example, to transfer an instance of the class `C1`, the whole class name `packageA.packageB.C1` must be transferred as well. If an instance of `C2` must be

C.2. KSN SERIALIZATION AND COLLECTIONS

transferred afterwards, the complete class name `packageA.packageB.C1` is transferred again. The online tree-compression assigns a hash value to each node of the tree. For the first instance of `C1` is transferred, we transmit the hash value associated with `packageA.packageB.C1`. For any subsequent instance of `C1`, it is sufficient to transmit the hash value instead of the whole class name. Additionally, in case of the transmission of an instance of `C2`, a large portion of the class path is equal to the previously transmitted class path of `C1`. Thus, the tree compression ensures that the hash value associated with `packageA.packageB` and the class name `C2` are transmitted. Again, subsequently transmitted instances of `C2` only require retransmission of the hash value associated with `packageA.packageB.C2` afterwards. Our evaluation shows that this reduces the message size of serialized messages significantly.

C.2.2 Study of Serialization Overhead

As stated at the beginning, the advantages of serialization for transferring objects come at the cost of increased message size compared to "manual serialization". This section investigates the overhead induced by the KSN Serialization and shows that the class-name compression reduces this overhead drastically.

Experimental Setup

To measure the overhead of serialization, we assumed that an application has to send a linked list of simple values from one node to another. The application generates between 10 and 1.000 elements for the list randomly and serializes the list into a string of bytes. The length of this string in bytes is the result of the experiment. We used four different serialization mechanisms which are outlined in the following.

Manual Serialization This approach resembles a program that does not run any kind of serialization and thus requires the programmer to manually write the whole serialization/deserialization code. Therefore the programmer can suit the serialization to the data that is expected in his application and thus reduce the amount of data that must be transferred, since the structure of the serialized objects as well as references / pointers are not serialized. It is expected, that this approach performs very well regarding data size compared to KSN Serialization.

The program was written by an experienced programmer with in-depth knowledge of the internals of Java serialization and the linked list data structure. Including tests and debugging, the development of the manual serialization took a few hours. This approach is tightly integrated into the written application and the reusability of the written code is very limited. Changing the communication protocol or the type of list that is used, e.g., from the linked list to an array-based list, would require re-writing large portions of the code.

Manual Serialization with ZIP compression This serialization mechanism used the software developed above in combination with the compression layer of the KSN Radio Stack. The compression layer of the KSN Radio Stack is a customized ZIP algorithm that has been fine-tuned to the characteristics of radio communication between sensor nodes. It is expected that this mechanism will result in the lowest data size of all approaches presented.

KSN Serialization The approach uses the KSN Serialization, which is generally applicable for the serialization / deserialization of all objects that implement the KSNSerializable interface. The expected data sizes for this approach are expected to be the largest in this evaluation, since all structural information of the transferred objects and references must be transmitted together with the data.

Writing the serialization code for the linked list was a matter of minutes. Due to the object-oriented approach, only a few classes had to be modified for serialization and writing the code does not require in-depth knowledge of the communication protocol or any other part outside of the list. More importantly, the serialization code for the double-linked list has been reused extensively: We integrated the serialization code into the collections delivered with KSN software packages. Since most collection data structures have a similar structure, the code originally written for the double-linked list has been partially reused in other collection classes as well, e.g., the array-based list implementations.

KSN Serialization with ZIP compression This approach is analogous to the manual serialization with ZIP compression: The data produced by the KSN Serialization is compressed by the compression layer integrated in the KSN Radio Stack. This approach should result in data sizes lower than those achieved with the KSN Serialization, but higher than any of the manual serialization approaches.

Summary Summing up, the setup for our experiment heavily favours the manual serialization, mainly for two reasons: First, a linked list is a very simple data structure compared to object structures typically encountered in object-oriented programs. For example the data structures required for the spatio-temporal query processor contain all kinds of collection data structures, inheritance and many other features not covered by this example. Second, the elements are randomly created which reduces the compression rate of the ZIP algorithm contained in the KSN Radio Stack. In typical applications, the data sent is correlated in some way which allows better compression ratios.

Results and Analysis

Figure C.4 shows the result of the experiment for KSN Serialization without any compression mechanism (cf. Section C.2.1). The data sizes obtained with the basic KSN Serialization are much larger than the data size with manual serialization. This is because the structural information in the form of class names but also for primitive data types increases the amount of information that

C.2. KSN SERIALIZATION AND COLLECTIONS

must be transmitted: The manual serialization only transmits the values required to reconstruct the object. Contrary to that, the KSN Serialization has to send the structural information, e.g., in case of our list pointers to the next and the previous object as well as class names. For long package paths, this overhead can be 50 bytes and more per object.

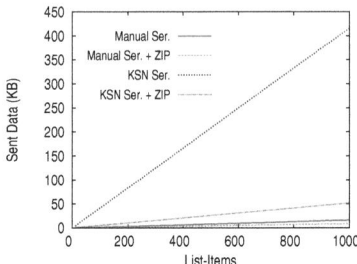

Figure C.4: Performance of basic KSN Serialization

Comparing the results of KSN Serialization with compressions to those without serialization shows that the potential for compression mechanisms is large: While the uncompressed list of 1000 elements requires 415 kilobytes, the compressed list is only 52 kilobytes.

Figure C.5 shows the result of the experiment with the KSN Serialization that encodes the structural information for primitive data types into single bytes. Compared to the results in Figure C.4, the improvement is obvious: The primitive data type compression reduces data size by a factor of two: 415 kilobytes for 1000 list elements are reduced to 225 kilobytes without compression. The compression of the serialized data reduces the amount of data that is transmitted to ≈ 50 kilobytes. The manual serialization still requires only 50% of that, i.e., ≈ 25 kilobytes, but as stated above, the manual serialization does not transmit the structural data that make up a large part of the information one has to transmit.

While the compression of primitive types is advantageous as shown in Figure C.5, the class names are still serialized as strings. To illustrate the problem, consider the following example: Our application produces list objects of the same type with different/random content. Assume the list elements are from the package `ksn.somePackage` and their class name is `ListElement`, i.e., the full class path is `ksn.somePackage.ListElement`. Without class name compression, the complete class name is transmitted for every element of the list. Thus, independently of its random content, every element requires 15 + 11 + 1 = 27 bytes just for class names. Considering a list of 1000 elements, the class names for list elements already use 27 kilobytes, despite the fact, that all elements are of the same type.

Figure C.6 shows the result of the experiment with compressed class names as described in Section C.2.1: The improvement compared to Figure C.5 is significant. Generally the KSN Serial-

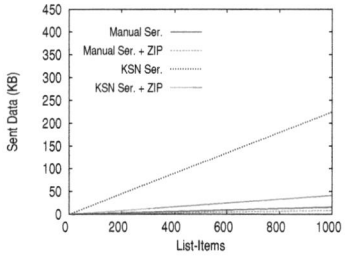
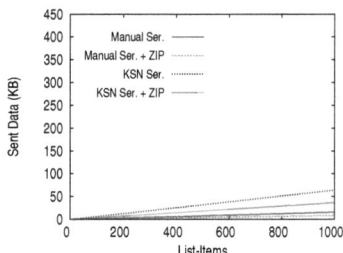

Figure C.5: Performance of basic KSN Serialization

Figure C.6: Performance of KSN Serialization with Class-Name Compression

ization with compression is closer the the manual serialization. Recall that the whole setup is still favorable for the manual serialization and that the effort for programming the manual serialization is relatively high compared to the few lines of code required for KSN Serialization.

C.3 KSN Radio Stack

During the development of the spatio-temporal query processor and other components for software, we had to work around the unreliability of the default radio stack many times. In particular, over-the-air software distribution was problematic as soon as the applications distributed were significantly larger than, for example, a "Hello-World demo".

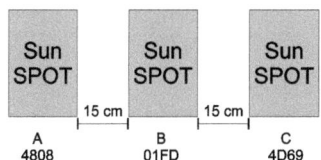

Figure C.7: Node topology for the radio stack reliability experiment

We investigated the reliability of the standard radio stack delivered with Sun SPOTs with a simple experiment: SPOT A in Figure C.7 generates a message of 100.000 bytes containing random numbers. This message must be sent to SPOT C. By reducing the output power of the radio chip on each Sun SPOT, we made sure that SPOT A (4808) cannot sent data directly to C (4D69), but the messages must be relayed via SPOT B (01FD). To test, if the message was forwarded

C.3. KSN RADIO STACK

successfully, we computed a checksum on SPOT A and C. A run of this experiment was considered to be successful if the checksums on both nodes were equal.

We repeated the experiment for the default radio stack six times and it never finished successfully. Even more problematic was the fact that only two of these runs actually finished at all. In both cases, the checksum was wrong but since the message was actually passed from the radio stack to the application shows that using the default stack would require handling even checksum calculation at the application level. The remaining four cases never finished, i.e., even if the application handled all communication errors, these four errors would not have been detected and thus not have been handled.

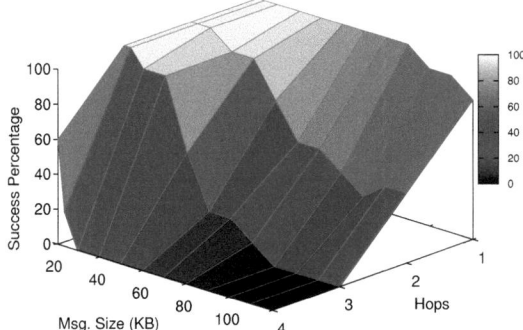

Figure C.8: Reliability of the default radio stack for Sun SPOTs

Figure C.7 shows the result of an advanced version of the setup above: For this experiment, we varied the number of hops, i.e., 1-4 hops, and the message size between 10 and 100 kilobytes of data. For each set of nodes and data size, we repeated the experiment 15 times. The result shows clearly, that the existing radio stack becomes very unreliable for data sizes of several kilobytes. Furthermore, forwarding messages even for small numbers of hops is very unreliable.

Since several modifications of the default radio stack were unsuccessful, we decided to develop our own radio stack for Sun SPOT sensor nodes. This radio stack has been used for all of our evaluations and we describe the design decisions in the following. At the end of this section, we repeat an advanced version of the above experiment that demonstrates that the KSN Radio Stack reliably forwards messages even if the network topology changes during transmission. Furthermore, the evaluation of the KSN Management application consist of an experiment where an application of more than 800 kilobytes was distributed over-the-air via multiple hops. This would not be possible without a reliable radio stack implementation.

C.3.1 Design Targets and Overview

Similarly to other well-known communication stack implementations, e.g., TCP/IP, the KSN Radio Stack uses a layer architecture to handle the different aspects of communication between Sun SPOT sensor nodes. To obtain 802.15.4 compatibility, we use the 802.15.4 layer provided by Sun and implement every layer above. Figure C.9 provides an overview of the radio stack and its layers. Every layer has a specified task and we provide a more detailed description in the following.

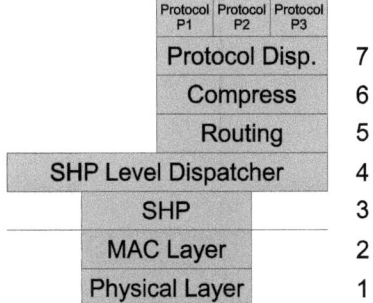

Figure C.9: Overview of the KSN Radio Stack

Considering the problems with the default Sun SPOT layer, the main design target for the KSN Radio Stack was increasing the reliability for communication between Sun SPOTs, particularly over multiple hops. In addition to that, the KSN Radio Stack offers the following features:

- **Flexibility**: Every layer implements a generic interface. Thus, users can change the order of the layers above the SHP Dispatcher, e.g., for some applications it makes sense to move the compression layer below the routing layer. Furthermore, this eases the implementation of new, user-defined layers because integrating new layers is achieved simply by implementing an interface. Changing or integrating layers during runtime is also possible.
- **Link-Quality Awareness**: The radio chip used on most sensor nodes provides link-quality information. This information is useful, for example when choosing routes, because the higher the quality of a link, the higher the probability that transmissions do not fail or have to be repeated. This quality information is automatically aggregated through the stack and applications may access it.
- **Multi-Stack Support**: In addition to the possibility to replace each layer with another implementation, one can use multiple stacks at one time. In the KSN Radio Stack this is

done by the SHP Level Dispatcher. For example, we typically use different stacks for the real application and for the management tools during experiments. This allows us to collect statistics, e.g., the number of messages sent or received, without disturbing the application or having to subtract the messages for statistics collection from the statistics itself.

C.3.2 Layers of the KSN Radio Stack

This section describes ever layer of the radio stack, its designated task and the most important facts about the implementation briefly. For more details, refer to [9]. Figure C.9 shows the default layers of the KSN Radio Stack and we describe each layer now separately using a bottom-up order.

SHP – Single Hop Protocol

To increase the reliability of communication, the first step is increasing the reliability of the communication between nodes that are communication neighbors (cf. Definition 20), i.e., nodes that can communicate directly with each other. The MAC layer provided by 802.15.4 already provides reliable communication, but only for single packets of 127 bytes at most. In most applications, packets of larger sizes occur, i.e., communication for messages of much larger sizes must be reliable as well. Thus, the main objective for the *Single Hop Protocol (SHP)* is reliable communication between communication neighbors for messages of arbitrary size.

For practical reasons, the amount of data that may be transmitted between Sun SPOTs is limited by the memory available on the nodes. But the design of the layer should avoid a tight limit on the message size, because it is likely that future sensor nodes will have more memory. The current implementation of the SHP layer can transmit 2^{32} bytes = 4096 megabytes using a unicast. This boundary stems from the maximum size of an array that can occur on a 32-bit virtual machine as it is used on Sun SPOTs. The broadcast has a lower limit: only 6.881.280 bytes can be transmitted by a single broadcast, but since broadcasting data of more than 10 kilobytes results in high loss rates, it is unlikely that this is a limitation. We discuss the packet flow of the SHP layer for unicast and broadcast separately in the following.

Unicast Figure C.10 illustrates the packet layout for the different types of packets occurring during unicasts at the level of the SHP layer. Note that the first bytes of every packet are reserved by 802.15.4. For every packet, the first part is a byte the indicates the type of the packet. The semantics of each of these packet types are as follows:

Data Request Packet: When $\mathcal{S}_{send}$ must send a message to a communication neighbor $\mathcal{S}_{recv}$, it indicates this by sending this packet. Prior to sending this packet, $\mathcal{S}_{send}$ generates a unique *Request Number* which uniquely identifies this transmission. All packets exchanged in the following use this identifier to associate each packet with a transmission. The packet contains the number of bytes, the checksum and how many packets will be required to transmit the message.

OK, go ahead: This packet is the response to the request above and indicates that S_{recv} is ready to receive the message. Nodes could indicate that they are not ready in case they do not have sufficient unused memory or other problems that prevent receiving/forwarding the message, e.g., low battery.

Data Packet: This packet contains a fragment of at most 100 bytes of the actual message. To allow S_{recv} to get the fragments ordered correctly to allow reconstruction of the actual message, each of these packets contains a sequence number that indicates the position of the fragment in the overall message.

Data Acknowledgement: The receiver S_{recv} sends an acknowledgement that the packet with the sequence number was received correctly.

Complete Packet: The packet indicates that S_{recv} was able to reconstruct the message successfully and the computed checksum equals the checksum of provided during the data request at the beginning.

Checksum Error Packet: This packet indicates that an error occurred during transmission and the checksum computed from the message received does not equal the checksum provided at request time.

Each of these packets has a specific role during the transmission. The control flow for a multi-packet transmission at SHP level is illustrated in Figure C.11: The transfer starts with a request which is answered by the receiver S_{recv} as soon as the receiver is ready to receive the message. If this request is not answered, this could have two reasons:

1. The node S_{recv} is not a communication neighbor of S_{send} or vice versa, i.e., either the request never arrives at S_{recv} or the sender does not get the corresponding acknowledgement.
2. S_{recv} has failed.

Independently of the reason for the failure, the SHP layer will abort the transmission with an error and report the error to one of the upper layers, e.g., the routing layer. The upper layers then may decide to deliver the message via another route or abort the transmission altogether.

An important detail at this point is the sequence number provided in the data packet: For large messages, e.g., for over-the-air deployment of software, messages may have more than 256 fragments, i.e., the byte used for sequence numbers is insufficient. If such an overflow occurs, the sequence number restarts at 0 and the SHP layer enforces that the S_{recv} sends an acknowledgement for the fragment with sequence number 0 before this overflow occurs.

The MAC layer of the 802.15.4 layer sends acknowledgements as well for every packet. Obviously, these are redundant as the SHP layers sends acknowledgements as well. Thus, for most of our experiments, we switched the MAC layer acknowledgements off to reduce the contention that might occur if several nodes send at once.

Broadcast Broadcasts are not acknowledged because the broadcast messages are intended for to be received by all communication neighbors. There are two types of packets for broadcasts whose format is illustrated in Figure C.12:

C.3. KSN RADIO STACK

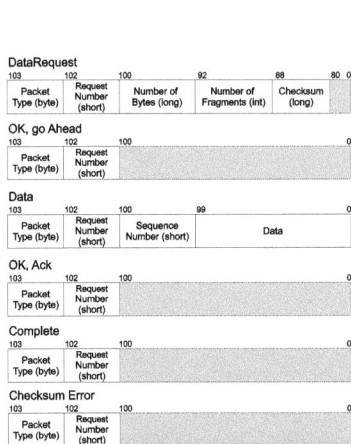

Figure C.10: SHP – Unicast Packets

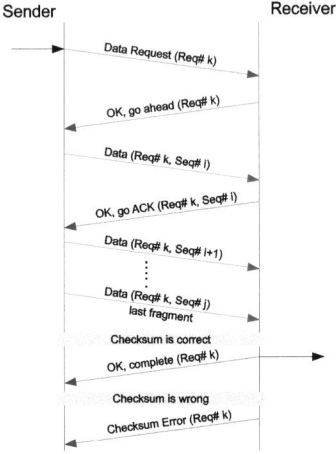

Figure C.11: SHP – Unicast Control Flow

Broadcast with more Fragments: This packet contains a fragment of a broadcast message and indicates that there will be more fragments, i.e., the message is not complete. As with unicasts, the sender $\mathcal{S}_{send}$ generates a unique identifier which allows receivers to identify packets associated with different transmissions.

Broadcast Last Fragment: Analogous to the packet above, this packet contains a fragment of a broadcast message. It also indicates that the whole broadcast transmission is finished, i.e., every node that received all fragments (as indicated by the sequence numbers) should be able to reconstruct the message.

As shown in Figure C.13, a node must receive all fragments of a broadcast message before it can reconstruct it. The sequence numbers start at 0 and increase by one for every packet. Since packets are not acknowledged, nodes can determine if a fragment is missing if the sequence numbers are not a complete sequence.

Error Handling and Route Quality In the description above we have omitted several packets and cases related to errors. After the transmission, receiver and sender can generate quality information regarding the link quality that occurred while transmitting the message. This information is returned to the application. For further information on both subjects refer to the KSN Radio Stack Manual [9].

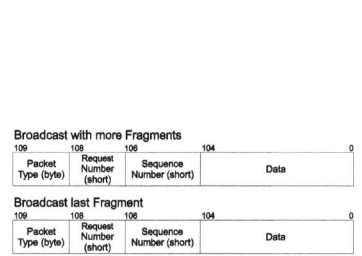

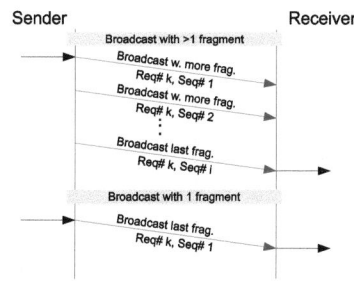

Figure C.12: SHP – Broadcast Packets

Figure C.13: SHP – Broadcast Control Flow

SHP Dispatcher

The SHP dispatcher allows nodes to have more than one independent series of upper layers using the reliable single hop communication provided by the SHP layer. The motivation behind this layer is a lesson we learned from our testbed deployment described in Section C.1: For an evaluation of the query processing mechanism, we deployed the latest build of the query processor which also included a modified version of the radio stack. The deployment was accomplished over-the-air and after the software was deployed on every node, the node restarts and uses the new version of the query processor. Unfortunately, the radio stack modification contained a bug and as soon as the node restarted, it was unable to communicate with any other node. To fix this bug, we had to collect all nodes and re-deploy an error-free version via USB because we could not access the nodes anymore "over the air". To avoid such situations in the future, we introduced the SHP dispatcher. This allows us to have a radio stack that is proven to work for over-the-air deployment and a different one for query processing. After the aforementioned incident, we could rely on the stack for over-the-air deployment whenever the stack for query processing contained bugs that prevented accessing nodes.

The implementation of the SHP layer is simple: The SHP layer attaches a stack identifier to every message. When the message is forwarded to another node, this stack identifier is used to determine which stack should be used to process the message and forward it to the application. The stack also allows changing stacks at runtime, i.e., the dispatcher provides an interface to replace stacks without restarting the node or deploying new software.

High-Level Layers

All layers above the SHP dispatcher are *dynamically stackable*, i.e., the structure of the stack can be changed at runtime. To allow this, every layer has to implement a common interface LayerInterface and inherit from an abstract superclass called AbstractLayer. Thus, every layer

C.3. KSN RADIO STACK

implementation has to implement the following methods:

sendBroadcast(): This method passes data from the layer above the current layer to the layer below. The use of this method indicates that the data must be broadcasted.

sendData(): As with the method above, the method passes data from the current layer to the layer below to send it via unicast to a given destination.

receiveData(): This method is used by lower layers to pass incoming data to the layers above.

At the construction of the layer, it must be specified how the layer forwards outgoing messages passed to it from an upper layer and how it handles incoming data from lower layers. The layer below a high-level layer is always either another layer or the SHP dispatcher described in Section C.3.2. In the following we describe several implementations of high-level layers which we used during our experiments.

Routing Layer To allow communication between nodes that are not communication neighbors, i.e., intermediate nodes must forward the message, we implemented a routing layer based on the AODV routing protocol [103]. AODV is an experimental routing protocol designed for mobile ad-hoc networks. The protocol ensures that routes are loop free and avoids problems such as the well-known "count to infinity"-problem. Routing with AODV requires every node to store a routing table. We describe this table later and provide an overview of the route finding process of AODV first:

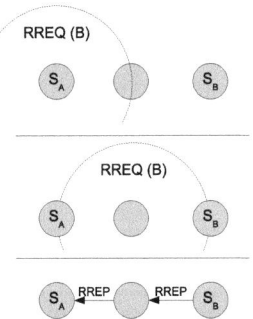

Figure C.14: AODV – Route requesting and reporting

1. Assuming a node $\mathcal{S}_A$ must send a message to a destination $\mathcal{S}_B$ and has not send messages previously to $\mathcal{S}_B$, $\mathcal{S}_A$ must initiate a so called *Route Request (RREQ)*. $\mathcal{S}_A$ can do this by broadcasting a route request message which initially does not contain any information except the originator of the request as well as the destination $\mathcal{S}_B$.

2. Any intermediate node that receives the RREQ will rebroadcast the RREQ unless it already has a route to the destination requested, e.g., S_B. When rebroadcasting the RREQ, any intermediate will insert its own node identifier into a list contained in the RREQ. Thus, the list contains a sequence of nodes that previously received the RREQ and forwarded it. Additionally, intermediate nodes store the information contained in the RREQ. For example, if the list of previous forwarders contains nodes S_X and S_Y, the intermediate node can derive that there is a route to S_A via S_X and S_Y, a route to S_X via S_Y as well as a route to S_X.
3. If the RREQ arrives at a node S_i that has a route to the destination of the request or the destination itself receives the request, S_i will send a *route reply (RREP)* to the initiator of the node. This reply is sent using the list of forwarders contained in the RREQ.

For further details on AODV refer to RFC 3561 [103]. Some of our experiments have shown that the route invalidation used by AODV is not well-suited for sensor networks where nodes do not move. Thus, we have modified the AODV protocol and tailored our implementation our needs. We focus on this modification in the following.

Routing Table Every node in the network manages a local routing table that contains entries for every known route. Each element of the routing table contains the following entries:

***Destination*:** Address of the destination node of this route.
***Next Hop*:** Address of a communication neighbor to which messages must be sent to reach the destination corresponding to this entry.
***Hop Count*:** Number of hops which have to be taken in order to reach the destination if the message is forwarded to the node with the address stored in *Next Hop*.
***Sequence Number*:** This number is used by AODV for route management and ensures that routes are loop-free.
***Route Quality*:** Aggregated information on the quality of the connections belonging to this route. Whenever the node storing this table sends a messages over this route, the aggregate is updated.

As illustrated by Table C.3 which contains the routing table for the network topology in Figure C.15, this table may contain several entries for the same destination, i.e., the routing table is 2-dimensional. This is advantageous, because it avoids *route flapping* as Example 18 illustrates.

Example 18: Assuming the link between S_B and S_C in Figure C.15 is weak, i.e., the probability to lose packets or whole messages when transferring over this link is high, particularly if the message is large. If S_B could only store a single entry for each destination and S_B must transfer a large message to S_B, it is likely that route flapping would occur. First, S_B would try to send the message directly and it is likely that this fails, i.e., S_B deletes the route to S_C from the routing table. Since there are no other routes to S_B stored in the routing table, S_A must initiate a RREQ and wait for a new route. The RREQ is only a single packet, thus it is likely that this transmission succeeds

C.3. KSN RADIO STACK

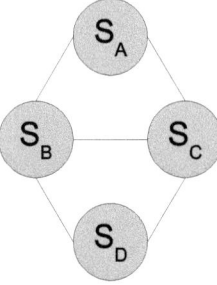

Destination	Next Hop	Hop Count
S_B	S_B	0
S_C	S_C	0
S_D	S_B	1
S_D	S_C	1

Figure C.15: Network topology example with four nodes and their links

Table C.3: Routing Table of S_A

and hence S_B will end up trying to send the message again to S_B instead of an indirect route over S_A or S_B. ♦

The route flapping described in Example 18 is avoided, because nodes have several entries for a single destination and try these routes before trying to discover new routes. A node creates multiple entries for the same destination if it receives multiple RREP messages. Using the topology in Figure C.15, S_A would receive a RREP from S_B and S_C regarding a RREQ for S_D. This would indicate that there are multiple routes to S_D and hence these entries are created.

Depth First Search Routing In the following we illustrate the major difference between the standard AODV routing and the implementation used by the KSN Radio Stack. Our implementation distinguishes between the following packets:

Route Request (RREQ): As aforementioned, this packet is broadcasted to search for a new route.

Route Reply (RREP): This is a reply that is sent back to the initiator of a route request to indicate that a route was found.

Data Packet: Whenever a valid route has been established from the routing table, these packets are sent towards the destination of a message to transmit the actual message.

Data Acknowledgement: Once the destination has received all fragments of a message, it sends this acknowledgement to indicate that the transmission was successful. Note that this acknowledgement is different from the acknowledgement sent by the SHP layer described in Section C.3.2. The latter acknowledgement indicates that a transmission between two communication neighbors was successful, while this acknowledgement is a *end-to-end acknowledgement* indicating successful transmission between nodes that are not (necessarily) communication neighbors.

Route Error (PERR): This packet indicates that there was a broken link on the way to the destination. When a node receives this packet, it checks if there is an alternate route to the destination and tries to find a way around the broken link.

When standard AODV encounters a broken link on a route while forwarding a message, the corresponding node generates a so called *Route Error Packet (PERR)*. This packet is the forwarded back to the original sender of the message and all nodes on the way "backward" invalidate the whole route, i.e., remove it from the routing table. After the PERR has arrived at the original sender, it tries to find a new route. Instead of restarting the routing, we use a depth-first search approach to circumvent broken links. We illustrate this in the following using a step-by-step example.

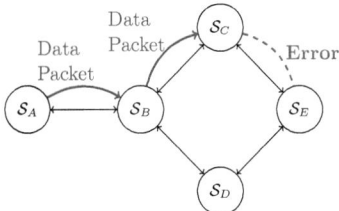

Figure C.16: Multi-Hop message forwarding with a broken link

Figure C.16 illustrates a sensor network with five nodes where $\mathcal{S}_A$ has to send a message to $\mathcal{S}_E$. The routing table contains a single entry where the destination equals $\mathcal{S}_E$ and the next hop for this destination is $\mathcal{S}_B$. Thus, $\mathcal{S}_A$ starts by sending the first data packet to $\mathcal{S}_B$. According to the routing table of $\mathcal{S}_B$, there are two routes to $\mathcal{S}_E$ and $\mathcal{S}_B$ choses $\mathcal{S}_C$ as the next hop for the message it received from $\mathcal{S}_A$. Similarly $\mathcal{S}_C$ tries to forward the message, but fails to do so, e.g., because an external influence prevents the use of the link between $\mathcal{S}_C$ and $\mathcal{S}_E$ at this time.

Since the link between $\mathcal{S}_C$ and $\mathcal{S}_E$ is currently unavailable, $\mathcal{S}_C$ removes the corresponding entry from its routing table. Due to the fact that the routing table stored at $\mathcal{S}_C$ does not contain any further entries for the destination $\mathcal{S}_E$, $\mathcal{S}_C$ sends a Route Error packet back to $\mathcal{S}_B$ from which it obtained the message previously. This is illustrated in Figure C.17. Based on the Route Error packet, $\mathcal{S}_B$ can derive that the route to $\mathcal{S}_E$ via $\mathcal{S}_C$ is invalid and remove it from the routing table as well. Contrary to situation at $\mathcal{S}_C$, there is another entry for $\mathcal{S}_E$ in the routing table of $\mathcal{S}_B$. Thus, to circumvent the broken link between $\mathcal{S}_C$ and $\mathcal{S}_E$, the message is routed via $\mathcal{S}_D$ as shown in Figure C.18.

When the message from $\mathcal{S}_A$ finally reaches $\mathcal{S}_E$, the data transfer is finished. To allow $\mathcal{S}_A$ to determine that the message was successfully received, $\mathcal{S}_E$ sends an acknowledgement back to $\mathcal{S}_A$. The acknowledgement is routed via the nodes that successfully forwarded the message as shown

C.3. KSN RADIO STACK

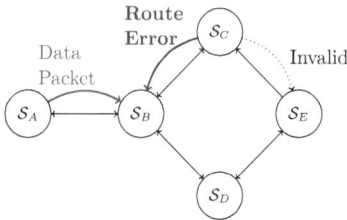

Figure C.17: Reporting and invalidating broken links

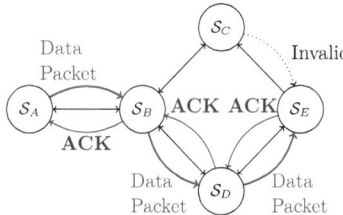

Figure C.18: Successful multi-hop communication and end-to-end acknowledgment

in Figure C.18. When the acknowledgement flows back to the initiator, nodes update the route quality information for the route used in their routing table.

Compression Layer As indicated by the name of the layer, this layer compresses the data that must be sent and decompresses data received. The layer itself can use any compression algorithm available. For our experiments we used an implementation of jzlib[2] and ported it to Sun SPOTs.

The experiments for serialization as well as other experiments have shown that compressing the application data in this way is highly efficient and reduces congestion considerably for large messages. During over-the-air deployment of new software for the query processor, the compression rates often reached 50-60%, i.e., the time it took to update software was halved.

Protocol Dispatcher The protocol dispatcher allows the conversion of incoming and outgoing data for different applications. As with the SHP dispatcher, the protocol dispatcher allows the application to chose how to communicates at application level, e.g., stream based, packet based etc.

---

[2]http://www.jcraft.com/jzlib/

While there are several protocols that have been implemented by users of the KSN Radio Stack, we only mention those implemented by us initially here:

Packet-Port Protocol: This protocol provides a similar interface for communication to desktop Java: Each node has virtual ports and may listen or send data using different ports. This protocol allows porting libraries or applications that have been used on PCs previously to Sun SPOTs without much re-implementation.

LoWPAN-Emulation Protocol: The default radio stack for Sun SPOT used an implementation of LoWPAN [95]. To allow users of this stack to use the KSN Radio Stack, this protocol emulates the LoWPAN implementation used on Sun SPOTs and allows stream based communication.

For more information on these protocols refer to the KSN Radio Stack Manual [9].

C.3.3 Evaluation and Summary

We repeated the experiment we conducted with the default stack with the KSN Radio Stack using a similar setup. Figure C.19 shows the setup, where the SPOT with the address 4808 has to send 100 kilobytes to 4D69. As with the experiment above, the output power of the radio chip was reduced in such a way that 4808 cannot send the data directly to 4D69, i.e., 01FD had to forward data sent by 4808 to 4D69. The main difference between the previous experiment and this one is that we remove 01FD during the experiment and replace it with 01EF. This setup is more challenging than the one above, because the route over which fragments of the 100 kilobyte message must be forwarded to 4D69 must be adapted on-the-fly.

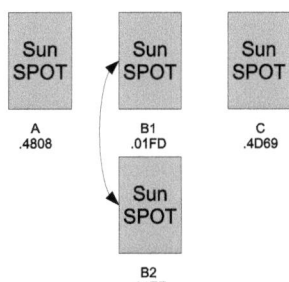

Figure C.19: Node topology for the reliability experiment using the KSN Radio Stack

The removal of the nodes simulates changing external influences that impact data transfer. An example of such an influence could be the fire doors in the KSN testbed shown in Figure C.1: We had several occasions where software had to be deployed and people walking in our office floors opened or closed these doors. Whenever the doors are open, the topology of the network among the nodes surrounding these doors changes.

The experiment above was repeated more than 20 times with 3 nodes and never failed to complete the sending of the message. Repeating the experiment with 4-6 nodes had the same result, even if multiple nodes were moved during the data transfer. This indicates that our main goal of increasing the reliability of data transfers, independently of their size, has been reached.

A more sophisticated application that demonstrates the capabilities of the stack is shown in Section C.5 where the radio stack is used for over-the-air software deployment in sensor networks. In particular, the KSN Management Application tries to exploit parallelism when distributing software among several nodes. Compared to the experiment above, this adds another difficulty the radio stack has to cope with: Since software is not distributed sequentially but in parallel on several different nodes, several nodes send large amounts of data at the same time resulting in congestion. We show that the radio stack can cope with this as well.

C.4 KSN Simulator

The development of the KSN Simulator had two main design targets:

1. Testing of Sun SPOT software prior to deployment on sensor nodes without requiring a re-implementation.
2. Conducting experiments to investigate the scalability of our measures.

We provide a high-level description how to accomplish both steps here. To enable the execution of the same software within the simulator as on Sun SPOTs, we implemented a node framework that adapts the interface of the Squawk virtual machine used on Sun SPOTs. Some details of this framework are presented after some of the main components of the simulator have been introduced.

C.4.1 Components of the Simulator

Figure C.20 shows the three major components of the KSN Simulator. The *environment* is the component that simulates the actual "world" which has to be modeled. Thus, this component contains simulated nodes, moving objects and any other entities that has to be simulated, interacts with sensor nodes or affects the simulation in any way.

The *clock* ensures that a virtual time among all nodes progresses at the same speed for every node. This is important, because nodes and other components have to be executed in separate threads and processes which are subject to the scheduling of the operating system. The scheduling might result in some threads/processes getting more time on the CPU to execute and could thereby result in asynchronous execution of the code on different nodes. For example, a node $\mathcal{S}_i$ sends a message at same time t_1 where another $\mathcal{S}_j \in \mathcal{CN}_i$ sends a message as well. Normally this would

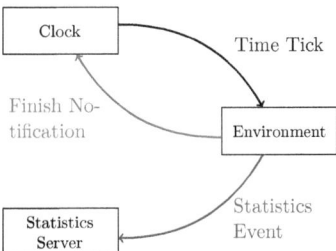

Figure C.20: Components and their interactions in the KSN Simulator

result in a collision, but if the thread for S_i would receive more execution time, this collision would not be simulated by the simulator. The clock ensures that the virtual time proceeds at each entity in the environment at the same pace independently of the scheduling as follows: Every entity is registered at the clock and executes so called *operations*. For each instant of time at most one operation is executed. For a moving object such an operation could be moving a certain distance through the environment, for a node an operation could be sending/receiving or switching one of the LEDs on. Whenever an entity finishes an operation, the entity notifies the clock and the thread or process is made inactive. The clock marks the entity it received such a notification from in a local data structure. When the clock has received a notification from all entities in the environment, it starts a new time cycle by unmarking all entities and sending a *time tick* to the environment. The environment re-activates all entities at once and each entity starts the execution of a new operation.

The third component is the *statistics server*. This component is required for experiments that measure the performance of a mechanism is some way. The performance measurements require that the environment reports *event* to the statistics server. For example, while a node S_i sends a message to another S_j, the environment raises several events related to the number of packets that are transmitted, collisions and other performance relevant indicators. The statistics server stores these events for every experiment and after the experiment has finished, the events are written to a disk or a database server.

C.4.2 Squawk Adaptation Layer

To execute the same software on SPOTs as well as simulations, we introduced the KSN node framework which provides an adaptation layer that separates the actual hardware from the application running on a node. This adaptation is accomplished by the *Squawk Adaptation Layer* shown in Figure C.21.

As explained above, the simulator is built around the concept that each node executes an operation for each clock tick generated by the clock component. Whenever the clock starts a new time

C.4. KSN SIMULATOR

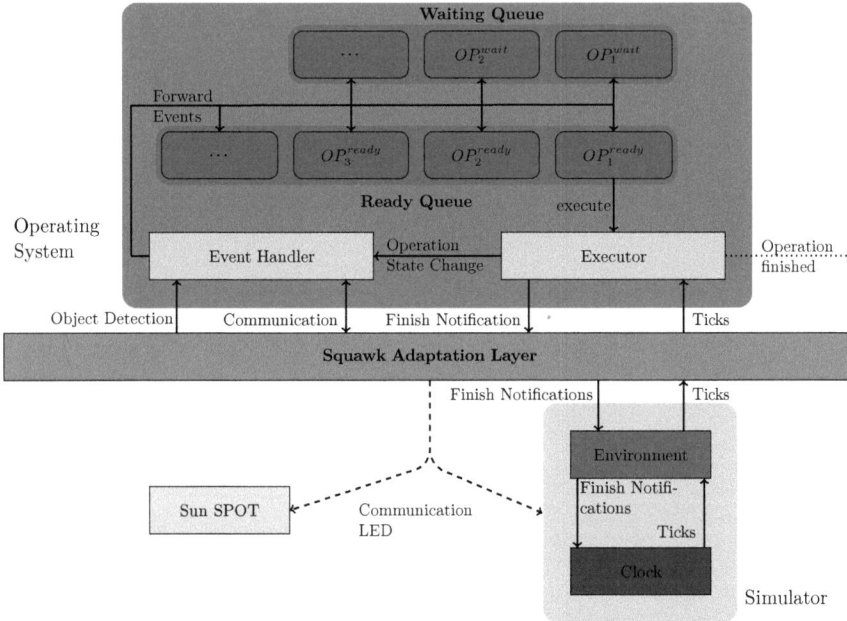

Figure C.21: KSN Node Framework and Squawk Adaption Layer

cycle by sending a tick to the environment, the tick is forwarded through the adaptation layer to the *operating system* of each simulated node. The operating system consists of four parts:

Waiting queue: This queue contains operations that are waiting for an external event to occur. Until such an external event occurs, the operations are not executed. An example of such an event would be an object detection, a message received or an event raised by another operation.

Event handler: The event handler forwards events to all operations. An operation can register for an event with the event handler and if this event occurs, the operation is notified. How the event is handled by the operation depends on the operation.

Ready queue: This queue contains operations that are ready for execution. If there are multiple operations ready for execution, the order of execution depends on the queue implementation. While the default implementation enforces first-in-first-out ordering, there are other implementations using priorities or other orderings.

Executor: This component halts all execution on a node until a tick from the clock arrives and executes the operations. After an operation has finished execution, the clock is notified. Events raised during the execution of an operation are passed to the event handler.

These components exist on SPOTs as well and the only difference between the execution on SPOTs and in the simulator is that the SPOT may continue executing operations without waiting for clock ticks. The mechanism that ensures this is completely transparent for the application and implemented in a straightforward way: If the Squawk Adaptation Layer is executed on a SPOT, it issues a clock tick as soon as the executor has indicated that the operation previously selected for execution is finished. Otherwise, the finish notification is forwarded to the Clock via the Environment component as shown in Figure C.21.

Every *time cycle* in the simulator starts when the clock issues a clock tick to the environment. The environment wakes up every node and forwards the clock tick to each one. Each node receiving the clock tick starts the time cycle by raising an *time tick event* through the event handler. This is required because operations may pause their execution for a limited time. For example, an operation could pause its execution until a timeout expires or an external event occurs such as an incoming message. The time tick event ensures that the operation is reactivated in time, i.e., such an operation would receive the time tick event and handle it in such a way that it is moved from the waiting queue to the ready queue.

After the time tick event, the executor acquires the next operation from the ready queue and executes it. During this execution, the operation may raise other events which are processed by the event handler. Furthermore, the execution may indicate that it has to wait, i.e., request that it is moved to the waiting queue. For example, an operation that has to send a unicast message to a nearby node has to wait until either a timeout expires or an acknowledgement of the message has been received. Thus, after the operation has called the appropriate interface function of the Squawk Abstraction Layer, it indicates that it has to wait for an event associated with the acknowledgement for the message sent. Depending on whether the node is a real SPOT or simulated, the message sent is passed to the KSN Radio Stack which either uses the 802.15.4 MAC of a SPOT or an 802.15.4-emulation layer of a simulated node. If the acknowledgement is received at some time, the operation may indicate that it is ready for further execution.

When operations are moved from the ready to the waiting queue or vice versa, the event handler issues another event to the other operations to indicate this. Similarly, if operations finish their execution, other operations waiting for the corresponding event are informed. This is useful, because in some cases operations wait until another operation finishes its execution.

When an operation either finishes its execution or indicates that it has to wait, the time cycle on the node ends. The executor notifies the squawk adaptation layer that the time cycle ended which either forwards it to the clock or issues a time tick event as described above. The Squawk Adaptation Layer handles all access to detection hardware, radio or LEDs as well and either forwards these calls to real hardware or the environment.

C.5 KSN Management Application

Management of single sensor nodes or the whole sensor network is a crucial task during the development or the evaluation of software for sensor networks. Examples of management activities are:

- Updating software executed on sensor nodes.
- Resetting system properties, e.g., the output power of the radio chip or the length of a timeout.
- Collecting statistics and evaluation results from sensor nodes, e.g., the number of messages sent/received.
- Restarting some or all sensor nodes,e.g., after an experiment has finished.

If there are many nodes or the nodes are physically inaccessible, executing these tasks manually is inefficient or impossible. For example, updating software for our testbed (cf. Section C.1) by walking into every office is not feasible. The KSN Management application is a flexible solution for managing large sensor networks over the air.

Contrary to real deployments of sensor networks, sensor nodes in a development testbed are usually connected to a permanent power supply. Therefore, management applications do not have to maximize efficiency, e.g., by minimizing the number of messages transferred, but have to execute tasks reliably. To ensure reliable communication, we base our approach on the KSN Radio Stack which was described in Section C.3.

The software provided with Sun SPOT sensor nodes provides a management application, but this application has some major drawbacks: Most importantly, updating software with this management application is very unreliable, particularly due to the problems associated with the default radio stack. Another problem is that all management tasks provided by this application are *base-station centered*. Figure C.22 illustrates why this is problematic. Assuming the software on nodes $\mathcal{S}_1$, $\mathcal{S}_2$ and $\mathcal{S}_3$ must be updated. In this application, $\mathcal{S}_1$ would receive the software first. Afterwards, the base station $\mathcal{BS}$, would start sending the software to $\mathcal{S}_2$ via $\mathcal{S}_1$. Next, $\mathcal{S}_3$ must be updated, which results in forwarding the software again via $\mathcal{S}_1$ and $\mathcal{S}_2$. In the following, we call this scheme for executing management tasks in a sensor network *serial distribution scheme*. We compare our approach with this one and show that it is inefficient.

In the following, we only introduce the major concepts of the management application. The KSN Management manual [8] provides a more detailed description.

C.5.1 Main Concepts

During the execution of a management task, the KSN Management Application distinguishes between three roles:

Executor: This role is assigned to a node that is currently executing the job associated with the management task, e.g., restarting or changing system preferences.

Figure C.22: Serial distribution scheme

Figure C.23: Domino distribution scheme

Controller: A node that performs this role controls the execution of the job at the executor.

Observer: This node receives notifications that indicate the progress of the execution of the management task. This role is typically assigned to the base station, e.g., when a node out of the set of target nodes restarts, it sends a message to the base station after the restart is completed.

To keep our system flexible, we distinguish between the following three orthogonal parameters for a given task:

- **Job**: This is the activity that must be executed on a given set of nodes.
- **Target nodes**: This is a set of nodes where the aforementioned activity must be executed.
- **Distribution Scheme**: This indicates how the job is distributed among the nodes in the network.

The distribution scheme determines the order and how the management task is executed by the different nodes in the set of target nodes. There are three distribution schemes that are currently supported by the KSN Management Application: With the serial scheme illustrated in Figure C.22, the base station always performs the role of the controller and the observer. The role of the executor is assigned to the node that currently executes the management job. The main drawback of the serial distribution is that nodes potentially forward the same job more than once. Using the example of updating software, with this strategy the software is sent once from the base station $\mathcal{BS}$ to $\mathcal{S}_1$. Afterwards, $\mathcal{S}_2$ becomes executor and assuming $\mathcal{S}_2$ is not a communication neighbor of the base station $\mathcal{BS}$, the software is sent to $\mathcal{S}_2$ via $\mathcal{S}_1$. After all nodes in Figure C.22 received the software, $\mathcal{S}_2$ has received it twice and $\mathcal{S}_1$ even three times. For large networks, this is clearly impractical.

The *domino distribution scheme* illustrated in Figure C.23 circumvents this problem by forwarding step-wise from one node to another. First, the base station is observer and controller at the

C.5. KSN MANAGEMENT APPLICATION

same time. Using Figure C.23, the first executor is S_1. After the management job has been finished on S_1, the executor-role is passed to S_2 and S_1 becomes controller. This continues until all target nodes have finished the task.

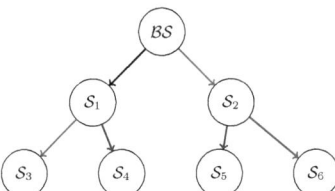

Figure C.24: Tree distribution scheme

The most sophisticated distribution scheme is the *tree distribution scheme* illustrated in Figure C.24 because executes management tasks in parallel. Continuing the example of updating software on nodes, the software is sent from the base station BS to S_1 first, i.e., the base station is controller and S_1 is executor. Afterwards, the base station starts sending the software to S_2 while S_1 starts transferring the software to S_5 or S_6. Thus, S_1 becomes controller and nodes S_2 and S_5 become executors. This continues until all nodes have been executor once. The coloring of the arrows in Figure C.24 indicates which executions of management tasks occur in parallel. As we show, this scheme reduces the time it takes to distribute software in a sensor network significantly.

C.5.2 Evaluation

In this section we evaluate the management application. First, we compare its reliability and performance to that of the management software provided with the default package. Second, we show that the different distribution schemes significantly impact the performance of the management application and reduce the time it takes to update software in a sensor network.

Comparison with the default management software

To compare the KSN Management Application with the existing over-the-air management capabilities of Sun SPOTs, we deployed six sensor nodes (red dots) and a base station (black square) at the Institute for Program Structures and Data Organization as shown in Figure C.25. For this comparison, we assumed that the software of node 58DE requires an update. The update process was started every time by the base station and the nodes are deployed in such a way that the software must be forwarded via several hops. While the actual number depends on the routing protocol, we determined that this was 6 hops in most cases. We also varied the size of the software update: First, we send an update consisting of a well-known demo application (Bouncing Ball) for Sun SPOTs which has about 25 kilobytes. Second, we increased the size of the software update to

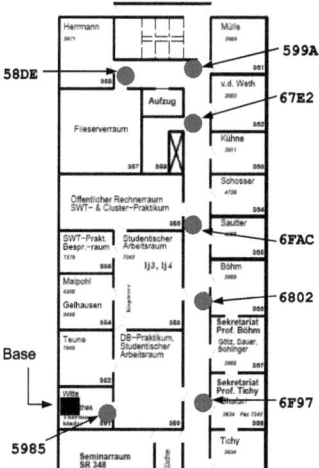

Figure C.25: Node Setup for the Evaluation of the KSN Management Application

834 kilobytes by updating the library on 58DE. An update was considered to be successful, if 58DE could execute the update after it was received completely. In addition to counting the number of successful updates, we also measured the time it took to successfully complete an update.

The result of the evaluation is shown in Table C.4: As expected from our results with the default radio stack in Section C.3, the size of the software update influences the success rate. While almost half the updates finished successfully with the default node management system, updating the library never finished successfully. This must be attributed to the unreliability of the default radio stack. Even though updating the library took about 14 minutes with the KSN Management Application, it always finished successfully. Thus, we conclude that our design target to obtain a reliable node management tool has been reached.

Performance of the KSN Management Application

To investigate the performance of the KSN Management Application in terms of speed when updating software, we deployed 14 Sun SPOTs and a base station on a desk. We assumed that the user wants to update the software on all 14 nodes and conducted this update using all three distribution schemes. We repeated the experiment with two different software updates: The first one was the demo we already used for the experiment above, i.e., 25 kilobytes. The second software

C.5. KSN MANAGEMENT APPLICATION

	Default Node Management		KSN Management Application	
	Success Rate	Avg. Duration	Success Rate	Avg. Duration
Bouncing Ball (25 KB)	4/10 = 40%	75 sec.	10/10 = 100%	59 sec.
Library (834 KB)	0/3 = 0%	-	3/3 = 100%	14 min.

Table C.4: Reliability and performance results for the KSN Management Application and the default node management

update contained a HelloWorld-application of about 1.5 kilobytes. The software update task was considered successful if all nodes had been updated successfully and we measured the time it took the KSN Management Application to complete the task. Since updating the software worked every time, we do not provide the success rate in the following and only show the time.

This setup has an important detail that demonstrates the reliability of the KSN Radio Stack as well: Since all nodes are put on the desk, they are all in communication range. This results in heavy contention particularly when several nodes send messages in parallel, i.e., with the tree distribution. Since all updates were successful, we conclude that the radio stack as well as we the KSN Management Application are applicable to collision-rich setups.

	Distribution scheme		
	Serial	Domino	Tree
HelloWorld (1.5 KB)	2 min. 20 sec.	3 min.	1 min. 15 sec.
Bouncing Ball (25 KB)	5 min.	6 min. 35 sec.	2 min. 35 sec.

Table C.5: Duration of the software updates for 14 Sun SPOT sensor nodes

Table C.5 shows the result of the experiment. For both software updates, the tree distribution scheme was the fastest. This is unexpected because with all nodes placed on a desk, collisions occurring when nodes try to send software simultaneously should reduce the performance of the tree distribution scheme significantly. To further investigate this, we repeated the experiment with increasing numbers of nodes. The result was that somewhere between 35 and 40, i.e., 40 nodes are placed in such a way that each node can communicate with 39 others, there is a point were the collisions prevent routing and communication causing the software deployment with tree distribution to be slower or fail. We consider this scenario to be sufficiently unlikely to occur in reality that we conclude that the tree distribution is the best distribution scheme regarding performance. Further investigation shows that the advantage of the tree distribution over the other schemes increases when the sensor network is less dense and the number of nodes increases.

Another unexpected result is that domino distribution is slower than the serial distribution. First off all, this changes as soon as the base station requires more than 1 hop to reach a node. Second, the main reason for this result is that reading flash memory is slow: With the serial distribution, the base station reads the application from the main memory of the computer it is attached to and then sends it. Contrary to this, with the domino scheme, nodes read from flash and then send the software to the next node. Since the flash memory is much slower than the main memory of the computer the base station is attached to, the domino distribution is slower overall.

C.5. KSN MANAGEMENT APPLICATION

Appendix D
A Topology Discovery Protocol

The optimizer for the rebroadcast parameter P for probabilistic query dissemination developed in Chapter 4 is based on the hop-set model. According to Definition 46, a hop set $\mathcal{HS}_h$ is a node set containing all nodes that have a distance of h hops to the base station. As shown in Section 4.4, our prediction of reachability and energy consumption for probabilistic query dissemination requires the following information:

Hop-Set size: The hop set size $|\mathcal{HS}_h|$ which equals the number of nodes in the hop set $\mathcal{HS}_h$.
Inter-Connectivity: Inter$[h]$ equals the average number of nodes in $\mathcal{HS}_h$ that will receive a broadcast by an arbitrary node from $\mathcal{HS}_{h-1}$.
Intra-Connectivity: Intra$[h]$ is the average number of nodes in $\mathcal{HS}_h$ that an arbitrary node from the same hop set can reach.

There are several ways to acquire such information, e.g., by using gossip protocols or by extracting topology information from meta-data of the routing protocol [4, 71, 90, 112]. However, these approaches strongly depend on the underlying communication protocols, hardware and system architecture. To avoid such dependencies, particularly for our evaluation, we decided to develop a lightweight topology discovery protocol based on the principle of the *echo algorithm* [23] and used it during our evaluation. This part of the appendix describes the implementation of our topology discovery algorithm in detail.

D.1 Overview – Echo-based Topology-Discovery

The *echo algorithm* [23] consists of an *expansion* wave, where messages are flooded from the base station to distant nodes, and a *contraction* wave that flows back to the base station. We use this concept to transport a request for topology information in the expansion wave, and we aggregate and return this information in the contraction wave. In particular, the base station initiates the topology discovery by broadcasting a *Topology-Discovery Request Message* (TDReq), thus starting

D.2. EXPANSION WAVE

Name	Description	Data Type
TDReq.sender	Sender of the TDReq	Node Identifier
TDReq.hop	Hop Number	Integer

Table D.1: Contents of a Topology-Discovery Request Message TDReq

the expansion wave. Table D.1 describes the content of a TDReq message. The small network in Figure D.1 with a base station $\mathcal{BS}$ and seven nodes will illustrate the topology-discovery process. Edges between nodes in Figure D.1 represent bi-directional links. In this example, the topology discovery is started by the base station broadcasting a TDReq to Nodes $\mathcal{S}_1$, $\mathcal{S}_2$, $\mathcal{S}_3$ and $\mathcal{S}_4$.

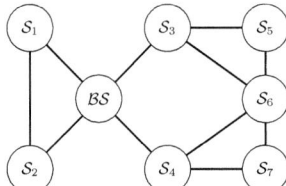

Figure D.1: Example network to illustrate the topology-discovery process

D.2 Expansion wave

When a node $\mathcal{S}_i$ receives a TDReq for the first time, the receiver must accomplish four steps, as illustrated in Algorithm 26:

1. Create three empty node lists Uncles, Siblings and Children (Line 3) and mark the sender of the request, i.e., TDReq.sender as the parent node of $\mathcal{S}_i$ (Line 5). $\mathcal{S}_i$ also extracts the hop number TDReq.hop and stores it (Line 4).
2. $\mathcal{S}_i$ replaces TDReq.sender with its own identifier and rebroadcasts the request with an incremented hop number (cf. Lines 6-8).
3. Start a timeout $t_{children}$ (cf. Line 9) to ensure that $\mathcal{S}_i$ does not wait forever for potential children. The length of the timeout should be sufficiently long to allow the children to receive, process and rebroadcast the Topology-Discovery Request.
4. $\mathcal{S}_i$ waits until the timeout expires or messages belonging to the contraction wave have been received from all children. Afterwards, $\mathcal{S}_i$ continues/starts the contraction wave by generating a Topology Discovery Response Message (TDResp) and sending it to its parent node.

In the example in Figure D.1, nodes S_1, S_2, S_3 and S_4 receive the TDReq from the base station, thus mark the base station as their parent node, rebroadcast the TDReq with an incremented hop counter and start a timeout to wait for further TDReq messages (cf. Lines 5-9 of Algorithm 26).

Algorithm 26: Handling of incoming TDReq messages

1 **When** S_i receives *TDReq* **do**
2   **if** S_i has not received any *TDReq* previously **then**
3   create empty lists Uncles, Siblings and Children ;
4       $S_i.hop \leftarrow$ TDReq.hop;
5       $S_i.parent \leftarrow$ TDReq.sender;
6   Increment TDReq.hop by 1;
7   TDReq.*sender* $\leftarrow S_i$;
8   rebroadcast TDReq;
9   start timeout $t_{children}$;
10   **end**
11   **else**
12   **if** *TDReq.hop* = $S_i.hop$ + 2 **then**
13   Add TDReq.sender to Children
14   **end**
15   **if** *TDReq.hop* = $S_i.hop$ + 1 **then**
16   Add TDReq.sender to Siblings
17   **end**
18   **if** *TDReq.hop* = $S_i.hop$ **then**
19   Add TDReq.sender to Uncles
20   **end**
21   **end**
22 **end**

After receiving the first TDReq and while waiting for the timeout of Line 9, a node can receive further TDReq messages, since every node broadcasts its own TDReq message (see Step 2 above). As illustrated in Section 4.4.1, a TDReq can reach any node either as a direct, indirect or reverse broadcast. Depending on the sender of the TDReq, i.e., TDReq.sender, a node that receives a TDReq must modify one these lists:

- Uncles: This case corresponds to a direct broadcast where a node with a distance of h hops to the base station receives a TDReq from a node with distance $h-1$. The first TDReq received is from the parent node in the previous hop set $\mathcal{HS}_{h-1}$. Every further TDReq corresponds to an additional connection from the h-th hop set to the previous hop set $\mathcal{HS}_{h-1}$. After the first TDReq has been received by a node S_i, every sender of a subsequent TDReq is added to Uncles stored by S_i.

D.2. EXPANSION WAVE

- **Siblings:** A node that rebroadcasted a TDReq must be added to Siblings by the receiver of this rebroadcast, if the rebroadcaster and the receiver have a distance of h hops to the base station. This case corresponds to an indirect broadcast. The sender is a sibling of the receiver and therefore must be added to Siblings (Line 16).
- **Children:** This case corresponds to a reverse broadcast, i.e., $\mathcal{S}_i$ receives a TDReq from another node $\mathcal{S}_j$ whose distance to the base station is larger. If TDReq.hop equals $\mathcal{S}_i.hop + 2$, then $\mathcal{S}_j$ is a child of $\mathcal{S}_i$. Hence, $\mathcal{S}_i$ inserts $\mathcal{S}_j$ into Children. If TDReq.hop > $\mathcal{S}_i.hop + 2$, $\mathcal{S}_i$ ignores the message.

In the example in Figure D.1, $\mathcal{S}_1$ receives a TDReq from $\mathcal{S}_2$. Since $\mathcal{S}_2$ has incremented the hop counter before rebroadcasting, $\mathcal{S}_1$ adds $\mathcal{S}_2$ to Siblings and continues to wait until the timeout $t_{children}$ expires. Similarly, $\mathcal{S}_2$ adds $\mathcal{S}_1$ as a sibling and start the contraction wave once the timeout expired, sine both $\mathcal{S}_1$ and $\mathcal{S}_2$ do not have any children. Assuming that $\mathcal{S}_2$ rebroadcasts TDReq prior to $\mathcal{S}_4$, $\mathcal{S}_3$ is parent of $\mathcal{S}_5$ and $\mathcal{S}_6$. When $\mathcal{S}_3$ receives TDReq from $\mathcal{S}_5$ and $\mathcal{S}_6$, both are added to Children. Once $\mathcal{S}_4$ rebroadcasts TDReq, $\mathcal{S}_6$ receives it and adds $\mathcal{S}_4$ to Uncles.

Algorithm 27 shows the possible transitions from the expansion to the contraction wave.

Algorithm 27: Transitions from expansion to contraction phase

1 **When** *the timeout* $t_{children}$ *expires on* $\mathcal{S}_i$ **do**
2   **if** Children ≠ ∅ **then**
3   Wait until all nodes in Children have sent a reply;
4   **else**
5   Initiate a TDResp message according to Algorithm 28   // $\mathcal{S}_i$ is a leaf node;
6   send TDResp to $\mathcal{S}_i.parent$;
7   **end**
8 **end**
9 **When** $\mathcal{S}_i$ *has received a TDResp from every node in* Children **do**
10   Use Algorithm 29 to aggregate topology information into one TDResp;
11   send TDResp to $\mathcal{S}_i.parent$;
12 **end**

Leaf nodes like Nodes $\mathcal{S}_1$, $\mathcal{S}_2$, $\mathcal{S}_5$, $\mathcal{S}_6$ and $\mathcal{S}_7$ in Figure D.1 end up with Children = ∅. Thus, they start the contraction phase by generating a TDResp using Algorithm 28 (cf. Line 5 in Algorithm 27). An arbitrary node $\mathcal{S}_i$ uses Children to determine when the topology information of all child nodes has been collected, e.g., $\mathcal{S}_3$ will wait for $\mathcal{S}_5$ and $\mathcal{S}_6$ to send their aggregated topology information. Afterwards, the node aggregates the topology information received from the children with its own as defined by Algorithm 29. The resulting TDResp is sent to the base station/parent node (Line 11 of Algorithm 27). The initiation of the contraction wave and the aggregation of topology information is described next.

D.3 Contraction wave

The contraction wave starts on leaf nodes where the timeout (cf. Step 3 above) expires without any incoming response messages from children. After the timeout has expired, the leaf node will execute Algorithm 28 in order to generate a *Topology-Discovery Response Message* (TDResp)). Table D.2 illustrates the structure of such a TDResp message.

Name	Description	Data Type
TDResp.sender	Sender of the TDResp	Node Identifier
TDResp.$|\mathcal{HS}_h|$	Size of the hop set $\mathcal{HS}_h$	Integer
TDResp.Inter[h]	Tuple to compute Inter[h]	[Integer,Integer]
TDResp.Inter[h]	Tuple to compute Intra[h]	[Integer,Integer]

Table D.2: Contents of a Topology-Discovery Response Message TDResp

The contraction wave starts, when a node sends the resulting TDResp to its parent node. For leaf nodes, TDResp must be generated in such a way that the parent node can aggregate the contained values for hop set size $|\mathcal{HS}_h|$, inter-connectivity Inter[h] and intra-connectivity Intra[h] as defined in Section 4.4.1. Note that Inter[h] and Intra[h] are average values, i.e., the corresponding entries in TDResp are tuples that represent the sum of uncles/siblings and the size of the corresponding hop set.

Algorithm 28: Generating TDResp messages at leaf nodes

1 **When** *the timeout $t_{children}$ expires on $\mathcal{S}_i$ and* **Children** = ∅ *at $\mathcal{S}_i$* **do**
2     $h \leftarrow \mathcal{S}_i.hop$;
3   Generate new TDResp message;
4   TDResp.$|\mathcal{HS}_h| \leftarrow 1$ // Set hop set size to 1;
5   TDResp.Inter[h] $\leftarrow$ [count(Uncles)+1,1] // take parent node into account => +1;
6   TDResp.Intra[h] $\leftarrow$ [count(Siblings),1];
7   return TDResp   // $\mathcal{S}_i$ sends this to parent node;
8 **end**

Continuing the example in Figure D.1, the responses generated using Algorithm 28 by $\mathcal{S}_1$, $\mathcal{S}_2$, $\mathcal{S}_5$, $\mathcal{S}_6$ and $\mathcal{S}_7$ are sent to the corresponding parent node. In case of $\mathcal{S}_1$ and $\mathcal{S}_2$ this is the base station. The parent node of $\mathcal{S}_5$ and $\mathcal{S}_6$ is $\mathcal{S}_3$ and $\mathcal{S}_4$ is the parent node of $\mathcal{S}_7$.

In case the node has children, i.e., **Children** is not empty, the node will wait for all children to return their response message (cf. Line 9 in Algorithm 27). To avoid endless waiting because a child fails to return its response message, we limit the waiting time for children with a sufficiently large timeout. If either this timeout expires, or if all children have responded, the lists of all children

D.3. CONTRACTION WAVE

must be aggregated as illustrated in Algorithm 29.

Algorithm 29: Aggregation of TDResp messages

1 **When** S_i *has received a TDResp from every node in* **Children do**
2   Aggregate $|\mathcal{HS}_h|$-values of all TDResp messages;
3   Aggregate Inter$[h]$-tuples from all TDResp messages from child-nodes;
4   Aggregate Intra$[h]$-tuples from all TDResp messages from child-nodes;
5   Generate new TDResp from these aggregates;
6   $h \leftarrow S_i.hop$;
7   Increment TDResp.$|\mathcal{HS}_h|$ by 1;
8   TDResp.Inter$[h]$ + = $[\text{count}(\text{Uncles})+1,1]$;
9   TDResp.Intra$[h]$ + = $[\text{count}(\text{Siblings}),1]$;
10 return TDResp   // S_i sends this to parent node;
11 **end**

The aggregation is straightforward: The corresponding values of TDResp messages from child nodes of a node S_i are added. For example, if the response messages of two nodes S_1 and S_2 contain hops set sizes $|\mathcal{HS}_h^1|$ and $|\mathcal{HS}_h^2|$, these are aggregated by computing $|\mathcal{HS}_h^1| + |\mathcal{HS}_h^2|$. In case of tuples, either for inter-connectivity or intra-connectivity, the respective attribute values of the tuple are added to each other. As a last step, the topology information of the current node is aggregated by counting uncles and siblings (Lines 7-9) and writing them into the TDResp message. The results are sent to the parent node of the current node, as described in Line 11 of Algorithm 27.

This continues until the base station $\mathcal{BS}$ has received all TDResp messages from nodes in the first hop set $\mathcal{HS}_1$, i.e., all communication neighbors of the base station. Similarly to the aggregation of the TDResp messages by intermediate nodes as illustrated in Algorithm 29, the base station aggregates the topology information as well. As a last step, the base station computes average values from the tuples representing inter-connectivity and intra-connectivity in the TDResp messages.

List of Figures

1.1 Illustration of a surveillance application 14
1.2 Illustration of an animal-tracking application 14

2.1 A Sun SPOT sensor node and its components 20
2.2 Mica motes: Mica2 (left) and Mica2Dot (right) 22
2.3 Illustration of B-MAC [105] 27
2.4 9-Intersection Model for two spatial entities **a** and **b** 32
2.5 Spatial Predicates for object/region relations 32
2.6 9-Intersection representation of spatial predicates (**a** = o_i and **b** = **r**) 32
2.7 Development graph for object-region predicates 35
2.8 Development tree for developments starting
    with $Disjoint$(**O**, **R**) 35

3.1 Illustration of the node model 43
3.2 $\mathbf{PE}_t^\mathbf{O}$ (S_1) based on $\mathcal{D}_{max}$ 44
3.3 $\mathbf{PE}_t^\mathbf{O}$ (S_1) with a distance estimating detection mechanism 44
3.4 $\mathbf{PE}_t^\mathbf{O}$ (S_1) with a position-precise detection mechanism 44
3.5 Illustration of the space partitions for a zone $\mathcal{Z}$ 47
3.6 Example of detection areas, detection ranges and a region 49
3.7 Development graph for an object **O** and a region **R** 63
3.8 Development Graph for an object **O** and a zone $\mathcal{Z}$ 64
3.9 Development tree with root $Disjoint$(**O**, **R**) 65
3.10 Development tree with root $Meet$(**O**, **R**) 65
3.11 Development tree with root $Inside$(**O**, **R**) 65
3.12 Development tree with root $Disjoint$(**O**, $\mathcal{Z}$) 67
3.13 Development tree with root $Meet$(**O**, $\mathcal{Z}$) 68
3.14 Development tree with root $Undetected$(**O**) 69
3.15 Development tree with root $Inside$(**O**, $\mathcal{Z}$) 70

4.1 Additional area covered by a rebroadcast of node S_B after receiving a query from S_A 82

LIST OF FIGURES

4.2 Additional area covered by a rebroadcast of node S_C after S_A and S_B received the query 82
4.3 IPD-Setup for the evaluation of existing dissemination algorithms 91
4.4 Grid-Setup 91
4.5 Setup for broadcast reachability study 97
4.6 Direct broadcast 102
4.7 Indirect broadcast 102
4.8 Reverse broadcast 102
4.9 Illustration of the Hop-Set model 103
4.10 Example: Uniform Topology (Node Degree 12) 109
4.11 Example: Gaussian Topology (325 Nodes) 109
4.12 Simulation result for uniform distribution with average node degree 4 (125 nodes) . . 111
4.13 Simulation result for uniform distribution with average node degree 8 (225 nodes) . . 111
4.14 Simulation result for uniform distribution with average node degree 12 (325 nodes) . 111
4.15 Simulation result for uniform distribution with average node degree 16 (425 nodes) . 111
4.16 Simulation result for Gaussian distribution with 125 nodes 112
4.17 Simulation result for Gaussian distribution with 225 nodes 112
4.18 Simulation result for Gaussian distribution with 325 nodes 112
4.19 Simulation result for Gaussian distribution with 425 nodes 112
4.20 Map of 17 Sun SPOTs and a Base Station deployed at the IPD 115

5.1 Border Nodes 125
5.2 Detection events when $\mathbf{O}$ moves into $\mathcal{Z}$ ($S_1 \in \mathcal{Z}, S_2 \in \overline{\mathcal{Z}}$) 127
5.3 Detection events when $\mathbf{O}$ leaves $\mathcal{Z}$ ($S_3 \in \mathcal{Z}, S_4 \in \overline{\mathcal{Z}}$) 127
5.4 Sensor network before S_2 leaves the zone $\mathcal{Z}$ ($S_2, S_3 \in \mathcal{Z}$) 132
5.5 Sensor network after S_2 left the zone $\mathcal{Z}$ ($S_3 \in \mathcal{Z}$) 132
5.6 Example for redundant notifications 137
5.7 Illustration of the filter layer with a zone $\mathcal{Z} = \{S_7, S_8\}$ 139
5.8 Scalability of data-collection strategies 142
5.9 Communication per detection-scenario 142
5.10 Case Study: Sun SPOT positions and object path 143
5.11 Outdoor Deployment of 50 Sun SPOT nodes 145
5.12 Ground view of nodes deployed on trees 145
5.13 Scalability with dynamic zones 147

6.1 Approximating detection neighbors based on communication neighbors 154
6.2 Reduction of radio output power to approximate detection neighbors 154
6.3 Link-quality based detection neighbor approximation 154
6.4 Detection neighbor approximation based on 2-hop neighbors 154

A.1	Circuit diagram for energy measurements	158
A.2	Sensor Node Management Device [60] and attached Mica Mote	158
A.3	Node lifetime measurement result	159
A.4	Energy Consumption for communication	161
A.5	Energy consumption with B-MAC [105]	162
A.6	Illustration of B-MAC [105]	162
B.1	OutsideDetected^v – Node detected object before joining $\mathcal{Z}$	169
B.2	OutsideDetected^v – Node detected object after joining $\mathcal{Z}$	169
B.3	OutsideDetected^v – Node detected object while joining $\mathcal{Z}$	169
B.4	OutsideDetected^v – Node detected object while leaving $\mathcal{Z}$	169
B.5	InsideDetected^v – Node is in $\mathcal{Z}$ while detecting object	171
B.6	InsideDetected^v – Node detects object while leaving $\mathcal{Z}$	171
B.7	InsideDetected^v – Node detects object while joining $\mathcal{Z}$	171
B.8	InsideDetected^v – Node joins and leaves $\mathcal{Z}$ while detecting object	171
C.1	The KSN Testbed: 41 Sun SPOTs deployed at the IPD	180
C.2	Structural information requiring serialization in a double linked list	182
C.3	Hierarchical class names in Java	187
C.4	Performance of basic KSN Serialization	190
C.5	Performance of basic KSN Serialization	191
C.6	Performance of KSN Serialization with Class-Name Compression	191
C.7	Node topology for the radio stack reliability experiment	191
C.8	Reliability of the default radio stack for Sun SPOTs	192
C.9	Overview of the KSN Radio Stack	193
C.10	SHP – Unicast Packets	196
C.11	SHP – Unicast Control Flow	196
C.12	SHP – Broadcast Packets	197
C.13	SHP – Broadcast Control Flow	197
C.14	AODV – Route requesting and reporting	198
C.15	Network topology example with four nodes and their links	200
C.16	Multi-Hop message forwarding with a broken link	201
C.17	Reporting and invalidating broken links	202
C.18	Successful multi-hop communication and end-to-end acknowledgment	202
C.19	Node topology for the reliability experiment using the KSN Radio Stack	203
C.20	Components and their interactions in the KSN Simulator	205
C.21	KSN Node Framework and Squawk Adaption Layer	206
C.22	Serial distribution scheme	209
C.23	Domino distribution scheme	209
C.24	Tree distribution scheme	210

BIBLIOGRAPHY

C.25 Node Setup for the Evaluation of the KSN Management Application 211

D.1 Example network to illustrate the topology-discovery process 216

Bibliography

[1] D. J. Abadi, S. R. Madden, and W. Lindner. REED: Robust, efficient Filtering and Event Detection in Sensor Networks. In *VLDB '05: Proceedings of the 31st international conference on Very large data bases*, pages 769–780. VLDB Endowment, 2005. ISBN 1-59593-154-6.

[2] R. Adler, M. Flanigan, J. Huang, R. Kling, N. Kushalnagar, L. Nachman, C.-Y. Wan, and M. Yarvis. Intel Mote 2: an advanced platform for demanding sensor network applications. In *SenSys '05: Proceedings of the 3rd international conference on Embedded networked sensor systems*, pages 298–298, New York, NY, USA, 2005. ACM. ISBN 1-59593-054-X. doi: http://doi.acm.org/10.1145/1098918.1098963.

[3] Advantaca, Inc. TWR-ISM-002-I Radar: Hardware User's Manual, 2002.

[4] A. Ahmed and B. Far. Topology discovery for network fault management using mobile agents in ad-hoc networks. *Electrical and Computer Engineering, 2005. Canadian Conference on*, pages 2041–2044, may. 2005. ISSN 0840-7789. doi: 10.1109/CCECE.2005.1557387.

[5] N. Ahmed, S. S. Kanhere, and S. Jha. The holes problem in wireless sensor networks: a survey. *SIGMOBILE Mob. Comput. Commun. Rev.*, 9(2):4–18, 2005. ISSN 1559-1662. doi: http://doi.acm.org/10.1145/1072989.1072992.

[6] A. Arora, P. Dutta, S. Bapat, V. Kulathumani, H. Zhang, V. Naik, V. Mittal, H. Cao, M. Demirbas, M. Gouda, Y. Choi, T. Herman, S. Kulkarni, U. Arumugam, M. Nesterenko, A. Vora, and M. Miyashita. A line in the sand: a wireless sensor network for target detection, classification, and tracking. *Comput. Netw.*, 46(5):605–634, 2004. ISSN 1389-1286. doi: http://dx.doi.org/10.1016/j.comnet.2004.06.007.

[7] Z. Benenson, M. Bestehorn, E. Buchmann, F. C. Freiling, and M. Jawurek. Query Dissemination with Predictable Reachability and Energy Usage in Sensor Networks. In D. Coudert, D. Simplot-Ryl, and I. Stojmenovic, editors, *ADHOC-NOW*, volume 5198 of *Lecture Notes in Computer Science*, pages 279–292. Springer, 2008. ISBN 978-3-540-85208-7.

[8] M. Bestehorn, S. Kessler, and A. Leppert. KSN OTA Management System Manual, 2009. URL http://www.ipd.kit.edu/KSN/Management.

[9] M. Bestehorn, S. Kessler, and A. Leppert. KSN Radio Stack Manual, 2009. URL http://www.ipd.kit.edu/KSN/RadioStack.

[10] M. Bestehorn, S. Kessler, and A. Leppert. KSN Serialization Manual, 2009. URL http://www.ipd.kit.edu/KSN/Serialization.

[11] M. Bestehorn, Z. Benenson, E. Buchmann, M. Jawurek, K. Böhm, and F. C. Freiling. Query Dissemination in Sensor Networks - Predicting Reachability and Energy Consumption. *Ad Hoc & Sensor Wireless Networks*, 9(1-2):85–107, 2010.

[12] M. Bestehorn, K. Böhm, P. Bradley, and E. Buchmann. Deriving Spatio-temporal Query Results in Sensor Networks. In M. Gertz and B. Ludäscher, editors, *SSDBM*, volume 6187 of *Lecture Notes in Computer Science*, pages 6–23. Springer, 2010. ISBN 978-3-642-13817-1.

[13] M. Bestehorn, K. Böhm, E. Buchmann, and S. Kessler. Energy-efficient processing of spatiotemporal queries in wireless sensor networks. In *Proceedings of the 18th SIGSPATIAL International Conference on Advances in Geographic Information Systems*, GIS '10, pages 340–349, New York, NY, USA, 2010. ACM. ISBN 978-1-4503-0428-3. doi: http://doi.acm.org/10.1145/1869790.1869838. URL http://doi.acm.org/10.1145/1869790.1869838.

[14] M. Bestehorn, K. Böhm, E. Buchmann, and S. Kessler. Energy-Efficient Processing of Spatio-Temporal Queries in Wireless Sensor Networks (Extended Version). *Technical Report of the Karlsruhe Institute of Technology*, 2010. http://dbis.ipd.kit.edu/english/1588.php.

[15] B. J. Bonfils and P. Bonnet. Adaptive and decentralized operator placement for in-network query processing. In *IPSN'03: Proceedings of the 2nd international conference on Information processing in sensor networks*, pages 47–62, Berlin, Heidelberg, 2003. Springer-Verlag. ISBN 3-540-02111-6.

[16] P. Bonnet, J. Gehrke, and P. Seshadri. Querying the physical world. *Personal Communications, IEEE*, 7(5):10–15, oct 2000. ISSN 1070-9916. doi: 10.1109/98.878531.

[17] P. Bonnet, J. Gehrke, and P. Seshadri. Towards Sensor Database Systems. In K.-L. Tan, M. J. Franklin, and J. C. S. Lui, editors, *Mobile Data Management*, volume 1987 of *Lecture Notes in Computer Science*, pages 3–14. Springer, 2001. ISBN 3-540-41454-1.

[18] R. Braunling, R. M. Jensen, and M. A. Gallo. Acoustic target detection, tracking, classification, and location in a multiple-target environment. *Peace and Wartime Applications and Technical Issues for Unattended Ground Sensors*, 3081(1):57–66, 1997. doi: 10.1117/12.280662. URL http://link.aip.org/link/?PSI/3081/57/1.

[19] T. Brooke and J. Burrell. From ethnography to design in a vineyard. In *DUX '03: Proceedings of the 2003 conference on Designing for user experiences*, pages 1–4, New York, NY, USA, 2003. ACM. ISBN 1-58113-728-1. doi: http://doi.acm.org/10.1145/997078.997083.

[20] M. Buettner, G. V. Yee, E. Anderson, and R. Han. X-MAC: a short preamble MAC protocol for duty-cycled wireless sensor networks. In *SenSys '06: Proceedings of the 4th international conference on Embedded networked sensor systems*, pages 307–320, New York, NY, USA, 2006. ACM. ISBN 1-59593-343-3. doi: http://doi.acm.org/10.1145/1182807.1182838.

[21] H. Cao, O. Wolfson, and G. Trajcevski. Spatio-temporal data reduction with deterministic error bounds. *The VLDB Journal*, 15:211–228, 2006. ISSN 1066-8888. URL http://dx.doi.org/10.1007/s00778-005-0163-7. 10.1007/s00778-005-0163-7.

[22] A. Cerpa, J. Elson, D. Estrin, L. Girod, M. Hamilton, and J. Zhao. Habitat Monitoring: Application Driver for Wireless Communications Technology. *SIGCOMM Comput. Commun. Rev.*, 31(2 supplement):20–41, 2001. ISSN 0146-4833. doi: http://doi.acm.org/10.1145/844193.844196.

[23] E. J. H. Chang. Echo Algorithms: Depth Parallel Operations on General Graphs. *IEEE Trans. Softw. Eng.*, 8(4):391–401, 1982. ISSN 0098-5589. doi: http://dx.doi.org/10.1109/

BIBLIOGRAPHY

TSE.1982.235573.

[24] G. Chen, R. Shetty, M. Kandemir, N. Vijaykrishnan, M. J. Irwin, and M. Wolczek. Tuning garbage collection for reducing memory system energy in an embedded java environment. *ACM Trans. Embed. Comput. Syst.*, 1(1):27–55, 2002. ISSN 1539-9087. doi: http://doi.acm.org/10.1145/581888.581892.

[25] Chipcon/Texas Instruments. *CC1000: Single Chip Very Low Power RF Transceiver*, 2010. URL http://focus.ti.com/lit/ds/symlink/cc1000.pdf.

[26] Chipcon/Texas Instruments. *CC2420: 2.4 GHz IEEE 802.15.4 / ZigBee-ready RF Transceiver*, 2010. URL http://focus.ti.com/lit/ds/symlink/cc2420.pdf.

[27] D. Chu, A. Deshpande, J. M. Hellerstein, and W. Hong. Approximate Data Collection in Sensor Networks using Probabilistic Models. In *ICDE '06: Proceedings of the 22nd International Conference on Data Engineering*, page 48, Washington, DC, USA, 2006. IEEE Computer Society. ISBN 0-7695-2570-9. doi: http://dx.doi.org/10.1109/ICDE.2006.21.

[28] A. Coman and M. A. Nascimento. A Distributed Algorithm for Joins in Sensor Networks. In *SSDBM '07: Proceedings of the 19th International Conference on Scientific and Statistical Database Management*, page 27, Washington, DC, USA, 2007. IEEE Computer Society. ISBN 0-7695-2868-6. doi: http://dx.doi.org/10.1109/SSDBM.2007.26.

[29] A. Coman, M. A. Nascimento, and J. Sander. On Join Location in Sensor Networks. In *MDM '07: Proceedings of the 2007 International Conference on Mobile Data Management*, pages 190–197, Washington, DC, USA, 2007. IEEE Computer Society. ISBN 1-4244-1241-2. doi: http://dx.doi.org/10.1109/MDM.2007.35.

[30] J. Considine, F. Li, G. Kollios, and J. Byers. Approximate Aggregation Techniques for Sensor Databases. In *ICDE '04: Proceedings of the 20th International Conference on Data Engineering*, page 449, Washington, DC, USA, 2004. IEEE Computer Society. ISBN 0-7695-2065-0.

[31] V. T. de Almeida and R. H. Güting. Supporting uncertainty in moving objects in network databases. In *GIS '05: Proceedings of the 13th annual ACM international workshop on Geographic information systems*, pages 31–40, New York, NY, USA, 2005. ACM. ISBN 1-59593-146-5. doi: http://doi.acm.org/10.1145/1097064.1097070.

[32] K. A. Delin, R. P. Harvey, N. A. Chabot, S. P. Jackson, M. Adams, D. W. Johnson, and J. T. Britton. Sensor Web in Antarctica: Developing an Intelligent, Autonomous Platform for Locating Biological Flourishes in Cryogenic Environments. In *34th Lunar and Planetary Science Conference*, March 2003.

[33] A. Dunkels, B. Grönvall, and T. Voigt. Contiki - A Lightweight and Flexible Operating System for Tiny Networked Sensors. *Local Computer Networks, Annual IEEE Conference on*, 0:455–462, 2004. ISSN 0742-1303. doi: http://doi.ieeecomputersociety.org/10.1109/LCN.2004.38.

[34] P. Dutta and D. Culler. Epic: An Open Mote Platform for Application-Driven Design. In *IPSN '08: Proceedings of the 7th international conference on Information processing in sensor networks*, pages 547–548, Washington, DC, USA, 2008. IEEE Computer Society. ISBN 978-0-7695-3157-1. doi: http://dx.doi.org/10.1109/IPSN.2008.59.

[35] P. K. Dutta, A. K. Arora, and S. B. Bibyk. Towards radar-enabled sensor networks. In *IPSN '06: Proceedings of the 5th international conference on Information processing in sensor networks*, pages 467–474, New York, NY, USA, 2006. ACM. ISBN 1-59593-334-4. doi: http://doi.acm.org/10.1145/1127777.1127848.

[36] M. J. Egenhofer and R. D. Franzosa. Point Set Topological Relations. *International Journal of Geographical Information Systems*, 5(2):161–174, 1991.

[37] J. Elson, L. Girod, and D. Estrin. Fine-grained network time synchronization using reference broadcasts. *SIGOPS Oper. Syst. Rev.*, 36(SI):147–163, 2002. ISSN 0163-5980. doi: http://doi.acm.org/10.1145/844128.844143.

[38] M. Erwig and M. Schneider. Developments in Spatio-Temporal Query Languages. In *DEXA '99: Proceedings of the 10th International Workshop on Database & Expert Systems Applications*, page 441, Washington, DC, USA, 1999. IEEE Computer Society. ISBN 0-7695-0281-4.

[39] M. Erwig and M. Schneider. Spatio-Temporal Predicates. *IEEE TKDE*, 14(4):881–901, 2002. ISSN 1041-4347. doi: http://dx.doi.org/10.1109/TKDE.2002.1019220.

[40] ETH Zürich. BTnodes – A Distributed Environment for Prototyping Ad Hoc Networks, 2010. URL http://www.btnode.ethz.ch/.

[41] X. Fan, C. Ellis, and A. Lebeck. Memory controller policies for DRAM power management. In *ISLPED '01: Proceedings of the 2001 international symposium on Low power electronics and design*, pages 129–134, New York, NY, USA, 2001. ACM. ISBN 1-58113-371-5. doi: http://doi.acm.org/10.1145/383082.383118.

[42] Federal Communications Commission. FCC 94-102. In S. Shekhar and H. Xiong, editors, *Encyclopedia of GIS*, page 313. Springer, 2008. ISBN 978-0-387-30858-6.

[43] A. Flammini, P. Ferrari, D. Marioli, E. Sisinni, and A. Taroni. Wired and wireless sensor networks for industrial applications. *Microelectron. J.*, 40(9):1322–1336, 2009. ISSN 0026-2692. doi: http://dx.doi.org/10.1016/j.mejo.2008.08.012.

[44] R. Fonseca, O. Gnawali, K. Jamieson, S. Kim, P. Levis, and A. Woo. The Collection Tree Protocol (CTP), 2007. URL http://www.tinyos.net/tinyos-2.x/doc/html/tep123.html.

[45] C. L. Fullmer and J. J. Garcia-Luna-Aceves. Solutions to hidden terminal problems in wireless networks. *SIGCOMM Comput. Commun. Rev.*, 27(4):39–49, 1997. ISSN 0146-4833. doi: http://doi.acm.org/10.1145/263109.263137.

[46] S. Gaal. Point Set Topology. *Academic Press*, 1964.

[47] C. Gamage, K. Bicakci, B. Crispo, and A. S. Tanenbaum. Security for the Mythical Air-Dropped Sensor Network. In *ISCC '06: Proceedings of the 11th IEEE Symposium on Computers and Communications*, pages 41–47, Washington, DC, USA, 2006. IEEE Computer Society. ISBN 0-7695-2588-1. doi: http://dx.doi.org/10.1109/ISCC.2006.143.

[48] M. R. Garey and D. S. Johnson. *Computers and Intractability; A Guide to the Theory of NP-Completeness*. W. H. Freeman & Co., New York, NY, USA, 1990. ISBN 0716710455.

[49] D. Gay, P. Levis, R. von Behren, M. Welsh, E. Brewer, and D. Culler. The nesC language: A holistic approach to networked embedded systems. In *PLDI '03: Proceedings of the ACM SIGPLAN 2003 conference on Programming language design and implementation*, pages 1–

11, New York, NY, USA, 2003. ACM. ISBN 1-58113-662-5. doi: http://doi.acm.org/10.1145/781131.781133.
[50] J. Gehrke and S. Madden. Query processing in sensor networks. *Pervasive Computing, IEEE*, 3(1):46–55, jan.-march 2004. ISSN 1536-1268. doi: 10.1109/MPRV.2004.1269131.
[51] J. Gosling, B. Joy, G. Steele, and G. Bracha. *Java(TM) Language Specification, The (3rd Edition) (Java (Addison-Wesley))*. Addison-Wesley Professional, 2005. ISBN 0321246780.
[52] A. Grilo, K. Piotrowski, P. Langendoerfer, and A. Casaca. A Wireless Sensor Network Architecture for Homeland Security Application. In *ADHOC-NOW '09: Proceedings of the 8th International Conference on Ad-Hoc, Mobile and Wireless Networks*, pages 397–402, Berlin, Heidelberg, 2009. Springer-Verlag. ISBN 978-3-642-04382-6. doi: http://dx.doi.org/10.1007/978-3-642-04383-3_34.
[53] R. H. Güting, M. H. Böhlen, M. Erwig, C. S. Jensen, N. A. Lorentzos, M. Schneider, and M. Vazirgiannis. A foundation for representing and querying moving objects. *ACM Trans. Database Syst.*, 25(1):1–42, 2000. ISSN 0362-5915. doi: http://doi.acm.org/10.1145/352958.352963.
[54] R. H. Güting, V. Teixeira de Almeida, and Z. Ding. Modeling and Querying Moving Objects in Networks. *VLDB J.*, 15(2):165–190, 2006.
[55] G. P. Halkes, T. van Dam, and K. G. Langendoen. Comparing energy-saving MAC protocols for wireless sensor networks. *Mob. Netw. Appl.*, 10(5):783–791, 2005. ISSN 1383-469X. doi: http://doi.acm.org/10.1145/1160143.1160161.
[56] A. v. Halteren, R. Bults, K. Wac, D. Konstantas, I. Widya, N. Dokovski, G. Koprinkov, V. Jones, and R. Herzog. Mobile Patient Monitoring: The Mobihealth System. *The Journal on Information Technology in Healthcare*, 2(5):365–373, October 2004. URL http://doc.utwente.nl/66488/.
[57] T. He, S. Krishnamurthy, J. A. Stankovic, T. Abdelzaher, L. Luo, R. Stoleru, T. Yan, L. Gu, J. Hui, and B. Krogh. Energy-efficient surveillance system using wireless sensor networks. In *MobiSys '04: Proceedings of the 2nd international conference on Mobile systems, applications, and services*, pages 270–283, New York, NY, USA, 2004. ACM. ISBN 1-58113-793-1. doi: http://doi.acm.org/10.1145/990064.990096.
[58] T. He, S. Krishnamurthy, L. Luo, T. Yan, L. Gu, R. Stoleru, G. Zhou, Q. Cao, P. Vicaire, J. A. Stankovic, T. F. Abdelzaher, J. Hui, and B. Krogh. VigilNet: An integrated sensor network system for energy-efficient surveillance. *ACM Trans. Sen. Netw.*, 2(1):1–38, 2006. ISSN 1550-4859. doi: http://doi.acm.org/10.1145/1138127.1138128.
[59] M. Heavner, R. Fatland, E. Hood, C. Connor, T. L. Hansen, M. S. Schultz, T. LeFebvre, and A. Esterline. Sensor Webs in Digital Earth: Monitoring Climate Change Impacts. In G. Uzochukwu, editor, *Proceedings of the 2007 National Conference on Environmental Science and Technology*, pages 211–217. Springer, 2007. ISBN 978-0-387-88482-0.
[60] A. Hergenröder, J. Wilke, and D. Meier. Distributed Energy Measurements in WSN Testbeds with a Sensor Node Management Device (SNMD). In *GI/ITG Energy-aware Systems and Methods*, Feb. 2010. to appear.

[61] J. Hill, R. Szewczyk, A. Woo, S. Hollar, D. Culler, and K. Pister. System architecture directions for networked sensors. *SIGPLAN Not.*, 35(11):93–104, 2000. ISSN 0362-1340. doi: http://doi.acm.org/10.1145/356989.356998.

[62] H. Huang, P. Pillai, and K. G. Shin. Design and implementation of power-aware virtual memory. In *ATEC '03: Proceedings of the annual conference on USENIX Annual Technical Conference*, pages 57–70, Berkeley, CA, USA, 2003. USENIX Association.

[63] F. Ingelrest, G. Barrenetxea, G. Schaefer, M. Vetterli, O. Couach, and M. Parlange. SensorScope: Application-specific sensor network for environmental monitoring. *ACM Trans. Sen. Netw.*, 6(2):1–32, 2010. ISSN 1550-4859. doi: http://doi.acm.org/10.1145/1689239.1689247.

[64] Institute of Electrical and Electronics Engineers, Inc. (IEEE). *802.15.4 – Wireless Medium Access Control (MAC) and Physical Layer (PHY) Specifications for Low-Rate Wireless Personal Area Networks (LR-WPANs)*, October 2003.

[65] C. Intanagonwiwat, R. Govindan, and D. Estrin. Directed diffusion: a scalable and robust communication paradigm for sensor networks. In *MobiCom '00: Proceedings of the 6th annual international conference on Mobile computing and networking*, pages 56–67, New York, NY, USA, 2000. ACM. ISBN 1-58113-197-6. doi: http://doi.acm.org/10.1145/345910.345920.

[66] C. Intanagonwiwat, D. Estrin, R. Govindan, and J. Heidemann. Impact of Network Density on Data Aggregation in Wireless Sensor Networks. In *ICDCS '02: Proceedings of the 22 nd International Conference on Distributed Computing Systems (ICDCS'02)*, page 457, Washington, DC, USA, 2002. IEEE Computer Society. ISBN 0-7695-1585-1.

[67] ISO. *ISO/IEC 14977:1996: Information technology — Syntactic metalanguage — Extended BNF*. International Organization for Standardization (ISO), Geneva, Switzerland, 1996. URL http://www.iso.ch/cate/d26153.html.

[68] ITRS. International Technology Roadmap for Semiconductors, 2010. URL www.itrs.net.

[69] P. Juang, H. Oki, Y. Wang, M. Martonosi, L. S. Peh, and D. Rubenstein. Energy-efficient computing for wildlife tracking: design tradeoffs and early experiences with ZebraNet. *SIGARCH Comput. Archit. News*, 30(5):96–107, 2002. ISSN 0163-5964. doi: http://doi.acm.org/10.1145/635506.605408.

[70] P. Juang, H. Oki, Y. Wang, M. Martonosi, L. S. Peh, and D. Rubenstein. Energy-efficient computing for wildlife tracking: design tradeoffs and early experiences with ZebraNet. *SIGARCH Comput. Archit. News*, 30(5):96–107, 2002. ISSN 0163-5964. doi: http://doi.acm.org/10.1145/635506.605408.

[71] A. M. Khedr and W. Osamy. A topology discovery algorithm for sensor network using smart antennas. *Computer Communications*, 29(12):2261 – 2268, 2006. ISSN 0140-3664. doi: DOI:10.1016/j.comcom.2006.03.002. URL http://www.sciencedirect.com/science/article/B6TYP-4JKJSF1-1/2/2106d315f8e9adbb10eda5ead37cb8c6.

[72] K. Klues, G. Hackmann, O. Chipara, and C. Lu. A component-based architecture for power-efficient media access control in wireless sensor networks. In *SenSys '07: Proceedings of the 5th international conference on Embedded networked sensor systems*, pages 59–72, New York,

NY, USA, 2007. ACM. ISBN 978-1-59593-763-6. doi: http://doi.acm.org/10.1145/1322263.1322270.

[73] D. E. Knuth, J. H. J. Morris, and V. R. Pratt. Fast Pattern Matching in Strings. *SIAM Journal on Computing*, 6(2):323–350, 1977.

[74] W. Koenig, D. Van Vuren, and P. Hooge. Detectability, Philopatry, and the Distribution of Dispersal Distances in Vertebrates. *Trends in Ecology & Evolution*, 11(12):514 – 517, 1996. ISSN 0169-5347. doi: http://dx.doi.org/10.1016/S0169-5347(96)20074-6. URL http://www.sciencedirect.com/science/article/B6VJ1-3WJG223-7P/2/32968219bb7a42b8ecd35f84bc6fb666.

[75] B. Krishnamachari, S. Wicker, R. Bejar, M. Pearlman, and C. Critical Density Thresholds in Distributed Wireless Networks. In *Communications, information and network security*, 2002.

[76] L. Krishnamurthy, R. Adler, P. Buonadonna, J. Chhabra, M. Flanigan, N. Kushalnagar, L. Nachman, and M. Yarvis. Design and deployment of industrial sensor networks: experiences from a semiconductor plant and the north sea. In *SenSys '05: Proceedings of the 3rd international conference on Embedded networked sensor systems*, pages 64–75, New York, NY, USA, 2005. ACM. ISBN 1-59593-054-X. doi: http://doi.acm.org/10.1145/1098918.1098926.

[77] P. Langendorfer, A. Grilo, K. Piotrowski, and A. Casaca. A Wireless Sensor Network Reliable Architecture for Intrusion Detection. In *Next Generation Internet Networks*, pages 189–194, Apr. 2008. doi: http://dx.doi.org/10.1109/NGI.2008.32.

[78] Laura Marie Feeney, editor and Can Basaran and others. Critical evaluation of platforms commonly used in embedded wireless sensor networks research. Public report, Embedded Wisents Project FP6-004400, 2006. URL http://www.embedded-wisents.org/studies/survey_wp2.html.

[79] H. Lim and C. Kim. Multicast tree construction and flooding in wireless ad hoc networks. In *MSWIM '00: Proceedings of the 3rd ACM international workshop on Modeling, analysis and simulation of wireless and mobile systems*, pages 61–68, New York, NY, USA, 2000. ACM. ISBN 1-58113-304-9. doi: http://doi.acm.org/10.1145/346855.346865.

[80] N.-H. Liu, C.-A. Wu, and S.-J. Hsieh. Long-Term Animal Observation by Wireless Sensor Networks with Sound Recognition. In *WASA '09: Proceedings of the 4th International Conference on Wireless Algorithms, Systems, and Applications*, pages 1–11, Berlin, Heidelberg, 2009. Springer-Verlag. ISBN 978-3-642-03416-9. doi: http://dx.doi.org/10.1007/978-3-642-03417-6_1.

[81] S. Madden, M. J. Franklin, J. M. Hellerstein, and W. Hong. TAG: a Tiny AGgregation service for ad-hoc sensor networks. *SIGOPS Oper. Syst. Rev.*, 36(SI):131–146, 2002. ISSN 0163-5980. doi: http://doi.acm.org/10.1145/844128.844142.

[82] S. Madden, M. J. Franklin, J. M. Hellerstein, and W. Hong. The design of an acquisitional query processor for sensor networks. In *SIGMOD '03: Proceedings of the 2003 ACM SIGMOD international conference on Management of data*, pages 491–502, New York, NY, USA, 2003. ACM. ISBN 1-58113-634-X. doi: http://doi.acm.org/10.1145/872757.872817.

[83] S. R. Madden. *The design and evaluation of a query processing architecture for sensor networks*. PhD thesis, University of California at Berkeley, Berkeley, CA, USA, 2003. Chair-Franklin, Michael J.

[84] S. R. Madden, M. J. Franklin, J. M. Hellerstein, and W. Hong. TinyDB: an acquisitional query processing system for sensor networks. *ACM Trans. Database Syst.*, 30(1):122–173, 2005. ISSN 0362-5915. doi: http://doi.acm.org/10.1145/1061318.1061322.

[85] A. Mainwaring, D. Culler, J. Polastre, R. Szewczyk, and J. Anderson. Wireless sensor networks for habitat monitoring. In *WSNA '02: Proceedings of the 1st ACM international workshop on Wireless sensor networks and applications*, pages 88–97, New York, NY, USA, 2002. ACM. ISBN 1-58113-589-0. doi: http://doi.acm.org/10.1145/570738.570751.

[86] T. L. Martin. *Balancing batteries, power, and performance: system issues in cpu speed-setting for mobile computing*. PhD thesis, Carnegie Mellon University, Pittsburgh, PA, USA, 1999. Adviser-Siewiorek, Daniel P.

[87] K. Martinez, J. K. Hart, and R. Ong. Environmental Sensor Networks. *Computer*, 37(8): 50–56, 2004. ISSN 0018-9162. doi: http://dx.doi.org/10.1109/MC.2004.91.

[88] M. Mazzu, S. Scalvini, A. Giordano, E. Frumento, H. Wells, K. Lokhorst, and F. Glisenti. Wireless-accessible sensor populations for monitoring biological variables. *Journal of Telemedicine and Telecare*, 14(3):135–137, March 2008. ISSN 1357-633X. doi: 10.1258/jtt.2008.003010. URL http://dx.doi.org/10.1258/jtt.2008.003010.

[89] C. Mbarushimana and A. Shahrabi. Comparative Study of Reactive and Proactive Routing Protocols Performance in Mobile Ad Hoc Networks. In *AINAW '07: Proceedings of the 21st International Conference on Advanced Information Networking and Applications Workshops*, pages 679–684, Washington, DC, USA, 2007. IEEE Computer Society. ISBN 0-7695-2847-3. doi: http://dx.doi.org/10.1109/AINAW.2007.123.

[90] S. Mehta, W.-S. Yoon, S.-W. Min, and S. Yu. Topology generation algorithms for home sensor networks. *Software Technologies for Future Embedded and Ubiquitous Systems, 2004. Proceedings. Second IEEE Workshop on*, pages 166–168, may. 2004. doi: 10.1109/WSTFES.2004.1300435.

[91] J. M. Metsaranta. Assessing Factors Influencing the Space Use of a Woodland Caribou Rangifer Tarandus Caribou Population using an Individual-Based Model. *Wildlife Biology*, 14 (4):478–488, Dec. 2008. ISSN 0909-6396. doi: http://dx.doi.org/10.2981/0909-6396-14.4.478.

[92] A. Mohammed, M. Ould-Khaoua, and L. Mackenzie. An Efficient Counter-Based Broadcast Scheme for Mobile Ad Hoc Networks. In K. Wolter, editor, *Formal Methods and Stochastic Models for Performance Evaluation*, volume 4748 of *Lecture Notes in Computer Science*, pages 275–283. Springer Berlin / Heidelberg, 2007. URL http://dx.doi.org/10.1007/978-3-540-75211-0_20. 10.1007/978-3-540-75211-0_20.

[93] A. Mohammed, M. Ould-Khaoua, and L. Mackenzie. Improvement to Efficient Counter-Based Broadcast Scheme through Random Assessment Delay Adaptation for MANETS. *Computer Modeling and Simulation, 2008. EMS '08. Second UKSIM European Symposium on*, pages 536–541, sep. 2008. doi: 10.1109/EMS.2008.69.

BIBLIOGRAPHY

[94] A. Mohammed, M. Ould-Khaoua, L. Mackenzie, and J. Abdulai. Performance evaluation of an efficient counter-based scheme for mobile ad hoc networks based on realistic mobility model. *Performance Evaluation of Computer and Telecommunication Systems, 2008. SPECTS 2008. International Symposium on*, pages 181–188, jun. 2008.

[95] G. Montenegro, N. Kushalnagar, J. Hui, and D. Culler. Transmission of IPv6 Packets over IEEE 802.15.4 Networks. RFC 4944 (Proposed Standard), Sept. 2007. URL http://www.ietf.org/rfc/rfc4944.txt.

[96] G. E. Moore. Cramming more components onto integrated circuits. *Electronics*, 8(4), apr 1965.

[97] L. Nachman, R. Kling, R. Adler, J. Huang, and V. Hummel. The Intel®Mote platform: a Bluetooth-based sensor network for industrial monitoring. In *IPSN '05: Proceedings of the 4th international symposium on Information processing in sensor networks*, page 61, Piscataway, NJ, USA, 2005. IEEE Press. ISBN 0-7803-9202-7.

[98] S.-Y. Ni, Y.-C. Tseng, Y.-S. Chen, and J.-P. Sheu. The broadcast storm problem in a mobile ad hoc network. In *MobiCom '99: Proceedings of the 5th annual ACM/IEEE international conference on Mobile computing and networking*, pages 151–162, New York, NY, USA, 1999. ACM. ISBN 1-58113-142-9. doi: http://doi.acm.org/10.1145/313451.313525.

[99] K. Obraczka, K. Viswanath, and G. Tsudik. Flooding for reliable multicast in multi-hop ad hoc networks. *Wirel. Netw.*, 7(6):627–634, 2001. ISSN 1022-0038. doi: http://dx.doi.org/10.1023/A:1012323519059.

[100] R. U. Pedersen, J. Nørbjerg, and M. P. Scholz. Embedded programming education with Lego Mindstorms NXT using Java (leJOS), Eclipse (XPairtise), and Python (PyMite). In *WESS '09: Proceedings of the 2009 Workshop on Embedded Systems Education*, pages 50–55, New York, NY, USA, 2009. ACM. ISBN 978-1-4503-0021-6. doi: http://doi.acm.org/10.1145/1719010.1719019.

[101] W. Peng and X. Lu. AHBP: An efficient broadcast protocol for mobile Ad hoc networks. *Journal of Computer Science and Technology*, 16:114–125, 2001. ISSN 1000-9000. URL http://dx.doi.org/10.1007/BF02950416. 10.1007/BF02950416.

[102] W. Peng and X.-C. Lu. On the reduction of broadcast redundancy in mobile ad hoc networks. In *MobiHoc '00: Proceedings of the 1st ACM international symposium on Mobile ad hoc networking & computing*, pages 129–130, Piscataway, NJ, USA, 2000. IEEE Press. ISBN 0-7803-6534-8.

[103] C. Perkins, E. Belding-Royer, and S. Das. Ad hoc On-Demand Distance Vector (AODV) Routing, July 2003.

[104] C. E. Perkins, J. T. Malinen, R. Wakikawa, A. Nilsson, and A. J. Tuominen. Internet Connectivity for Ad Hoc Mobile Networks, 2002.

[105] J. Polastre, J. Hill, and D. Culler. Versatile low power media access for wireless sensor networks. In *SenSys '04: Proceedings of the 2nd international conference on Embedded networked sensor systems*, pages 95–107, New York, NY, USA, 2004. ACM. ISBN 1-58113-879-2. doi: http://doi.acm.org/10.1145/1031495.1031508.

[106] R. Powers. Batteries for Low Power Electronics. In *Proceedings of the IEEE*, pages 687–693. IEEE, April 1995.

[107] A. Qayyum, L. Viennot, and A. Laouiti. Multipoint Relaying for Flooding Broadcast Messages in Mobile Wireless Networks. In *HICSS '02: Proceedings of the 35th Annual Hawaii International Conference on System Sciences (HICSS'02)-Volume 9*, page 298, Washington, DC, USA, 2002. IEEE Computer Society. ISBN 0-7695-1435-9.

[108] J. M. Rabaey, J. Ammer, T. Karalar, S. Li, B. Otis, M. Sheets, and T. Tuan. 12.3 Pico-Radios for Wireless Sensor Networks – The Next Challenge in Ultra-Low Power Design. In *Proceedings of the International Solid-State Circuits Conference*, feb 2002.

[109] A. Rahman and P. Gburzynski. Hidden Problems with the Hidden Node Problem. In *in Proceedings of 23rd Biennial Symposium on Communications*, pages 270–273, 2006.

[110] J. W. Rettie and F. Messier. Hierarchical Habitat Selection by Woodland Caribou: Its Relationship to Limiting Factors. *Ecography*, 23(4):466–478, 2000. ISSN 09067590. URL http://www.jstor.org/stable/3683077.

[111] R. Riggs, J. Huopaniemi, A. Taivalsaari, M. Patel, and A. Uotila. *Programming Wireless Devices with the Java 2 Platform, Micro Edition*. Sun Microsystems, Inc., Mountain View, CA, USA, 2003. ISBN 0321197984.

[112] R. RoyChoudhury, S. Bandyopadhyay, and K. Paul. A distributed mechanism for topology discovery in ad hoc wireless networks using mobile agents. In *MobiHoc '00: Proceedings of the 1st ACM international symposium on Mobile ad hoc networking & computing*, pages 145–146, Piscataway, NJ, USA, 2000. IEEE Press. ISBN 0-7803-6534-8.

[113] E. Shih, S.-H. Cho, N. Ickes, R. Min, A. Sinha, A. Wang, and A. Chandrakasan. Physical layer driven protocol and algorithm design for energy-efficient wireless sensor networks. In *MobiCom '01: Proceedings of the 7th annual international conference on Mobile computing and networking*, pages 272–287, New York, NY, USA, 2001. ACM. ISBN 1-58113-422-3. doi: http://doi.acm.org/10.1145/381677.381703.

[114] N. Shrivastava, R. M. U. Madhow, and S. Suri. Target tracking with binary proximity sensors: fundamental limits, minimal descriptions, and algorithms. In *SenSys '06: Proceedings of the 4th international conference on Embedded networked sensor systems*, pages 251–264, New York, NY, USA, 2006. ACM. ISBN 1-59593-343-3. doi: http://doi.acm.org/10.1145/1182807.1182833.

[115] B. S. I. G. (SIG). Bluetooth Core Specification Version 4.0, apr 2010. URL http://www.bluetooth.com.

[116] D. Simon, C. Cifuentes, D. Cleal, J. Daniels, and D. White. Java™ on the bare metal of wireless sensor devices: the squawk Java virtual machine. In *VEE '06: Proceedings of the 2nd international conference on Virtual execution environments*, pages 78–88, New York, NY, USA, 2006. ACM. ISBN 1-59593-332-6. doi: http://doi.acm.org/10.1145/1134760.1134773.

[117] D. Simplot-Ryl, I. Stojmenovic, and J. Wu. *Energy efficient backbone construction, broadcasting, and area coverage in sensor networks*. John Wiley & Sons, nov 2005. ISBN 978-0-471-68472-5.

BIBLIOGRAPHY

[118] J. Song, S. Han, A. Mok, D. Chen, M. Lucas, and M. Nixon. WirelessHART: Applying Wireless Technology in Real-Time Industrial Process Control. In *Real-Time and Embedded Technology and Applications Symposium, 2008. RTAS '08. IEEE*, pages 377–386, Apr. 2008. doi: 10.1109/RTAS.2008.15.

[119] G. P. Succi, T. K. Pedersen, R. Gampert, and G. Prado. Acoustic target tracking and target identification: recent results. *Unattended Ground Sensor Technologies and Applications*, 3713 (1):10–21, 1999. doi: 10.1117/12.357130. URL http://link.aip.org/link/?PSI/3713/10/1.

[120] SUN Microsystems Inc. Small Programmable Object Technology (SPOT), 2009. URL www.sunspotworld.com.

[121] D. Thompson and R. Miles. *Embedded programming with the microsoft .net micro framework*. Microsoft Press, Redmond, WA, USA, 2007. ISBN 9780735623651.

[122] R. Tilove. Set Membership Classification: A Unified Approach to Geometric Intersection Problems. *Computers, IEEE Transactions on*, C-29(10):874–883, oct. 1980. ISSN 0018-9340. doi: 10.1109/TC.1980.1675470.

[123] G. Tolle, J. Polastre, R. Szewczyk, D. Culler, N. Turner, K. Tu, S. Burgess, T. Dawson, P. Buonadonna, D. Gay, and W. Hong. A macroscope in the redwoods. In *SenSys '05: Proceedings of the 3rd international conference on Embedded networked sensor systems*, pages 51–63, New York, NY, USA, 2005. ACM. ISBN 1-59593-054-X. doi: http://doi.acm.org/10.1145/1098918.1098925.

[124] G. Trajcevski, O. Wolfson, F. Zhang, and S. Chamberlain. The Geometry of Uncertainty in Moving Objects Databases. In *EDBT '02: Proceedings of the 8th International Conference on Extending Database Technology*, pages 233–250, London, UK, 2002. Springer-Verlag. ISBN 3-540-43324-4.

[125] G. Trajcevski, O. Wolfson, K. Hinrichs, and S. Chamberlain. Managing uncertainty in moving objects databases. *ACM Trans. Database Syst.*, 29(3):463–507, 2004. ISSN 0362-5915. doi: http://doi.acm.org/10.1145/1016028.1016030.

[126] T. van Dam and K. Langendoen. An adaptive energy-efficient MAC protocol for wireless sensor networks. In *SenSys '03: Proceedings of the 1st international conference on Embedded networked sensor systems*, pages 171–180, New York, NY, USA, 2003. ACM. ISBN 1-58113-707-9. doi: http://doi.acm.org/10.1145/958491.958512.

[127] J. Werb. Making Sense of the Sensor Network Value Chain, 2008. URL www.adaptive-wireless.co.uk/wp-content/uploads/2008/09/making_sense_of_the_sensor_network_value_chain.pdf.

[128] B. Williams and T. Camp. Comparison of Broadcasting Techniques for Mobile Ad Hoc Networks. In *Proceedings of the ACM International Symposium on Mobile Ad Hoc Networking and Computing (MOBIHOC)*, 2002.

[129] N. Wirth. What can we do about the unnecessary diversity of notation for syntactic definitions? *Commun. ACM*, 20(11):822–823, 1977. ISSN 0001-0782. doi: http://doi.acm.org/10.1145/359863.359883.

[130] O. Wolfson, B. Xu, S. Chamberlain, and L. Jiang. Moving Objects Databases: Issues and Solutions. In *SSDBM '98: Proceedings of the 10th International Conference on Scientific and Statistical Database Management*, pages 111–122, Washington, DC, USA, 1998. IEEE Computer Society. ISBN 0-8186-8575-1. doi: http://dx.doi.org/10.1109/SSDM.1998.688116.

[131] XBow Technology Inc. Wireless Sensor Networks, 2009. URL http://www.xbow.com.

[132] X. Yang, H. B. Lim, T. M. Özsu, and K. L. Tan. In-network execution of monitoring queries in sensor networks. In *SIGMOD '07: Proceedings of the 2007 ACM SIGMOD international conference on Management of data*, pages 521–532, New York, NY, USA, 2007. ACM. ISBN 978-1-59593-686-8. doi: http://doi.acm.org/10.1145/1247480.1247538.

[133] Y. Yao and J. Gehrke. The Cougar Approach to In-Network Query Processing in Sensor Networks. *SIGMOD Record*, 31(3):9–18, 2002.

[134] W. Ye, J. Heidemann, and D. Estrin. An energy-efficient MAC protocol for wireless sensor networks. In *INFOCOM 2002. Twenty-First Annual Joint Conference of the IEEE Computer and Communications Societies. Proceedings. IEEE*, volume 3, pages 1567 – 1576, 2002. doi: 10.1109/INFCOM.2002.1019408.

[135] M. L. Yiu, N. Mamoulis, and S. Bakiras. Retrieval of Spatial Join Pattern Instances from Sensor Networks. In *SSDBM '07: Proceedings of the 19th International Conference on Scientific and Statistical Database Management*, page 25, Washington, DC, USA, 2007. IEEE Computer Society. ISBN 0-7695-2868-6. doi: http://dx.doi.org/10.1109/SSDBM.2007.41.

[136] H. Yu, E.-P. Lim, and J. Zhang. On In-network Synopsis Join Processing for Sensor Networks. In *MDM '06: Proceedings of the 7th International Conference on Mobile Data Management*, page 32, Washington, DC, USA, 2006. IEEE Computer Society. ISBN 0-7695-2526-1. doi: http://dx.doi.org/10.1109/MDM.2006.113.

[137] M. Zennaro, A. Floros, G. Dogan, T. Sun, Z. Cao, C. Huang, M. Bahader, H. Ntareme, and A. Bagula. On the Design of a Water Quality Wireless Sensor Network (WQWSN): An Application to Water Quality Monitoring in Malawi. *Parallel Processing Workshops, International Conference on*, 0:330–336, 2009. ISSN 1530-2016. doi: http://doi.ieeecomputersociety.org/10.1109/ICPPW.2009.57.

[138] W. Zhang and G. Cao. Optimizing tree reconfiguration for mobile target tracking in sensor networks. *INFOCOM 2004. Twenty-third AnnualJoint Conference of the IEEE Computer and Communications Societies*, 4:2434–2445, mar. 2004. ISSN 0743-166X.

[139] X. Zhu, H. Gupta, and B. Tang. Join of Multiple Data Streams in Sensor Networks. *Knowledge and Data Engineering, IEEE Transactions on*, 21(12):1722–1736, dec. 2009. ISSN 1041-4347. doi: 10.1109/TKDE.2009.38.

[140] ZigBee Alliance. ZigBee Specification, Jan. 2008. URL http://www.zigbee.org.

I want morebooks!

Buy your books fast and straightforward online - at one of world's fastest growing online book stores! Environmentally sound due to Print-on-Demand technologies.

Buy your books online at
www.morebooks.shop

Kaufen Sie Ihre Bücher schnell und unkompliziert online – auf einer der am schnellsten wachsenden Buchhandelsplattformen weltweit! Dank Print-On-Demand umwelt- und ressourcenschonend produziert.

Bücher schneller online kaufen
www.morebooks.shop

KS OmniScriptum Publishing
Brivibas gatve 197
LV-1039 Riga, Latvia
Telefax: +371 686 204 55

info@omniscriptum.com
www.omniscriptum.com

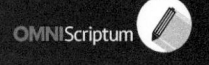

Printed by Books on Demand GmbH, Norderstedt / Germany